outlook

A journal of opinion

Selected Articles

T0345825

outlook

A journal of opinion

Selected Articles

Editor: I. H. Burney

OXFORD

UNIVERSITY PRESS

OXFORD
UNIVERSITY PRESS

Oxford University Press is a department of the University of Oxford.
It furthers the University's objective of excellence in research, scholarship,
and education by publishing worldwide. Oxford is a registered trade mark of
Oxford University Press in the UK and in certain other countries

Published in Pakistan by
Ameena Saiyid, Oxford University Press
No.38, Sector 15, Korangi Industrial Area,
PO Box 8214, Karachi-74900, Pakistan

ISBN 978-0-19-940769-9

Typeset in Adobe Garamond Pro
Printed on 55gsm Newsprint Paper

Printed by The Times Press Pvt. Ltd., Karachi

Contents

Introduction

IT is March 1971. Pakistani army tanks are rolling into (Dacca), the provincial capital of the eastern wing of the country. The next nine months see an orgy of killing, rape, and destruction across the land. People in the western wing of the country appear detached. They stay uninformed—deliberately or otherwise. News from western sources that trickle in is rubbished as propaganda, conspiracies against Pakistan. However, it is a conspiracy of silence in which there are many willing and eager participants. Because it is a matter of the country's unity. Because India, our enemy since birth, is involved ...

All Pakistani publications—and, by and large, the Pakistani people buy the official line. It is only when the Pakistan Army surrenders on 16 December 1971 and over 90,000 become prisoners of war (POWs) in India that the Generals are questioned. There is a mixed and mostly angry reaction to a short clip showing 'Tiger' Niazi signing the surrender document on Pakistan Television. The new Information Minister's effort to defend the broadcast by questioning if Pakistanis were 'a nation of ostriches' is severely criticized and the historic news footage is not shown again.

When *Outlook* begins publishing in April 1972, its editor, I. H. Burney, ensures that the weekly embodies the country's conscience on all that has happened in Pakistan, the former East Pakistan, and the present Bangladesh. Suddenly, pent-up opinions and feelings find space and *Outlook* provides ample opportunity to diverse points of view.

This compilation of articles published primarily on Bangladesh is both an indictment of those governing Pakistan during the most tragic phase of its history as well as a reminder to the present powers-that-be to take stock of unaddressed disillusionment with the concept of a united Pakistan in parts of the country. The denial of history and its distortion are sadly widely prevalent in Pakistan, whether in school textbooks or intellectual discourse. This collection from *Outlook* is a sharp reminder of the saying: 'those who do not learn from history are condemned to repeat it'.

This collection truly represents a diversity of ideas and attitudes. Hamida Khuhro, perhaps feeling the deprivation of Pakistan's smaller provinces, wrote in 'The Catharsis of Pakistan' (27 May 1972) about the 'blind indifference of the urban middle class intellectual' to the tragedy unfolding in East Pakistan, terming it a 'crisis of conscience'. She noted, 'the elementary distinction between mob violence and the policies of the government carried out by its armed forces was not made;' the few voices of conscience she observed belonged to the Baloch people (the most backward province).

However, not all opinions expressed in *Outlook* on the emergence of Bangladesh are as understanding or conciliatory. A letter from a 'Muhajir' accuses Khuhro of being pro-Hindu and against the Pakistani ideology. A 'roving reporter' sent to Dacca to interview Shaikh Mujibur Rahman after his release reveals all the prejudices held by West Pakistanis against Bengalis. He chooses to comment disparagingly on the cultural practices of Bengalis, betraying the feeling of superiority held by West Pakistanis—an attitude that was partly responsible for the rise of Bengali nationalism. It is unclear why this particular reporter was given the assignment.

If Pakistan was a pariah state post 1971, Bangladesh became the world's cause. The suffering Bengalis experienced as a result of the military action led to unquestioned support for the young country. The wave of sympathy for Bangladesh drowned out critical voices. This is amply clear in David Frost's interview of Shaikh Mujib conducted in Dacca on 26 January 1972 and reproduced in *Outlook's* issues of 22 and 29 April 1972 in two parts. A man known for putting world leaders in tough spots appears totally enamoured by Bangladesh's Prime Minister, unquestioningly accepting his version of events. However, even without the uncomfortable questions, the interview is rather revealing of the Shaikh's weakness of leadership and governance. (Of course, this interview was reproduced at a time when copyright was not a hindrance.)

A very different interview is of Zulfikar Ali Bhutto (President at the time) given to Dilip Mukherjee of *The Times of India*, published in *Outlook* in its issue of 15 March 1972. The focus of this interview is on a pressing humanitarian problem that both the governments of Pakistan and Bangladesh were in no mood to address. Mukherjee asks compelling questions on the plight of non-Bengalis (or Biharis as they were known) in camps in Dacca and the future of the Bengalis stuck in Pakistan, many of whom were also in camps but not in the dire conditions experienced by those in Bangladesh. While Bhutto makes many promises, the majority of the stranded Pakistanis (as they like to identify themselves) remain where they are. Reading Bhutto's interview is a sharp reminder of promises broken at the altar of political expediency.

The humanitarian issue of divided people—Bengalis in Pakistan and Biharis in Bangladesh was taken up in an article by Walter Schwarz of *The Observer* written after his visit to the camps in Dacca and in a full page article published in June 1972 titled: 'Bengalis here, Biharis there—a deepening tragedy' which gave an insightful account of the persecution of both by the two countries.

Outlook also took up the cause of Pakistani prisoners of war. Lawyer Aziz Kurtha contributed an article explaining the principles of the Geneva Convention that dictate the treatment of prisoners of war. India, of course, was accused many times by Pakistan of violating the Geneva Convention. It was also possibly the only publication to highlight the predicament of businessmen who had to leave all their assets and enterprises in East Pakistan and were confronted with apathy from the government in Pakistan.

The weekly continued to cover issues related to the birth of Bangladesh throughout the early seventies untill it was banned in 1974. It did not spare any of the main actors of the tragedy. It condemned the brutality of the Pakistan Army as well as the desire for vengeance shown by the government of Bangladesh when it passed the Bangladesh Special Collaborators (Special Courts) Order 1972 to punish collaborators of the Pakistan Army with retrospective effect—that is from 26 March 1971. It covered wide-ranging offences, even for statements made in favour of the Pakistan Army and provided for arrest without warrant. While the government of Shaikh Mujib did not invoke this law, it was a precursor to the war crimes tribunal set up by his daughter, Prime Minister Sheikh Hasina Wajid, decades later.

In December 1972, Bhutto sent two journalists, highly respected in Bangladesh, to Dacca to explore the prospects of a dialogue with Shaikh Mujib prior to recognition of the new country by Pakistan. Syed Najiullah and Mazhar Ali Khan reportedly enjoyed Mujib's confidence and had many friends in key positions in Bangladesh. Syed Najiullah's three-part report is among those written with rare understanding and empathy.

Outlook's first editorial set the tone: 'The pith of the matter is that we, the people of West Pakistan, the silent majority and the not-so-silent minority, all of us were mute witnesses to an avoidable human tragedy. Not a political or economic tragedy.'—8 April 1972. This collection captures *Outlook*'s efforts to examine all the dimensions of this human tragedy. And if one were to place this tragedy in a wider context, this collection also includes articles on developments in Afghanistan and on a key player of the time—Zulfikar Ali Bhutto.

The articles on Afghanistan read like a premonition of things to come. They refer to the growing Russian interest in the country as well as the desire of Bangladesh and India to play a role. These were the days of the 'London Plan'—a deliberate campaign to discredit the leaders of the secular National Awami Party—Ghaffar Khan, the Frontier Gandhi, and his son Wali Khan. *Outlook*'s correspondent, Askar Ali Shah, makes several references to the broadcasts of Radio Kabul as indicative of a conspiracy in the offing. These broadcasts are monitored with consternation and the role of Russia and India are considered suspect. As has historically been the case with the Pakistani state, its own policies and their repercussions are never examined closely. Outsiders—regional states—are blamed for the fault lines that appear frequently.

Of course what happened in Afghanistan, beginning from the late seventies to the present, is part of a traumatic phase of the country's history. A country with regional—even if misplaced ambitions—ended up being pushed back centuries to a version of Islam violently enforced by the Taliban. In Pakistan's N.W.F.P. (now Khyber-Pakhtunkhwa), the transition from Pakhtun nationalism to Islamic extremism has been engineered at great cost not just to the people of the province but the country at large. The secular politics of the vanguards of the NAP is now a thing of the past. Were the seeds of change in Afghanistan and the Frontier sown in the early seventies?

Pakistan in the early seventies was all about Zulfikar Ali Bhutto. He was President, Chief Martial Law Administrator, and leader of the largest party in the country—the Pakistan Peoples Party. Mr Bhutto's personality and populism evoked strong feelings of admiration as well as revulsion.

He was a poster child of the media in some ways and also its *bête noire*. He had little tolerance for criticism or differing points of view. Bhutto, of course, was responsible for the ban on *Outlook*. The articles on Bhutto included in this collection capture the essence of the man—the leader as well as the demagogue. Air Marshal (Retd) Asghar Khan was an early critic of Bhutto's government. Writing in the issue of 5 April 1972, he lamented the fact that the nature of dictatorship had not ended with the coming into power of an elected government due to Bhutto's authoritarian style of governance. The editor of *Outlook* was among the journalists who became victims of Bhutto's intolerance of a critical press. The articles on the period cover the crisis developing over Bhutto's confrontation with the provincial governments of N.W.F.P. and Balochistan. The undemocratic actions taken in the seventies started the process of disenchantment with the federation in the two provinces. While it has intensified in Balochistan, Khyber Pakhtunkhwa has gone its own way in redefining its identity.

So what lessons can we learn from this insightful collection? The words of an editorial published in the 15 April 1972 issue of *Outlook* still ring true. It is, in fact, a succinct statement on present-day Pakistan:

> 'In a crisis-ridden country like ours, one learns to live on the verge of hope and despair. Illusions come to be traded as facts of life. Lessons are learned only to be forgotten. Few seem to realize that we are living on the brink of disaster.'

— Zohra Yusuf, 29 June 2017

Part I
Bangladesh

NEARLY six years af[...]
business of attempti[...]
our soul. The country we kr[...]
defeat have yet to visit us in a[...]
uncertain. In the circumstances[...]
of the commercialized values and[...]
can only be rationalized in terms of[...]
is a journalist's special burden. 'The[...]

Three periodicals have been struck[...]
not confined to only one side of the po[...]
set of periodicals which were all in the op[...]
which bodes ill for the country. It has to be[...]

This society, once so static and resistant [...] The winds
of change are swirling around us. Perhaps the [...] preserving. Perhaps a change can
only be for the better. The social order, the production relations, greying concepts like patriotism
and nationalism, [and] dusty old human values which we claimed to have inherited in an ideological
handbag and never practised, nearly everything is crying for a re-definition. Even the conceptual basis
of the country itself. Surely, the Two-Nation Theory is dead like dodo. No one with a heart can tell
the 1.5 million Biharis crying from the remote lush green wilderness of Bangladesh that Pakistan was
conceived and created as a homeland for the Muslims of the subcontinent. If it was so conceived, it was
wrong. Let us have the courage to admit it. And no one with a heart can tell the 50,000 or 3 million
(or whatever the number, only the vultures can tell) dead Bengalis that Pakistan was carved out as a
haven of safety for Muslims as Muslims. If it was so conceived, recent history belied the assumption.

It matters little whose fault it was and how truly international the conspiracy was. The pith of the
matter is that we, the people of West Pakistan, the silent majority and the not-so-silent minority, all
of us were mute witnesses to an avoidable human tragedy. Not a political or economic tragedy. Like
partition itself, it was perhaps inevitable. Like history, the tide of aspirations rolls on, regardless of

offers us no vicarious

is a lesson for what is left

essarily underwrite viable new

minated by inexorable geopolitical

and inter-class relationship which need a

d. What is needed is a prescription. Speaking

. We only hope to project an inquiring mind, feed

discussion on issues that matter. All points of view, if

accommodated within the limitations of a cramped space.

favour of a liberal, democratic, secular, and a more just and

ized. The people seem to be ahead of parties, way ahead of their leaders.

lloping ahead of resources viewed in terms of concrete, conscious planning.

situation exists without the infrastructure of a disciplined, dedicated party

nnelize this bubbling fervour of unrest into a deliberately chalked out, constructive,

al goal. Events happen, they are not designed. The reforms ushered in by the present

re not to be underrated. A qualitative change in the political processes has already occurred.

t all seems to be a mixed bag of improvisation, hasty thinking, and calculated exaggeration. The

eadership, irrespective of party affiliations, does not seem to have the vision to foster a controlled, productive change. There are grounds for fearing that the country may drift towards the risky shores of anarchy. Both internal and external pressures will be ascendant in the trying days to come.

What this country, or whatever is left of it, needs above all is a sense of committment. Pakistan makes sense only in terms of the good of the people who inhabit it. This country deserves to be preserved for the sake of its 60 million people. This commitment is partly the reason for *Outlook's* re-emergence. To our mind this is justification enough.

Mujib in Power: A Portrait

8 April 1972

DATELINE: SUNDAY EVENING: I'm going to Dacca via Calcutta. Honestly this is the last thing in the world I would like to do, after having seen the massacre on 18 December by the Mukti Bahini with their bayonets. I had promised myself never to set foot in that hateful city. But my director wants me to interview 'Mujib'. Frankly speaking he is right. Since Mr Bhutto had freed him, everyone speaks of him constantly. He is becoming [the] number one star of the subcontinent. Journalists rush in squads to see him. Photographers flock wherever he is. Television has lost all sense of proportion. David Frost of the 'David Frost Show' went from London with a group of twelve technicians to interview him for an entire programme. NBC and CBS have spent huge fortunes to televise his return to Dacca. They say that to greet him, there were more than three hundred thousand persons. When he stepped off the plane, the diplomats who were waiting for him on the platform, were stampeded and one ended up in the hospital. When he was driven through the streets of the city, many children were crushed and one old man found himself with only one shoe. What sort of a man will he be? My colleagues affirm that he is a great man, a superman, [and] the only one in a position to save the country and lead it to democracy. Maybe this is possible. I remember that when I was in Dacca on 18 December, people said 'had Mujib been here, it would not have happened. As soon as Mujib arrives, such things will not happen anymore'. But, then, why did the Mukti Bahini kill another fifty innocent Biharis yesterday? Why did *Time Magazine* publish a headline with a question mark 'Great Man or Rabble Rouser'? I'm astonished specially after having read what he told Aldo Santini who interviewed him in November 1969: 'I am the most courageous and feared man in the country. I am the tiger of Bengal, the Sandokhan of politics ... modesty would be out of place...' I don't know...

Monday Afternoon

I am now at the Intercontinental Hotel and my perplexity is more than doubled. I have seen *the* 'Mujib'. But, for only a few minutes: I will interview him later. But those few minutes were enough to fill me with suspicions and doubts. I arrived in Dacca, and at the airport whom do I meet? No one else but Mr Sarkar, the Bengali who was my interpreter the last time I was here. He was in the middle of the runway, and I cannot figure out just why: perhaps he did not have anything better to do, and the moment he saw me, he asked what he could do for me. I answered that he could take me to Mujib's house. He took me straight away and fifteen minutes later we were entering a gate that was guarded by Mukti Bahini with machine guns. We entered the kitchen where Mujib's wife was eating. Mujib was not there. Eating with her were her nephews and cousins who were sticking their fingers in a common plate taking the rice with sauce to their mouths. This seems to be the usage here. The wife gave me a warm welcome. She caressed my face with her oily fingers dirtying my face. She, then, caressed my suede leather jacket, on which the finger-prints remained and which no laundry or dry cleaning will ever succeed in cleaning. After doing this, she started to chatter without my understanding a word. It was then that Mujib arrived. He appeared suddenly on the threshold of the kitchen. He was dressed in a sort of white toga which made him look like an ancient Roman. Under this toga, he looked tall and straight. Inspite of his fifty-one years of age, he is a handsome man. Fair complexioned with Caucasian features, looking intellectual with a large moustache and his spectacles, one can see that he is the type that people like and who likes to lead the crowds. He looked healthy, but after eight months of jail and the sufferings which he claims to have received, his appearance should have been less prosperous. Pakistanis must have been feeding him in ample measure and with tenderness.

I went to him directly and introduced myself and explained what my mission was. Mr Sarkar fell at his feet and kissed them fanatically then slowly climbed up his legs, the hips, the stomach, and the shoulders without the slightest protest from Mujib or a thought of my presence. I stood there dumbstruck. Then again Sarkar kneeled at his feet kissing the toes which stuck out of the sandals. I intervened fearing that Mr Sarkar, if he continued in this manner, would contract a disease. I took Mujib's hands and said, 'I'm very happy Mr Sheikh to see you back here in the city which feared you would never return'. He looked at me with scorn and with a disdainful smile and replied, 'Speak to my Secretary'. Then he stepped over the body of Sarkar who was at this point completely exhausted on the floor, and went to the table to eat, belching as he sat down.

You can now understand my suspicion and doubt. After all, Mujib was reported to be a democrat and socialist who shunned honours. While I was gasping for breath, a young man arrived and introducing himself as Assistant Secretary, asked me what I wanted. After I explained to him, he started making excuses and at long last promised that I would be given ten minutes, if I appeared at the White House at 4 pm. The White House is the official residence of Mujib where he receives people. It was 3.30 pm and the city was taking its afternoon rest. There were only Mukhti Bahinis on the roads with guns on their shoulders. The war is over for well over a month now, and they still have their arms. They roam day and night like vagabonds shooting in the air and killing people. When they are not killing, they loot shops. No one can stop them, not even Mujib. He is either unable to stop them or he does not wish to. According to a Bengali intellectual, whom I met, he is unable to stop them: 'the only thing he is very good at is to dirty walls with his poster photographs. He wants to see his photographs everywhere'. Strange. This Mujib resembles someone whom I've known, but I cannot figure out just who. Is he Cassius Clay?

Monday Evening

No. He cannot be Cassius Clay although many of his features which come to the mind (belching) bring them very close together. He looks like Mussolini. The same megalomania, the same expression, the same manner of throwing his chin forward, his jaw tightly clenched and even the same voice—arrogant, provocative, war-like voice. Even when he asks what time it is, he seems to be leading a mob to an exhilarating venture. The only difference is that Mussolini admitted to being a fascist. Instead he hides himself behind the mask of liberty, freedom, democracy, and equality. I interviewed him. It was a disaster. Indeed, I have my doubts about his mental capacities. Is he mad? Could it be that prison and the fear of death have shaken his nerves and brain? I cannot explain otherwise his lack of equilibrium. At the same time … well I mean the story of the prison is not very clear to me. How was it that he was simply arrested the night that everyone was killed? How is it that he and his family did not have one hair of their heads touched? How is it that he was allowed to escape from a cell that was to be his tomb? Was he secretly plotting with Bhutto? There is something suspicious about him. The more you observe him, the more one is convinced that he is hiding something. Even his aggressiveness appears to be a form of self-defence. This is the way the interview went this afternoon.

At 4 o' clock sharp I was at the White House. The Assistant Secretary asked me to sit in a corridor crowded with at least fifty persons and walked into the office to inform Mujib of my presence. I heard a terrible growl, and the poor man reappeared shaken asking me to wait. I waited. One hour, two hours, three hours, four hours, then at eight o' clock I was still there in that damned corridor. At eight thirty a miracle: Mujib was ready to receive me. I was asked to enter. I entered into a large room with a sofa and two armchairs. On the sofa, there was the Mujib sprawled all over it. Two fat ministers were seated on the armchairs with their bellies in the air. No one rose. No one made a greeting, and no one responded to mine. There was a very, very long silence until Mujib gestured me to sit down. I sat on the sofa and opened the tape recorder preparing the first question. But, I didn't have time in that he started to shout:

'Hurry up quick, understand?' 'I have no time to waste, is that clear? The Pakistanis have killed three million of my people, is that clear? Yes, three, three, three'! (How he arrived at that figure, I'll never understand. The Indians speaking of victims have never gone over one million. But it was not even the false figure that counted, it was the way in which he said it which seemed as if I killed those three million persons).

'Mr Prime Minister …' 'They killed my women in front of their children and husbands, the husbands in front of their sons and wives, the sons before their fathers and mothers, the nephews in front of their grandfathers and grandmothers, the grandfathers and mothers in front of their nephews, the cousins in front of their cousins, the aunts in front of their uncles, the brothers-in-law in front of their sisters-in-law…'

'Mr Prime Minister, I would like…'

'Listen to her, she would like: she would like: What would you like? You have no right to want anything, understand? Is that clear?'

A very uncomfortable beginning indeed. In fact, my first reaction was to send him to hell and quit. But I wanted to know more on the question which does not convince me.

'Mr Prime Minister, were you tortured when arrested?'

'No, Madam, no: They knew that it would have been useless. They knew my character, my strength, my courage, my honour, my values, my heroism, understand? They wanted to hang me that's all, understand?'

'I understand. But how did you come to know that they wanted to hang you? Was the death sentence to be carried out by hanging?'

'No. No sentence: There was no sentence'.

'Then how did you come to know it?'

At this point he became confused and started to tell stories.

'I knew it because on 15 December they dug a ditch to bury me'.

'Where was it dug?'

'In my cell'.

'Was not there a flooring in your cell?'

'No'.

'While digging the ditch, did they tell you that you would be hung?'

'No'.

'Then how did you find out?'

'I guessed it when I saw them digging a ditch near my cell'.

'Inside the cell or beside the cell?'

'Near my cell'.

'I understood that it was in your cell'.

'You understood wrong'.

'How were you treated Mr Prime Minister?'

'I was put in solitary confinement. I was not even allowed interviews, to read newspapers, to receive the mail, nothing, understand'.

'Then what did you do?'

'I did a lot of thinking, reading'.

'What did you read?'

'Books and other things'.

'Then you read something?'

'Yes, I read a bit'.

'I understood that you were not allowed to read anything?'

'You understood wrongly'.

'Yes, yes, Mr Prime Minister. How was it that they did not hang you?'

'The jailor allowed me to escape from my cell and sheltered me in his home'.

'Why? Had he received an order?'

'I don't know. I didn't talk to him and he didn't talk to me'.

'Had you become friends in spite of the silence?'

'Yes, we had many discussions together, and he decided to help'.

'You, therefore, talked with him'.

'Yes, I spoke with him'.

'I was led to believe that you did not speak to anyone'.

'You misunderstood'.

'Of course, Mr Minister. Don't you feel grateful to this man who saved your life?'

'No. Why should I?'

'Because he saved your life, Mr Prime Minister'. 'It was fate. I believe in fate'.

He then spoke of Bhutto. But this time without any contradictions. He was very careful. He told me that on 26 December, Bhutto went looking for him with a helicopter and some soldiers, to take him back to Rawalpindi. 'Bhutto behaved like a gentleman. He is a gentleman', and he reported that there had been a war; a thing that Mujib had suspected from the blackouts and the roaring of planes. He explained that he was now President and wanted to make some proposals. 'What proposals Mr Prime Minister?' 'Why should I tell you? This is a personal affair, a private affair. Ha, listen to her, I should tell her'. 'Not to me, Mr Prime Minister, but to history. You know very well that this will go down in history'. 'I am history'. 'Exactly', I stopped him immediately. 'I told Bhutto proudly, "Am I free? Because if I'm not free, I refuse to speak to you." Then Bhutto respectfully replied, "You are free although I cannot release you, only after one or two days—but not immediately." Having said this, Bhutto started making plans for West Pakistan and Bangladesh. I answered proudly again, that I could not make plans without first consulting my people'. 'However, it was a friendly conversation, Mr Prime Minister?' 'Certainly, it was very friendly. We knew each other well, I did not know that Pakistanis had committed such barbaric acts against my people; I did not know that they had killed mothers in front of their sons and husbands, fathers in front of sons and their wives, the sons in front of their fathers and mothers, nephews in front of grandfathers, grandfathers in front of nephews, cousins...' 'I know, Mr Prime Minister, I know'. 'You do not know anything ... The aunts before their uncles, cousins in front of their cousins, brothers-in-law in front of brothers-in-law. I did not know that they had killed my scientists, lawyers, dentists, my engineers, my architects, my servants, my houses, my lands, my properties'. 'Oh…'

On his properties, he made a tremendous groan. It was so tremendous that I felt the need to ask him whether he was really a socialist and he replied 'Yes…' with a rather uncertain voice, I asked him what he meant by socialism and he replied, 'the socialism', thus showing that he did not have an exact idea of socialism. After this came the big drama.

I burst out with my long-intended question on how he felt about the massacre of 18 December. Following is taken from tape-recorder: 'Massacre? What massacre?' 'The one committed by Mukti Bahini at the Dacca Stadium'. 'There has never been any massacre at the Dacca Stadium. You are lying'. 'Mr Prime Minister, I am a not a liar, I saw that massacre with other journalists and other fifteen thousand persons. If you'd like, I'll show you the photographs. My paper has published them'. 'Liar, those were not Mukti Bahini'. 'Mr Prime Minister, do not repeat, please, the word, liar, they were Mukti Bahini, they were led by Abdul Kader Siddiqui and wore uniforms'. 'Then it means that those Razakars had opposed resistance and Siddiqui was compelled to eliminate them'. 'Mr Prime Minister, no one has proved those people were Razakars and no one opposed resistance. They were quiet, frightened, immobile with their hands tied'. 'Liar'. 'For the last time, I will not permit you to call me liar'. 'Well then what would you have done?' 'I'll tell you immediately what I would have done. I would have first ascertained if those persons were Razakars and guilty and after satisfying myself that they were so, I would have executed them by a firing squad, thus avoiding that shameless lynching'. 'It means that my people had no bullets'. 'Yes, they had bullets. They had lots of bullets. They still have lots of bullets, they do nothing else but shoot from morning to night. They shoot at trees, at clouds, at the sky, at persons, only to amuse themselves'.

My God, what happened then; even the two fat ministers who had been snoring all this time woke up. I did not even know what he was shouting. He screamed in the Bengali language and to avoid being killed, I did not wait to be kicked out. I sneaked out quietly.

Monday Night

All of Dacca knows what happened between me and Mujib. Not all of Dacca is on my side. Mujib's nephew, however, is on my side. His name is Shamsher Wadud, a handsome young man, gentle, with a smooth voice. He is the son of the eldest sister of Mujib and has a Bengali restaurant in New York called the 'Nirvana'. He came to Dacca at his own expense to call on his uncle. But is already sorry he did. 'If you only knew how he has treated me; like a dishrag; and to think that I even brought him flowers; presumptions scoundrel, egoist. Power must have driven him mad. He has always been like that, but now he is exaggerating. If he continues on this road, he'll end up badly. He will at least lose his great popularity. This is what we all say in our family. Poor uncle. On the other hand you must understand him—he has never been very intelligent. Just imagine, he finished high school when he was 22 years old. He entered politics as the Secretary of the Awami League President. He could not do anything else. He arranged appointments, read the mail; who would have ever suspected that my uncle would rise so high and become the Prime Minister? However, this is not a good reason to act haughtily with his relatives. In fact, my mother will lead a family protest delegation consisting of people who have been offended by him to death. It will be quite a show. My uncle has always feared my mother. Not only because she is the eldest daughter and therefore authoritative, but because my mother is not the type of obedient Muslim who accepts abuses. I will tell her what he has done to you, so that she will reproach him for this. However, you should not let him get away with it. You must protest. Why don't you go to the Government Headquarters and speak to some of the ministers? Try to speak to the President of the Republic who is a real gentleman'.

I shall do it, as tomorrow I cannot leave. I have just learned that to leave Bangladesh one needs an exit visa. I must get it before it is too late. I'm starting to feel uneasy here in Dacca.

Tuesday Afternoon

First of all, I have gone to get an exit visa. The police gave me a hard time. 'Why do you want to leave so soon? What is the reason for such a hurry, you have just arrived, etc., etc.' But when I said that I was a friend of Mujib, they stamped my passport at once. After this I went to the Government Headquarters. I could not see the President of the Republic who was still sleeping. I met the Foreign Minister. He was a young man who lived for many years in Rome as a diplomat in the Pakistan Embassy. He knew me by name and this helped things a bit. I told him everything, including my indignation. He let out a sigh that came from the bottom of his heart, shook his head and said that he apologized on behalf of the Government, promising me that I would meet Mujib again. 'Please go to him again, we will arrange it in such a way that all will go smoothly'. I doubt it very much. However, inspite of insults received, I am not against the idea of seeing Mujib again. One must always give a second chance. To judge on the basis of one meeting is unfair. Let us be sure before giving a definite judgement. To be a journalist is a great responsibility. Suppose Mujib was nervous last night, for some good reason? Suppose I irritated him with a wrong remark? Yes, I'll see him again, I must go back.

Moreover, the information which I have collected on him is catastrophic. Listen to this: Early in 1971 Bhutto came to Dacca. He was accommodated at the Intercontinental Hotel, apt. No. 911-913. Guess who was his guide? It was Shaikh Mujibur Rahman, now just 'Mujib'. It was actually him. They were always together like two very good friends. In the hotel apartment, they ordered whisky and snacks and were always happy and smiling. One morning they went on a picnic on a boat. Yet they could not agree on a settlement. But, why all this if they were enemies? Then they met again in March 1971 and at 10 o'clock on 25 March the tragedy happened. Bhutto witnessed like Nero from the last floor of the Intercontinental Hotel, drinking and laughing, while the city was burning and guns wildly shooting. At 7 o'clock the next morning he left. But, before leaving, he made a telephone call. Could he have wanted to make sure that nothing happened to his friend? At Dacca the truth always comes to the surface. I have even found out that those who were afraid of Pakistanis are now afraid of Mujib. There is a lot of talk of democracy, freedom, but it is always said in a whisper and with fear. 'Don't write my name, he will take revenge'. 'Do not disclose the source. I will be jailed'. And so whispering with tears in their eyes they tell you that the price paid by Mujib is nothing compared to the price paid by others. The others have been killed, but Mujib has lost little property. Yes, he is rich, very rich. The day after his return he had helicopters at the disposal of foreign journalists. Do you know why? So that they could go to see for themselves the damage caused to his properties. And yet he chats of socialism, of nationalization. He protests but will he nationalize all of his lands, his houses, the splendid villa he is building and the luxurious Mercedes which he drives? Let him take off his mask and confess who his friends are: the British and the Americans. He is servile when he meets an Englishman or an American. He embraces English and American journalists. If this was not so, why did he go to London and not to New Delhi when he was freed? There were no connections between Karachi and New Delhi, it is agreed. But there were connections between Karachi and Tehran, between Karachi and Athens and by landing in Athens or in Tehran, he could reach India and spend twenty four hours with Indira Gandhi, who had arranged a warm welcome. Instead, he spent twenty four hours in London and only fifty minutes with Mrs Indira at the airport that night.

His first argument came with Bhutto in 1965 because West Pakistan had left East Pakistan's border with India undefended. As a statesman, he is of little value. His only talent is to send the illiterate to ecstasy. He is a magician of rhetoric, of lies—the most extravagant lies. Sometime back, during a public speech, he said the streets of Karachi were covered with gold, and if one was to walk on them, one would be blinded. He does not understand a thing about economics. For him agriculture is a mystery. Politics for him is an improvisation. Do you know why he won the elections in 1970? The cyclone had destroyed all crops etc. Even the Mauists voted for him and their leader Bhashani decided to transfer his votes to the Awami League. If the people were asked to vote again, Mujib would be in an entirely different position, unless he imposes his will by the use of guns. This is why he does not ask the Mukti Bahini to hand over their arms; and we must remember that his personal adviser is named Abdul Kader Siddiqui—the bloodthirsty henchman who wanted and led the massacres at the Dacca Stadium. The Indians had arrested him, and Mujib had him freed. Now we come to democracy. A word that fills the entire mouth. Can a man who does not allow opposition be democratic? If anyone does not agree with him, he accuses him of being a Razakar. The least that will happen to him is that he is sent to jail. He has the makings of a dictator, and it suits his vanity—which is part of his natural character. Poor Bengalis, they have gone from the frying pan into the fire. With regard to Bengali women, it is better not to speak. He shuns women. There are no women in his government. Not even a lady typist. And you should see how he deals with his wife. Have you seen what condition she is in at only 38?

Now I am going once again to the White House. The Foreign Minister telephoned me and informed me that the second appointment with Mujib has been arranged and this time all will go well. Instructions have been issued by the President of the Republic.

Tuesday Evening

The President of the Republic hasn't had much success. Just imagine, to have his instructions carried out, he had to send two officials. But all they could obtain was a growl and the authorization to wait in a room instead of the candour. I waited from four o'clock in the afternoon until nine o'clock in the evening. A servant filled my tea cup as soon as it was empty and I drank 18 cups of tea. At the 19th cup of tea, I threw the tea cup on the floor and went away. The Secretary, and the Assistant Secretary of Mujib, rushed after me to the hotel. They apologized and told me that Mujib had fallen ill at seven o'clock and had fainted. This is why I had to wait and they told me that Mujib wanted to see me very much the next morning at seven thirty. I don't know what to do.

Wednesday Afternoon

I am now on a plane that is taking me to Calcutta and to New Delhi. I was able to board the plane thanks to the help of five Australian businessmen and two Indian officers. If it wasn't for this, I would still be in Dacca, certainly not alive, but cut in pieces like Razakars and Biharis. This is because I lost my temper and I treated Mujib badly and told him that he was a charlatan. He took it badly, but let me tell you the story which starts at six o'clock in the morning. I got ready and packed my things to rush to the airport immediately after my meeting with Mujib, and then I went to the White House punctually like an automatic watch. There was no one at the White House except a butterfly over a flower, and a dog which was peeing against a tree. There was no one at eight o' clock, eight thirty or nine. At long last—at nine thirty—Mujib arrived in his Mercedes. I went to meet him. He wouldn't deign to look at me. I said good morning, he did not answer. I followed him, he groaned and then suddenly said 'Are you still here?' I reminded him that the evening before he had sent his Secretary and Assistant Secretary to my hotel to fix an appointment at seven thirty. He didn't say a word and entered his office. I also entered the office and then he screamed 'Get out'. I left. And he screamed 'Get in here'. I returned and there appeared three men with his photograph the size of a poster. They threw themselves at his feet and start licking them like Mr Sarkar. Touching and kissing they climb up his legs, the belly, and the shoulders. They show him the posters in which Mujib is looking up with his chin out forward, and his eyes with a wild look. He looked at it and said 'Beautiful. Show it to the lady journalist'. They show it to me. I repeat, 'Beautiful'. This was a very serious error. Just like a thunder storm he went into a wild rage, he threw the picture to the floor screaming that it wasn't beautiful at all, it was a disaster. I don't understand anything. I should keep still.

How I was able to calm down I don't know. However, I was successful. Diplomacy was necessary since I wanted to know his relationship with Bhutto. I wanted to know up to what point his conscience was dirty. This was an illusion. As soon as I mentioned the name of Bhutto, I found myself with my eardrums deaf. Bombarding my ears, he screeched that he only wanted to answer questions on the future of Bangladesh. I had to listen to him. I asked him if he considered the possibility of Bangladesh uniting with West Bengal, which is a part of India. He remained confused. 'For the time being I am not interested anymore? Just imagine Indira Gandhi's surprise to hear that Mujib wanted to grab Calcutta'. 'Do you mean that in the past you were interested and in the future this could be reconsidered', I insisted. 'Oh God'. Through the dense clouds of his obtuseness, he realized that I had led him into a trap, and he might have given a wrong answer. Instead of correcting himself, he slapped the table with his fist and started to scream that I was not a journalist but a public minister; I was not interrogating him, but accusing him, I was to get out immediately and never set foot in his country again. At that point I didn't know how to hold myself back. The patience with which I had kept an appearance in the last few days flew out of the window. The exasperation which had accumulated within me, exploded. I said that he was a charlatan, a hysterical madman, and that he would end up badly. While he looked at me with his mouth wide open, incredulous, I left to find a rickshaw. I went to the hotel, paid my bill, grabbed my suitcase and rushed to the airport. When I started to leave, the Mukti Bahinis were waiting for me out in the hall. The most brave of these said that I had insulted the Father of the Country and that I would pay dearly for this. He flew at me, and I landed a punch at him square in the face. In the fray that followed, the Mukti Bahini started to hit each other, and I was able to escape into the car of five Australians (businessmen) who kept saying 'quickly; hurry, quick'. At the airport two Indian officials took me to the plane and here I am. I am writing a letter to my editor.

Letter to the Editor

Dear Director, I've been to Dacca, as I said I would. But I would have preferred not to have gone. That Mujib is not serious. To write it in the form of an interview would be a laugh. I will not write it. To convince you, I am sending you all my notes. Do what you will, sincerely,

Oriana Fallaci
Courtesy Europeo, Milan

The Laws and Facts about POWs

15 April 1972

Dr Aziz N. Kurtha

WITH some 98,000 of our troops, and over 8000 civilian government employees plus nearly 300 sick and wounded members of our armed forces presently in Indian (and Bangladesh) captivity, it is understandable that almost every day we should be subject to some report or the other about our prisoners of war. A number of demonstrations and protests—particularly from Lahore and Pindi—have been held by the families of captive prisoners of war emphasizing the human problems concerning the question of repatriation.

Incidentally, there seems to be same confusion about the exact number of our POWs in captivity. According to the latest list of POWs supplied by India to the International Committee of the Red Cross and reported in *Dawn* on 7 April, the Indians say they hold about 17,600 *more* POWs than our government claims. Even if this extra figure includes the civilian internees (8000), which we list separately, it still leaves some 7600 POWs unaccounted for in our books. This raises the horrendous implication that we did not know that almost half an army division was fighting on our side!

We have no exact information about the real condition and plight of the POWs themselves. But one thing is clear—it must have been a traumatic experience for most of them to find themselves in captivity after fighting and being fed on the idea that they were the greatest fighting force in the world. The experience must have been even more harrowing for those who find themselves in captivity at a variety of skeletal camps in India, without ever having wholeheartedly joined the battlefield. Victims of gross military miscalculation and 'CIA-ish' chicanery, many of them must be as bewildered as impotent men incarcerated on charges of rape.

The provisions of law, however, are always printed in cold and callous print, with innumerable schedules and appendices, through which one has to meander in order to find the meaning. The Geneva conventions of 1949 are very lengthy and are couched in language which seems almost deliberately designed to deter any intelligent layman from reading them. Nevertheless, they are very comprehensive and contain many humanitarian provisions protecting war victims. There are, of course, four Geneva conventions namely (i) the Prisoners of War Convention (ii) the Civilians

15

Convention and (iii) and (iv) the conventions relating to the sick and wounded at sea and on land. These conventions are not the first of their kind; but they are the most detailed and, to a large extent, were dictated by the experiences of the Second World War in which the many deficiencies of previous conventions like the one of 1929, became apparent. One of the greatest drawbacks of previous conventions relating to the laws of war was that they contained what is technically known as a 'general participation clause'. This, in effect, meant that even if there were six state participants in a war, and even if only one of them was not a party to a particular convention, then the conventions applied to none of the parties at all. In other words, the conventions apply to all those participating in the conflict or do not apply to any of them at all. One of the arguments of the Germans during the Second World War was that none of the previous conventions applied to any state during the global conflict because Poland was not a party to any conventions. Mercifully, the 1949 Geneva Conventions deliberately omit such a requirement.

Secondly, the 1949 conventions, which largely replace all previous conventions relating to war victims, contain novel provisions whereby they apply not only to international conflicts but also, in a limited manner, to other conflicts, including civil wars. The wordings of Article 2, which is common to all four of the conventions, read as follows:

> The present convention shall apply to all cases of declared war or of any other armed conflict which may arise between two or more of the Contracting Parties, even if the state of war is not recognized by one of them. The convention shall also apply to all cases of partial or total occupation of the territory of a High Contracting Party even if the said occupant meets with no armed resistance.

The same provision totally does away with the need for any declaration of war for a legal state of war to come into operation. But of course, it is the provisions relating to repatriation which are of immediate concern. Article 118 of the POW conventions which states 'that prisoners of war shall be released and repatriated without delay after the cession of active hostilities,' has been learnt by heart by every *awami* politician and every member of a *jawan's* family. The provisions of Article 109 are, however, rather less well known. They provide inter alia that sick and wounded POWs are entitled to be sent back to their own country as soon as they are cared for and are fit for travel. In view of this unusually unadvantageous stipulation it is a source of constant amazement to the relatively uninitiated as to why nearly one lac of our POWs have still not returned home. Here we have to face the stark reality that international law exists in a twilight zone between law and big power politics. The distressing truth is that, in international law as much as in international affairs, might is right.

Thus, the fact is that our prisoners of war are not being repatriated, in clear violation of international law, simply because the Government of India does not wish to repatriate them and the big powers are happy to acquiesce in this situation. For, the provisions of Article 129 to 131 of the conventions also very clearly provide that every party to the convention, which includes the majority of states in the world, is under an obligation to ensure compliance with the stipulations of the conventions. Under the Geneva Accords of 1954 relating to Vietnam, Article 21 provided for repatriation of POWs 30 days after the ceasefire. It would be painful to labour this picayune platitude of international life.

Nevertheless, certain matters relating to our POWs which seem to be causing a great deal of confusion need clarification. For the time being we shall bypass the controversial subject of war crimes. But, our representative at the UN is quite right in stating that it would be illegal for India to hand over our POWs to Bangladesh.

There has been a great deal of wild speculation in our press about mass exchanges of Bengali populations in West Pakistan for our captured POWs. It may come as a rude surprise to many of these self-appointed spokesmen that, generally speaking, exchanges, as opposed to a repatriation, are not governed by the Geneva Convention at all. The only article which marginally touches on the question of exchanges is Article 109. In fact, during the first and second world wars no such exchanges took place at all, except for wounded POWs.

The technical term for exchange of prisoners is cartels. Of course, there is nothing to prevent exchanges taking place, but exchange is generally related to members of the armed forces. Therefore the opinion that the Bengali uncaptured civilian population in West Pakistan could be exchanged for captive prisoners of war in Bangladesh and India, who have to be repatriated in any case by the captors, is as reckless as speculation on the stock exchange.

As regards the recently reported shootings of our POWs in Indian camps, it is pertinent to Article 42 of the POW Convention.

'The use of weapons against POWs especially those who are escaping or attempting to escape, shall constitute an extreme measure, which shall always be preceded by warnings appropriate to the circumstances.' Needless to say there were no warnings of the prospective murder of the unarmed POWs.

On the question of transfers of our POWs from Indian captivity to the Bangladesh authorities the provisions of Article 12 of the POW Convention are again clear and state that 'POWs may only be transferred by the Detaining Power (in this case India) to a Power which is a party to the Convention.' As the POW Convention came into operation on 12 August 1949 and the nascent state of Bangladesh was delivered by mother India and baptized by father Kosygin on 20 December 1971, there is no question of Bangladesh being a party to the convention. However, on 5 April 1972, Bangladesh was reported to have formally applied for accession to the Geneva Convention and thus a legal headache arises as to whether the convention can have retrospective effect for a new signatory.

Transcript I: David Frost Interviews Mujib

22 April 1972

EDITOR'S note: This is the first part of a transcript of the interview given to Mr David Frost by Shaikh Mujibur Rahman on 26 January 1971, at Dacca. It was recorded from television by an English girl in London and transcribed by her. There are, therefore, some mistakes in names and places which the girl could not catch because of their unfamiliarity and because of Shaikh Mujib's accent.

A few deletions have been made to remove repetitions and to make the material more manageable. These, however, do not detract from the veracity of the statement and this account is faithful and authentic, and not coloured in any way.

This television show, we are given to understand, was a departure from David Frost's usual format. Mr David Frost was invited by Shaikh Mujib, as is mentioned later in the interview, and himself appeared several times on Dacca Television. Both on Dacca Television, and in this interview, Mr Frost made no secret of his identification with the Bangladesh movement.

This interview is being printed primarily for two reasons. Firstly, to acquaint people with Shaikh Mujibur Rahman's thoughts before 25 March 1971. Part II of the interview, to be printed next week, has some bearing on the view recently expressed by Gen. Tikka Khan that 'Mujib was preparing for a showdown'.

And, secondly, it is intended to show how great a barrier Shaikh Mujib's stance will be in any talks between him and a West Pakistani leader. In any case, the record must be set straight in regard to the events which took place in Bangladesh.

The Frost Programme from Bangladesh
The plane touches down

Frost: It's good to see you after the delay.

Reporter: Just say something for the television viewers of Bangladesh.

Frost: I just share your joy that the dark days are over and I hope that the sunshine that greets me here will be apparent throughout the nation as soon as possible. It's been a thrill for the whole world and when Shaikh Mujib arrived in London last Saturday, I think that the whole world rejoiced. I certainly rejoiced and I rejoice to be here.

Reporter: Well, will you please sum up our revolutionary struggle?

Frost: I will do that better when I leave, I think. I don't think I'm an expert yet, do you? But I am just very happy, that's all. Happy to be here and happy at the outcome. It's a pleasure to be here and thank you very much. (Frost travels on through people)

Frost: It is so good to see you.

Mujib: I am so happy to see you. Just now I am holding a press conference.

Frost: So, we can't do our interview now, but we shall listen.

Mujib: Tomorrow.

Frost: Tomorrow would be lovely. (Man shouts)

Frost: As you can probably see here in Sakharipatti, life in the new-born State of Bangladesh is returning to normal … or at least as normal as it possibly can, considering the events of the past few months.

(Events like this: These were houses, and then what happened here in Sakharipatti was simply terrifying. A West Pakistani army tank at that end, a West Pakistani tank at this end. First of all shelling in this densely populated area. The results you see all around me. Then the resistance was softened up with light machine guns and then the troops moved in, simply and terrifyingly to each house, abusing the surviving residents upto the roofs, where they were bayoneted and in many cases thrown back down into the streets again. It's estimated that 10,000 people died here in Sakharipatti alone.)

But now a new nation has been born. Today Shaikh Mujib, the beloved leader of that new nation, talks on television for the first time. His story of the past few months of bloodshed out of which Bangladesh has been born. Joy Bangla. (Loud shout goes up)

Frost: On the night that you were arrested, on the night when in fact West Pakistan was about to invade, they had been talking with you for some time and disguising their intentions, and then they invaded. Now, you were at home at eight o'clock on the night you were arrested. And you got a warning, I believe by telephone that the army was on the way. Why did you decide to stay and be arrested?

Mujib: You see there is a most interesting story on this point. Early in the evening they almost surrounded my house with commandoes and they wanted to kill me if I came out of the house, and then blame the outrage on my own people. Mujibur Rahman, they would say, had been killed by the extremists of Bangladesh while the government was negotiating with him, and Yahya Khan had no alternative but to take action against that.

Frost: Certainly that's, oh I see.

Mujib: That was the first idea. Next I knew they were brutes.

Frost: Brutes?

Mujib: Brutes. Uncivilized. They would kill my whole people, who would be massacred. I thought it was better that I should die and at least save my people who loved me so much.

Frost: You didn't want to run. I mean you could have gone to Calcutta perhaps, and flown.

Mujib: I could have gone any place if I had used money and if I was ready to go. But how could I leave my people? I am the leader of a nation, I can fight and die. But I asked my people to resist.

Frost: You were right, of course, this is what in the past nine months made you such a symbol for your people to believe in. They think of you now as almost a god, don't they?

Mujib: I don't say that. I wanted to save the lives of the patriots, but the brutes, in arresting me, destroyed my precious home. Both my father, ninety, and my mother, eighty years of age were living in my precious house, in the centre of the village. The army dragged my father from the house and burned the house in front of them. They had no shelter.

This is the way they burned everything. I thought that if they get me, at least they would not kill my unfortunate people, for I knew my party was sufficiently strong. I had organized the party and the people behind it. They would fight it out. And I had told them, you must fight every inch. I had told them it might be my last order. Until we were emancipated, we would continue to fight and struggle.

Frost: How did they actually arrest you? It was one thirty in the morning, wasn't it? What happened?

Mujib: I was staying with my family in my bedroom and this—they started machine gunning from this side, shooting from this window, all broken you know and the bullet entered my bedroom. My six year child sleeping on the bed—I will show you.

Frost: But where were you?

Mujib: I was here. This is my bed.

Frost: And the machine gun bullets came through?

Mujib: From these windows.

Frost: Your wife was here?

Mujib: Yes. With two children.

Frost: Where did the Pakistani troops come in?

Mujib: All sides.

Mujib: They were shooting from that side. Then I told my wife to sit here with my two children. I went out.

Frost: You went out this way?

Mujib: Yes. I came here, took leave of my wife.

Frost: Leaving her here?

Mujib: Yes.

Frost: What did she say?

Mujib: She did not say a word. I only kissed her. A farewell kiss.

Frost: Just a farewell kiss.

Mujib: A farewell kiss and we came out. They were shooting from that window. The door opened. I opened it. I came out. I said you can stop shooting; I am here. What are you shooting for? Then they start moving from all sides … to charge me. Then accidentally, one officer was here. He caught hold of me like this. 'Don't kill him', he said.

Frost: Just one officer stopped them?

Mujib: This time. Then they took me, dragged me from here and they started raining blows from the back on my head and then from there guns in the back. You know. They started pushing me here and there. The officer caught me but still they started pushing. And dragged me down and said, 'Come on'. I said, 'Wait'. Allow me to bring my pipe and tobacco and say goodbye to my wife. I grabbed my pipe, then came again. I saw my wife standing here with my two children. Nobody was there and they brought the pipe for me, and clothes and something in a small suitcase. I went away. But I could see the fire from all sides burning everywhere, shooting the mortars all over Dacca. They took me from here.

Frost: And as you left 32, Dhanmandi, did you think you would see it again?

Mujib: I knew I would not—I thought that was the end. If I died as the leader, at least they (my people) will not be ashamed, but if I surrendered to them, my nation, my people of my country would not be able to show their face to the world.

Frost: You once said you could not kill someone who was ready to die, didn't you?

Mujib: I did. You can kill a man physically but you cannot kill a man's soul. You can't. It's my fate. I am a Mussalman. And a Mussalman dies only once. I am a leader of this nation. There is nothing I cannot expect from them. They are giving everything for me, because I want to give everything for them. And to make them free, I want to see my children happy—by my children I mean these unfortunate people of Bangladesh. And today they are free. I am willing to die. This is my last wish, you know.

They have taken my furniture, my chairs, my mirrors, my clothes and my children's clothes and everything. I only mind the fact that they have taken my life's history. I had diaries for 35 years of my political life. I have a wonderful library. They have taken every book of mine. And all my documents. Everything has been taken by the Pakistani army.

Frost: Again, again the question comes so often, why? Why did they? Why take everything?

Mujib: I don't know. They are not human beings. They are … They are …They are fanatics. They are inhuman, uncivilized creatures. This is a small thing of mine. I don't mind it. Think of all this when they have killed a two-year-old child, a-year-old child. Five-year-old children, women. Think about that. They have no heart, no homes, I have shown you how they burned the poor cottages, they are absolutely hungry people. With the fire burning people rush from their houses, they can't live there. They rush to stand outside in the thousands.

Frost: Forced out of their houses and when they're in the open, gun them down.

Mujib: That's right.

Frost: They just did it to anybody?

Mujib: Any people. They feel that everyone is Shaikh Mujibur Rahman's follower. Everyone should be killed.

Frost: When you see people, human beings do something like that do you feel that human beings are basically good or does that make you feel that the human being is basically bad?

Mujib: There is good and bad everywhere. People have animal qualities I know; but these people are worse than animals. They kept torturing my people, five days, ten days, fifteen days, torturing and having them killed. They made a court martial with five military officers and one civil officer and that trial is *in camera*. That is inside Lyallpur Jail.

Frost: What did they charge you with?

Mujib: The charge is treason. One against the Pakistan Government. Against their armed forces. Wanted to make Bengal Independent! In all 12 charges. And for six charges [the] punishment is hanging.

Frost: And did you have any defence? Did you have a defence?

Mujib: The government had given defence first. Mr Brohi. But when I saw the situation and the position, I thought, no use of it.

Frost: Pardon?

Mujib: No use of defending me, because this was a mock trial. It is a farce. Then I got up in court and said, Mr Justice kindly ask the defence lawyers to go away. Because you know it is a comic trial. I am a civilian. I am not a military person. And they are giving me a court martial. And Mr Yahya Khan is not only the president, he is the chief martial law administrator, who administers it. He is the confirming authority. He is the confirming authority of this court.

Frost: Did you carry on going to the court or did you stay away?

Mujib: I had to. I was a prisoner.

Frost: You didn't have much freedom of choice. Did they ever reach an official verdict, I mean, this group?

Mujib: After the court finished the sittings on 4 December. Immediately he (Yahya) called all judges to Rawalpindi. To dictate the judgement, there they decided to hang me.

Frost: And indeed I believe that you discovered that in the next cell to you, they were digging a grave.

Mujib: Yes. When I—they removed me from Lyallpur Jail to Mianwali Jail again, just near my cell they are digging the grave.

Frost: You knew they were doing that?

Mujib: Yes. I have seen that with my own eyes. And I say I know this is my grave perhaps. Alright I am ready.

Frost: Did they say, 'Yes this is your grave.'

Mujib: No, no they don't say that.

Frost: What did they say?

Mujib: They said, no, no, no, no, we are making some of these [so that], in the event of a bomb attack, you can take shelter. I said the wall in all sides is small, very thin. Don't try to fool me, I understand.

Frost: And at that moment in time, what were your thoughts. Had you thought that you were about to die, all the nine months, or were you suddenly?

Mujib: No, no, I know all the nine months that, any time I can die.

Frost: And how did you face up to that? Did you pray?

Mujib: I always. I can always because I can face my conviction. I can face for my principle. I can face for my 75 million people.

Frost: Do you think first of your country for instance, or your wife and children?

Mujib: No, I think for my country and my people.

Frost: Because they need that?

Mujib: And you know that I know that human beings have to die one day, today tomorrow or the day after tomorrow, then every human being should die later than this man.

Frost: Like a courageous man.

Mujib: Yes, like a courageous man.

Frost: And how were you saved? How were you—who saved you from that grave?

Mujib: I think the God, the Almighty God saved me and the inspiration of my people who had started fighting, yes.

Frost: Did the jailer move you at one point? Did he move you away when Yahya Khan came to collect you, to kill you, I read one account?

Mujib: They created a situation inside the jail. They sent some assassins to the jail and they mobilized the prisoners in the jail to create a disturbance. The guards would use this disturbance as an excuse for killing me. The one officer, who was in charge of me, started moving me. Something like that. As far as he knew Yahya Khan's days were numbered. At 3 o'clock at night, he took me out of the jail and took me in his bungalow for two days without any police or military guards. After two days, from there they took me to another deserted area of Chashma Barrage, a colony, Chashma Barrage colony. They kept me for five, six days. Nobody knew where I was except the four officers.

Frost: I wonder what has happened to them.

Mujib: I don't know. I don't think they can do anything to them. But I wish them good luck.

Frost: And missed even when Yahya Khan was handing over to Mr Bhutto. I gather he again suggested that you should be hanged. Is that right?

Mujib: Absolutely.

Frost: Mr Bhutto, told you?

Mujib: That is a most interesting story. Mr Bhutto told me that when Yahya Khan wanted to surrender power to Mr Bhutto, he said, Mr Bhutto I have committed a gross blunder in not killing Shaikh Mujibur Rahman before.

Frost: He said that?

Mujib: Yes. Now kindly allow me before handing over the power to kill Mujibur Rahman giving the order a back date. Hang him now and then I hand over the power. But Bhutto refused.

Frost: Did Bhutto tell you what he said?

Mujib: Yes.

Frost: What did Bhutto say?

Mujib: Bhutto said that I can't allow, because there will be a serious reaction … One lac twenty thousand armed forces and civilians have been arrested in Bengal in the hands of the allied forces of Bangladesh and Indian army. If you kill Mujibur Rahman now, and I take over the power, not a single soul will come from Bangladesh to West Pakistan again. And the reaction in West Pakistan, and my position will be precarious.

Frost: And today there …

Mujib: I am grateful to Mr Bhutto, no doubt about it.

Frost: No doubt about it yes. And today there is Yahya Khan. If you came face to face with him today, what would you say to him.

Mujib: He is a criminal. I don't like to see his photo even.

Frost: You don't?

Mujib: He has killed my three million people of Bangladesh by his forces, his soldiers.

Frost: Mr Bhutto has him under house arrest. What should Mr Bhutto do, do you think?

Mujib: Do no obvious harm. You know what else has happened in Bengal? I'll tell you. 3,000,000 people have been killed including children, women, intellectuals, peasants, workers, students and at least 25 to 30 per cent houses burnt and looted. All the food godowns have been destroyed.

Frost: And how do you know that the number was as high as 3 million?

Mujib: I have my machinery you know. You know that before my return, they had started collecting information. Moreover, I have my own militia, my own Awami League Party has a base in every village, every union, every subdivision and messages come through from all over the areas. We have not finally calculated, and the number might be more.

Frost: And this was just pointless killing? They just dragged people out of their houses?

Mujib: Yes, they were absolutely peaceful people who lived in their houses, in the village, knew absolutely nothing of the war.

Frost: Why, why, why?

Mujib: I don't know. I can't understand it. It never happened in this world, never in the history of the world has such a thing happened. This is most unfortunate.

Frost: And it was Muslim killing Muslim?

Mujib: Ya, they claim to be Muslims. How could a Muslim kill a Muslim girl?

Frost: How did they do that?

Mujib: They have done it. We have rescued thousands. We still get them from out of the camps. The husbands were killed, the fathers were killed.

They have raped daughters in the presence of their fathers and mothers and raped mothers in front of their sons. You can't think of this. I can hardly stop my tears. How these people can do it [when] they claim to be Muslims.

Do you know the story of some of the killings? I have a friend, one of the top leaders of my party. Mr Mushir Rahman, he was minister in the government of Bangladesh. He was killed. They tortured him for four days. They first cut one of his hands and then the other. Then his ears, then his legs. For 24 days they tortured that poor man.

He was not the only one, many leaders, many workers, many people, many government officials were taken into custody and killed after being subjected to torture from seven to ten days. Even if a tiger kills, a man it does not kill like this.

Frost: And what did they hope to achieve?

Mujib: They wanted to control the administration. They wanted to keep this land a colony.

Frost: And they took out and killed 130 intellectuals even as the war was ending, here in Dacca?

Mujib: Just one day before the surrender in Dacca. They killed 300 not 150, 300 intellectuals from the University; from the medical college.

Frost: Where did they take them?

Mujib: They take them to Kurmitola. They kill them in their own houses. They have given curfew and people are in the house then they enter the house and kill them.

Frost: Was Yahya Khan using the curfew so nobody knows what's going on? Do you think Yahya Khan was a weak man, lead into evil by others or was he an evil man himself?

Mujib: He is certainly an evil man and his own friends who were his colleagues, they were evil too. He cannot shuffle off his responsibility to others. He is an absolute hypocrite, a dangerous man from what I could see of him during my talks with him when he was the president and I was leader of the majority party.

Frost: He mislead you, didn't he?

Mujib: He could not mislead me. *I understood what he was going to do. But I was preparing to hit and he has got hit.*

Frost: Preparing to do what?

Mujib: Hit him back. And he has got the hit-back. My people migrated.

Frost: Did you see him after you were imprisoned?

Mujib: No, no.

Frost: What do you think would be the right thing for Mr Bhutto to do to him now?

Mujib: He should give him a full trial—open trial, I think.

Frost: Do you think Mr Bhutto will do that?

Mujib: He should.

Frost: What do you think now of Mr Bhutto? Do you think now that one day, as Prime Minister or President of Pakistan, Mr Bhutto will ever visit free Dacca? Will he ever come here for talks?

Mujib: I don't know. I don't know. But let him realize the reality now, that Bangladesh is an independent country and that there is no good of shouting now that Bengal is his territory. It is not. If they still stick to that *claim of one Pakistan* they do know I am the majority and I could have claimed that I was the president and personal administrator of Pakistan and that all Pakistan was my territory.

I can call a meeting of the National Assembly, declare the name of the whole country as Bangladesh, and tell them that West Pakistan is my territory. I can ask Bhutto to get out and tell him that I am appointing the governors of Punjab, Sind, and Baluchistan. I can tell him that it is in my territory and you withdraw, or I will send my army with the allied forces, and occupy West Pakistan.

But I don't want this trouble. I have no ambition for territory. Let Mr Bhutto be happy with West Pakistan, if they want to use the name of West Pakistan. Let them do it, I have no objection. I want to be happy with my people in Bangladesh. And Bangladesh is a sovereign independent country.

(To be continued next week)

Transcript II: David Frost Interviews Mujib — Was Mujib preparing a showdown?

29 April 1972

*T*HE *date of Shaikh Mujib's interview with David Frost was inadvertently printed as 26 January 1971 last week. It should be 26 January 1972.*

This interview is being printed courtesy of London Weekend Television.

—Editor.

Frost: How many of the 75 million people of Bangladesh are hungry today? Are in a state of famine today?

Mujib: I think about 75%.

Frost: 75%?

Mujib: Yes, because they have destroyed everything. Even the people who have the capacity to eat something from their own godowns have been looted. Even the people who have some money have been looted. Even the people with small units of property have been looted. And I think it is not 75%, but 85% of the people who are hungry today.

My people have full confidence in me, and that is the thing, they are waiting, and I hope that I will be able to arrange something for them. And I am glad that India has recognized us and has come to our help so that my machinery can function. And it is functioning. They did it before my arrival, and I am grateful to Mrs Gandhi and the Indian Government. Communications should be restored, because before the Pakistanis have surrendered, they destroyed the oil tanks, they destroyed my industries. They destroyed everything humanly possible, in the time that they had.

Frost: You have had so much to do in the first week of the new country. You have also selected, for instance, a flag and a national anthem?

Mujib: Yes. That was the flag we used long before. That was also a song, which was our national song, long before. But I want [to] give to it official recognition, and I have given them official recognition, now only making a small change in my flag, because in my flag there was a map of Bangladesh and no country can give a map of territory in its flag. My people have accepted it gladly; they have agreed to drop the territory map and keep the rising sun.

27

Frost: The rising sun, and who wrote the national anthem? Is it an old song?

Mujib: It is an old song of Rabindranath Tagore.

Frost: What does it say in English?

Mujib: In English it says, 'I love all my golden Bengal'.

Frost: And this is a song that has been sung in Bangladesh for many years?

Mujib: Many years. When on 7 March last I held the last meeting, one million people were there and they were shouting independent Bengal slogans, and boys started singing the song and all of us—10 lac people—got up and stood to attention to salute these songs. That was the time when we accepted. That is the national song of Bangladesh.

Frost: Do you wish that on 7 March, at the race course, you had declared the independent state of Bangladesh?

Mujib: *I knew what is coming up. And I declared at that meeting, 'This time the fight is a fight for the liberation, emancipation, and freedom'. That was my speech.*

Frost: If you had said that day, 'I declare the independent state of Bangladesh', what would have happened?

Mujib: I did not want to do it that day particularly, because I would not allow them to tell the world that Mujibur Rahman had declared independence. We had no alternative but to hit them back. They hit us first and my people were ready to resist it, and they have resisted it.

Frost: But you did not want to start it?

Mujib: I wanted that they should start it first.

The Frost Programme Part II

Frost: All of this was burnt?

Mujib: All burned. Nothing was left here.

Frost: Burnt by the fighting Pakistan forces after ... Really ... And slowly they will try to start to rebuild, yes?

Mujib: No, no, no, they have left.

Frost: Yes, no, I mean your people first will start...

Mujib: When I have the money after liberation, they come and start it.

Frost: It is a hungry city but it is a happy city, isn't it? (PAUSE) How much do you know yet, how much money you need to repair what was done?

Mujib: I can't say now. I have nothing. I can tell you nothing. When they went from here, they burned even the bank notes.

Frost: And then there is the other money of East Pakistan, as it then was, that is in West Pakistan, isn't it?

Mujib: I am hoping, I am asking my people to give gold; whatever they have they will give it.

Frost: But where will people be able to give you gold from? Their teeth?

Mujib: Where there is gold … if they have it in the teeth, they will give the teeth.

Frost: Will you ever see any of the reserves that are in West Pakistan again?

Mujib: You know that they have a commitment to the world, and they are taking about 2,000 gross loan only a small portion of which they spent in Bangladesh. I do not own the responsibility, let them pay all the loans they are taking. With 2,000 gross loan and no market for their industry they have grown, they will have serious unemployment. What do you think?

Frost: They say, Well you know the quotation. You now have the great power of leading Bangladesh, and there is that old quote, 'power corrupts, and absolute power corrupts absolutely'. How will you stop power corrupting you?

Mujib: That you know that if man like a Pharoah comes to Bengal by accident he can be corrupt. But if the man comes through a process of struggle, suffering, fighting whatever power he gets will not corrupt him because there's also a process.

And so where my party and I am concerned, all my leaders have suffered jail, their families have suffered, they lost their houses. Many of them lost their family members in the long struggle for these 24 years—up to the achievement of independence. Thus have my people come to power. Now if they get absolute power there is very little chance of corruption, because they have not come through a process like that which brought Yahya Khan and others to power, with force behind it. My people have not come to power through guns, my people have come to power through a process, a struggle. And not only that, they have achieved this independence after making sacrifices, and they have love for the people and the country. Everybody wanted to be peaceful and live with his children but they have lost everything and still they fought. I enjoy the confidence of my leaders and the party workers and the average people.

Frost: You mentioned leaders. What is a leader, if you had to define the word leadership? For instance what is true leadership?

Mujib: True leadership comes through a process. A man can't be a leader by accident. A leader must be above personal interest, he must be prepared to sacrifice his life for the cause of humanity and the cause of the people. He must have his principles and he must have his ideal. If a person has those qualities, he is a leader.

Frost: Who are the leaders in the history of the world whom you admire? Who have been great leaders, who are the great leaders of the world?

Mujib: I – er – er – I think of many nice leaders. I don't like to mention them today—who are the leaders you know?

Frost: Well, looking back on history, who are the people who inspired you?

Mujib: I admire Abraham Lincoln. I admire Mao Tse Tung, I admire Lenin, I admire Churchill. I used to like Mr Kennedy, the ex-president.

Frost: Did you meet the ex-president?

Mujib: I did not meet him, but I have read his books and I like him.

Frost: What about Mahatma Gandhi?

Mujib: I have great respect for Mahatma Gandhi.

I admire A. K. Fazlul Haq of Bengal. I admire Mr Shaheed Suhrawardy of Bengal. I admire Mrs Nitaji Subaschandra Bose who fought against the British. I used to admire Dr Sukarno who fought for the emancipation of the people. I had great admiration for ... the people who came to power through the process of fighting.

Frost: At this moment in time, as you look back, what would you say was your gladdest moment in the past year? What was the moment of greatest happiness for you?

Mujib: The day that I heard that my people, had been liberated. My people are independent and I have got Bangladesh as an independent sovereign country.

Frost: That was the day?

Mujib: That was the day. That was the happiest day of my life.

Frost: Of your whole life?

Mujib: Whole life.

Frost: How long had you been dreaming of a day like that?

Mujib: Long time.

Frost: When did you first go to prison in your fight for freedom? It was many years ago?

Mujib: Long time. I started going to jail in so-called Pakistan in 1948. I was in jail from the age of 19. I was arrested in 1949. I was in jail up until 1952 then I became a minister in 1954; again I was arrested in '54. It continued upto 1955; again I was arrested in 1958 by Ayub Khan. I continued in ... about five years in jail and two years in internment and faced trials for many cases including Agartala case. Again I was arrested in '62 when my leader Mr Suhrawardy ex-prime minister of Pakistan was arrested. Again I was arrested by Yahya Khan and I came out after a long struggle, long suffering... not only I, many of my colleagues too...

Frost: And when you heard what had happened to some of your colleagues in the fight for freedom in the past nine...

Mujib: The worst time of my life was when I heard they had killed about 3 million people of mine, unfortunate people of my country.

Frost: These pictures I have are pictures that we will never forget. They are... you know the pictures that moved the world. The pictures of what was done. When you saw those pictures for the first time...

Mujib: Don't show me, I become emotional.

Frost: You must. What did you say when you first saw those pictures?

Mujib: What could I say? I had no words. I became emotional, I started weeping, tears came to my eyes; innocent boys, innocent girls, innocent people who had been killed mercilessly by the Pakistani army, which burnt their houses, hurt my people, hurt my sisters, and my brothers. That was the worst time of my life, I am a strong man and nobody has seen tears in my eyes, that was the time tears came to my eyes. I could not stop it.

Frost: How many times have you wept in front of your people in the past month?

Mujib: Many times have I wept. I wept for them.

Frost: When you heard what had been done?

Mujib: Yes. I think every time when I remember it, tears come to my eyes. They are still coming. I can't even think of this, my friend. Really it is an unfortunate position. I am a jealous man. *I will not live and forgive and forget because these were cold-blooded planned murders.* Do you think that any human being can tolerate this thing? These people must be punished, there is no question about it. I can't talk now. Why have you shown me these photos?

Frost: Because they have …

Mujib: I can't think of this, believe me. I become emotional on this particular point. And I don't expect that any power should do politics with my people any more for the sake of humanity. I appeal to them to help my unfortunate people, the people who are still suffering.

I did not want to be prime minister. I am more than anything to my people. What can a prime minister get, what I have got from my people? I have been to the hospitals and I saw these people. They have lost their hands, they have lost their legs. You know that we have lost everything. We don't mind. We have come back. That is our satisfaction. We are happy with that. Prime Ministership or presidency means nothing to me. I have got the love and affection of my people. I want to die with that; nothing more do I expect. I am happy. My people are today independent, they can develop themselves. They can live like an independent country.

I am grateful, really, I am grateful to the Indian people and Mrs Gandhi. The way they have helped my ten million people who have migrated to India; and the people of India giving them food, shelter, accommodation. You have 80 countries in the world whose population is less than 10 million but my 10 million people had to migrate from their houses and you know what the suffering was. I want to rehabilitate them, and I want help from everybody who has human feelings.

I want the world to comfort my people. I have no malice against anybody. I already declared my foreign policy: friendship with all, malice to none. I want to save my country, I want to give them accommodation. I want to give them education. I want to give them employment. I want to make them a happy society. That's what I want, nothing else.

Frost: Joy Bangla. I am sure the world will come forward and I am sure that if it doesn't, God will never forgive us.

Mujib: Thank you very much, thank you very much. Bye. Thank you all very much. Sorry I have to rush now.

Who is a Pakistani?

29 April 1972

A correspondent writes:

THE pathways of politics are tortuous and perfidious. In our own lifetime a hundred million Mussalmans of the subcontinent fought for Pakistan. When on 14 August 1947 the new state was born, nearly fifty million of these devotees became aliens overnight. Many writers have likened Pakistan to Israel because both are—or were—regarded as states created to serve as the homelands of particular religious communities. Could this be true? Israel passed a Law of Return under which any Jew could return to Israel from any part of the world at any time he chooses. Pakistan—on the contrary—passed a law that no 'alien' Muslim could cross the border and enter the promised land after a particular date. Since then it has been easier to become a British national than a Pakistani national even for the erstwhile voters for Pakistan. So far so good. Those poor blokes across the border were, after all, Indian subjects, and in principle, they were 'aliens'. But what about the 'Biharis'?

The state of Pakistan, which denied entry to Indian Muslims, is now allowing two million of its own nationals to be wasted away in Bangladesh. They are dying a cruel and slow death only because they were stupid enough to call themselves Pakistanis, naive enough to have trust in the forces of Yahya Khan, [and] short-sighted enough to depend upon the age-old (now outdated?) concept that every state stands by its nationals. We hear that the President of Pakistan is still doing some mathematical calculations for exchange of one Bengali against one Bihari. He is not prepared to allow the repetition of the history of Red Indians. I wonder how the Sindhis would allow themselves to be compared to the backward Red Indians of America and how the poor Biharis of Bangladesh can be treated as strong civilized colonizers from Europe who had the support of their home countries. True, Sind is the land of Red Sindhi bulls and of oppressed Haris and of king-size landlords—but not of Red Indians.

However, the President will feel relieved now that the Biharis have given up hope of returning to their homeland and are getting ready to give up the ghost. Their ultimate end is nearing. Their only request is that they should be transferred to some other country or desert where they could die in peace. The tragic picture of the last days of Biharis is being painted now by the British press—which

32

can also take credit as a supporter of Bangladesh and therefore not biased in their favour. Here is an article by the Observer correspondent in Dacca. You will find in the article a statement by Shaikh Mujib who is reported to have said: 'At least I allow the Red Cross in, which is more than Pakistanis do for the Bengalis over there'. Readers would know better than I do, how Bengalis are being treated 'over there'. But before you read the article, may I tell you that a very senior Bengali broadcaster landed in London from Karachi the other day [and] I asked him how did he manage to leave Karachi. 'Very easy', he said with a chuckle, 'all those bastard Custom-Immigration people in Pakistan are corrupt. You pay them Rs. 300/- and they will let you go. Anyone can come out.'

A couple of days later, I asked him how the Bengalis are being treated by West Pakistanis and with a great show of anger he said: 'Short of being murdered, they are suffering in every way.' I reminded him that they could pay Rs. 300/- and come out. He pondered for a while and then said: 'You see, the rates have gone up recently. You have to pay Rs. 1000/- to get out of Pakistan. Moreover, the West Pakistanis have entered into a diabolical conspiracy not to buy any household goods from Bengalis, otherwise at least some of them, could raise money by selling cars, frigidaires etc.' So Pakistanis are conspirators, their Immigration staff is corrupt, and 'their' government is not allowing the Red Cross to look after the suffering ex-Pakistanis and present Bangladesh nationals. But who is really a Pakistani? One who dies for Pakistan or one who lives off it?)

We Want: A Peaceful Death

29 April 1972

THE Observer published the following despatch by Walter Schwarz from Dacca in its issue of 15 April 1972:

When diplomats and officials here say 'The Biharis are better off now' they mean only that they are no longer being massacred. But this weekend the Biharis face a new horror—starvation and disease in camps into which 300,000 of them have fled for safety in the Dacca area alone.

Today the International Red Cross Committee, which has been feeding, inoculating, and housing them, is handing over to the Bangladesh Red Cross. This body is led and run by members of the Bangladesh Awami League—the Biharis' worst enemy.

Food supplies are in danger of drying up altogether. The crisis comes when the pre-monsoon rain storms have begun, turning the camps into quagmires and threatening to flood them out altogether by the end of May. The Bangladesh Red Cross is supposed to work with the League of Red Cross Societies, which in practice means mainly the Indian Red Cross. The ICRC handed over most of its food stocks in India to the Indian body—which has not released any for the Biharis.

The situation is even worse at Chittagong, Khulna and other towns where 800,000 Biharis live. It is only a month since 1,000 were killed in Khulna and tensions there are worse than in Dacca. Shaikh Mujibur Rahman, the Prime Minister, explained to me that he was 'under pressure to give my own people priority. Many of them are ex-refugees who themselves live in camps. At least I allow the Red Cross in, which is more than the Pakistanis do for the Bengalis over there.'

The camps in Mohammedpur and Mirpur, Dacca's Bihari quarters, make Palestinian camps in Gaza look like luxury resorts. The Red Cross has been using its last days to inoculate as many as possible. As a stopgap measure, United Nations officials this week obtained permission from the Bangladesh Government to divert 4,000 tons of wheat from the UN relief effort for Bihari use. But the camps have no milling facilities and corn soaked in water ferments and becomes poisonous. Rice stocks were almost exhausted last week and only one small distribution a day is being made.

In Mohammedpur, I tried to walk through a camp to a disused girls' school (no schools are open), but the refugees, three or four families in and around each tent, were so thick on the ground, and the remaining spaces were so deep in mud and excrement, that it was impossible to pass through.

Tiny children, apparently immune to suffering, took the needle without flinching. A young Norwegian doctor picked his way through the mud to treat people too ill to attend his dispensary; Bangladesh hospitals refuse to admit them.

The Red Cross has been preparing a new, more spacious camp for 4,000 refugees to replace the one in the girls' school before the monsoon. But it is expected to be swamped by twice that number within weeks. More Biharis are still leaving their homes, which are steadily being taken over by Bengalis at the point of a gun.

After the massacres of January and March, the Bangladesh Government took steps to protect the Biharis. It has put their districts under night curfew and sent in police patrols and a special force of riflemen. These have stopped the killings, but not the looting and the free-enterprise evictions. The police—poorly paid and many of whom have lost their own homes—sometimes join in the looting.

Shaikh Mujib promises that all the Biharis who want to stay as citizens can stay and all who want to go can go, but for the moment no exit visas have been granted. The situation is bedevilled by Bangladeshi insistence on trying 'hundreds' of war criminals, including both local Biharis and Pakistani officers now in custody in India. Doubts were also thrown on Mujib's promise by an official who told a Bihari leader: 'We cannot let Biharis back into business because they will send their money abroad, and we cannot afford that.'

One of the many typewritten appeals and petitions handed out by students in the Bihari quarters concludes: 'Our immediate request is repatriation to any part of the world, either en masse in one country, or in small numbers to different countries. As the Indian tactics and the inimical mood of Bangladesh seem to kill us ultimately, will the world take the trouble to save these naked, hungry, homeless, diseased, poor, and helpless Biharis by repatriating them even in the desert, so that they could peacefully die there?'

The Newsprint Noose

6 May 1972

Mohsin Askari

THERE are many subtle variations to the hangman's noose which is perpetually dangling over the opposition press. Hopefully grouped under the single word 'law' or the phrase 'in the interests of the nation', they are all variations on the same dirge. Pathetic manifestations of the administration's single-track mind and its lust for authoritarianism, they are timely warnings of the shape of things that might come. The most favoured minion in Karachi today is Amanullah Sardar, a man whose hands are sullied by the blood of the many skeletons now reposing in his cupboard. All the perfumes of Araby…

There are many sides to the hangman's noose. They are all designed towards creating a uniformly servile press *a la* National Press Trust. A half-turn of the screw here, a quarter turn there… The current favourite in the administration's bristling arsenal is newsprint allocation.

When the mass sedition of 70 million culminated in Bangladesh, the country lost its only internal source of newsprint, the Khulna Newsprint Factory. With Khulna gone, the supply source shifted to other countries, and the meagre money at the country's disposal caused an 'acute shortage' of newsprint. But the warped thinking of the powers-that-be turned this economically distressing fact into a politically advantageous one. The overly eager rationing of newsprint followed and consequently its allocation degenerated purely into a matter of political and business patronage—to the winner the spoils.

Initially, newsprint distribution was done by the Ministry of Information through officers separately designated for the purpose. The regional information directorates, keeping daily contact with the newspapers in the sphere of news and views, were not directly concerned with it. But having realized the value of a two-edged knife, the regime has now merged the two functions in the regional directorates. And the regional directors, always keen to curry favour, have joined the fray with a vengeance.

Mr Amanullah Sardar's overriding passion in life is building houses, preferably his own. He has so far baptized three of his own in Karachi alone, and when he was PRO of WPIDC …well… He has the remarkable capability of adjusting his sails to the prevailing wind. With him it is a case of 'the king is dead, long live the king.' His type abounds in the Ministry of Information and, with a few honourable exceptions, they all have been rewarded for their shifting loyalties. Mr Sardar has now been posted to Tokyo for good work done right since the days of Ayub Khan.

The Ministry's busy little axe almost fell on the *Sun* when that newspaper took the words freedom of the press literally. But the *Sun's* cries of blue murder and threats of legal action deterred the Ministry who then looked elsewhere. *Jasarat* was the administration's victim. *Nidai Haq,* a Rawalpindi daily, filed suit on the government to revoke some newsprint decisions. In Karachi a new paper started publication from 2 May *Hilal-i-Pakistan,* a Sindhi pro-PPP paper, was given a newsprint quota for 10,000 copies—and this in the face of a regulation banning supply of newsprint to all new publications without a certificate from the ABC. Prior to this, *Hilal-i-Pakistan* was being published from Hyderabad and doing well. Many other papers including *Dawn* and *Jang* have been conveyed the displeasure of the Ministry one way or the other.

'Do not blame me if the people mob your offices, and burn and stone it' were Minister Pirzada's prophetic words to a couple of Karachi publishers. What the Minister, perhaps justifiably, was objecting to was the rather incendiary language being used against the President. Some weeks later I walked into a roaring, restless mass of people, thus validating Minister Pirzada's powers of prophecy. The people had gone to the extent of procuring trucks and jeeps. They came in trucks and they were outfitted with banners and sticks and invectives and they were out for blood. They were at the *Jasarat* offices and they were invoking their gods to strike down the 'dirty rightists'. They roughed a lone, bearded reporter who was halfheartedly standing guard, and rushed upstairs to proclaim their sovereignty. Nowhere could I see a policeman.

This, I am told, was a relatively peaceful demo. They had come on 20 March with some incendiary material—and made use of it. These demonstrations, violent or otherwise, are daily occurrences at the *Jasarat* offices. They appear to be part of a well organized campaign to chisel away at the last vestiges of defence that a beleagured *Jasarat* can put up. It seems geared to the administration's less vociferous, but equally effective, offensive aimed at bringing a bleeding and cornered *Jasarat* to its knees.

'Mr Mohammed Salahuddin, editor, Daily *Jasarat,* Karachi, has resigned from the membership of the Press Consultative Committee as a mark of protest against the arrest of the Lahore editors and publishers and the banning of their journals', so went the story in the *Sun* of 7 April. On the same day he was informed that *Jasarat's* newsprint quota was being cut by 75 per cent—from 25 reels per week to 6 reels per week.

Jasarat is a right-wing paper which faithfully reflects the policies of the Jamaat-i-Islami. It has been viciously anti-government—both Yahya and Bhutto, and its writers have indulged in blistering tirades against Mr Bhutto, dripping with venom, and with very few compunctions about descending to the level of making snide and catty comments on his non-political life. Of late, however, these lapses have been few and far between.

It first came out from Karachi in May 1970 under the editorship of Mr Altaf Hussain Qureshi of *Urdu Digest* fame. Its circulation hovered around the 10,000 figure for a long time. Only recently has it spurted to reach an estimated 25,000. *Jasarat* was being granted newsprint on an ad hoc basis until the regional directorate decided to review the quota. The result was that the department decided to revert to the circulation figures of 1970 and simply newsprint on that basis. *Jasarat's* plea that a fresh audit be taken to determine the present circulation was ignored. Soon after that *Jasarat* had to reduce its pages to four and start a campaign to collect as many contributions as it could. The money is trickling in, rupee by rupee. Newspapers with small circulations can survive a reduction in newsprint allocation. But for dailies with large circulations the additional expense of buying paper on the market might run into lacs of rupees.

On 13 April, a peon cycled up to the *Jasarat* offices in the evening. He was carrying a message which almost proved to be the *Jasarat's* death knell. It still might. It was from the National Press Trust presses where *Jasarat* has been printed since its inception, and it said that from that date the paper could no longer be printed there.

In March the paper owed the NPT some 40,000 rupees—about two month's printing charges. To NPT's demand for money the paper asked till 15 April, for payment. To this there was no reply and by the time the quit-printing notice came, *Jasarat* had payed up most of the money. (By the way, *Jasarat* had in all paid Rs. 478,000 to NPT as printing charges since May 1970.) Prior to this, *Jasarat* was being intermittently bothered by Mr G. M. D. Paracha, NPT press incharge, whose rather misguided love for the country transcends all bounds. Mr Paracha evidently took it upon himself to interpret the press code and ensure that *Jasarat* printed matter that would be helpful in reconstructing the country.

'I think now the time has come to warn you' wrote Mr Paracha on 6 April, 'that you should stop such writings while the NPT Press is your printer and nation is passing through unparalleled crisis of the living memory. Please refrain from such writings and help to reconstruct the country.' As a self-appointed enforcer of the press code, Mr Paracha had occasionally deleted material from the editorials of the paper. On three consecutive days, *Jasarat* had left its editorial space vacant as a token of protest against this censorship.

The present and past chain of coincidences which have so suddenly and mysteriously afflicted this paper appear to be aimed at bringing the attrition of *Jasarat.*—and perhaps serve as a grisly reminder to those who might be thinking of following in its foot steps.

A Rape is a Rape

6 May 1972

Our correspondent writes:

SHE was hardly twelve—a slip of a girl. Her big, black eyes, set in a thin, emaciated and sad face seemed bigger as she stared at you with glassy looks. She was lying on a hospital bed, ready to be operated upon. She was the youngest of them all, but the others too, lying in a row on similar beds were not more than sixteen or seventeen.

The twelve-year old, said the TV commentator, had been raped by ten Pakistani personnel during its 'occupation' of the country now known as Bangladesh. It was impossible to say whose child the twelve year old had been carrying, perhaps the father is now in India but she would get rid of this shame soon.

The BBC-TV had shown pictures of many such girls who claimed—rightly or wrongly—to have been raped by our personnel or *razakars*. Peter Preston of the *Guardian* wrote on 25 February that Bangladesh's 'official estimate of the number of Bengali girls raped in the last nine months of a united Pakistan touched 200,000. Of these, it is reckoned, thousands are now pregnant.'

Shaikh Mujibur Rahman has called these girls the 'heroines of war'. A hospital has been set up in the suburbs of Dacca, where 100 abortions are being performed every day. A British doctor, who returned to London recently said in a TV interview that 'tens of thousands' of Bengali girls were raped during this period. The interviewer asked him if he was sure that the number was not inflated, or that Pakistanis alone were responsible for these criminal acts. Perhaps the Indians also had a hand in it? This is very likely. But, he replied, he was pretty sure of his facts. Reports have also come in that after the surrender, hundreds of Bengali girls were rescued from bunkers. According to the *Guardian* 'one reliable witness counted 500 women in a single camp shortly before the fall of Dacca'.

Truth, it is said, is the first casualty in a war. The recent war—whatever you may be pleased to call it—a civil war, a war of liberation, or an Indo-Pakistan war—was no exception. The Government-controlled media in Pakistan were not above suppressing facts, the British media very often slanted the news, the AIR and the PTI often carried baseless stories, the supporters of the Bangladesh movement indulged in relentless propaganda.

For instance, except for the Pakistani press, the others overlooked to mention facts such as the forced white slave traffic of non-Bengali girls between Bangladesh and India. This featured prominently in the statement of Mr Badre Muneer, a journalist who was allowed to leave Bangladesh after its occupation by Indian forces. He also commented on the merciless and unprovoked killing of non-Bengalis, and the pressure brought on Bengalis to refrain from harbouring any 'Biharis'.

But, inspite of the conflicting mesh of propaganda, the discerning reader could extract some truth. For instance, the Indians lied blatantly when they said that ten million refugees had crossed into India. But surely some did cross, and the number must have been in lakhs, not thousands.

Similarly one can safely assume that by far the majority of the Pakistani personnel and *razakars* did not go about raping women from March to December. The number of their victims—200,000—is also definitely exaggerated. We can also safely say that all these pregnant women were not actually 'raped'. Maybe some of the men were paying well for 'goods and services rendered.' Moreover, in a land of abject poverty there must be many among these women who were simply availing themselves of the opportunity to make money, get free food or medical treatment, and housing and other amenities.

But, after all is said and done, the behaviour of at least some of our men can hardly be explained, especially in view of the fact that they belonged to a disciplined group. Don't shrug your shoulders and say 'Well, in times of war and turmoil all this does happen. How else can one live under a strain for months?' The question is: 'Whatever was happening, was it not happening, in a part of our country? Were these girls any different from other nationals of Pakistan? Or were these men reverting to the old custom of claiming legitimate booty in the form of "*kaneezes*" from a conquered people?'

It is true that some men were punished for this offence but obviously this was not enough to deter other rapists. When we talk of 'retaining some kind of link' between East and West Pakistan, we should not overlook these factors. The few men who killed and raped may now have been killed or may now be safe from the Bengalis' revenge. But they did not realize that the consequence would be a blood-thirsty lust for the Biharis' lives who have been left behind in Bangladesh at the mercy of Bengalis. Vengeance is as much a part of Bengali character as of any other person. Something must be done, and done pretty soon, to pour water on this consuming fire of hatred and revenge.

Many of the men who commuted these offences considered them a just reprisal for the atrocities of the Bengalis against non-Bengalis prior to 25 March. Their acts could have been justified if they had been aimed at the guilty Bengalis, for, after all, legal justice is nothing but a formalized kind of vengeance. The shape which their actions assumed, however, has to be deplored.

One can only hope that in the future our men will be more disciplined, and dedicated to the basic human values which transcend material and geographical boundaries. In fact, this is what our trained and disciplined men are expected to be and are. But their image and reputation has suffered due to the actions of an undisciplined, stupid minority.

Bhutto talks to *Times of India*

6 May 1972

THIS is the text of a despatch filed from Karachi by Dilip Mukerjee of *The Times of India* on 15 March last after his interview with President Bhutto at Larkana. This has not been printed in Pakistan. Later Dilip Mukerjee wrote a series of four articles which have already been reproduced in *Dawn*.

—Editor

Pakistan's President, Zulfikar Ali Bhutto, has a new formulation on Kashmir, the basic problem in the dispute with India. It is not for Pakistan to secure the right of self-determination for Kashmiris; it is up to them to fight for it if they want a different future.

He now takes the stand that just as a revolution cannot be exported, the basic struggle for self-determination cannot be inspired from outside. India and Pakistan have gone to war three times since 1947 but the fact remains that Pakistan has failed to resolve the problem by military means. 'India has also failed to achieve a satisfactory political solution'.

'It is for India to find a way out. Pakistan cannot set the pace any more'. Bhutto's comments on Kashmir highlighted an interview lasting almost eighty minutes at his family estate in Larkana last night. I, along with another Indian journalist, were flown from Karachi to this Indus valley town close to the ruins at Mohenjo Daro to meet him just before he plunged into his final preparations for a visit to Moscow beginning on Thursday.

As Bhutto sees it, Pakistan can no longer afford to pursue a policy of confrontation towards India he was advocating at one time. It was undoubtedly the right policy then; 'it was to our advantage and it served our national interest'. But in today's changed circumstances Bhutto wants to promote consultations and negotiations as staunchly as he advocated confrontation.

Bhutto is clear in his mind that India has no aggressive designs against Pakistan. 'Unless you go completely *gaga* you will not attack us again'. He accepts that responsible opinion in India does not want further disruption or disintegration of Pakistan although a lunatic fringe may keep harking back nostalgically to the dream of a united India.

Bhutto's evaluation is that the people of Pakistan want peace. They want an end to hostility and conflict not merely because of the recent military defeat but because tensions have proved

41

unproductive and hindered economic development and growth. Discussing modalities of future talks with India, Bhutto indicated that he would utilize his meetings with Soviet leaders this week to convey through them his wishes to New Delhi. But Moscow's role will be only that of a communication channel. Bhutto does not want any third party to intercede for Pakistan in its negotiations with India. 'I am allergic to third party intervention'. It is high time that nations of the subcontinent solved their disputes without having to turn to outside umpires for help.

Bhutto would like to proceed step by step in resolving India-Pakistan problems. The Pakistan President recalled that Nehru was in favour of this gradualistic approach. When you resolve all issues in one day as at Tashkent it simply does not work out. This is the lesson to be drawn from our past experience.

The Pakistani President clearly indicated that he would prefer non-Bengalis in Bangladesh to remain there. The best solution would be for Shaikh Mujib to give them a sense of security in the East where they have made their home and where a whole new generation has come up since partition. But Bhutto recognizes that Shaikh Mujib is faced with a very difficult and complicated problem.

The Pakistani President says that he and his party has made herculean efforts to protect Bengalis living in Pakistan. At the same time he is offering them an option to move to the East if they wish to. If there is a large-scale movement of population both East and West will suffer. Pakistan will be thrown back to the slums and shantytowns of 1947. All its hopes of an improvement in living standards will be dashed—at least for quite a time. Yet Pakistan cannot be indifferent to the fate of non-Bengalis. 'There is good deal of feeling and sympathy for them here', Bhutto added.

Discussing Pakistan's political future, Bhutto said that the quantum of autonomy to be allowed to the provinces remains to be settled between him and his new ally, Wali Khan, leader of the N.W.F.P. based National Awami Party. Bhutto would like to settle the question on the basis of a consensus among all parties when the National Assembly's Committee of the House sits down to hammer out a new constitution. But if a consensus does not emerge, he would have to accept the less desirable alternative of going by the verdict of the majority.

Discussing the future role of the army in Pakistan's life, Bhutto said that the recent changes in the army and air force commands were intended to emphasize civilian control. He poohpoohed the notion that General Gul Hasan and Air Marshal Rahim Khan were planning a coup. 'There was no concerted plan for a military takeover but they made some rather silly remarks suggesting they were not reconciled to civil control. The remarks implied that the way things were going in Pakistan the military would be back in the saddle sooner than anyone expected—in six months rather than two years. 'You cannot take this sort of comment lightly.' Bhutto does not think that the army will want to make a comeback. Only if the democratic experiment fails, their ambitions may revive and people may accept army rule as a last resort. But any bid by generals at present will touch off trouble on as big a scale as in the East wing after last March. Bhutto's answers to some of the more important questions now follow in fuller detail.

In dealing with Kashmir, Bhutto argued, 'We must take into account the genesis of the problem beginning with the two nation theory on the basis of which India was divided in 1947. We have also to take into account the commitments made by leaders of both India and Pakistan to the Kashmiri people and also the internationally accepted concept of self-determination. Even when all this is taken into account, we still have to reckon with the fact that the struggle for self-determination cannot be inspired from outside. Like revolution it cannot be exported. It has to be an indigenous struggle.

'If the people of Kashmir want a different future, you cannot stop them nor can we. If the people of Kashmir believe that they have been deprived of the right of self-determination, they will rise. Their struggle will be basically theirs. Outside support cannot solve their problem. This is the clear lesson to be drawn from the sad history of Palestine despite all the help given by Egypt. 'We have been to war several times, over Kashmir. Let us not argue about who fired the first shot. Each time Kashmir has been the key issue in the conflict directly or indirectly. The problem has not been resolved for us by military means. You have not resolved it politically either. In today's situation it is for you to solve the problem. You set the tone. I cannot set the pace anymore.

'Kashmir is a basic problem. Quite frankly I am greatly attached to the principle of self-determination. There was a time when we thought in terms of confrontation militarily and politically. It was to the advantage of Pakistan. Today, the situation is not there, it is a qualitative change, I cannot pursue the policy of confrontations. I want to turn to consultation and negotiation. I will make as deep a search for peace along this direction as when I was seeking to resolve the problem through confrontation'.

'You will find me reasonable at the negotiating table. I will agree to nothing which runs counter to Pakistan's national interest but I am fully prepared to take into account the sweep of history. It is unfortunate that there is so much misunderstanding in India of my posture.

'I believe that the situation in East Pakistan or Bangladesh as you prefer to call it, has made the problem more difficult. If an indigenous province can become independent, a disputed area like Kashmir can claim the right to be on its own with much greater validity. But I do not want to go into this now. I have not dwelt on Kashmir on my taking over—not in the way I did before. I am not making it my dominant theme.

'Let us have some understanding which would make sense. For too long we have been going to the world chanceries arguing against each other. The world is fed up with this. There is a new leadership in India. Mrs Gandhi fought with the old guard not only for office. She in fact, risked her office to give the country a breath of fresh air. Let us hope that she can also bring a new approach to India-Pakistan relations. I am prepared to make my modest contribution. Like Mrs Gandhi I also have a massive mandate from my people.

'Let us not treat the prisoners of war issue on the basis of legal fictions. Our people cannot believe that the Mukti Bahini had any role in the East. Even assuming that there is joint jurisidiction of India and Bangladesh over the prisoners, it is for you to make the right suggestions to Shaikh Mujib. He will be amenable. I do not think he will resist. In fact, he should be happy because a settlement will help to get me and Shaikh Mujib together more quickly'.

Asked whether he feared that India or any other power might work for the further disintegration of Pakistan, Bhutto said: 'I cannot speak about other countries but only about India. After all, we were the same country 25 years ago. I know you do not stand to gain from any disintegration. Some people might be nostalgic about the past. They may feel it will be better to break up Pakistan but I do not think anyone sensible has such ideas. If I felt that you were hell-bent on destroying Pakistan I would not go at all to Delhi for talks.

'Fissiparous tendencies go up and down in the subcontinent. You were fortunate, you got yourself a constitution early. When you have institutions you can take many knocks. We are determined to consolidate our country—what you have left of it—and to restore democracy.

'We have been prisoners of words in the past. Mention confederation and it puts up the backs of lots of people in Pakistan. Let us not get bogged down in semantics. Let the factors of geography and history assert themselves in the natural course of things. Let us start modestly. Why should we imagine that every problem has to be resolved today. Let us do our bit and future leaders can build on it.'

'If you use the prisoners to milk Pakistan, there will be only two alternatives open to me. Either I capitulate and accept whatever line you wish to draw in Kashmir or elsewhere—whether it runs through Lahore or further west still. Or I go to my people and tell them that there is no alternative to confrontation. As long as prisoners of war remain in Indian camps, it gives rise to tensions in Pakistan. A political crisis or instability in Pakistan is not to your advantage.

'Yes, I know about the argument that Bangladesh is a new state and not a successor state. Problems about debts and liabilities can always be resolved. It is only a question of setting accountants to work on the ledgers. But my concern is with non-financial problems—the human and psychological ones.

'When I came back from Washington after the surrender in Dacca, I told Yahya Khan that I am not seeking power by anybody's grace. I was seeking it as leader of a party which had a decisive mandate from people of West Pakistan. General Gul Hasan and Air Marshal Rahim Khan also accepted that position. No, they are not my special friends. When I was having trouble with Yahya Khan last year, they did not help. But, of course, we sometimes met socially.

'Their behaviour pattern was unfortunately too conditioned by the past. It was unacceptable because I want the services to be accountable to political authority. I want to emphasise civil control. This is why I am keeping the defence portfolio to myself'.

The Option of Recognition

13 May 1972

THERE is no agreed scale to measure the distance which has always separated Bangladesh from the rest of Pakistan. Nostalgia apart, the primacy of geo-political compulsions could not have been, and cannot now be blinked away. The Lahore Resolution, perhaps inadvertently, reflected the shape of things to come. An ideological plastering could not conquer the physical distance which separated the two regions, bridged only by a yawning 1,000 miles of hostile territory. Added to it were the ever sharpening divergencies in the field of language, culture, topography and rising middle class aspirations, capped, of course, by the wanton abuse of power on this side. What could have held this seemingly impossible edifice together was the bond of common interest buttressed by other factors including, importantly, religion. To our mind, this bond of common interest was resilient enough to have withstood the corrosive impact of time and of a certain residuary seed of conflict. It didn't. Instead, it was washed away by a man-made tidal wave of blood, rapine, and revenge. Men, more often than not, are smaller than the problems they help create.

What now? Bangladesh has emerged as a fact of life, whatever its character, structure, status, or its future. The foremost consideration should be to minimize the ghastly, endless burden of human suffering, the inevitable legacy of the follies of the past. Inspite of its inevitability, it is maddening, haunting like a curse, ubiquitous like life itself, saturating like sorrow incarnate. A sizeable mass of humanity, in either part, lies trapped in what till yesterday was 'my country' and now is an alien, hostile environment. The fetters of prejudice and the perverted doctrine of nationalist necessity cut deeper into their withered skins than the absence of mere bread and water or the stench from over-filled latrines. The enormity of it all should shake our conscience, even if it may not be enough to cause a change in the hallowed ground rules of repatriation, or even a change in the leadership's grand vision of a prosperous Pakistan free of *jhuggis* and shanty towns.

The issue of recognition is now squarely in Pakistan's lap. Mr Bhutto has been dealing with it adroitly and with a *finesse* expected of him. He needs, and deserves, all our support in dealing with this sensitive, delicate problem. He has, rightly, paved the ground for recognition by preparing public opinion to be reconciled to the idea. But the timing and modalities involved are surcharged with equal import. Shaikh Mujibur Rahman too has to observe certain rules of the game. It is to be hoped that he will oblige.

In this regard, there are no clear cut precedents to go by. International law and practice offer a variety of examples. Which does not necessarily mean that a strictly legalistic approach to the problem will be in our interest. According to one theory, however, a new state, exercising effective authority over a given territory and capable of discharging its internal and external obligations, is entitled to recognition as an international person. Others advocate that it is a matter of discretion for the members of the existing international community to recognize a new state. It is in pursuance of the second doctrine that the recognition of the Soviet Russian regime was held in abeyance for years and years by a large number of countries. Even today the United States and some other countries do not recognize the reality as represented by the Peoples Republic of China.

Regardless of this theoretical controversy, it remains a fact that in the case of a secessionist state, which Bangladesh is, it is *only* recognition by the mother state which sets the seal of finality on international acceptance. Diplomatic experts in Bangladesh and in Islamabad are well aware of the finer points of this issue. This is precisely why Bangladesh is keen to extract Pakistan's recognition while President Bhutto is willing to concede it, but only after a meeting with Shaikh Mujib. From Pakistan's point of view there are other irons in the fire. And, it is a wholly legitimate point of view.

The objective situation is that Bangladesh has already been recognized by about sixty countries. Recognition was extended even while Indian troops remained on the soil of Bangladesh. Even today Shaikh Mujib's hold on Bangladesh is tenuous and his writ hardly seems to run beyond Dacca. His recurring references to internal and external 'intrigues' and his 'shoot at sight' orders against leftist insurgents speak for themselves. His dependence on India and Russia is complete. Bangladesh has undoubtedly emerged as a one-party state. Nevertheless, what happens inside Bangladesh is not our concern. We would like to wish Bangladesh well, tranquillity at home, and the assertion of independence in its relations with other countries. Even after recognition and a possible resumption of some degree of communication and contact, Pakistan's capacity, to influence the course of events within Bangladesh will remain severely limited. For good or evil, it is better if it remains so.

It is encouraging that some contacts between Pakistan and Bangladesh have already been made. It is welcome again that the Bangladesh authorities have offered to drop the trial of Pakistani personnel in exchange for the writ of recognition. These are pleasant whiffs in an otherwise poisoned atmosphere. There is a good deal of weight in President Bhutto's argument; that a meeting between him and Shaikh Mujib should be held outside this subcontinent. Mr Bhutto has an open mind on whether or not Bangladesh would like to retain any links with Pakistan, apart from trade, communications, etc. The choice is entirely theirs. He has also said that the problem of assets and liabilities can be looked after by accountants working on the ledgers, once some understanding, however limited, has emerged. The minorities, living in either part, may also get a respite. There is nothing on the debit side to pre-empt a meeting which should not prejudice Bangladesh's inherent right to recognition. The viewpoint that recognition will wreck the ideological basis of Pakistan, or will legalize the fruits of aggression, or will nullify the chances of a reunion, is spurious.

An agreement between Mr Bhutto and Sh. Mujib might help in straightening out relations between India and Pakistan. Both leaders owe it to themselves and to their suffering people to make a try. They have something to gain and nothing to lose by meeting. The point is: will sanity be allowed to prevail?

Drastic Law for 'Collaborators' in Bangladesh

20 May 1972

Our correspondent writes:

THE Bangladesh Collaborators (Special Tribunals) Order, 1972, was promulgated by the President of the People's Republic of Bangladesh on 24 January 1972. The purpose of the order as stated in the preamble is to effectively and adequately punish all persons, individuals or members of organizations, who have been collaborators, directly or indirectly, of Pakistan armed forces, which had 'illegally occupied' Bangladesh by 'brute force'. The order has been given retrospective effect from 26 March 1971.

Under this order, special tribunals have been constituted to deal with and punish collaborators. The expression collaborator has been given the widest possible connotation and not only includes persons who had participated, aided or abetted the 'occupation' army, but also all those who had rendered material assistance in any way whatsoever to the army, whether by word, sign, or conduct. The expression also includes all persons who actively resisted or sabotaged the efforts of the people and the liberation forces of Bangladesh in their struggle against the 'occupation' army. Even those persons who had made public statements or voluntarily participated in propaganda within and outside Bangladesh or who had participated in any delegation or committee or in the by elections, are included in this definition. All persons who performed their functions in good faith required by law in force at the material times, have been excluded from the definition, unless in performance of such functions such a person was responsible for or caused the death of any member of the civil population of any member of the liberation forces, or caused destruction of property or committed rape, even if such an act was done under a law passed by the 'occupation' army.

The police officers have been authorized to arrest, without warrant any person who is reasonably suspected of having been a collaborator. The officer is required to report such arrest forthwith to the Sub-Divisional Magistrate and furnish materials on the basis of which the arrest had been made; and the magistrate has the power, on receipt of such information, to detain such a person for an initial period of six months, which may be extended by the government, if further time is required to complete the enquiry. The special tribunal constituted under the order shall consist of only one member who may be a sessions judge, additional sessions judge or assistant session judge.

The procedure to be followed by the special tribunal will be that of summons cases in the Code of Criminal Procedure.

No adjournment will be granted at the trial unless it is in the interest of justice. The trial will not be adjourned by reason of the absence of the accused persons, but the tribunal will take steps to appoint an advocate to defend an accused who is not represented by a counsel. In the schedule to the order, offences are enumerated which the special tribunal shall try and punish. Significantly, in this schedule the offences are those which are offences under various sections of the P.P.C., but there is a rider that any act of a person who has been defined as a collaborator, as above, though not covered by any of the offences defined in the Penal Code, may also be deemed to be an offence.

There is a further article which provides for confiscation of property belonging to proclaimed persons who in the opinion of the government are persons required for the purpose of any investigation or enquiry or other proceedings connected with an offence punishable under the order, and who may be absconding or otherwise concealing themselves or remaining abroad to avoid appearance. The 'property' of such a person has been given wide meaning so as to include not only all his movables and immovables, but also all movables and immovables standing in his name or of his wife, children, parents, minor brothers and sisters, or dependents or benamidars. If the proclaimed person does not appear, his properties would be attached and forfeited to the government.

The order also provides for appeal to the High Court. The punishment provided for offences varies from death, transportation for life to a term not exceeding two years and fine. On conviction all the properties of the collaborators shall be forfeited to the government. An appeal will lie to the High Court on questions of fact as well as law.

Hate, Bigotry, and an Official Cloak

20 May 1972

Our correspondent writes:

THE plight of Biharis in Bangladesh raises a number of constitutional, political, social, and moral questions, from which even the political ostriches of West Pakistan cannot escape. They have to ponder over this problem because, who knows, they may suffer the same fate tomorrow? It is gratifying to note that inspite of the continuing violence in the backyard of Ulster and the rising tempo of war in Vietnam, *The Times* is able to devote so much space every week to raise the question of Biharis. Its latest verdict is horrifying and stunning; that unless the international community is able to intervene, these 'wretched people will slowly but surely face extermination.' By appealing to the international community, *The Times* correspondent by the same stroke of pen has pinpointed Pakistan government's impotence and the supine attitude of its 60 million people.

Read the despatch of *The Times* and answer the following questions:

Who is primarily responsible for the plight of the Biharis? Who is responsible for the protection of Pakistani nationals and its loyal subjects if they are caught and arrested by an alien government? What is the guarantee that in future minority groups in West Pakistan will not suffer the same fate and that Pakistan government will come to their rescue if they are caught in political chaos? If a government is unable to protect the nationals, should they prepare themselves to fight their own battle or should the Pakistanis be ready to change their loyalties and nationality and bow down before anyone who conquers them?

Is it not the duty of the socialist groups to agitate and work at international level if neo-fascist groups in Bangladesh are exterminating a minority? Is it not the duty of Islam pasand elements to work for the safety of their Muslim brethren who are being killed for being loyal to the Islamic concept of Pakistan? Is it not the duty of the Pakistan army and the bureaucracy to at least try to save those who are suffering only because they had provided a second line of defence in what was 'East Pakistan'? Clearly the army failed to defend the country. Perhaps it could not. Therefore, should it not be the first champion of the cause of its erstwhile supporters and open its arms for them? Does the Pakistan government believe that ethnic and linguistic minorities in every country have a right to exist? If it does, then it should stand by the Biharis and if not then it should withdraw the Kashmir

50

case from the UN and warn all minority groups in Pakistan, like Sindhis, Baluchis, Makranis, Pathans etc. to take care of themselves as best as they can because protection of its citizens—particularly the minorities—is not the responsibility of the government. Incidentally it may also state in clear terms what is the job of a government in our country. But the government need not be criticized too much. It represents the people. Do the people in Pakistan feel any pinch when their fellow men and women are being killed, starved, raped, and being slowly wiped out?

The fact of the matter is that a majority of the people in Pakistan would prefer the Biharis to rot where they are. To them they are not Pakistanis. They are Biharis. What am I raving about?

The Times published this dispatch in its issue of 10 May:

From: Peter Hazelhurst

Dacca, 7 May

If every nation can be judged by the way it treats its minority community, then 70 million Bengalis in Bangladesh must hang their heads in shame today. They are behaving in much the same manner as the Pakistanis did during the nine months of repression in Bangladesh last year. They have closed their eyes to reality and to the humanitarian aspect of the plight of the 1,500,000 Urdu-speaking minority which is living in stark terror in Bangladesh.

Non-Bengalis have been hounded out of their homes into crowded ghettoes. They cannot find employment and without protection, men, women, and children are systematically being slaughtered by fanatical Bengali mobs.

But, like the West Pakistanis, the Bengalis in Dacca refuse to believe the facts. Hate, bigotry, and an official cloak of ruthless indifference have brought Bangladesh to the threshold of pure and unadulterated fascism.

Sitting back with soft music in the Intercontinental hotel and the Dacca Club, the average Bengali repeats the official cliches in the Government-controlled press and waves the helpless non-Bengali community aside as 'miscreants, collaborators and thugs'. There is no compassion, no mercy and no comprehension of the word humanitarianism.

A well-known lawyer calmly declares that the minority community is getting what it deserves and borrowing some of ex-President Yahya Khan's cliches, brands all non-Bengalis as 'miscreants and collaborators' too. As the former regime did, Bengali government officials who have not bothered to go to see the ghettoes two miles away from their offices give the foreign press bland assurances that the minority community is contented and safe.

But a visit to the overcrowded non-Bengali area on the outskirts of Dacca would prove to them that most of these 'miscreants and thugs' are terrified women, starving children, the homeless, the aged, and weeping widows whose husbands have been slaughtered by fanatical Bengali nationalists. Non-Bengalis are pulled out of their homes almost every day, in most cases in front of the police. They simply disappear. The police remain indifferent to requests for assistance.

The facts have been suppressed until now, but I can reveal that an estimated 200 to 300 Biharis were slaughtered by mobs of Bengalis two weeks ago on the outskirts of Dacca when busloads of relatives of prisoners returned to Mirpur camp.

I spoke to an eyewitness of the slaughter, a weeping 15-year-old girl, who saw her father hacked to death together with scores of other inmates of the camp. The girl, who can only be identified as Shamim for obvious reasons, explained that the Bangladesh Rifles had entered the camp in February this year. They instructed the male and female inmates to assemble in different fields.

'My brother and thousands of other young men were arrested and taken away. In the middle of April, my father took me by bus with many other people to visit our relatives in jail. When we returned by bus, the police at the entrance of the camp demanded a permit and would not let us pass. Just then, I saw some women from the bus being dragged away by some Bengalis. I screamed to my father to run but we were surrounded.

'The police just turned away. I pleaded with the Bengalis and offered them 200 rupees and my watch but they laughed and took the money. One man said: "We are going to kill you Biharis." They dragged us across the road into a ditch.

'I saw them take my father a few yards away and they cut his throat with a large knife. Two men were doing the killings while the others were laughing and holding other people. The killings went on for several hours but they eventually let me go', the weeping girl said.

Other inmates of the camp said that the killings on 18 April started after the Bengali press had given wide publicity to the discovery of a pit of skeletons near the camp. A Bihari clerk claimed bitterly that the bones belonged to people from his community. 'In a few days the bones of the latest victims will be found, they will be called Bengalis and the killings will continue.'

Another witness to the slaughter, a 50-year-old weaver from Mirpur, said he saw mobs of hundreds of Bengalis roaming through the camp. 'They had long knives and dragged everyone they could find, including women and children, to a ditch out of sight. I don't know what happened to them but they have never come back.'

These are just a few examples of the terror which prevails in the ghettoes today. While we were speaking, a weeping woman entered the camp office to report that her husband had been dragged out of the camp by a group of Bengalis. 'We can't do anything about it', a Bihari camp administrator said. 'The road surrounding the camp is under curfew and we cannot cross it.'

'They come in and drag our people across the road. When we appeal to the Bangladesh Rifles outpost they say the matter does not fall under their jurisdiction.'

Another woman from the Murapapa camp, 23 miles away, said the Bengalis were cutting through the wire and kidnapping women. The girls were usually raped and never reappeared, she said. Police protection was inadequate and officers were usually indifferent to the appeals of the women.

There is no sign of a police presence at Mohammadpur either. At the insistence of militant chauvinists in the Government, the International Red Cross has been forced to hand over supervision of the camps and the distribution of food to the Biharis to Bengali nationalists belonging to the

Bangladesh Red Cross. But the Bangladesh Red Cross is completely indifferent to its task. During many visits to the camps I could not discover a single Bangladesh Red Cross or Government official. For all practical purposes, the Biharis have been left to fend for themselves.

Mirpur was originally a Bihari middle-class suburb, but most of the original inhabitants have been evicted from their homes either by the Awami League, the police or mobs. Most of the original inhabitants are living in crowded houses or huts in a section of the suburb.

A Government servant who has been unemployed for five months says that he was forced to move from his house on 23 March. 'This was my own house I had purchased from my life savings [.] But on 23 March the Bangladesh Rifles and the Superintendent of Police told me to vacate the house in two hours. Sixteen thousand other people were also evicted and their houses were given to Bengalis.'

Most non-Bengalis have been unemployed since December and they are now selling the last of their clothes and belongings to remain alive. They are simply too terrified to leave the camp. Previously they needed permits to leave and enter the ghettoes, but now they have been told that they can leave the area but cannot return.

Food supplies are inadequate: two ounces of cornflower per person per day. Foreign observers have also discovered that food supplies have been pilfered and tampered with since the Bangladesh Red Cross insisted on handling the distribution of foreign assistance to the non-Bengalis. There are some pitiful sights in the camps. Mr Paul Connett, a member of the mission led by Mr David Ennals, discovered hungry people eating grass in the Mohammadpur camp this week.

A weeping woman explains that she is 80 and alone in the world. Her two soils were slaughtered by Bengali mobs and she was evicted from her house. A boy, of 12, Ishan, is attempting to fend for his sister, aged 10. Their entire family was slaughtered by Bengali mobs in the district of Mymensingh in March last year.

Heads of families show me their dismissal notices. 'What is to become of us? Pakistan will not have us, India will not have us and we will either be liquidated or starved to death here', a young accountant said.

Ultimately, the blame for the deteriorating plight of the non-Bengali community must lie squarely on the shoulders of the Prime Minister, Shaikh Mujibur Rahman. Apart from his initial plea for harmony the Shaikh has refused to take a firm stand on the question of their security.

Apparently he does not have the courage to oppose the narrow chauvinists and the bigoted student leaders who surround him. Essentially, the Shaikh has found it easier to ignore the question and to swim with the tide of hatred and unreasoned emotions.

And as time passes it would seem that his public utterances are becoming more irresponsible and prone to further inflame public feeling against the minority community. For instance, in response to the British mission's appeal for tolerance, the Shaikh has made a public statement which can only aggravate the issue.

Speaking to trade unionists over the weekend the Shaikh reverted to pure demagoguery and called on his people to launch a movement against the 'collaborators who are conspiring with foreign collaborators to undermine the freedom of Bangladesh'.

Under the circumstances the average Bengali would accept this as open licence to hunt down the non-Bengalis. Unless the international community is able to intervene, these wretched people will slowly but surely face extermination.

The Catharsis of Pakistan

27 May 1972

Hamida Khuhro

THE saddest and most striking feature of post Bangladesh Pakistan is the almost total unconcern of the people of Pakistan with the events that have rent the country for the past year—but the most amazing of all is the bland indifference of the urban middle class intellectuals to the basic issues behind the events. There are elevated articles about 'foreign policy' and 'the need to unite the nation', about fringe problems such as 'the Biharis' and 'why we lost the war', even sometimes articles displaying a strange *schadenfreude* about conditions in Bangladesh—but nowhere is there any sign of a crisis of conscience which should follow a cruel and bloody civil war such as we have just passed through—a war which was deliberately let loose on the country by its rulers and was tacitly if not openly supported by the intellectuals.

Let us recall some of the circumstances of this war: a highly trained professional army was used against the civilian population, the only justification offered by the government (and apparently accepted by the intellectuals) being that West Pakistanis and Biharis had been attacked first by the Bengalis. The elementary distinction between mob action and the policy of a government carried out by its armed forces was not made. This action did not take place secretly or even for a short period of days or weeks, it was carried on for a period of several months—more than six months before any foreign intervention took place. And all this time no middle class intellectual of Pakistan raised a voice in doubt, let alone in protest.

Surely 1971 will go down in the history of the Muslims of the subcontinent of India as infamously as the Nazi regime in Western civilization. It is difficult to recall any similar event in the history of Islam apart from Yazid's massacre of the Innocents. The nation that proudly calls itself the largest Muslim country in the world and whose citizens used to commonly (and with perfect seriousness) denounce Muslims from other parts of the world for their decadence and un-islamic ways, stood by and watched one of the bloodiest and most inhuman civil wars in history without a flicker. Even if we admit as an excuse, feeble though it may be, that a Genghis Khan was ruling us and that protest would have been no use or that we did not know what was happening—although this last excuse scarcely holds water—surely now when the whole story is before us in hideous detail, some sign is due from the conscience keepers of the nation that they recognized the enormity of the events that have occurred. Surely, they have a clear duty to inform the public of what actually happened, to analyse the events and to explain what went wrong with the body politic of Pakistan that such events should have occured. They must isolate the diseased bits of our anatomy and tell us why a country which came into existence with such hopes scarcely twenty-five years ago could perpetrate such crimes against its own citizens and where half the people watched while the other half were being suppressed and where half the people were so disaffected that force was felt necessary to keep them in the country. Such self-examination is absolutely essential for our very survival as civilized beings. It has occured in every historical situation and surely Pakistan is not so afraid of what it might find in its behaviour or its psyche that it is not able to fulfil this basic requirement necessary to intelligent human beings.

There are a few, a very few, people who have tried to pinpoint the nature of the crisis in Pakistan and the necessity for recognizing the completely changed situation obtaining in Pakistan after the secession of Bangladesh. The voices in the wilderness belong not as one might expect, to the political commentators and treatise writers of Karachi and Lahore but to Baluch political leaders, the inhabitants of that 'backward' region of Pakistan where there is no university and scarcely a newspaper. To reiterate the stark truth of Pakistan's situation in 1972, the country that came into existence in 1947 has been destroyed as has the two nation theory on which it was based. The regions that form West Pakistan had not voted for Pakistan in its present form and therefore if it is to survive and flourish, the country needs a new identity. It needs a *raison d'etre* which it can only get if there is the will among the people who live in these regions to live together as one country. They have to decide anew on what terms they will live together. Geographical contiguity is not necessarily a criterion if there is not also cultural affinity, and, above all, affection and goodwill. In order to find this new basis for the nation we must re-examine the true circumstances and aspirations of the people of these regions, to see what their expectations were at the creation of Pakistan and how far these expectations were honestly striven for and how far betrayed. Such a reappraisal would be impossible without another look at the pre-partition political situation in India and particularly the Muslim situation before 1947.

Muslims of India expected from independence a flexible and open society in which there would be opportunity and the possibility of breaking out of the straitjacket of 'backwardness' and underdevelopment, a possibility which was remote in a system of open competition. This was a problem which the Muslims of India had experienced for nearly a hundred years after English education and the British legal system had been applied to India. Beginning with Sir Syed Ahmed Khan's efforts to educate and westernize the community, Muslims had been engaged in a struggle to gain their fair share of jobs and opportunities. They found that in practice it was very difficult to break through the Hindu monopoly of education and services.

Muslims had to rely heavily on the government's provision of special reserved places for 'backward' communities and on 'nomination' to get into the services when open competition failed to get them places. The basic demand of the middle class Muslim political movement in provinces like U.P. was this demand for representation in the services and it was channeled through the middle class Muslim political organization—the Muslim League.

In the provinces where Muslims were not 'bourgeoised' such as Sind and Bengal, they looked for emancipation from economic and bureaucratic domination by an assertion of their political as well as economic rights as majority communities. To some extent this was true of the North West Frontier provinces also where, however, the Hindu presence was much less noticeable. The Muslim League had comparatively little strength. The Punjab Muslims had long been the blue eyed boys of the imperial government. They formed the bulk of the army and the civil service, the two main pillars of British rule in India, hence the independence movement here was off to a slow start and the Muslim League lacked middle class elitist support right up to 1946 when, finally, the Muslim middle classes switched their support from the Unionists to the Muslim League.

The Muslim League though essentially a middle class movement brought together on one platform Muslims from different regions of India with their varied stages of development and their widely different demands and expectations. The aim of the Muslim League under Jinnah was to unite Muslims in order to strengthen their bargaining position on an all-India level. He would use the strength of the Muslim position in one area i.e. their great majority in Sind, to gain bigger numbers to represent them in the Assembly of U.P.—this was the idea behind 'weightage' which the Muslim League insisted should form part of the package in the settlement in the Government of India Act of 1935. In the post-1935 period of provincial autonomy, the Muslim League sought to cushion the position of Muslims in minority provinces from their vulnerable positions under Congress governments, by presenting their problems on an all-India stage. As the prospect of independence came closer, however, it was no longer enough to make a case to the imperial government and obtain special 'safeguards' as the situation arose, but to win such 'safeguards' on a permanent basis with a guarantee not from the imperial government but from the majority community—a community which had the advantage not only in numbers but also was far more advanced educationally and economically. If the British had not been on the scene or if they had withdrawn, say in 1918 or even in the 1930s, no doubt some workable settlement would have been arrived at within the framework of a united India but, as it happened, this remains one of the tantalising *ifs* of history, and the British remained in India to act as arbitrator between the two communities while at the same time, furthering their own interests.

The British presence distorted the situation in India and complicated the relationship between the two major communities. The two communities, instead of coming to a practical arrangement with each other, could always turn to the third party for arbitration—a third party which would, in the interests of preserving its own preeminence and continued influence, pander to each in turn and thus make more difficult an eventual settlement. It was the great misfortune of the Indian subcontinent that the leadership available to the two communities, especially to the majority community, could not see far enough and had not enough statesmanship to forestall imperial designs, and fell readily into the trap so cleverly designed for them.

It did not suit the great powers of the post-1945 era to have a united independent India. The cold war game had to be won and it would be easier to establish client states in Asia and Africa if the new Asian and African states were small, weak, and fragmented. In India the Congress crowned its long career of short-sighted policies by sabotaging the Cabinet Mission plan of 1945 and then accepting the ill-considered partition plan of Lord Mountbatten. Although the Muslim League leadership was not a particular fount of wisdom and discretion either, its culpability is lesser than that of the Congress because, as it was the minority party, it bore a lesser burden of responsibility. There can be no doubt that until 1946 at least the demand for Pakistan was a mere 'bargain counter'. Mr Jinnah accepted the Cabinet Mission plan and only abandoned it after Nehru's rather ambiguous attitude towards it became clear. Even at the last minute he put forward a scheme for a 'corridor' across north India to link the two wings of the proposed Pakistan—a scheme which would be clearly unacceptable to the Congress and the British. It is possible to see in this demand a last minute gambit to torpedo the Pakistan scheme and arrive at some other arrangement. Most historians now accept that the scheme, as drawn up by Mountbatten, was hasty and ill-conceived. There is room for suspicion that in the execution of the partition scheme, the imperial power was serving interests other than the welfare of the people of the subcontinent of India. The fact that Mr Jinnah accepted the scheme was a measure of his despair with the Congress and the British, a last resort rather than a genuine demand or the irreducible minimum demand as popular theory would have it.

The result of the partition was an unforeseen holocaust: large scale killings and a massive transfer of population. In the dislocation that occurred, all calculation of balance and security to be achieved by retaining the Hindu population in Pakistan areas went awry. Most of the Hindus, who were few to begin with, in the western areas of Pakistan emigrated and large numbers of refugees flooded into Pakistan, particularly into Sind and into East Bengal.

These were the facts we inherited at partition. A scheme for self-governing Muslim majority areas with Hindu minorities to act as security for Muslims in Hindu majority areas had gone wrong and instead a severely handicapped, geographically divided and economically backward country with an enormous refugee problem was created. Among the people of Pakistan, however, there was a great enthusiasm and a great idealism which could have been harnessed and used to create a just society incorporating the spirit of the early Islamic state of the *Khulfa-e-Rashidin*. The people of Pakistan were in the mood for change and for sacrifice so that their vision of an Islamic society could be realized. The leaders of Pakistan, however, instead of recognizing this mood and indeed the great need for revolutionary social reform and simple and honest leadership, inaugurated the new regime by an incredible display of arrogance, extravagance, bombast, and a crude manipulation of power. The executive government at the centre as inherited by Pakistan was the authoritarian centralized system of the Indian viceregal government—although at the provincial level, democratic governments had been functioning partially since 1919 and fully since 1935, albeit subject to the exercise of Section 92.

As a result of the high-handed policies of the central government, provincial autonomy was quickly undermined and thus the only source of life-blood to the democratic politics of the country began to dry up. At the centre itself the civil servants nominated to the cabinet soon became ascendant. After the death of Liaquat Ali Khan, power fell entirely into the hands of bureaucrats, first of all those who had been elevated to cabinet posts, and secondly to the permanent civil service. It is important to remember that these bureaucrats had no electoral mandate and no popular base and were, moreover, an elite which had been nurtured in the tradition of service to the empire. Exactly the same could be said of the army. The Indian army was a mercenary force which had fought in Mesopotamia against fellow Muslims. Both the army and the civil service were well organized and, more important, they had an *esprit de corps*. The civil service were already in charge of the day to day working machinery of the government. Without any political or ideological convictions, with the departure of their imperial masters, they owed loyalty only to themselves. This elite was not widely based in all the provinces of Pakistan but was largely drawn from the Punjab middle classes and from westernized middle classes who had come from India.

Of all the sections of Muslim population in India, the civil service and the army had the least consciousness of the nationalist spirit and felt the least passion for the attainment of freedom. The civil service knew the working of government in an authoritarian state and not the far more subordinate role that a civil service has to play in a free country. After independence, therefore, when fortuitously put in control of some key positions in the government, the civil service moved like Frankenstein's monster, uncontrolled and irresponsible, to seize power and destroy the liberty of the people. In this, their task was made easier by the fact that the Muslim League political organization was extremely weak at the centre and dominated by the personality of Mr Jinnah. After his death the Muslim League was left a highly centralized organization with a powerless Council and a tradition of being a rubber stamping body to whoever assumed the position of president. Presidentship under Jinnah and Liaquat Ali Khan was combined with high office in the state which destroyed any independence the organization may have developed or any role it might have played as a channel for the political views of the people. Even provincial organizations were strictly controlled from the centre and refused any autonomy in their affairs. The Muslim League organization also fell into the hands of the 'anti-politician' civil servants who were in control at the centre.

The fate of democracy was thus sealed in Pakistan. From now on all vestiges of independence would be ruthlessly and inexorably stamped out—whether this meant dismissal of Fazlul Haq's government in East Bengal or politicians' victimizations under PRODA in Sind and the Punjab or Nazimuddin's dismissal at the centre or the dissolution of the Constituent Assembly. Historians will have to determine when evidence becomes available as to how much of the strength of the 'anti-politicians' backed by the army was their own determination to monopolize power and how much support and encouragement they enjoyed from the great powers who wished to use Pakistan as a pawn in their cold war battles. That this hidden hand was manipulating Pakistan's rulers at least in the 1958 *coup* is obvious now and it is within the bounds of probability that this hand was operating in Pakistan politics at least as early as Ghulam Mohammed's *coup* in 1953 and Bogra's installation as prime minister.

Once the channels of democracy had been blocked, the economic exploitation of regions without representation in the ruling elite was a natural corollary. The ruling groups wanted to perpetuate their power by all means at their disposal. To this end both political and economic devices were to be used. Among the more important political devices used were one unit in West Pakistan to make the smaller provinces toe the line, and 'parity' between the east and west wings of Pakistan (surely this is where the distrust began which created Bangladesh), Although, East Bengal was theoretically given equal share in the services (no question of proportionate share for Sind and Baluchistan); care was taken to see that no key departments went to any region not fully worthy of trust. Economic injustice was perpetrated through highly sophisticated techniques. Thus projects given to East Pakistan were usually found to have been 'non-feasible' at the end of 5-year plans and somehow funds earmarked for projects in East Pakistan were found to be still unspent because East Pakistan had proved 'incapable of absorbing' these funds. Crude and thorough exploitation of regions in the western half of the country, of Sind and Baluchistan particularly, was carried out with impunity. The object was to keep power in the hands of the bureaucratic-military elite and wealth in hands where it would be readily available to the rulers, that is, in the hands of their closest supporters. Under Ayub the practice of rewarding some of the faithful by licences and loans for industry and of others by cushy jobs was commonplace. The public life of Pakistan was so demoralized that corruption in every sphere was accepted as the norm.

Thus while the reality in Pakistan was that a corrupt and tyrannical oligarchy ruled the country in its own interests, using such doses of the stick and the carrot as would enable: it to rule with the greatest possible ease, the fiction was maintained that Pakistan was an 'Islamic state', established for the express purpose of revealing God's will to the rest of the world. The rulers of Pakistan ruled by a Divine Right such as Louis XIV would have hesitated to claim in his heyday, and to hold an opinion contrary to the accepted creed (whether that was to doubt the infallibility of Ayub Khan or Yahya Khan or to denounce one unit or to doubt the claim of Urdu to be the 'chosen' language), was treason to the state of Pakistan and to the religion of Islam. These trends of intolerance were strengthened till it became impossible to write a mildly different interpretation of certain aspects of Islamic theory without being hounded out of one's job and the country, or to differ with some theory of Iqbal without being in danger of detention. Pakistan, the pre-eminent Islamic state, put to shame the basic concept of tolerance pioneered by the Prophet of Islam and negated the right of reinterpretation as allowed by *ijtehad*. Pakistan outdid the intolerance of mediaeval Christianity and the early Protestant puritan states because it lacked even the excuse of a narrow belief firmly held. In Pakistan all this purity was a charade to hide the reality of a corrupt and materialist power-wielding minority which had imposed itself on a simple and utterly oppressed people.

The real tragedy, however, was not the existence of this ruling elite and its tyranny but the fact that the educated class—the middle class intellectuals of Pakistan—prostituted themselves to the service of this elite. They applauded every turn of the screw and every blow at the freedom and dignity of the people. They did so not only out of fear which would itself be a betrayal of trust but out of self-interest. The Pakistan press and intelligentsia produced no martyrs for the truth. They watched and said nothing while armed force was used to crush Baluchis, while trains were run over striking railway workers, and while people were imprisoned without trial and they remained silent still when brute force was unleashed on the hapless people of East Pakistan. Surely no person of reasonable intelligence can believe that mob action or even organized killings by disaffected groups required that armed strength should be sent into action to systematically kill civilian citizens. What difference does it make that those killed, were 30,000 or 3,000,000—why should a single citizen be killed without trial by proper judicial process? Where were the press and the leaders now clamouring on behalf of 'Biharis' and 'pro-Pakistan elements' when Bengali Pakistan elements were being butchered and their wives and daughters raped? Surely we cannot seriously believe that the 'Awami League' or the 'Yahya clique' or Indian agents destroyed Pakistan. The blame must be laid on the educated bourgeoisie of Pakistan, on the writers, the newspapers, the conscience keepers of Pakistan who failed us in our hour of need and allowed tyranny to run amok in the land. If there had been protests and defiance and sympathy displayed for *our* Bengali fellow citizens during the year of their agony, they would still be with us in Pakistan, and the Muslims of the subcontinent would not have had to suffer the shame and humiliation of a Hindu army coming to save a Muslim people from a Muslim army.

The question now is whether any lessons have been learnt from the experiences of the past? It is a crucial question because on it depends whether Pakistan will continue to exist and if a consensus can be found among its people for its existence. It is highly significant that there is a resurgence of nationalism in the different regions of West Pakistan. Basically this is due to the fact that with East Pakistan gone, the smaller regions feel they must assert their rights against a possible reimposition of an elitist rule which would once again deprive them, and this time they cannot rely on a bigger 'have not' region like East Bengal to redress the balance. Pakistan will no doubt continue to exist as a geographical entity as long as the great powers will it, but it is up to us to decide whether the carcass will have life. If Pakistan can show that it can build a free and democratic society and does not need to hide behind chauvinistic slogans, it may yet achieve its salvation.

Let us openly acknowledge the errors of the past and make friends with Bangladesh and Bharat. The only way Pakistan can still discharge its obligation of being security for the Muslims of India is by being true and just and *in friendship* with the other two countries of the subcontinent. It is no use at all to make hollow appeals for unity—it is not enough just to paper over the cracks. We must destroy the faulty edifice and build again on a secure foundation. At each step in our progress we must analyse and re-analyse ourselves and our history until we find the right answers.

The Defection of K. M. Kaiser

3 June 1972

Jamil Akhtar

WHILE Dacca was still rife with stories that Bengalis in Peking were being harassed, ill-treated, kept in confinement etc. etc. by the Chinese, the last batch of Bengali officers and staff of the Pakistan embassy in Peking, headed by the ambassador, Khwaja Mohammed Kaiser, entered the British colony of Hong Kong on [the] way to Bangladesh. Dacca and Hong Kong press had shown so much interest in the fate of the Bengalis trapped in Peking that the smooth departure of this last batch came as something of an anti-climax. There was no story. The sensation-seeking Hong Kong reporters were flabbergasted to learn from these diplomats that the 'unfriendly' Chinese had been nice to them.

Khwaja Kaiser deservedly took pride in his efficacious efforts in arranging the officially sanctioned defection of all his Bengali subordinates. He was right in saying that he left only after he had safely sent away all of his Bengali colleagues with explicit permission and at the expense of the Government of Pakistan. With all facilities, allowances and travelling expenses, he got them transferred to convenient points, Bangkok, Rangoon etc. He himself was transferred to Islamabad but was asked to travel via Bangkok instead of the usual and, in case of government servants almost obligatory, Shanghai-Karachi PIA route. There were no doubts where the Khwaja would go as the rumours were already there in Peking that of late he had been having frequent meetings with Indian diplomats who served as the contact channels. People also believed that he had started advocating Bangladesh point of view in diplomatic gatherings and probably also with the Chinese. Nevertheless, he was given a respectful and almost moving send-off by Pakistanis, their wives and children and an equally warm welcome by the Pak Trade Mission in Hong Kong. Not exactly knowing what sort of an award awaited this rather belated defection, Khwaja Kaiser, coming from the much talked about Nawab family of Dacca, told a confidant before boarding the Russian-made Illushyn at Peking airport, 'I am an old-time Awami Leaguer, Shaikh Saheb knows it'. He had another big consolation, 'I know better Bengali than Dr Kamal Hussain'. He had also made it plain to the Bengalis accompanying him that he would be nothing less than foreign secretary if he decided to go to Pakistan.

A police-officer-turned-diplomat, Khwaja Mohammed Kaiser, who had started using the 'son of the soil' vocabulary during the days of Awami League non-cooperation movement, and had a heart attack immediately after Yahya's military operation, had early this year suddenly started remembering how intimate he had been with President Bhutto all these years. Those close to him had, by now, almost got by heart the innumerable anecdotes which revealed Bhutto's immense liking and warmth for him.

There was a time when he gave the appearance of a broken man. But as he recovered from his squeamishness, he was quoted as saying, 'after all we did not, work for twenty four years to see the country divided'. But possibly the signal from Dacca was very clear whereas that from Islamabad was jammed somewhere. According to one report (Khwaja Kaiser himself being the source), among the first few questions that Shaikh Mujib asked President Bhutto in the Rawalpindi meeting was one about three senior Bengali officers, Khwaja Saheb being one of them. So ultimately the old Khwaja was left with no alternative but to decide 'to serve and rebuild his country under the leadership of the great leader, Banglabandhu'. He is now in Dacca and has joined the Bangladesh Government.

With Khwaja Kaiser, and so with all the Bengalis, the attitude of the Chinese had always been one of strict non-involvement. The farewell party given by Premier Chou en-Lai in honour of the outgoing ambassador proceeded in warm and friendly atmosphere (an expression reserved for receptions for guests from friendly countries like Pakistan). It meant that the Chinese pretended not to know anything, although it was rumoured that the Khwaja had lately tried to establish some sort of contact between Dacca and Peking. The Chinese had always been cautious on the defection issue. When the personnel of the Chinese consulate in Dacca were allowed by the Bangladesh Government to return to their country, it was suggested in the Dacca press that there had been some understanding between Dacca and the Chinese Government about the repatriation of the Bengalis in Peking. It was also reported that the Dacca Government had decided to charter a Burmese plane to bring the Bengalis back. The Chinese never made any comment. It was three months after the return of the Chinese consulate staff that the first batch of three Bengali officers left for Bangkok on transfer.

It is difficult to say how the Chinese would have behaved had there been a defection in the classic style. One Bengali officer had actually thought about it. Encouraged by the possibilities of immediately becoming a hero in case the Chinese refused him an exit visa, thereby compensating his failure to defect before the fall of Dacca, he had almost drafted a statement for the foreign correspondents. Later, he dropped the idea when it occurred to him that if the Chinese decided to be fussy, they might deport him to Pakistan. In that case, by the time he reached Dacca, the stories of his heroism would almost be forgotten or there will be too many heroes from Karachi and Islamabad. Nobody was prepared to go to Hong Kong at his own expense and risk, and announce his allegiance there, although it had been hinted that the Chinese would have no objection to it.

Bitter Memories, Bitter Faces

3 June 1972

INEXORABLY inching towards the stage where total, corroding disillusion begins to bore its remorseless way into a man's soul, the non-Bengalis who fled the bloody shambles of Bangladesh are today a struggling, uncertain lot. They are lost, unsure, in a strange world into which they have been so unceremoniously dumped. The young ones still have a spring in their step, a mock-jaunty air, for their lives are beginning, and dreams are still dreams. But the old ones, most of them are totally lost, with bitter lines etched on their faces, for the acrid taste of defeat is still fresh in their mouths, the shattering impact of watching a lifetime crumble before their eyes still fresh on their minds. And the most cruelly laughable thing is that it was a defeat in which they had no hand, a loss not of their own making, but an irrevocable slide of massed passions in the face of which they were helpless.

These words might bring a spark of recognition to the eyes of those who have been in Bangladesh. The rest, these words will probably leave them cold, or at most cause a pitying clucking. Just as well. A man cannot be expected to take on the burden of the whole world. But a man can have some share in relieving the burden, if not for altruistic reasons, then for the simple fact that when tragedy is stalking in your midst you never know when it is going to turn on you. But many in this country of mine are not even prepared for that.

I have read with disbelief stories in newspapers about the repugnance which some people here have towards the non-Bengali East Pakistanis. The disbelief was gradually and reluctantly replaced by a certain philosophic resignation, repeated onslaughts have turned the disbelief into cold cynicism. I read about an organization in Sind which held province-wide demonstrations to prevent East Pakistanis from settling here. I read about a procession in Karachi led by two MNAs with the same objective in mind.

And I read elsewhere that the grand old man of Sind, Mr G. M. Syed, is somewhere behind all this muck, omnipotently pulling strings to add yet another feather to his cap. But what use are all those feathers, *Saeen*, when they are dripping with blood? These actions speak for themselves. And they come from the proud upholders of truth, justice and a lot of similar bunk. My people. Add to this President Bhutto's pregnant allusion to the Red Indians in his Sanghar speech and a hazy, though

BITTER MEMORIES, BITTER FACES

firm picture begins to form. His words are now famous, they have been bandied around the world. No retraction has come, nor any explanation. Obviously the king can do no wrong.

There is still a feeling of unreality about the whole affair. The *it can't happen to us* sentiment persists, in the face of overwhelming evidence that it can. So says the soldier until he is shot. The non-Bengali East Pakistani in Karachi still clings to this forlorn illusion. *There will be a one-Pakistan again, Bhutto is a wise man—he will make some arrangement with Mujib. I will get my business back—they can't take it.*

But even this slender thread of hope is fast disappearing. The immense confidence that Mr Bhutto had so brashly generated in the non-Bengalis is now dissipating in the face of the government's obviously desultory interest in the problem. And the inane statements which some of the ministers are making are not helping any; instead they are pushing the people towards the brink of total despair. Listen to this: *The people of East and West Pakistan share limitless devotion and their souls rise above and meet across alien barriers in joint dedication to a common faith.* Is Maulana Niazi making a bad joke? Or is he trying to pull wool over the eyes of those whose eyes have seen everything?

It is disheartening for the non-Bengalis when they compare the frantic interest which the government is showing in its army in India which is well-fed, properly housed and which is going to return anyway; and its perfunctory interest in the non-Bengali population in East Pakistan which is starving, living in holes, and whose lives depend on the itchy trigger fingers of a people trying to remove the chip which has always been on its shoulder.

Admittedly, there is not much that the Pakistan government can do about the non-Bengalis in Bangladesh, except for raising a stink about it and showing a bit more concern than it is presently. It is doing neither, and what is really contemptible, it is almost cold-shouldering those who are daily escaping from Bangladesh. While there are paeans of praise for the armymen who have escaped, very few of whom have done so despite the fact that they are duty-bound to try and escape, the fleeing civilians are greeted with a bare toleration. What does it do to a man who is fleeing from a nightmare to what he believes is his country, to be so greeted?

Those who have escaped through Burma speak of the nights they have spent at the Pakistan embassy there lying on newspapers, living on bad food awaiting their turn to be flown to Pakistan. And once they get to the promised land, what awaits them? A few bouquets, a few more brickbats, and a lot of indifference.

The lucky ones are those who have relatives here, on whom they can go and impose, live from day to day, spend their time tramping from office to office, looking for jobs, letting their expectations sink lower until they are ready to accept whatever crumb is offered them. And the unlucky ones for them the hellholes of Orangi, live on filth and sneers, live on the charity of people like the ladies of APWA, live on the two anna bucket of water when the truck comes round.

The non-Bengalis in Karachi have done all they can to get some attention. They have formed associations, they have gone on roadside hunger strikes, they have taken out processions. And perhaps one indication of the government reaction is the *lathi*-charge on the processionists who had gone to the President's Clifton house in March—and in the procession were women and children also. The uproar that followed was calmed by the establishment of an enquiry commission—that all-purpose sop, a few comforting words and gestures from Mr Bhutto, and a warning to the press not to give so much attention to such insignificant bits of news—in the national interests, of course.

Also indicative of some people's attitude is this letter which was printed in the Punjab Punch of 2 April:

...It is an obvious fact that Biharis, after coming over to Pakistan, have taken over the administration and economy of the country. They have mercilessly exploited the poor local populace, Bengalis, Punjabis and Sindhis all alike. The poor masses have been enslaved by Biharis in their home provinces and have been subjected to tremendous mental and physical torture. It will be a humanitarian duty if you will take up the cause of downtrodden Punjabis and Sindhis in order to save us from total annihilation...

And from another part of the world, from the remote wilderness of Dacca comes a cry: ...will the world take the trouble to save these naked, hungry, homeless, diseased, poor, and helpless Biharis by repatriating them even in the desert, so that they could peacefully die there?

I wonder what the like of Mr G. M. Syed will use to mop up the shreds of their conscience with?

—M. A.

Take-Over Ordinances

10 June 1972

A. S. Pingar

RECENTLY, the Bangladesh government has promulgated a series of orders dealing with the sequestration and management of Pakistani property including banks, insurance companies, and buildings. The following is a commentary on these measures:

1. THE BANGLADESH ABANDONED PROPERTY ORDER OF 1972 was promulgated on 26 February 1972. All the properties (movable and immovable) left by the citizens of Pakistan vest in the Govt. of Bangladesh which has the power to administer, control, manage and even dispose of such property. The conditions required for the taking over of such properties are that the owners are not present in Bangladesh or their whereabouts are not known or that they are not looking after their properties or have become enemy aliens. Enemy aliens are those persons who are citizens of Pakistan, which state, according to the Bangladesh Government, conducted military operations and war against Bangladesh after 25 March 1971. The term thus covers a very large number of people. By this order, the government has already taken over properties like industries, corporate companies, shares and stocks, banks, insurance companies, land, transport, buildings and houses, tea gardens, gold and silver etc.

These properties are initially taken over by the deputy commissioner or subdivisional magistrate concerned who, after making a proper inventory, hands them over to the relevant ministries. Shops and godowns are handed over to the Ministry of Commerce; industrial undertakings to the Ministry of Industry; trucks, buses, and cars to the Ministry of Communications; negotiable instruments and securities such as shares, stocks, bonds, debnetures etc. to the Ministry of Commerce, and so on. Unauthorized persons who are in possesion of such properties are asked by the order to surrender the properties to the deputy commissioner or subdivisional magistrate. Those who refuse to comply are liable to ejection and also prosecution.

The government has been given wide powers under which it can constitute boards to look after such acquired properties, or appoint administrators who cannot only run the properties but can take action for the recovery of any debt, claim or right. They have all the rights and liabilities of a private individual. The courts have been denied the power to issue any orders in respect of such properties and the only relief that is provided is that an affected person can make an application within three months from the date of the publication of this order to the relevant authority, though the relevant authority is not named and the aggrieved person can make a further appeal to the relevant authority against the rejection of his application within one month.

2. THE BANGLADESH RESTORATION OF EVACUEE PROPERTY ORDER was promulgated on 17 February 1972. Some relief is provided by this order to those persons who left their homes or business during the widespread disturbances on or after 25 March 1971, or before 16 December 1971, and took shelter somewhere either in Bangladesh or in some other country. Such persons, on returning to Bangladesh, can oust the unauthorized persons in occupation of their homes and houses on an application to an arbitration court whose members are chosen from the secondary and primary school teachers, and the provisions of the Criminal Procedure Code and the Civil Procedure Code do not apply to this court. If the parties do not agree to the arbitration award, the court can then refer the matter to the *thana* magistrate who may conduct a further inquiry and give his findings which will be binding on both the parties, though a further appeal lies to a tribunal, whose decision is final. Similar provision has been made in respect of the claim of compensation in case any property is misappropriated or damaged or lost during its possession by an unauthorized person, though it would be very difficult to prove an allegation of misappropriation, loss or theft, because the property or properties must have passed through so many hands.

The civil courts are not debarred from entertaining the plaints by way of suits for the establishment of the right of the affected persons, but the courts are not permitted to question the orders passed under this law.

3. THE BANGLADESH BANKS (NATIONALIZATION) ORDER was promulgated on 26 March 1972. As the title suggests, the government has by this order, nationalized all the existing banks and converted them into new banks though these banks may use their old names and seals till the government finds suitable substitutes. The order provides that the government shall honour all the existing contracts, agreements and bonds, and that pending proceedings in a court of law shall not be affected by the said order. The order provides that the banks shall continue to be run in the same way as they used to be run by the previous owners and shall enjoy their previous rights and liabilities, except that in place of the old directors, there will be a new board of directors consisting of seven members inclusive of the managing director, who shall all be appointed for three years by the government. The managing director is a wholetime officer and he is the chief executive of the bank.

The previous owners of the banks are entitled to compensation but such compensation would not exceed the total paid-up value of the shares held by the share-holders among whom such compensation is to be distributed. The government was to frame rules for awarding compensation, and these must have been published by now. The accounts of the bank are to be audited by government appointed auditors who will scrutinize the accounts, and submit their report to the government. Banks are permitted to carry on their business as they used to do, except that they cannot make any advance or grant in contravention of the Bangladesh laws; nor can they make any unsecured loan to any director or to any concern in which a director is interested. The winding up proceedings are not applicable to such banks but the order does not say whether or not a bank can question the validity of such an order. The former employees of the banks shall continue to be in the service of the new banks, and their remuneration, rights and obligations remain unchanged.

4. Under the BANGLADESH INSURANCE (EMERGENCY PROVISIONS) ORDER, promulgated on 26 March 1972, the government has pending nationalization, taken over the management of *certain* life and general insurance companies, and a custodian is to be appointed to manage their affairs. It is not known how many companies are affected by this order, but the government intends to pay compensation and the amount of compensation will be determined under the rules which the government will publish, or may have published by this time. All the persons who are in control of the insurance business have been asked to hand over all the properties of the insurance business, including account books, to the custodian and failure to do so entails imprisonment upto six months along with a fine. Winding up proceedings are not applicable to this order and the custodian is also protected in respect of legal proceedings for acts done in good faith. The order is silent in respect of the courts power to examine it.

5. Under the BANGLADESH (VESTING OF PROPERTY ASSETS) ORDER, promulgated on 26 March 1972, all the properties and assets that formerly vested in the Government of Pakistan now vest in the Government of Bangladesh.

Conclusion - We thus find that the government of Bangladesh has legalized the taking over of vast properties belonging to private citizens of Pakistan and of the Government of Pakistan itself. How far the Bangladesh Government will succeed in the efficient running of these vast and complex enterprises and to what extent it will modify these orders will depend upon the result of the negotiations between Pakistan and Bangladesh which will probably begin after a settlement with India. It would appear that the chances of any such understanding are remote.

A Plea for Recognition

10 June 1972

S. J. Hussain

O N the eve of the crucial Indo-Pakistan talks at the end of this month, and in view of the President's call for a debate, a reflection on the knotty problem of recognition of Bangladesh would be most pertinent.

At the outset I would like to remark that, as is usual with a particular section of the press, this rather sensitive issue has been given a highly emotional treatment and looked at from a purely subjective angle. Of course, a lot of confused thinking has gone into proving that recognition of Bangladesh would be tantamount to signing the death warrant of 'Islamic ideology' and legalizing Indian military intervention.

I, for one, do not agree with this view and feel that by recognizing the new state we would not only be accepting a *fait accompli* but would also be exposing the hypocritical rigmarole of 'Islamic ideology' and the supposedly theocratic rationale of Pakistan.

Briefly, following are the points which could be considered in favour of recognition:

i)   In the famous Pakistan Resolution (1940), which had the blessings of Muslim Bengal, there was a clear mention of two separate and sovereign Muslim states.

ii) The Pakistan ideology itself was based on secular and democratic principles, and in the struggle for a separate Pakistani nationhood, economic and cultural motivation played a dominant role. The decision, therefore, to recognize Bangladesh will not in any way harm that basis. On the contrary it will strengthen it.

iii) The two-nation (Hindu-Muslim) or three-nation (Hindu-Muslim-Bengali) concept may be considered (for a while) a politically viable concept, but not the 'Islamic ideology', which was only a sentimental political slogan of an obscurantist group in the Muslim League hierarchy. It was never a rational and well-grounded ideology in the sense of socialism, communism and similar other ideologies.

iv) The unity of East Pakistan and West Pakistan was a misnomer throughout the last 25 years because of:

a) geographical distance

b) cultural and linguistic differences

c) geopolitical compulsions.

v) Even if there was some semblance of unity and the common bond of religion between the two parts, it was destroyed by the misrule of the autocratic regimes and exploitation of the capitalist class, which unfortunately enough, was identified with the western wing.

vi) The six-points programme of the Awami League was in fact a charter of secession, and when the Awami League got an overwhelming majority in East Pakistan in 1970 elections, it was a clear indication that the people of that wing wanted to exercise the right of secession—a right enshrined in both the federal and unitary constitutions of the world. Specific examples could be given from the Swiss and USSR constitutions.

vii) Recognition of Bangladesh and the re-establishment of cultural and economic links with that country will indirectly help the socialist forces on both sides to wage a common and united struggle against the exploiters and oppressive forces of all hues—the capitalists, chauvinists, fascists, and parochialists.

In view of the above points I would give my vote in favour of recognizing Bangladesh.

The 'Catharsis': A Rejoinder

17 June 1972

Khurshid Hyder

A GREAT deal has been written about last year's civil war in Pakistan and its aftermath. Much more will be written on it in the years to come. The controversy associated with it is endemic. The passage of time is not going to still or terminate it but may heighten and extend it. Like the partition of India, it will remain one of those historical happenings which is suffused with emotions and will defy a rational and objective assessment. There can be no justification whatever for the killings and rapes which took place. All life Hindu, Muslim, Bengali, non-Bengali is sacred. Mutual killings are disgusting and revolting and indicate a fatal flaw in our national character.

It is tragic to recall that bloodshed and violence have been a recurring feature of our political life. The revolt of 1857 was marked by unprecedented acts of ferocity and savagery on both sides. Our own century is replete with incidents of violence and bloodshed; the massacre at Jallianwala Bagh, the Moplah rising, the Great Calcutta Killings followed by similar ones in Bihar and Noakhali, and the bloodbath which accompanied the partition are recorded historical events. In Punjab alone, it is estimated that nearly half a million perished in communal killings. The tradition of bloody violence has been carried over in both India and Pakistan in the post-1947 era. The assassinations of Mahatma Gandhi and Liaquat Ali Khan, communal riots of varying intensity in India, are vivid illustrations of it. The anti-Ahmadiyya riots in the Punjab in 1953, in which hundreds of innocent people lost their lives, occasioned the imposition of the first martial law in Pakistan. Killing of the Biharis is a daily occurrence in Bangladesh and is openly connived at by the ruling authorities there.

Generalization of violence does not make it any less reprehensible. But the civil war in Pakistan should not be singled out as an unparalleled event in the otherwise peaceful chronicle of the Indian subcontinent. Happenings in East Pakistan are not an aberration from the pacific traditions but a continuation of the bloody methods which are an integral though less creditable part of our heritage. Nor should our righteous indignation at the doings of the army make us forget the thousands of non-Bengalis who were massacred before the army action began in various parts of East Pakistan. They should not go unmentioned, unmourned, and unremembered whenever a history of the civil war of 1971 is written. Currently, it is more important to publicize the present than to investigate the past. The dead cannot be resurrected to life but the lives of thousands of non-Bengalis, precariously hovering between life and death may be saved. There is all the time for self-examination and emotional catharsis but there is very little time for over a million non-Bengalis who, in the words of Peter Hazelhurst, 'are systematically being slaughtered by fanatical Bengali mobs.'

So much for the 'killings'. As for the secession of East Pakistan, it may have been precipitated by Yahya's policies but was certainly not brought about by them. Given the lack of any well-defined community of interests and conflicting attitudes on economic, political, cultural, and linguistic matters, the two wings could not have indefinitely existed as a political unity. It is a miracle that despite fundamental and conflicting differences, the people of the two wings managed to live together for so long. The two common factors between the two wings were common religion and the fear of Hindu domination. But religion alone could not reconcile or resolve the differences between them. Geographically, the two wings belong to different regional groupings. West Pakistan is more an extension of the area called the Near East or the Middle East, whereas East Pakistan belongs to South and South East Asia. Thus the foreign policy orientations and strategic compulsions are widely apart. Many of the Indo-Pakistan disputes—notably canal waters and Kashmir—of paramount significance to West Pakistan in the context of its economic viability and strategic defence were totally irrelevant to the people of East Pakistan. Their economic and trade interests were also divergent. Linguistic and cultural differences also stood in the way of any abiding links.

The common fear of Hindu domination had created the need for a united struggle and brought the people of the two wings to a single platform. After the partition that fear in East Pakistan gradually became insubstantial and receded into the background. Instead, resentment began to grow against the political and economic domination of West Pakistan. And as the rising intelligentsia became conscious of the lack of any community of interests and values between the people of the two wings, separatist tendencies began to emerge. In the case of the Muslims of North India, the controversy over Urdu brought to the surface Muslim consciousness of separateness and provoked Sir Syed Ahmad Khan into saying that 'I am convinced the two people will not be able to cooperate in any venture. This is only the beginning; later because of the educated classes this hostility will increase. Those who live long enough will see it grow.' Similarly, the language controversy in East Pakistan sparked off the Bengali nationalist movement. Had the rulers in West Pakistan shown vision and foresight, the movement could *perhaps* have been contained. But their obduracy, intolerant, and narrow policies widened the base of resentment till it culminated in last years' tragic happenings.

To continue on the parallel of the Muslim freedom movement in India, the rise of an educated middle class among the Muslims of India created the inevitable demand for a share in the services and economic life of the country and when that could not be fully satisfied, constitutional safeguards were demanded which the majority community did not concede and thereby pushed the Muslims towards seeking a separate homeland of their own. The emergence in East Pakistan of urban intelligentsia aroused the very natural and legitimate demand for participation in the power processes and an access to the benefits of government. And when it was denied there was clamour for autonomy which was tantamount to complete independence.

Mujib in his recent statements has confessed that he had been working for the independence of East Pakistan since 1948. The Agartala conspiracy case was not a trumped up affair but based on incontrovertible evidence revealing the fledgling plan of secession. The defeat of the Muslim League by the United Front in 1954 was a clear assertion of the will of East Pakistan to resist the non-Bengali domination at the centre. The successive governments at Karachi and Islamabad took no serious note of the political trends in Pakistan. Instead of conceding their demands, they sought to suppress them. The rift between the two wings began to widen and in the decade of the Ayub *raj*, with almost total centralization, the gulf became unbridgeable and culminated in last year's irrevocable split.

It has often been alleged that if the 1956 constitution had been allowed to work and the political processes had not been abruptly halted by the proclamation of martial law in 1958, some kind of consensus between the two wings would have gradually evolved. Like all 'ifs' of history, there is no way of establishing or repudiating the validity of this assertion. Speculation on this can be indefinitely batted about. But such a view completely overlooks the inherent conflict of interests between the people of the two wings. Sooner *or* later, with the inevitable consequences of majority rule, (Bengali domination at the centre and the diversion of development funds, both domestic and foreign to East Pakistan where they were needed to correct the disparity and imbalance in the economic growth of the two wings) West Pakistanis, conditioned to exercise power since 1947, would have chafed under the control of Bengal and would have worked for the formal political bifurcation of the country. This is precisely what happened last year. The immediate cause of the crisis was the refusal of the political leadership in West Pakistan to accept and implement the results of the elections of 1970. So the inevitable break. Therefore, to suggest that but for the army action, East Pakistan would not have made a bid for independence is to ignore the fundamental clash of interests which in the absence of countervailing factors would have sooner or later led to the parting of ways. What could have been avoided was the army action. We should have seen the writing on the wall and agreed to part as friends as Malaya and Singapore did. The bloodshed, misery, and suffering and the overall mess and confusion in which we find ourselves could have been avoided. We should have accepted the verdict of the people and withdrawn gracefully after a warm handshake.

The emergence of Bangladesh in no way affects the continued viability of West Pakistan. The Muslims of India in demanding the partition of the subcontinent on communal lines challenged the one-nation theory and affirmed that Hindus and Muslims were not separate communities but different 'nations'. That they continue to be. Instead of two states, there are now three states in what was previously the subcontinent of India. The 1940 Lahore session of the Muslim League, where Quaid-e-Azam enunciated the two-nation 'theory unequivocally resolved that the areas in which the Muslims are numerically in a majority, as in the north-western and eastern zones of India, should be grouped to constitute 'independent states' in which the constituent units shall be autonomous and sovereign. The phrasing of the resolution makes it abundantly clear that it was intended to establish two Pakistans, each of which was to contain sovereign independent units. At the annual session of the Muslim League in Madras in 1941, a major portion of the Lahore Resolution, drafted in slightly different terms, was adopted as one of the aims and objectives of the All India Muslim League, thereby amending the League constitution.' The draft said that the north western and eastern zones of India shall be grouped together to constitute independent states as Muslim Free National Homelands in which the constituent units shall be autonomous and sovereign. Thus according to the Muslim League Constitution, the Muslim League was commited to the establishment of two Muslim 'Independent States' in the North-Western and Eastern zones of India. Khalid bin Sayeed, Pakistan; *The Formative Phase,* (Karachi, 1960), p. 124.

Allama Iqbal in his celebrated speech at the Allahabad session of the Muslim League had envisaged a Muslim state in India comprising of the north western regions only. The word Pakistan coined by Chaudhri Rahmat Ali in his pamphlet, *Now or Never,* stood for the north-western areas of India which presently constitute Pakistan. The Muslim majority areas in the north west were to form the projected Pakistan and the Muslim majority areas in the east were to a separate state to be called Bang-i-Islam.

Notwithstanding the foregoing, it is futile to engage in a meaningless controversy on the theoretical basis of Pakistan. The ultimate basis of Pakistan, as indeed of all countries, lies in the corporate will of its people and their cumulative resolve to live together as a separate independent identity. There are numerous instances of a single nationality being split into different independent units. The two Germanys and Austria are illustrative of this point. The Arabs, on the basis of a common religion, culture, and language, should form a single nation. Yet they are bifurcated into a number of large and small political units. As against this, Great Britain consisting of four different nationalities English, Welsh, Scots, and Irish, has continued to exist as a political nationalism Soviet Union is a multinational state *par excellent.* Canada is binational.

India could have continued to exist as a single political unit if the Congress leadership had not adopted a rigid and uncompromising attitude towards the constitutional safeguards sought by the Muslims of India. To say that if the transfer of power had taken place in 1930, a workable settlement would have been arrived at within the framework of a united India, is to ignore the basic facts of history. The constitutional proposals which were drafted by the Congress in the late twenties repudiated the principle of separate electorates which it had accepted and endorsed earlier in the Lucknow Pact of 1916. But both in the resolutions of the Congress on political, religious and other rights of minorities passed in December 1927 at its Madras session and the Nehru Committee proposals regarding communal representation and adopted by the All Parties National Convention held at Allahabad in 1929, joint electorates were substituted for separate electorates. Quaid-i-Azam in his Fourteen Points, presented in March 1929, had demanded, inter-alia, that 'representation of communal groups shall continue to be by means of separate electorates as at present, provided it shall be open to any community, at any time, to abandon its separate electorate in favour of joint electorate. Even this reasonable proposition was turned down by the Congress, thereby foreclosing the possibility of Hindu-Muslim cooperation.

At the Second Round Table Conference in 1931, where Congress was represented by Mahatma Gandhi, no settlement of the communal problem could be worked out thereby necessitating Ramsay MacDonald's Communal Award of 1932 (by which both Punjab and Bengal had to forgo their majorities for the sake of the weightage being granted to the Muslims in the Hindu majority provinces). For instance, in the Punjab, Muslims formed 57% of the population but were given 49% of the total seats. (86 out of 175) and in Bengal the Muslims formed 55% of the total population and were given 48% representation—(119 out of a total of 250 provincial assembly seats). If the Congress had agreed to the constitutional safeguards demanded by the League, the history of the subcontinent may have taken an entirely different course. It is one of the ironies of history that a secularist like Mr Jinnah became the leader of the movement for the partition of India on a communal basis.

Pakistan as presently constituted is a more rational and viable political entity than before and there is no reason to assume that the 'will' to continue as a single political entity is lacking among its constituent units. If anything, the separation of Bengal and the war have strengthened it and made it a vibrant living force. There is an underlying unity between the people of the various regions of Pakistan. They share a common historical past; linguistic differences are not fundamental, or too glaring, because all the languages have the same script, a common fund of vocabulary and their generic source is the same. The dress and dietary habits are more similar than dissimilar. Their strategic interests are indivisible and their economies complementary. Therefore, undisturbed by contrary tendencies, these factors will exercise their unifying influence. There is as strong a base for united West Pakistan as for any country in the world. Moreover, provinces in West Pakistan, do not have the option of independence before them as was the case with East Bengal. They can either continue to exist in the form of Pakistan or be prepared for eventual absorption into India and total obliteration of their identity and culture. If the people of the different regions of Pakistan have to choose between continuing as Pakistanis, or merger with India, one can confidently predict what the verdict of the overwhelming majority will be.

It is altogether futile to conduct a post-mortem of last year's happenings now. It will be conducted in due course by historians and political analysts. What we need today is an institutionalized political system so that power cannot in future be personalized by any ruling clique. There should be maximum political autonomy with stern safeguards against excessive centralization of power. Each region should be assured effective participation in the political processes and must have its due share in the economic development. The less-developed areas should be given priority in the allocation of funds over developed regions. The bigger and more prosperous provinces should help the less developed regions overcoming the economic difficulties and obstacles. A balance must be evolved between the several and collective interests of the various provinces so that future conflicts and tensions may be eliminated or minimized. Once maximum political autonomy is granted, the question of domination by any one province will not arise.

Our past failings cannot be attributed entirely to the misdeeds of the army and bureaucracy. To do so is to ignore the selfish and ignoble role of the politicians, who completely failed the nation in not framing a constitution for eleven long years and thereby paving the way for the takeover by the army and the bureaucracy. If, as in India, the politicians had successfully framed a constitution and set up political institutions to operate it and decentralized the power base so that every province had a sense of participation in the government, the army and the bureaucracy would not have acquired a political role. The politicians deliberately associated and involved the army and the bureaucracy in the political system to impregnate themselves against their respective rivals and opponents. In Pakistan, the failure has not been only of the army, or the bureaucracy, or for that matter of the politicians but of the *entire* nation. Each one of us has contributed, directly or indirectly, by our action or inaction, to the present imbroglio in which we find ourselves. Therefore, let there be no selective condemnation or apportioning of blame. The failure is collective and total.

Corruption is a two-sided affair; it involves those who award favours and those who seek and receive them. If there are no persons eager and willing to be corrupted, it would cease to be a weapon with such strong leverage in politics. In the Ayub era, people were corrupted by the dispensation of licences, jobs and other favours. The fault lay not only with Ayub but also with those who were more than anxious to solicit and acquire them. Even the so-called intellectuals queued up for the favour of appointment as advisers, consultants and delegates to various international conferences.

So far as Indo-Pakistan relations are concerned, there is a general consensus in Pakistan that we must move from sterile confrontation to meaningful co-operation (but not to capitulation). There is no alternative to it. The uneasy co-existence of the past should be transmuted into peaceful co-existence for the future. But Indo-Pakistan friendship cannot be wished into existence. Notwithstanding the interludes of confrontation, Pakistan has on a number of occasions, taken the initiative to seek a *detente* with India but the latter has never reciprocated. In 1953, when Mr Mohammad Ali Bogra became the Prime Minister, he exerted himself to the utmost to bring about a settlement of Indo-Pakistan disputes so that a friendlier atmosphere could be created between the two countries. President Ayub in 1959, even went to the extent of offering joint defence to India but Pandit Nehru contemptuously turned down his offer. Confrontation was *never* a feasible policy; last year's war and the accompanying changes in the power balance in the subcontinent have made it altogether irrelevant. But the course and shape of Indo Pakistan relations will be determined by the attitude which India adopts at the forthcoming summit. The ball is in Mrs Gandhi's court. President Bhutto is more than keen to arrive at a mutually advantageous settlement. India should respond positively and constructively to Pakistan's overtures for peace and friendship. Above all, she must concede Pakistan's right to independent existence and enter into relationship with her on the principle of sovereign equality. Then and only then, can there be abiding peace and friendship between the two neighbours and co-operation on different levels of activity become possible.

Pakistan today faces intimidating difficulties. But all is not lost. A developing order can still be evolved from the confused and discordant situation consequent upon last year's war and defeat. The swarm of difficulties which confront us, should not weaken our faith and hopes in the future but should open before us a vista of challenge and opportunities. There is a real, even if inchoate, identity of interests between the various parts of Pakistan which can provide the basis for a strong, viable and progressive Pakistan. In the ultimate analysis, the destiny of Pakistan will be shaped by the people of Pakistan.

A country is nothing more than the totality of the people who inhabit it. The measure of its achievements and greatness depends on the ideals, aspirations and strivings of its people. Our individual and collective attainments will thus mould the image and future of Pakistan. Individual interests and regional considerations should be moderated to promote general welfare.

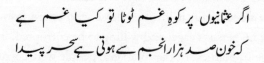

Peace at any Price, No! Freedom at any Price, Yes!

24 June 1972

Air Marshal Nur Khan (Retd)

THE Indo-Pakistan summit, due to be held in the next few days, has naturally led to a lot of discussion and debate in an attempt to evolve a national consensus. The issues are grave, and the consequences even more so. On the nature and character of a settlement will depend whether we survive as a free and self-respecting country or we pass into India's orbit of influence. Let us look at Pakistan's position dispassionately.

Since the loss of East Pakistan the impression is being created that it is the result of a *decisive* military defeat of the Pakistan armed forces as a whole. As a consequence, it is argued that at the present moment we are in no position to offer any physical resistance to India, if she were to decide to wage a war in pursuance of her policy objectives. In other words, the Indians are so superior to us militarily that they can, whenever they choose to do so, force us to our knees and make us accept their demands.

On this premise actually rests the whole case of those who are advocating the policy of 'peace at any cost' with India. A factual survey of the events that led to the last war and its dismal outcome might, however, warrant a different conclusion.

East Pakistan was lost primarily because of the gross mismanagement of our internal political affairs. The problem was basically political and had to be tackled as such. We failed to find a solution acceptable to the people of East Pakistan who formed a majority, although an under-privileged one, in the whole country. A cruel civil war was started in March 1971 which nine months later reached a stage when almost the entire population of East Pakistan had turned against the western wing. The strength of the ground forces stationed in East Pakistan was raised from one division to about four divisions. Contrary to popular notions, the increase in the strength of the armed forces there was not geared to meet the possible threat of Indian intervention but was purely conceived as a measure of internal security. There never was any serious plan for this force to take on India. Nor, for that matter, was there any plan, since the inception of Pakistan, for the armed forces in East Pakistan to deal effectively with any Indian invasion.

This is substantiated by the fact that the operating capability of the Pakistan Air Force was decreased in the eastern wing during this critical period when the strength of the army was being increased. The Pakistan Navy had only a nominal presence in that area. Whatever naval strength there was, it was merely to provide logistical support to the internal security operations of the Pakistan army.

East Pakistan was treated more or less as a colonial domain. The inter-wing gulf, inherent because of the geographical separation and linguistic difference, was accentuated after 1958. During these years, power was personalized. All inter-wing institutions like political parties and a representative legislature, were eroded. Yahya Khan capped it all by ignoring the election verdict of December 1970. After the military action, almost the entire Bengali population had been totally alienated and was actively hostile to us. The Indians in the meantime were forging ahead with their preparations, concentrating their forces along East Pakistan's borders and gearing up their logistical support to conduct interventionist operations at a time of their choosing. Other international forces were also at work. Of course, this was all to be expected.

The inept leadership at Islamabad had no clue of the implications of the developing situation. As the situation got totally out of control, our leadership—lacking the moral fibre to admit the failure of its policies and, as a consequence, compromise with our own people—simply lost its nerve. As an act of sheer desperation, it declared an emergency on 22 November 1971, on the plea that India had invaded East Pakistan. The fact is that at that time skirmishes between the forces of India and Pakistan were limited to the border areas and had not assumed the character of a full scale intervention. There was no all-out offensive on the part of India as occurred after 3 December 1971.

By declaring the emergency we actually warned India that we were about to escalate the conflict. The purpose of all this exercise was not to save East Pakistan, because it could not be saved, but only to get the Indians involved directly. What was sought to be achieved through this desperate gamble was to concede the loss of East Pakistan and later to internationalize the problem with a view to securing a ceasefire. It was also hoped that our marooned divisions in East Pakistan would be able to surrender to the Indian Army and not to the *Mukti Bahini*.

It may not be irrelevant to point out here that the maxim that the defence of East Pakistan lay in West Pakistan was always treated as a cliche. Successive regimes in Pakistan never really worked out any defence strategy. No strategic or tactical planning, was ever seriously undertaken or implemented to back up this much propagated assumption. It was used more as an excuse for not building up armed forces with a truly national composition and character. An effective defence of East Pakistan could only have been ensured if the armed potential was more or less equally divided between the two wings with the East Pakistanis primarily manning the eastern defences.

So was the case with the policy of confrontation which was in fact forced on us by India. On our part it was always a political confrontation carried out in the shape of a war of nerves conducted at home and abroad. Militarily it was never conceived seriously or pursued in terms of any concrete planning with a view to changing the borders of Pakistan including Kashmir through the use of force.

India, always bigger in size and resources, has been pressurizing us since 1947. Ours was a policy of reacting to it.

Physically, no country can be defended unless the people are prepared to defend themselves, and also if the people and the armed forces do not share a common sense of purpose. For developing any offensive capability in pursuance of national policy objectives, this cohesion and consciousness is all the more imperative.

With all these factors, it will be seen that the achievement of the Indian army in East Pakistan cannot be described as a feat of any intrinsic military significance. It was more a political debacle, brought about first through mindlessness and then by design, rather than a military disaster. The surrender occurred because it was the last desperate gamble by a crumbling regime, and because it was so planned. The Pakistan armed forces, isolated in the hostile surroundings of the eastern wing, were not in sufficient numbers or equipped to deal with a full-fledged Indian invasion. Nearly nine months of a bitter civil war conducted all over East Pakistan had affected the fighting ability and spirit of our armed forces. Coupled with the pressure exercised by the Indian border security forces and the hit and run tactics employed by the *Mukti Bahini* operating from safe sanctuaries across the border, it is no wonder that the morale and physical stamina of our forces had been seriously affected. Still they gave a tough fight. They did not run away from their positions or surrender without a fight. Actually, fighting in isolated pockets continued even after the surrender had occurred. Given the overwhelming disadvantages of not having sufficient air cover, it was a good performance by our fighting forces. They surrendered because they were under orders to surrender. It should be remembered that the total number of officers and men involved in the fighting in the eastern wing was less than four division with token air and naval forces.

The bulk of our armed forces was deployed in West Pakistan. Since the men in power in Islamabad only wanted to engineer a ceasefire, they only went through the limited motions of a war along the West Pakistan border. Had they struck deeper into Indian territory and with all their might, the war would have been a prolonged confrontation, and there would have been no ceasefire within a matter of two weeks. Since they did not want to fight in the first place, they did not push hard enough for a decisive fight.

Similarly, if India had been in a position to inflict a decisive defeat upon us, they would have prolonged the fighting, particularly since we had declared the war. From the Indian point of view, the decisive war had to be fought in the western sector where they could have gone in for a determined 'kill' to smash and humble our armed forces and finish Pakistan for good. As it happened, India declared a unilateral ceasefire on the evening of 16 December 1971.

Let us face facts squarely. The plain simple position is that the Indians were not in a position to inflict a decisive defeat on our armed forces in West Pakistan. It is true that they had achieved their limited objectives in the eastern wing and they were also aware of the international pressure working for a ceasefire. Nevertheless, the stark truth is that along the West Pakistan borders, a military stalemate had developed which the Indians knew was not easy to break in their favour. They had been forced to a halt. And let us not forget that during the course of the fighting on the western sector, the Indians at no place were able to penetrate our main defences. If they occupied a sizable chunk of territory in Sind and in Shakargarh, it was because these areas were not heavily defended by us. On the other hand, in the Fazilka and Lahore sectors, our forces did come into contact with the main Indian defences and were able to overrun them at certain points.

It is argued that with the fall of East Pakistan the balance of power has shifted for good in Indian's favour. Because India can afford to concentrate all her armed might along the western sector, it is deduced that they can force a military decision easily at a time of their own choosing. The factor of an undivided front works in our favour too. The fact that we do not have to disperse our forces or resources means that we can deploy our available potential to better advantage in the western sector alone.

A dear lesson that can be drawn from this analysis is that West Pakistan is militarily viable. The bulk of our forces are intact. If there is to be another war, our forces will be defending their own homes, their own near and dear ones. It was not quite the same case in East Pakistan. The motivation to fight was not there.

We now come to the crux of the matter, that is, the impending Delhi summit. What should be the nature of Indo-Pakistan relations? With what mandate should President Bhutto go to New Delhi?

Since we are capable of defending West Pakistan militarily, we should not sign an unfavourable peace settlement. We should not be in a panic to yield to unacceptable terms. We should not allow our 93,000 POWs to be used as a bargaining counter. They can stay in Indian camps pending a just and workable settlement.

This is not to say, however, that we should pursue a policy of chauvinism against India. The desirable alternative is to devise a workable, peaceful relationship with India which does not impinge upon our independence and sovereignty and which does not compromise our basic national objectives, it is not fair to suggest, as is being done in certain quarters, that not to accept a humiliating peace settlement must necessarily mean the adoption of a chauvinistic and jingoistic posture towards India. This is only an attempt to deliberately confuse the issue.

It is true that in trying to defend its basic interests the main effort has to be put in by the nation itself. At the same time, international support and alliances can also be useful adjuncts to national policy objectives. In the prevailing geo-political context, China is the only country which has a genuine identity of interests with us. China supports the right of self-determination for Kashmir and has a border dispute with India including the boundary of Kashmir. At every critical juncture in our history, it has provided us with massive aid, moral, economic and military, and without any conditions. In fact, we should aim at signing a treaty of friendship with China. It is hard to believe that China has changed her posture of friendship towards us because of the loss of East Pakistan or that they cannot share the burden of helping us out on a long term basis. These reports are obviously inspired. China, of course, cannot, and will not, fight our battles for us but it will remain our resolute friend provided we give them cause to trust our leadership and our policies.

It will always be useful to develop friendly and meaningful relations with USA and Soviet Russia. Both are super powers and can influence the course of events in this part of the world. Both have to safeguard their own interests which do not always and necessarily coincide with ours. Russia is too deeply committed to India and it also has a major interest in trying to check the Chinese influence from spreading further south. Russia is interested in a land route for their trade to and from India via Afghanistan and Pakistan. In case of a conflict between India and Pakistan, they are almost sure to always extend their support to India. Recent events bear this out to a large extent. In view of the deep Russian involvement with India, it would be advisable for us to treat our relations with Russia with circumspection. Our adherence to an Asian security pact, backed by Russia and India, will inevitably make us dependent on Russian military equipment. This will ensure that the Moscow-Delhi axis with their converging interests, will make us stay within the orbit defined by them. Inevitably it must alienate us from China.

The policies of the Americans in this area can also be understood in the context of the growing isolationist opinion at home and the gradual erosion of the American supremacy in South East Asia. We should endeavour to improve our friendly relations with the US and use the economic assistance from the West for our development purposes. This in no way contradicts our relations with China. Over eighty per cent of our requirements of military hardware can be secured from China on undoubtedly the most favourable terms. The rest can be purchased from other world sources.

This leads us to the conclusion that we must try to develop self-reliance and simultaneously seek the support of powers who have a basic interest in seeing us preserve our independent identity. Let me make it quite clear that the neglect of the armed forces should be remedied and a clear charter for the defence in depth of the country should be formulated by the government and the people, and it should be clearly understood by the armed forces. Our fighting men, howsoever they are organized structurally, should fit into the national political ethos. The armed forces of a country are indispensable instruments of its national political objectives. In our case this framework of objectives, and the instruments necessary for it, has not been defined yet. It is time it was done. Neither the confidence of the people in the armed forces nor the identification of the armed forces with the national purpose can be achieved unless those who were in command are brought to book. General Yahya Khan and his close military advisers should be given a fair trial either before a court martial or before a properly constituted special tribunal. Only after the responsibility for the debacle has been clearly established can we start on the task of genuine national reconstruction.

It is not a valid argument to assert that the armed forces as a whole have been a privileged, pampered class. It is true that since 1958 the top brass has maintained a position of vantage, but the younger officers and the lower echelons have not exactly been living on cream and butter and it is they who form the hard core of our fighting strength.

Quality wise, we have one of the best manpower material in the world. We are no worse off than many other countries placed in a similar situation. And they preserved and overcame their difficulties. Yugoslavia, in 1948, defied Russia, stood up to all the pressures and ultimately prevailed. Tiny Cuba is another example, which has stood up to the American giant next door. Turkey has been under constant Russian pressure over the last couple of centuries, but has managed to preserve its national identity and integrity. The Algerians fought an unequal but gallant war against France and ended up victorious. Nepal has been able to ward off Indian influence. In the early sixties, it appeared to be a backward outpost totally under Indian influence. The Indian presence was all-pervading in the army, in internal security, in her external affairs. Even her post offices, power houses and other communication installations were all run by Indians. Today, with a will to be free and through a dexterous exercise of diplomatic initiative, Nepal has been able to assert her independence, and identity. Similarly, Iran and Afghanistan have so far been able to keep the Russian influence at bay.

Compared to any of these countries, Pakistan today is more favourably placed vis-a-vis India. Where is the need for despondency? The prerequisite, of course, is that we mend our fences, set our house in order, promote a sense of national purpose, work for internal cohesion and international support will follow. If little Ceylon can try and cut down her dependence on foreign assistance, and in the process butress her independent status, there is no reason why we should be in a hurry to accept terms which are not just and honourable.

As far as we know, the Indians, in proposing what they term as a durable and lasting peace, would like to cut Pakistan down to size to an extent that she may not be in a position to play any significant role in the world of tomorrow. In other words, they would like to confine Pakistan to their own orbit of influence.

Secondly, we are being asked to recognize Bangladesh as part of a dictated peace settlement. India would like to set herself up as the arbiter of the subcontinent. Not that I am proposing that we should not recognize Bangladesh, but it should not come as a consequence of defeat. Rather it should evolve through a process of adjustment, compromise and give and take, to mutual advantage. The return of our POWs, the *unfair* threat to try some of our armed forces personnel, a possible demand for reparation, and the question of assets and liabilities should be discussed and settled before we recognize Bangladesh.

Thirdly, India has repeatedly made it plain that the ceasefire line in Kashmir must be accepted as the permanent international frontier, with adjustment in India's favour. A demand for 'minor' adjustments in our western borders is also on the cards. There is no justification to accept these demands. India, after its conflict with China, agreed to maintain the *status quo ante bellum*. Why must different standards be applied to us if India is interested in promoting friendly relations with Pakistan?

Fourthly, India, through a security agreement or some such other diplomatic understanding, may seek to limit the size and composition of our armed forces. Again, this should be totally unacceptable to us. We desire to live in peace with India and let us make it clear to them that Pakistan has no intention to alter the agreed borders, including Kashmir, by force. The *status quo ante bellum* should be restored, the POWs returned and only then the necessary environment for a peaceful, purposeful coexistence will be created.

Basically, our survival will depend on our ability to forge and define a sense of national purpose and identity and to supplement it with political unity at the national level. There is to my mind a consensus of interest among the four provinces. It only has to be defined, articulated, and spelled out in the form of a genuinely democratic constitution which would institutionalize the locus and exercise of power.

It is equally imperative that we set the economy moving. The reforms already promulgated should materialise to benefit the less privileged and to lessen the existing social tensions. Both in the agricultural and industrial sectors we need to increase production.

We are not an insignificant country, all we need is the will to survive and to fight for a place in the sun. Peace at any cost, no; but freedom at any price, yes. Do we have to debate the issue? Only those nations have a right to survive who are prepared to fight and suffer to preserve their freedom.

The Rape Business

24 June 1972

S. M. Asif Ali

I HAVE read the article entitled, 'A rape is a rape' from your London correspondent in the *Outlook* of 6 May 1972.

I am not trying to be critical of your correspondent for the simple reason that anybody in his place may have written in the same way. Rather I must give him credit for being as impartial as possible and for a very balanced view inspite of the extreme slant and viciousness with which the British press and radio in particular, have reported the East Pakistan affairs.

Anybody knowing the Pakistan armed forces personnel can say without fear of contradiction that they are a more disciplined people than perhaps anywhere in the world. I am certainly not trying to justify any acts by merely saying that these things happen in war. This may happen anywhere but not with Pakistani army boys, particularly so because, as your correspondent has very rightly pointed out, they were not in an alien country. You may also agree that the armed forces in East Pakistan had a giant size job before them. Is it possible for anybody to visualize that people who are constantly under pressure, defending the integrity of the country as also their own personal safety, could have found time to indulge in such matters? As for the figure of 200,000 women raped, I have only this to say: no individual check was made to arrive at this figure. Even if this figure is to be believed, then, on an average, from amongst 90,000 Pakistani soldiers, every one of them raped at least two women. Does it at all sound sensible?

On the other hand, imagine the undisciplined, unscrupulous, a people without objective, doing as they pleased. This description very correctly fits the *mukti bahini*, who are responsible for acts of unprovoked violence in a manner which could make even the Nazi concentration camps pale into insignificance.

I am not ruling out any acts of atrocity committed by the *razakars*, who were by no means part of the Pakistan army. As far as propaganda is concerned, the foreign press can make believe many impossibilities.

Our London correspondent writes:

Mr Asif Ali's comments on my despatch are thought provoking. If thinking persons like him begin to give attention to questions raised in the despatch, then one can feel that the object of its publication has been well and truly achieved.

Those of us like me who have lived in Britain during the last couple of years, are fully conscious of the part played by the British mass media in the events of the subcontinent. There is no doubt that the British press and radio/tv informed us about many facts of which Pakistanis were kept in the dark. In fact, if the press in Pakistan were free, the shape of things may have been somewhat different today.

Having no first hand knowledge about the tragedy, I can only read between the lines and my impressions are somewhat on the following lines:

1. Hair-raising atrocities were committed by the activists among Bengalis against their non-Bengali neighbours before 25 March (1971) which remained more or less unreported in the British (and Pakistani) press. Why?

2. There have been reports of excessive use of force against the civilians. To what extent are these reports true? Some one has to give a verdict on facts.

3. Figures of casualties of Bengalis propagated by the Indians and repeated *ad nauseum* by the British media were highly exaggerated. What was actually the approximate number of civilians killed?

4. The figure of ten million East Pakistani refugees given by the Indo-British media is palpably wrong. An enquiry is called for to get at least an approximate figure.

5. Shaikh Mujibur Rahman is insisting on 'war criminals' trials'. Why should we not insist on an international enquiry into the allegations of rape and killings against both parties by judges of a neutral country?

Furthermore, we all know, and even the foreign press has now admitted, that the *mukti bahini* or the goondas who joined it have shown incredible savagery, have publicly murdered non-Bengalis and are continuing to do so. Rape and slaughter of the non-Bengalis and even of the Bengali community which is suspected of sympathising with Pakistan are not unknown. Why is this going on? Is a political solution possible that could, even at this late stage, stop the total extinction of a minority?

I think that, we as Muslim, (a fact which we are not tired of asserting), as Pakistanis, and as human beings, must try to satisfy our own conscience. We cannot continue to exist as an honourable people just by constantly blaming others for our misfortunes and ignoring the shortcomings within our own society. The cobwebs of doubts must be removed to clear our name, because unless the guilty (who are few) are punished, the innocents (who are many) will remain suspects and the mud will continue to stick.

Are We Guilty?

24 June 1972

Parveen Daskawie

'IT has been proved beyond doubt that the massacre carried out by the Pakistan Army in East Pakistan in 1971 was presented accurately and without exaggeration in the western press'. Every time a foreigner makes this statement, why do we flinch? Why do we then hasten to deny, re-define and explain the facts and figures, using elaborate arguments to show that it was a retaliatory action justified by law as necessary to public order? But after the explanations have been made, why do doubts still linger in our minds? Is it that, beneath the facade, we really do fear that there may be some truth in the allegation? Surely an objective explanation should be forthcoming. Our conscience will not be at rest till then.

There is only one other nation in recent history that has suffered the same allegations and doubts that trouble us today. Germany, defeated in two wars, still carries on its conscience the scars of the Nazi massacres and bears a burden of guilt that the passage of nearly thirty years has not lightened. And yet the accusations levelled against the Germans take no account of the sacrifice of German lives and the sufferings of the many who suffered at the hands of their own oppressors or at the hands of their liberators, in the guise of justice meted out in war trials. In a sense, Germany has paid the price for two thousand years of western prejudice and hatred of the Jews. The intensity of western horror at the treatment of the Jews, the relative lack of intensity at the same treatment of millions of Slavs, Poles and others, and the absence of any horror at the Italian treatment of the Ethiopians, give rise to interesting speculations about the nature of humanitarian protest in the west. One of the elements which no doubt contributes to the intensity of the horror that characterizes western feelings about the Nazis is the guilt that many westerners themselves feel about their own prejudices against the Jews. For even today anti-Jewish prejudice in the west is hardly a thing of the past.

Similarly, one of the more obvious things about the press coverage of the struggle in East Pakistan last year, has been the difference in emphasis placed on the conflict in different countries. There appears to be a close connection between this emphasis and the basic problems in the particular countries. For example in the USA, the conflict was represented as a racial conflict between dark-skinned Bengalis and fair-skinned West Pakistanis. This may reflect the underlying preoccupations of American life today, but no one in East or West Pakistan would consider this to be more than superfluous. Colour prejudice does exist in Pakistan but it is not divided along provincial lines. The fact remains that Americans are bound to project their own problems on to any situation that arises elsewhere.

And what of the glee that the conflict generated in Britain? It certainly contains a triumphant note of 'I told you so', reflecting British attitudes towards Pakistan in general. Britain is trying to relive her imperial past, in fantasy, if not in reality. Britain was always opposed to the creation of Pakistan and its disintegration cannot bring tears to British eyes. In the old days, we blamed the colonial powers for their inhuman excesses and their love of violence. Now that they are no longer in a position to exercise control over the 'natives', western condemnation of Asian 'excesses' is a way of getting their own back at us. Now that they've got all the loot, they are in a position to espouse humanitarian causes!

The western preoccupation with violence is also reflected in the emotions that the conflict generated. There is an excitement in knowing that this is 'for real' while the distance of the theatre of violence and the knowledge that it can be dismissed from one's mind by the flick of the TV switch, does not detract from the exhilaration it arouses. What sweet horror!

And what of our neighbour, India? India's moral concern, political and economic considerations aside, is a reflection of it's own inability to deal with its own troublesome province of West Bengal and its unacknowledged problem of the assimilation of a large Muslim minority into a supposedly secular, but in fact hostile, Hindu state. One's own problems seen in the context of other people's situations always suggest easy solutions.

We have been branded as murderers and called inhuman. But 'have we not eyes? Have we not hands, organs, dimensions, senses, affections, passions? Fed with the same means, warmed by the same winter and summer? If you prick us, do we not bleed? If you tickle us, do we not laugh? If you poison us, do we not die? If you wrong us, shall we not revenge?' Our immediate reaction is to deny that any massacre took place and then to attempt to justify whatever did happen. In the last few months hundreds of articles, speeches, and essays have tried to fix the blame for whatever did happen on various conspiracies, foreign and indigenous. But all such explanations and justifications lack conviction and avoid the main issue: what really did happen in East Pakistan? It is true that foreign propaganda was definitely anti-Pakistani in bias, but can there be smoke without fire? That is the question that haunts us, for when the rhetoric is over, the doubts still remain. Is there any truth in the allegations levelled against us, and if so, does not each one of us share equally in the blame? For where were we when these massacres took place? Was there not even one in 120 million who was willing to sacrifice his safety and security to the cause of truth? Alas, even now we do not feel the need to face the truth.

There is no doubt that there is a gross unfairness in what has been said about us. After all, the hands of our accusers were soaked in blood. Why is the killing of Biharis 'justifiable' and not a massacre? Why is the death and destruction meted out by others in Ireland, Nagaland, by Israel not blameworthy? 'I'll be judge, I'll be jury, said cunning old Fury, I'll try the whole case and condemn you to death.' We have been condemned. And who takes note of the hundreds of lives that we have sacrificed, of our people who have given their lives for Pakistan? But then neither does anyone remember the victims of the Allied bombings of Dresden or the martyrs of Hiroshima and Nagasaki. How can we believe that our own men, our brothers our fathers, our sons are responsible for the horrors which the world assigns to us?

It is not only we who react protectively towards our own people. After the fall of Dacca, several Pakistani newspapers published photographs of Abdul Qadir Siddiqi and his hoodlums slaughtering Pakistanis in front of 'humanitarian' crowds of foreign correspondents and 'peace-loving' Bengalis. A Bengali friend who saw the pictures refused to accept their authenticity, even though he recognized some of the people: 'Bengalis could never do such a thing', he said,—but they did. So neither can we believe that our own people, could do the things of which they stand accused. Did they? We have a right to know the truth. For unless we know the truth, how can we ever trust ourselves, our soldiers, our existence as a nation? The honour and prestige of our soldiers will always be in doubt unless we know the truth. And what of the future generations? Will they condemn us for our moral cowardice and our hypocrisy? Will they suffer the doubt and the anguish that by right we ought to feel? Will our national psyche forever be tormented by the bitterness of defeat and the realization of our failures and our lack of courage?

Each one of us shares the responsibility for what our nation does: some by what they do, the rest of us by our acquiescence or indifference. We must accept this. Pakistan can only be what we are. Let's not opt out.

A Briton Protests

1 July 1972

IT is perhaps as well that I, a Britisher working in Pakistan, had developed the *Outlook* habit before you came out with your anti-British editorial on 10 June. This has now been followed by the article 'Are we guilty?' in your 24 June issue, in which the author talks of 'the glee that the conflict (in Bengal) generated in Britain', and says that 'Britain was always opposed to the creation of Pakistan and its disintegration cannot bring tears to British eyes'.

The last phrase is true; the preceding ones are utter rubbish. The conflict in Bengal was followed in Britain with horror and concern; there was certainly no feeling of glee over it. And although I am now in my forties, and was therefore taking an interest in politics at the time of partition, I was quite unaware that 'Britain was always opposed to the creation of Pakistan'—the vast majority of Britons have no views either way on the original desirability of creating Pakistan.

As to the events which led up to the rise of Bangladesh, they seem to me to be well enough summarized by your contributor Hafeez R. Khan in his book review, where he says that 'a majority of Pakistanis sought the help of India's armed might to liberate themselves from their countrymen'. That's certainly how the world sees it; is not it a true picture?

The 'Are we guilty?' article argues that 'we have a right to know the truth'; and this is echoed by your London correspondent, who says that 'the cobwebs of doubts must be removed to clear our name', and asks: 'Why should we not insist on an international enquiry into the allegations of rape and killings against both parties by judges of a neutral country?'

A SPLENDID idea (if a willing neutral can be found). Perhaps Bhutto will discuss this with Mrs Gandhi at Simla. But it is not very likely to happen Meanwhile Pakistanis concerned about the national conscience (as both your contributors are) will have to build up as full a picture as they can from all available sources.

They could well start by reading your article 'Raised Eyebrows in Delhi'. For there they will learn that Bhutto, in his interview with an Italian female reporter who asked him about the massacre in Dacca on the night of 25 March, did not deny that it happened, and described it as 'barbarous and stupid'. He blamed the 'disgusting drunkard' Yahya Khan for it. This view of Bhutto's corroborates what we learnt from the British media.

What about the British media? S. M. Asif Ali talks about the 'extreme slant and viciousness with which the British press and radio have reported the East Pakistan affairs'. He seems to me to be regurgitating Yahya's propaganda of last year. Perhaps he, living in Karachi, cannot help it; but there is less excuse for your London correspondent, who writes that the atrocities committed by Bengalis against non-Bengalis 'remained more or less unreported in the British (and Pakistani) press'.

What utter nonsense this is! The most horrifying item of TV news coverage ever shown in Britain consisted of film shots taken about a year ago which showed non-Bengalis tied together being led away by Bengalis; followed by bodies lying on the ground which then started to move. At this point the cameraman wanted to get help for them, but was pursuaded by his interpreter to flee for his life as the Bengali mob which had in fact murdered them was returning to the spot. Whatever the British public was or was not told, they were certainly not in any doubt that non-Bengalis had been killed by the Bengali mobs.

As to numbers, I have heard a figure of 100,000 non-Bengalis killed prior to 25 March from a well-informed West Pakistani. The same man thought the number of Bengalis killed from 25 March onwards was probably around a million. But do the numbers really matter? What surely matters is the type of action launched on 25 March, and the spirit in which it was conducted. On that subject I regarded as the most authoritative and detailed account the two articles which appeared in the SUNDAY TIMES which were contributed by a Pakistani journalist after visiting Bengal with a group of other Pakistani journalists. Have your contributors who are so concerned to know the truth read those articles? Perhaps you should reprint them for their enlightenment.

Three final points:

1. S. M. Asif Ali cannot believe that an army cracking down on a civilian population would have time to spare for rape. How long does he think rape takes?
2. How does your London correspondent know that the estimate of 10 million refugees is 'palpably wrong'? Did he count them himself?
3. As a Britisher I feel ashamed of the raid on Dresden—and indeed of all the indiscriminate bombing of German cities. But at least we had one man who protested publicly at the time. He was Dr Bell, the Bishop of Chichester. What did the maulanas of West Pakistan have to say?

—'A Britisher'

Beginning of the End

8 July 1972

THE process of licking one's wounds is painful enough. To be told that the wounds have been converted into marks of glory by the healing touch of a master surgeon is a crowning insult. President Bhutto should realize that there are limits to the achievements which can be scored through the gift of the gab. It certainly helped him win a landslide victory in the 1970 elections. More pertinently, the verbal and visual revolution he has wrought since he came into power, still breathes, though heavily, under a thin veil of credibility. The story, however, is going to be different with the Simla accord. Truth will catch up with him, and his verbiage, faster than he thinks.

What was agreed upon at Simla smells bad enough. It is worse to be told that it was a triumph of Pakistan's diplomacy or that national interests were not compromised in the process. The Indians, having won their main point and waiting patiently for the rest of the bag to come their way, are playing it cool.

Admittedly, President Bhutto was playing on a weak wicket. To that extent he had the nation's sympathy. He could not have achieved what was lost on the battlefield. Normalization of relations with India, after a debilitating 25-year-long confrontation, has its own inexorable logic. Having said all this, the unpleasant truth must also be faced that Mr Bhutto's own future was also part of the stakes at Simla. He has opted for the easy way out. As expected, he signed more or less on the dotted line. One tragic consequence of the follies of the successive regimes in Pakistan and of the defeat in 1971 is that the rump state which Pakistan today is, stands dangerously vulnerable to external pressures. Simla is only the opening reminder of an escalating story of subservience.

Elsewhere in this issue we have analyzed the consequences which will flow from the Simla accord. The root actually goes back to the military debacle of 1971. At Simla, however, the diplomatic sponge was thrown. Without being too harsh on President Bhutto, and it is possible to sympathize with his unenviable position, it must be said that it will be hard to shake off the consequences of the latest unequal peace settlement.

What are the essential ingredients of the agreement? From Pakistan's point of view, the gainful point centres around the promised withdrawal of troops from the western sector. With India occupying nearly 5,000 sq. miles of our territory, troop withdrawals were necessarily high on

93

our priority list. It has now been made contingent on two conditions. Firstly, due ratification of the agreement and, more important, on talks *in the meantime* on diverse issues including a *final settlement* of the Kashmir problem. In simpler words, troop withdrawals may be contingent on a *final settlement* of the Kashmir problem which, in order to be acceptable to India, must also include territorial adjustments in the ceasefire line, particularly in the Kargi area. This is precisely why the Kashmir sector has been specifically excluded from the provisions regarding troop withdrawals. That the ceasefire line (with adjustments) will be the new international frontier seems to have already been agreed to by the two parties.

Moreover, Pakistan has agreed to what the Indians claim to be 'more than a no-war declaration'. It can be validly argued, if we cannot wage a war, why not agree to a no-war declaration? But the ramifications are deeper. All issues are now to be settled bilaterally. Even a recourse to any international agency is barred except with India's consent. In respect of Kashmir, it means a waiver on the part of Pakistan of all UN resolutions. With a *final settlement,* due to crystallize before the troop withdrawals begin, the issue will become an *internal* affair of India. This cuts the ground even from under the feet of Sheikh Abdullah and such other groups who may now or ever again try to struggle for Kashmir's right of self-determination. This is perhaps the unkindest cut of all and India's major gain. It is manifestly untrue to suggest that principles have not been sacrificed in this search for an unequal peace.

Peace is not secured by agreements. Munich is one example. There are countless others. It may be secured by a willingness to fight for and defend what *is* right and just. Power has its own compulsions. In this part of the world it will be a gross stupidity to ignore the pulls of history. With the balance of power having decisively shifted against us and with India about to amass an atomic arsenal of its own, it will be the height of folly to bury our heads in the sands of Simla and expect India to play the good Samaritan. The shadows of Indian hegemony, despite protestations of a *durable peace*, will creep upon what is left of Pakistan almost as surely as the sun rises in the east. In the annals of history there is nothing like a durable peace in the context of a decisively unequal balance of power. This is not to suggest that we re-embark on a confrontationist and chauvinistic path. In the past there has been no dearth of exponents of this line of thought. But, in the name of greying heavens, let us at least be alive to the dangers that a pitiless future holds for us. The only straw we can clutch at is internal cohesion, a determined national effort and a search for support from quarters which have a genuine identity of interest with us. Unfortunately, as far as the latter category is concerned, Simla may be the harbinger of a trot in the opposite direction.

Not unexpectedly, the question of the 93,000 POWs has been left dangling in the air. They are prisoners of the 'India-Bangladesh joint command'. It is linked with the question of the recognition of Bangladesh which in turn is linked with the threat of 'genocide trials', reparations, assets and liabilities and what not. It is to be hoped that the performance at Simla is not repeated in negotiations with

Bangladesh, now right on the cards. The reality of Bangladesh has to be recognized but preferably not without an equitable understanding which might, if possible, bury the bitterness of the past.

It must be said in fairness that the price which Pakistan is now in the process of paying was perhaps inevitable. The cost could have been reduced by a leadership which had its priorities right and which, since the beginning, should have tried to evolve a national consensus. This was not done. The Indians are more intelligent students of history. The choice of Simla as the venue of the talks had its own sting. Unless we wake up, the fate that awaits Pakistan is that of a client state (or states?). Simla may be the beginning of the end. Who knows?

The 'Catharsis'—Last Installment

8 July 1972

Hamida Khuhro

I READ with great interest the 'rejoinder' to my article. I was happy to see that to a large extent the writer agreed with my analysis. The rest seemed a painstaking compilation of the more familiar shibboleths of Pakistan's Establishment. I feel that some of these points need to be discussed with less ambiguity.

In my article I suggested that from the beginning the middle class intelligentsia of Pakistan had not done its duty by the people of Pakistan by discussing frankly and fearlessly the political trends and developments in the country and that furthermore, they had connived at the infringement of people's liberties and at the strangulation of democracy. I then gave a brief analysis of the trends in Pakistan's history which in my view have led to the present tragic situation. Such analyses and constant vigilance on the part of the educated and articulate members of our society is essential to the safety of our democratic rights. Only thus can we prevent the repetition of the kind of deception that was practised on the nation last year, and in the shadow of which such horrors were perpetuated on the people of Pakistan. The writer denies the need for such analyses: 'It is altogether futile to conduct a post mortem of last year's happenings now.' Surely it is this kind of self-denial that has made us into a nation of sheep—sheep which are slaughtered from time to time.

It is a curious method of minimizing the bloodshed which resulted from last year's civil war. Surely there is a qualitative difference between the bloodshed as a result of a war of liberation against a foreign ruler and their reprisals as in 1857, bloodshed in the mad frenzy of communal killings in 1947, and the cold blooded butchery of a civilian population in a country in which the whole population had supposedly come together because they wished to live together as Muslims in a Darul Islam and not a Darul Harb. Still, let that pass. The writer does not wish us to consider Islam at all seriously as the basis for Pakistan—Well, what then was the basis for Pakistan and what is it today? If there was no 'well-defined community of interests' and we differed on economic, political, cultural, and linguistic matters and the two wings could not have existed as a political unity, if in fact religion was not a binding factor, then it follows that it is not a binding factor in the rest of Pakistan. A common

96

script (remember, not language), geographical contiguity and the fact that 'the dress and dietary habits are more similar than dissimilar' is hardly enough to keep us together. All these characteristics we share with the whole of North India. With one overwhelmingly powerful province and three or four smaller and weaker ones, other factors come into play which we are all perfectly familiar with. To carry the parallel of modern European history that the writer cites further, one could point out that Germany in the late 19th and the first half of the twentieth centuries was feared by her smaller neighbours. Czechoslovakia and Poland, among others, sought security in alliances with more powerful neighbours and history justified their fears. The provinces of Pakistan had developed a power balance in which the smaller provinces of west Pakistan could look to East Bengal to provide them with a counter-balance against the dominance of the Punjab. With this counter-balance gone, there is a great feeling of insecurity in the smaller provinces which is manifesting itself particularly in Sind—the most vulnerable and the most self-conscious province among them.

Of course I fervently echo the admirable and pious hopes: What we need today is an institutionalized political system so that power cannot in future be personalized by any ruling clique. There should be maximum political autonomy with stern safeguards against excessive centralization of power. Each region should be assured effective participation in the political processes and must have its due share in the economic development. The less developed areas should be given priority in the allocation of funds over developed regions. The bigger and more prosperous provinces should help the less developed regions in overcoming the economic difficulties and obstacles. A balance must be evolved between the several and collective interests of the various provinces so that future conflicts and tensions may be eliminated or minimized. Once maximum political autonomy is granted, the question of domination by any one province will not arise. *AMEN*. But is there any sign of such a consummation so devoutly to be wished? Even so fundamental and so simple a desire as to have Sindhi as the chief language of Sind is being combated fiercely. Can we not detect in this echoes of the arrogant attitude towards Bengali? And what of Sind's endemic struggle to get her fair share of Indus waters. Who will arbitrate when the province on the upper reaches of the river also happens to be the dominant province? For Sind the river is a matter of life and death, and our experience under one unit does not fill us with rosy expectations and unbounded optimism. It is easy to brush aside the terrible events of the past year with amazing nonchalance: 'If anything the war and the separation of Bengal have strengthened it [Pakistan] and made it a vibrant living force.' What a giveaway! The utterly disillusioned smaller regions cannot agree with this and are currently showing their apprehensions. A great deal more will have to be done to remove the accumulated injustices of the past twenty-five years before the 'have nots' of Pakistan can display the 'will' to live together which is always based on trust. If the writer wants to make economic viability the criterion of her state, surely the most viable of all—much more viable than West Pakistan—is the subcontinent of India as a whole. Make no mistake, however futile a discussion on the theoretical basis of Pakistan may be, the basis for Pakistan, theoretical or otherwise, has been knocked sideways by the emergence of Bangladesh. And dare we suspect some deep and sinister motive behind these bland assurances and warnings not to indulge in 'futile discussions'? The actual Pakistan as brought into being by the Independence Act of 1947 has now changed and now it is up to the different provinces to federate again if they *wish* to do so, as has been pointed out by that indomitable politician, Malik Ghulam Jilani. We, the people of Sind, because we feel deeply the tragedy which has befallen the Muslims of the subcontinent, would like to do everything to strengthen and rebuild the morale and unity of the Muslim peoples, but we will not be exploited in the name of Islam or Pakistan or whatever term it may suit the powers that be to use. The rebuilding of Muslim unity (because Pakistan is meaningless without it) will depend on intellectuals recognizing the facts as they exist and not gloss over the ugly realities in our past and our present.

Perhaps it is not the fault of Pakistan's intellectuals. As a distinguished political commentator pointed out recently:

'In Germany the only people that were really resistant to the Nazis were the simple proletariat who had no higher education. The people who were overwhelmingly in favour of the Nazis were the professors …' (R, Crossman, *Inside View,* p. 117.)

An Exposé of the American Role in the Dismemberment of Pakistan

22 July 1972

Our correspondent writes:

ABOUT 80 years ago Jose Marti wrote: 'When a strong nation gives food to another, it makes use of the latter.'

These prophetic words could to some extent be applied to describe the unequal US-Pakistan relations in which American foundations, operating in Pakistan under various labels, have over the years played a key role.

A glimpse into the role which these foundations, notably the Ford Foundation, played in the dismemberment of Pakistan is now available. A secret report entitled 'Conflict In East Pakistan: Background and Prospects', was recently published in a book called 'The Challenge of Bangladesh'. The report written in April 1971 throws interesting light on the international strings behind the East Pakistan crisis and the motives of the super powers in supporting the dismemberment of Pakistan.

The report was written by three American academicians, Edward S. Mason, Robert Dorfman, and Stephan A. Marglin. At least two of them are known to have spent a couple of years in Pakistan on assignments given by the Ford Foundation.

This report written 'to suggest the likely implications for international relations of the break-up of Pakistan' was not the only one of its kind compiled in America. It is known for example that research on this project was also carried out in the University of Philadelphia commissioned jointly by private American foundations and the US government. Much earlier the Rana Corporation had also authorized a study on similar lines.

The sum total of these research studies seem to have prompted the US State Department to encourage and support the emergence of Bangladesh as an independent nation state, (in saying this it is not intended to cover up our own criminal follies for which we have paid and will continue to pay a high price). The highlights, viewed in the context of the Simla accord, can be summed up as follows:

1. 'The longer the independence of Bangladesh is delayed, the more likely it is that the leadership of the movement will pass from the moderate Shaikh Mujibur Rahman to the more leftist NAP.'

99

2. 'The new Bangladesh will set up friendly relations with India.'
3. 'A major role of US foreign policy in this area has been to seek a reduction of tensions in South East Asia. West Pakistan is bound to tone down its policy of confrontation with India.'
4. 'The Kashmir issue will also subside in importance not because of any reduction in tension but because West Pakistan, without the economic support of the East will be unable to sustain the level of pressure it has been mounting until now.'
5. 'An independent Bangladesh will, if at all, have only marginal economic contacts with China. It is unlikely that it will become a satellite of China.'
6. 'In the past the USSR has not been sensitive to the aspirations of East Pakistan and it is unlikely to make the new Bangladesh an area for a super power competition for influence.'

It will be seen that as a result of the emergence of Bangladesh and the recently concluded Simla agreement, the first four objectives mentioned in the Mason report, have virtually already been fulfilled. The report was also on the ball in suggesting that Bangladesh was unlikely to become a satellite of China. At least on present showing this looks like being a fair and proper assessment of the trend of events in Bangladesh. India will ensure that Bangladesh is kept clear of Chinese influence to the extent that it can be managed. Not only that, the upsurge of national confidence and patriotic fervour in India which has developed as a result of its convincing victory over Pakistan, might even ensure that the Naxalite movement in West Bengal is curbed by India with a heavy hand. The arrest of Charu Mazumdar and two of his principal lieutenants speak of the vigorous drive which India has launched over the last six months to control and curb the movement. That it has not been entirely unsuccessful seems to be very obvious. It will surely have its repercussions in Bangladesh as well.

Where the Mason report has gone right wide off the mark, is its prediction: that the Russian influence will not be felt significantly in Bangladesh. Following the Indo-Soviet treaty and the timely support given by Soviet Russia to the nationalist movement in Bangladesh, the Soviet Russians have been able to reap a pretty full harvest.

A word about the authors. Edward S. Mason, now a professor emeritus at Harvard University was in Pakistan in 1954–55 and directed an eight man team to draw up the first development plan for Pakistan. Robert Dorfman, another professor, at Harvard, was appointed by the late President Kennedy at the request of ex-President Ayub Khan as an adviser on the problems of water logging and salinity in this country.

The text of the report is as follows:

US Economic and Military Aid to Pakistan

Since 1951 Pakistan has been a major recipient of US economic aid amounting to approximately $3 billion by 1969. Except for food aid donated under Public Law 480, the bulk of this assistance has been used to support industrialization in West Pakistan, with only a handful of projects undertaken in East Pakistan.

The quantum of US military aid to Pakistan is a classified figure but two estimates put it between $1.5 billion to $2 billion for the period between 1954 and 1965. The assistance has included F-104 Starfighters, Patton tanks, armoured personnel carriers, automatic, and recoilless infantry weapons. This impressive array of modem weaponry was given expressly for defensive purposes. With Pakistan an early member of SEATO and CENTO, this military aid was intended to bolster the armed containment of the communist bloc in the Dulles era of US foreign policy, but apart from the brief border war with India of 1965 the only active use of these sophisticated weapons has occurred against the unarmed and defenseless civilian population of East Pakistan.

The growth and maintenance of the superstructure of the armed forces which was built up with massive US military aid continued even after 1965 when the United States decided to put an embargo on the delivery of arms to both Pakistan and India. This was made possible by diverting resources from the much needed development projects. East Pakistan, poorer and less powerful politically than the West, suffered more by this irrational policy.

Surprisingly, the United States has just recently (October 1970) made an exception to its embargo on military sales to Pakistan. According to the information available, the United States has offered to supply Pakistan the following items:

(a) Armoured personnel carriers (approximately 300)
(b) Maritime reconnaissance aircraft (4)
(c) F-104 jet fighters (6)
(d) B-57 bombers (7)

Fortunately, no sales or deliveries have yet been made. It is not too late to rescind the offer, a move that would be of practical as well as symbolic value. American arms must not be supplied to a government which makes war on helpless civilians.

Economic and Political Domination of East by West

The basic facts seem to support the East Pakistan charge of economic domination by the West. The economic disparities between East and West Pakistan have been so serious for so long that the Pakistan Government's highest planning authority has been forced to take official note of them.

A recent report by a panel of experts to the Planning Commission of the Government of Pakistan provides authoritative documentation of the widening of economic disparities in the two regions. The most striking fact in this report is the widening gap between the income of the average West Pakistani and his eastern counterpart. In 1959–60, the per capita income in West Pakistan was 32% higher than in the East. Over the next ten years the annual rate of growth of income of West Pakistan was 6.2% while it was only 4.2% in East Pakistan. As a result, by 1969–70 the per capita income of the West was 61% higher than in the East. Thus in ten years the income gap doubled in percentage terms; it increased even more in absolute terms.

East Pakistanis blame three instruments of central government policy for their plight:

1. Pakistan's scant investible resources, plus foreign aid, are directed unduly to the development of West Pakistan—to the comparative neglect of East Pakistan.
2. In particular, East Pakistan's foreign trade earnings are diverted to finance imports for West Pakistan.
3. Economic policy favours West Pakistan at the expense of the East. Specifically, tariffs, import controls, and industrial licensing compel East Pakistan to purchase commodities from West Pakistan which, but for the controls, they could obtain more cheaply in the world market.

We believe the East Pakistani claims to be largely justified. First, it is indisputable that the bulk of public investment has been in West Pakistan though the majority of the population lies in the East. With 60% of the population, East Pakistan's share of central government development expenditure has been as low as 20% during 1950/51–1954/55, attaining a peak of 36% during the Third Five Year Plan period 1965/66 to 1969–70. East Pakistan has received an even smaller share of private investment, less than 25%.

It may be true, as defenders of Pakistan government policy claim, that the great bulk of worthwhile investment opportunities have been in the West, though the relative attractiveness of the West may be more the effect of overall government policy than a cause. In any event the fact remains that investments in the West have done little or nothing for the people in the East.

As for the second point, it is clear that foreign exchange has been allocated to the detriment of East Pakistan. Over the last two decades East Pakistan's share of total Pakistan export earnings has varied between 50% and 70% while its share of imports has been in the range of 25% to 30%. Until 1962–63, East Pakistan has shown significant surpluses on foreign account, which has changed in recent years to small deficits. By contrast the West's foreign trade has shown a substantial and chronic deficit that has absorbed virtually all foreign exchange made available through foreign aid.

With respect to the third point, general economic policy has clearly favoured West Pakistan. The West's preponderant share of imports and investments might have provided inexpensive necessities for all of Pakistan's people. In fact it has allowed the development of inefficient industries, which ironically have prospered largely because of tariffs and quotas that have made East Pakistan a captive market. 40% of all exports of West Pakistan are sold to East Pakistan; in 1968/69 the West sold 50% more to the East than it bought from the East.

An analysis of foreign trade data reveals that a net transfer of resources has taken place from East to West Pakistan. According to the official report refered to above, East Pakistan has transferred approximately $2.6 billion to West Pakistan over the period 1948–49 to 1668–69.

In short, Pakistan's economic policies are harmful to East Pakistan. 'Exploitation' may be a strong word but it seems clear, all in all, that East Pakistan's economic interests have been subordinated to those of the West, and that the East Pakistanis have had good cause to resent that fact.

The economic domination of East Pakistan has been facilitated by West Pakistani dominance of the central government. The military regime in Pakistan has existed, with modifications, since 1958, and decision-making authority rests with a well-entrenched civil service and their military bosses. All senior military members of the administration have been West Pakistani, and of the senior officers in the central civil services, 87% were West Pakistani in 1960, and the proportion has not changed much since. The Deputy Chairman of the Planning Commission and the Central Finance Minister, key individuals in resource allocation, have always been West Pakistanis.

The location of the Central Government in West Pakistan has encouraged the concentration of industry and the entrepreneurial class in West Pakistan. Such a concentration is to be expected in an economic system where direct allocation and control of resources by the government makes direct access to government authorities a prime business asset.

Background to the Break-up of Pakistan

The history of economic and political domination of East Pakistan by the West led naturally to increasing demands for provincial autonomy, spearheaded by Shaikh Mujibur Rahman's Awami League. Its 6-point platform for autonomy sought to transfer control over foreign trade, foreign aid allocation, and taxation powers to the provinces so that no province could be dominated through disproportionate control of the central Government's power over resource allocation.

At the polls last December this Awami League platform swept 167 of the 169 seats in the national Constitutional Assembly that were allotted to East Pakistan. The Awami League's 167 seats constituted an absolute majority in a chamber of 313. The political and military powers of West Pakistan tried to pressurize Shaikh Mujib into compromising on his 6-point autonomy mandate. In particular, Zulfikar Ali Bhutto, leader of the West Pakistan People's Party which had won 80 odd seats in the elections, demanded that control of trade and aid should remain with the central government. When Shaikh Mujib refused to compromise on these instruments of past economic domination, Bhutto announced a boycott of the Constitutional Assembly scheduled to meet on 3 March. General Yahya Khan used this pretext to postpone the Assembly indefinitely. This arbitrary postponement provoked demonstrations in Dacca and other cities on 1 March, which the military decided to control by force. The military authorities conceded 172 deaths in the disturbances (the Dacca correspondent of the *London Observer* put the figure nearer 2000). Despite the bloody provocation, the Awami League refrained from declaring independence. Instead they launched a campaign of civil disobedience to demand a return of troops to barracks and an enquiry into the firings. The campaign of non-cooperation effectively transferred civilian authority to Shaikh Mujib but even in the massive rally of 7 March Shaikh Mujib still spoke of a united Pakistan with autonomy of each province. His preparedness for negotiation and commitment to the unity of Pakistan was demonstrated by his continuation of talks for the next two weeks despite the well-advertised influx of West Pakistani troops. Indeed in retrospect it would appear that the West Pakistani officials were never negotiating in good faith; negotiations were a way to forestall an open break until sufficient numbers of West Pakistani troops could be brought on the scene to unleash a terror whose full dimensions are only now becoming known. The Awami League's commitment to a peaceful political settlement was convincingly demonstrated by the complete lack of preparation of the civilian population to the onslaught of military arms which was unleashed on them on the night of Thursday, 25 March.

International Implications of an Independent 'Bangladesh'

From news reports now available it would appear that the use of massive military firepower has broken the Awami League and its supporters in most urban centers. But control of urban centers at gunpoint in a country where 90% of the population lives in rural areas hardly constitutes a framework for any effective government, let alone a popular one. The immediate prospect is for ruthless military rule in urban centers, with tenuous control over a countryside which is likely to become increasingly the base for armed guerilla resistance.

The base for such a movement clearly exists. The overwhelming support for the Awami League's demand for autonomy was clearly shown in the election results of December when 167 out of 169 seats allotted to East Pakistan were won by the League. As reports of military massacres are carried by urban refugees to the rural areas, the democratically expressed sentiment for autonomy is likely to be converted to a militant desire for independence. It is possible that a West Pakistani army of occupation can suppress the Bengali nation for two months, six months, or a year, but the American experience in Vietnam illustrates only too painfully the impossibility of holding an entire population captive by force of alien arms alone.

The emergence of an independent Bangladesh appears to be inevitable in the long run. What remains in question is how much blood will flow before it occurs. Politically it is clear that the longer it takes to achieve independence, the more likely it is that *control of the independence movement* will slip away from the *moderate* leadership of the Awami League to the *more leftist* National Awami party (which did not contest the December elections).

Assuming that the independence movement succeeds while under Awami League control, certain predictions may be made about its relations with neighbours and superpowers. As expressed in public statements of Shaikh Mujib, an independent Bangladesh *will* establish *friendly relations* with India and set up economic trade to their mutual advantage. Up to now such trade—and all cultural ties—have been frustrated by the West Pakistanis who dominate the central government. They believe that, short of war, their only lever to force a settlement of their Kashmir claim is the economic interest of

India in trade with East Pakistan. By contrast, East Pakistan has never been aroused by Kashmir, and in the 1965 war no military activity took place within its borders. Strong *linguistic and cultural* ties with the state of West Bengal in India *are likely to help cement durable good relations* between the two countries and reduce tension in the area. Unable to share the burden of military expenditures with the East, West Pakistan *is bound to tone down its policy of confrontation with India,* a confrontation which for the past 24 years had diverted scarce resources of both these poor, populous countries from much needed economic development to defence.

As an independent nation Bangladesh might conceivably establish *marginal* economic contacts with communist China. But these are unlikely to be any greater than the current scale of trade and aid between China and Pakistan, and will certainly be less than the likely range and depth of Bengal's economic ties to neighbouring India. As long as India is the main trading partner (and both pronouncements of Awami League leaders and the economic geography of the region support this possibility), *it is unlikely that Bangladesh will become a satellite of communist China.*

The USSR has in the past three years become an active patron of the military clique that controls Pakistan. Soviet aid has included considerable economic aid (including agreements for a steel mill in West Pakistan) and some military aid. The Soviet initiative has been largely a response to growing communist Chinese ties with Pakistan. This competition between rival giants has rebounded to the benefit of West Pakistan where the central government and military establishment are based. The USSR has not been sensitive to the aspirations of East Pakistanis in the past, and *is unlikely* to make a new Bangladesh an arena for superpower competition for influence.

A major goal of US foreign policy in this area has been the reduction of the debilitating confrontation between India and Pakistan. This goal will surely be advanced by the existence of an *independent Bangladesh friendly to India.* Most observers believe that the Awami League leadership will follow a neutral foreign policy, particularly if the US and multilateral aid agencies like the World Bank are *major aid donors.*

Bengali independence will be inimical to American interest only if by following short-sighted policies we drive East Pakistan into the arms of another power—the USSR or China. To the extent that Bengali independence is delayed by means of American arms, the image of the United States will suffer, and rightly so. The offer of arms to Pakistan by the United States Government in October 1970, whatever its ostensible purpose, will, if implemented, oil a Pakistani military machine that is making war on its citizens. The United States Government must rescind this offer forthwith. No further military aid, or economic aid—which directly or indirectly provides foreign exchange that makes it possible to buy weapons abroad—should be given to West Pakistan until it withdraws its occupation force from East Bengal and *recognizes the independence* of the Bengali nation.

End of Report

It is obvious that most of these advisers and experts which are deputed to this country by various American foundations are not exactly doing the job they are supposed to do. A lot of extra-curricular activity seems to have been going on behind the mask of aided projects which may in fact be needed by the country. It is time to assess and scrutinize the role played by various American foundations which have been operating in the country. It may not be wholly unreasonable to suggest that the sphere of their activities should be restricted to specialized projects which may be beyond the capacity of this country to handle on its own.

In the early years of Pakistan, the Ford Foundation financed an eight man advisory group which virtually compiled the country's First Five Year Plan. Ex-prime minister Suharwardy had an American political adviser in the person of C. B. Marshall. In the days of Ayub Khan, the US military assistance group had access to every single section of the GHQ and even a US lieutenant-colonel could reach the C-in-C or even the President. The U-2 spy flights were apparently carried on from Peshawar without the consent or knowledge of the Government of Pakistan.

The eight man panel of economic advisers finally left the country around the middle of 1970. An unflattering comment on the group's role was carried by *Forum* of Dacca, in its issue of 22 November 1969. The Forum's Pindi correspondent reported:

'It seems that the Harvard Advisory Group is finally pulling out of Pakistan. The Group came to Pakistan 13 years ago ostensibly to train us in the techniques of planning but was soon involved in writing the First Five Years Plan under the leadership of David Bell, subsequently a member of the Kennedy cabinet. The Group was financed by the Ford Foundation and administered by Harvard University who, over the years, transmitted a stream of economists, to the Planning Commission and the Provincial Planning Departments. During the Ayub decade they became closely involved with the regime's conversion to the philosophy of economic liberalism and the promotion of local capitalism or what one of their team leaders, Gustav Papanek, termed the robber barons, in a highly laudatory book on development under Ayub. In return for ready acceptance of their philosophical guidance they became eloquent ambassadors of the Ayub regime both to aid givers and in the US academic world and even organized a high-powered conference at Harvard where a number of distinguished economists were conned into giving their blessings to Ayub and his Third plan.

The downfall of the Ayub regime promised to be a death blow not just to their role in Pakistan but to their professional reputation since they had been selling the durability of Ayub and his achievements with considerable skill and diligence to the world. In Pakistan they sought to salvage their reputation by climbing on the East Pakistan bandwagon by becoming eloquent spokesmen for higher allocations to this region. There was some irony in this, given their intimate involvement with those very policies which promoted the growth of disparity, indeed their group leader Richard Gilbert who was rushed back to his old post in Islamabad from Indonesia following the fall of Ayub, intervened personally to promote the candidature of Mahbubul Haq, the present chief economist, for this post at the expense of the East Pakistani candidate Dr R. H. Khandkar who is now in exile at the World Bank.

Their *volte face* has naturally generated resentment with the top brass in the Planning Commission but the *coup de grace* to their presence seems to have come from, of all quarters, the Jamaat-e-Islam. Some zealous functionaries of the party unearthed the fact that eight out of the ten members of the group with the Planning Commission were of Jewish origin. The Jamaat elements took this up and publicized the group as Israeli agents and intimidated them personally. The traumatic character of this experience, coming on top of the general deterioration in their standing both in Pakistan and in quarters where they were once honoured, has finally persuaded them to pack their bags and return home by next June.'

Even today the ramifications of the American influence in Pakistan are wide and deep and not an insignificant part in this undesirable penetration of foreign influence is carried out by private American foundations. The lion's share in this grey-black business seems to fall to the share of the Ford Foundation which, having assets of 2.4 billion dollars, is believed to be the largest organization of its kind in the world today.

On the face of it, the Ford Foundation is a private non-profit making institution serving public welfare. One of its official aims is to identify and contribute to the solution of problems of national and international importance. The Foundation works mainly by giving funds for experimental, demonstration, and development efforts that are likely to produce significant advances within its fields of interests. The Foundation was established in 1936. In 1950 the Foundation became a national organization and virtually all of its grants have been made since then. Till the end of 1969, grants totalling 3.95 billion dollars had been made to a total of 6,034 institutions and organizations in all 50 states of America and 83 foreign countries. In Pakistan the area of its interest seems to be economic planning, public administration, education, agriculture improvement, and population control plus, of course, the unmentioned areas of interest. There is no doubt that the Foundation seems to have played a worthwhile and significant role in helping promote the 'green revolution' in Pakistan and also in introducing improved strains of rice, in what is now Bangladesh. However, all the good work it may have done in the country may have been offset by the under-the-table political role which some of its designated advisers have played in promoting the secession of East Pakistan. Its functionaries have not helped our national interests either by giving a wholly capitalistic orientation to economic planning and by virtually buying up the sympathy and support of a large number of highly placed public officials in Pakistan by sending them on trips and study tours abroad. An assessment of the Harvard Group's advisory role in Pakistan was published in the form of a pamphlet 'Underdeveloping The World'. It was written by Students and Movement Research people in Cambridge (USA). The pamphlets, scathingly critical of the project, referred to the beneficiary countries as 'client states of US imperialism'. While the Advisory Group claimed Pakistan as a 'unique success story', the pamphlet put forward a radically different point of view, and accused the group of pursuing a policy aimed at 'stabilizing and rationalizing market economics which are thereby more reliable for international business.'

Mr McGeorge Bundy, President of the Ford Foundation, in his TV interview, during his 1968 tour of Pakistan, said, 'I think the reputation of Pakistan and her government and her authorities for economic planning and for the effective use of outside assistance is very high.' After 14 years of Harvard advisers in Pakistan, the advisory group reported in its annual review for 1967–68:

'Although the President's illness created a period of uncertainty, progress in economic policy and performance was excellent.'

According to the pamphlet, 'This public relations work would have been received with scorn by the Pakistani masses. While the (Advisory Group) was waving the flag of victory for Pakistan's capitalist development, the people of Pakistan were rioting in the streets of all major cities. Although a new military take-over in early 1969 forced calm upon the country, it is clear that animosity towards the ruling elite runs deep over corruption, repression, unemployment, and general poverty.'

The pamphlet took particular exception to the period of economic growth which the Advisory Group found to be highly impressive. 'The period began at the end of 1950. In 1958 political instability ended abruptly with the military coup which brought Ayub Khan to power. Martial law was maintained until 1962, the opposition was ruthlessly suppressed, and economic growth began. Per capita product grew at an annual rate of about 2.6% from 1960 to 1965.' Thereafter the decline the pamphlet came to the conclusion:

'A succession of capitalist governments operating with (Advisor Group) advice, have done nothing for the people of Pakistan. Income inequality, between classes and between East and West, shows no signs of decreasing. Repression and corruption are as common today as when Harvard first intervened in the 1950s. Capitalism in Pakistan is not an independent, developing system, but a very dependent client of the major capitalist powers, unable to finance its investment plans without massive foreign aid.

'Its ideological orientation prevents the (Advisory Group) from offering advice which can help the Pakistani people change their society. Pious declarations of good intent and juggling statistics in Five-Year plans are of little help. The success about which the (Advisory Group) boasts, an apparently temporary period of rising income per capita, means little as long as it occurs within the capitalist framework of inequality, repression, and dependence on foreign benevolence. The (Advisory Group) cannot change that framework; at its best, it can provide technical improvements in transportation, agriculture, planning methods, etc. At present such improvements far from leading to basic change, can only serve to stabilize an illegitimate military government. And the people of Pakistan undoubtedly view that government and its American advisers as 'part of the problem, not part of the solution'.

It may not be wholly valid to accuse the Ford foundation, other similar institutions or the US government to have brought about the secession of Bangladesh but there is no doubt that having sensed the trend of coming events, they certainly contributed their bit to hasten the separation. Not for any idealistic or humanitarian reasons but for well-defined US foreign policy objectives as has been borne out by the Mason report. It should always be kept in mind that more copious and more exhaustive studies on this subject have been carried out by various official and non-official American agencies since 1965 or thereabouts.

Whither Pakistan

22 July 1972

Benjamin H. Oehlert Jr.

*F*OLLOWING *is the transcript of a speech delivered by Benjamin H. Oehlert, Jr, a former US ambassador to Pakistan (1967–69), delivered at the Pakistan Council of Asia Society, New England Branch, Massachusetts, on 17 March 1972.*

Perhaps I should have called these remarks 'whether Pakistan' rather than 'whither Pakistan'—for I am not at all sure how long there will be a Pakistan.

I know you don't like to hear that, but I hope that I have sufficiently established myself as a friend of Pakistan so that at least you will not question my motive and that you will consider carefully what I am about to say.

East Pakistan has been forcibly torn away from Pakistan. I submit that three principal factors made this possible. One, of course, was the intervention of India and Russia, but I do not intend to address myself to that factor tonight. The other two factors were, first, a disposition on the part of too many Pakistanis to consider themselves as Pathans, or Bengalis, or Baluchis, or Punjabis, or Sindhis first and Pakistanis second.

The rape of East Pakistan is already fanning the flames of separatism in the North-West Frontier and in Baluchistan and in Sind. If this is allowed to continue, there may well soon be four or five countries in what once was so proudly Pakistan. And the trend may not stop even there. It is conceivable even to visualize a return to a tribal society.

How do you avoid that? At the risk of seeming like a meddlesome foreigner, I presume to suggest that you must forego a large measure of parochialism which too many of you have displayed in the past. You must think and act less in the modes which separate you and more in the modes which unite you. Cultural, religious, ethnic, economic, linguistic, and social backgrounds are important—but they cannot be allowed to be divisive—for they are not as important as the ideals which conceived and created Pakistan and without which it cannot long endure. So I beseech you to put away your differences and concentrate on your likenesses for the good of your national existence.

My country, too, was settled by men and women of many different national and cultural backgrounds and we too went through a bloody civil war, from which we emerged as one country, thank God. We have our differences today, but we have a strong sense of national unity and I would remind you that the government of the United States of America is the oldest continuous form of government in the world today—so it can be done and you can do it.

You don't need to turn your backs on your individual heritages to work together as brothers in a common cause. The other factor of which I wish to speak tonight is public relations.

When old British India was partitioned in 1947, the two new nations so created were officially named Bharat and Pakistan. But no one called Bharat by that name. Everyone called it India, and still does. The course of history might well have been different if Bharat had been called Bharat or Hindustan, which would have been a logical name.

India—What name with which to conjure!

India—land of romance, mystery, and empire.

India—land of Kipling, of Winston Churchill's early campaigns and of Kim's cannon. Land of the North-West Frontier, of the Khyber Pass, and of the Khyber Rifles. Land of the Punjab, of Shalimar Gardens, and of the Lahore horse show. Land of the smugglers' bazaar at Landikotal, of bandits and Pathans, of vast deserts and the high Himalayas.

Where are all those places now? In a sense they are where they always were, for places don't move. But in another sense, they have all moved because boundaries were changed. Those places are no longer in what is called India. They are in the Islamic Republic of Pakistan.

As you so well know, Pakistan was a coined name in which 'P' stood for the Punjab, 'A' for Afghania (North-West Frontier Province), 'K' for Kashmir, 'S' for Sind, and 'Tan' for Baluchistan.

No one had ever heard the name Pakistan before, whereas the lore of centuries attached to the name India, bringing with it sympathy, understanding, friendship, charity, interest, and concern. So Pakistan started its national existence under a tremendous public relations handicap vis-a-vis India.

Today, more than twenty years later, India is a household word in the United States, while Pakistan is relatively little known, despite the fact that, population-wise, it is (or was) the fifth largest country in the world, exceeded only by the United States of America; the Union of Soviet Socialist Republics (Russia), India, and the Peoples' Republic of China (Red China) in that ascending order.

Despite Pakistan's closeness to us for years, and our alliances with her while India grew ever closer to Russia, our relations with each other began to deteriorate after 1962. There were many reasons for this, with fault on both sides, but time is too short to dwell on all of them. We noted earlier that Pakistan started its national existence under a tremendous public relations handicap vis-a-vis India.

This should have indicated to Pakistan that she badly needed to work hard for understanding and friendship, and she should have realized that this could not be accomplished without the sympathy of the free press of the world and especially of the United States. But, she did the opposite. She not only made little or no effort to cultivate the press, but she actually seemed to take a perverse delight in antagonizing it.

I shall return to that subject in a moment to justify my conclusions but first let me point out that India took an opposite course from Pakistan. Although India began its national existence with all the good will in the world, she worked hard and intelligently at maintaining and improving her image. Even though she has no pacts or alliances with us; even though she has rarely supported us in the UN; even though she set herself up as the leader of a 'Third Force' in the world; even though she has grown closer and closer to Russia—internationally, politically, economically, and militarily; even though she has become increasingly a socialist state bordering on communism; even though she has frequently resorted to military conquest, as witness Kashmir, Hyderabad, and Goa among others, she is still regarded—even almost revered—in this country as a paragon of friendship, democracy, non-violence and peace.

How did this all come about? It didn't just happen, believe me. The image was consciously created through skillful public relations efforts. Remember I said a moment ago that Pakistan made little or no effort to cultivate the press and that she actually seemed to take a perverse delight in antagonizing it? Let me tell you why I say that.

Although, in her earlier years Pakistan was so close to the United States that she was sometimes called 'the most allied of our allies,' that was a government-to-government relationship rather than a people-to-people relationship. Any government-to-government relationship is bound to die out unless it is, or is made to become, a people-to-people relationship.

No matter how well disposed an American President, a Secretary of State, and an Ambassador may be, they cannot create a people-to-people relationship and they cannot maintain a government-to-government relationship unless the Congress is equally well disposed; and no Congress will be so disposed unless the individual citizens who elect it are. And the individual citizens are not apt to be unless their press is.

But Pakistan did not act to create a good public image. Although it is (or was) the fifth largest country in the world: although it is so close to us in religion, economic conviction and military alliance; little is known about Pakistan by the average American except for her calamities of nature and rebellion.

Pakistan should have exerted every effort to publicize who, where, and what she was in the hopes that she too could make her name a respected by word in the United States. Had she done so, many subsequent events would have been viewed here with far more understanding and sympathy. Not only did Pakistan fail to move efficiently to create a favorable image, she also failed to explain and justify some of the later events of her history.

The underlying necessities for Ayub's military takeover were never dramatized, nor were those which underlay the declaration of martial law in 1969. On the contrary, Pakistan seemed content for years to be falsely labelled a military dictatorship—with all the attendant negatives which that created in this country. How were the people of the United States to know why Ayub had to step in; how were they to know that he was later elected democratically by the free expression of full male and female adult franchise; how were they to know that the much maligned basic democrat system was both truly democratic and a massive extension of our own electoral college system to which we still cling tenaciously? They could not know unless Pakistan told them.

How were the American people to know what took place between November 1968 and March 1969 when martial law was declared unless Pakistan told them?

How were the American people to know the facts about Hyderabad and Kashmir unless Pakistan told them?

How were the American people to know the facts about Pakistan's remarkable progress in creating, from scratch, a governmental and an economic infrastructure and the outstanding success of its 'green revolution' unless Pakistan told them?

How were the American people to know all that took place between December 1970 and 25 March 1971, when President Yahya was finally forced to call on the army to suppress revolution— unless Pakistan told them?

But Pakistan not only did not tell us those things, she actually made it impossible to learn them from any credible source.

The Government of Pakistan took control of her press years ago, which somewhat unfairly, became known as a fully censored propaganda arm of the government. That not only caused its press despatches to be unbelieved and unused, but even worse, it aroused the enmity of the American press, which, as you well know, fights vigorously for its own freedom.

Over the years, Pakistan has systematically discouraged the presence of American press representatives, has expelled many and has closed down offices of the AP and the UPI among others. She has barred American newspapers and magazines for carrying displeasing stories.

All of this has forced the American press to rely on India and on American newsmen stationed in India for news of Pakistan. So of course the stories have been coloured. How could they have been otherwise?

If you were a Pakistani newsman in the United States who, along with your colleagues, had been banished to Canada, where you are warmly received, would you have friendly feelings for the United States?

It is for all of these reasons that, until very lately, all of the despatches about the revolt in East Pakistan have come either from the Indian press or from antagonistic American reporters stationed in India. The sources of the stories have been either Indian or from East Pakistanis who support the so called Bangladesh. Is it any wonder that those stories have been anti-Pakistan and pro-Indian and pro-Bangladesh?

I know that you do not like to hear these criticizms [*sic*], and I realize that I am not helping my own popularity by stating them, but I came here to try to help Pakistan and I can best do so by telling you the hard truth in the hope that I may convince you and that through you the situation may be improved.

It is my earnest recommendation that Pakistan take the following steps:

1. Remove all controls over the Pakistani press, radio and television;
2. Invite the AP, the UPI, *The New York Times* and all US papers, magazines and TV network maintaining their own overseas bureaus to establish permanent, fully staffed offices in Pakistan;
3. Give the staffs of those offices full freedom to travel and interview;
4. Extend frequent invitations for other press groups to visit the country;
5. Stop the banning of American newspapers and magazines;
6. Employ competent public relations counsel in the United States to encourage authors to write favourable books, newspaper[s], magazine features and TV documentaries;

To make a real effort to encourage tourism when the present violence stops—as it will some day.

So there you have it. I'm grateful, for the opportunity to tell you what I believe to be the root cause of many of Pakistan's problems of relationships abroad. I hope I haven't offended you. I hope that something constructive can and will come out of our meeting. There is a tremendous job to be done. It will be expensive in terms of time, talent, efforts, and money. But it can be done, it should be done, it must be done. Pakistan cannot afford not to do it. If it is done, the rewards will make it all worthwhile.

Pakistan Zindabad.

Bengalis Here, Biharis There—a Deepening Tragedy

19 August 1972

THE condition of Biharis in Bangladesh continues to be a source of increasing concern for most conscientious men. The adverse publicity which the Bangladesh government has been receiving in the world press seems to have had no effect on it and Biharis are still living the same harrowing existence. The British press particularly has been very vociferous in highlighting the plight of Biharis with newspaper and television stories.

In Pakistan too it appears that the government has been taking action against the Bengalis. Most Bengalis working in government organizations have been sacked, mostly without any benefits, and their salaries are being delayed. Armed personnel have been interned in special repatriation camps.

Such drastic action[s] can hardly be justified. When the news filters through to Bangladesh, it might result in more repressive action against the Biharis. Although no Bengali in West Pakistan is subject to any physical danger, the sacking or harassing of Bengalis in itself will be excellent propaganda material for the Bangladesh government and might be used as a reason for the action against the Biharis, who are 'asking for poison' anyway.

36,000 Bengali government employees plus about 10,000 serving in autonomous and semi-government organizations were sacked last month. Previously, a fortnight ago and prior to the Simla meeting, they had been asked to indicate whether they would opt for Bangladesh or Pakistan. The only reason for this query was that it was in connection with repatriation. Most Bengalis opted for Bangladesh, as could be expected. A short while later they received letters terminating their services because they had opted for so-called Bangladesh.

They were deprived of the various benefits which were due to them such as those of group insurance, benevolent fund, G. P. fund, pensions, gratuities, etc. Moreover payment of their salaries was delayed and many non-gazetted men have still not received their salaries for June. Bengalis claim that low-paid workers are being victimized and that some of them are being forced to do manual labour.

This arbitrary action of the government is contrary to the principles of democratic action. It is also in clear contradiction of President Bhutto's statements that Bengali employees would be treated well and that no opportunity for the creation of any bitterness would be given. Bengalis claim that this action is without precedent. They point out that during the partition of the subcontinent, Muslims who opted for Pakistan were allowed to revise their decision within six months and their services were terminated with full service benefits.

In Bangladesh, the relentless pressure on the Biharis and West Pakistanis continues unabated. Last week a new order for the screening of collaborators was put into effect. Under this amendment, the government has the power to constitute an additional screening board for the removal of corrupt officials, collaborators and all those who believed in the ideology of Pakistan. Moreover, the scope of the screening boards has been widened, so that now more categories of workers are under its jurisdiction: university teachers, members of associations, all government servants, full time servants, directors, members, officers, and other employees of corporate and nationalized enterprises, local authorities, and government-aided institutions.

According to an article published in the *Hongkong Standard* by Ben Whitaker, Director of the Minority Rights Group, the Biharis' morale has fallen so low that they are making almost no effort to solve their problems. Much more dangerous than mere physical privation, this psychological state is growing among the Biharis. This apathy, which is fast taking roots, is so great that the Biharis do not retaliate to any attacks when they can be assured of success, and do not even venture outside the camps to tell the government their problems.

According to Sh. Mujib, any Bihari who wished to leave the country 'could do so tomorrow'. President Bhutto has said that he is willing to exchange populations on a one to one basis—there are about 4 lac Bengalis in Pakistan. President Bhutto is unlikely to agree to the repatriation of Bengalis here, until the question of the POWs and the war criminals trial has been settled. For the present, the more than 15 lac Biharis can hope for no succour until the fate of 90,000 POWs is decided. On the contrary, they can hope for a worsening situation. According to Mr Whitaker, the trials of war criminals and collaborators can have two results: 'they could be cathartic for the Bengalis' bitter memories; or the publication of the evidence of atrocities could refuel public hatred against the Biharis'. Mr Whitaker goes on to say: *the very words "collaborator" and "miscreants" are rapidly becoming means of denouncing any element that the militant students wish to see eliminated'*. Between 5,000 and 10,000 Biharis have been arrested, and have either disappeared or taken to prison. The Bengali press, with the sole exception of the weekly paper *Holiday*, is both chauvinistic and subservient to the government's indifference.'

The Indian army, while it was in Bangladesh, had tried to protect the Biharis as much as it could. It had grouped the Biharis in ghettoes, or posted guards at important Bihari concentrations. Sh. Mujib himself was inclined to be well disposed towards the Biharis initially, more so because his wife had been helped by some Biharis during the army action. His first speech on return to Dacca had laid stress on the unity of all Bangladeshis. But being attuned to the peoples' thoughts he soon realized that the prevalent mood was strongly anti-Bihari. Consequently his efforts for the Biharis soon trailed into nothing and they were left more or less at the peoples' mercy. One was his tacit condoning of

Kadir Siddique's act by doing nothing: 'Tiger' Kader killed six Biharis in cold blood before a meeting in Dacca Stadium, which was seen widely on world television.

It is true of course that cries of peace and brotherhood are for the idealists and the freaks; that it is very difficult to translate them into action when the hard practicalities of race, religion, and economics come into play, and that at best a very precarious balance can be achieved. The situations in Pakistan and Bangladesh call for this balance. While it is futile to hope that the animosities of years can be wiped out, a balance can certainly be achieved. It needs a little bit of effort.

—M. A.

Aspects of Reality

26 August 1972

THE issue of recognition of Bangladesh, due to have been discussed by the National Assembly in the current session, has been indefinitely postponed. Since a meeting with Shaikh Mujib did not come off in July, President Bhutto, as a tactical move, has the issue on ice. Nevertheless, he is keeping his options wide open. His last address to the National Assembly was an unsophisticated attempt to prepare the ground for recognition, sitting at the same time on the freeze box.

The Indians, nursing a sense of disappointment, are accusing President Bhutto of backtracking on a private understanding reportedly given by him at Simla that he would recognize Bangladesh by 14 August. The Bangladesh spokesmen, meanwhile have shown no signs of relenting in their stand that formal recognition should precede any talks between the two states. The only chinks in the wall are the meetings which Shaikh Mujib has had with a few West Pakistani political leaders all of whom, at one time or another, are known to have had sympathies for the Awami League. None of them commands any significant political support in the country. Yet, these unofficial contacts can be useful in promoting an understanding which might lead to a formal recognition.

It is difficult to appreciate Dacca's rigidity in opening a dialogue with Pakistan unless it is presumed that a defeated nation has no rights or interests to defend. Any talks, official or unofficial, will automatically imply an equal status. Pakistan is in no position to dictate to Bangladesh. That bit of reality has been etched out for good on the geopolitical canvas of the subcontinent. The nature of inter-state relations is also wholly dependent on the wishes of Bangladesh, acting either on its own or under advice from its partners-in-security. President Bhutto may have his ideas, as he presumes to have, on the subject but it takes two to evolve a link or a special relationship. From whatever can be read from the logic of events or the signs of the times, it is futile to look for any link or special relationship as of now. It would be more sensible to start with a clean slate which is predicated on the recognition of Bangladesh as a sovereign, independent state.

President Bhutto has done well not to resurrect his earlier commitment that any solution must be framed within 'one Pakistan', howsoever loose the arrangement might be. On 20 December he had talked of 'Muslim Bengal' being an 'indissoluble part of Pakistan'. Today he still talks of a 'Muslim Bengal' and, mercifully, does not repeat the rest of the stipulation. It is this background which may have offered Shaikh Mujib an excuse to insist on an equal status and prior recognition. To put any store by what Shaikh Mujib promised while he was still Islamabad's prisoner is not a fair presumption. Promises extracted under a situation of duress are of no value, moral or political. At the same time, it is equally true that Dacca's unreasonable stance in the matter has been made possible only because India holds in ransom 93,000 POWs and civilian internees. This is a kind of blackmail which, to some, may be justified in view of the events of the past but which does not make a good beginning to build for the future. Now that the chances of Bangladesh joining the United Nations have been precluded by the Chinese veto, it is possible to visualize a more moderate attitude on the part of the Dacca government. It would be far more desirable if sanity could prevail for its own sake rather than being induced as a result of a parity in pressurization. There is substance in the Sino-Pakistan viewpoint that the Security Council resolutions of 5 and 21 December must be implemented before Bangladesh is admitted into the United Nations. It also emerges as the logical outcome of the Simla accord.

If nothing else, purely human considerations demand that the process of repatriation should be expedited to mitigate the undeserved hardship of people trapped in either wing. Even conceding the right of Bangladesh to hold on to a certain number of POWs suspected of war crimes, there can be no justification for the continued detention of the rest of the armed services personnel and civilians in Indian camps. Nor can the forced retention of Bengalis in West Pakistan be justified on any count. They are a weight on one's conscience. The sooner this deepening human tragedy can be resolved, the better. Rather it must be resolved, even pending recognition. All the more necessary, therefore, that talks between Islamabad and Dacca should be initiated, not necessarily at the official level. It is not beyond the capabilities of diplomacy to arrange it all [so] that recognition and the elevation of negotiations to an official level may be announced at the same time. Reasons of prestige or intended pressurization should make way for a climate of pragmatic accommodation.

The reality of Bangladesh has to be recognized, sooner rather than later. The ideology of Pakistan, if there be any such formulation, should be resilient enough to withstand the impact of reality. Which is that a majority of the population of what was once a unified Pakistan has chosen to snap the bond which held the two wings together. Foreign intervention was a material factor, not a decisive one. The old arrangement stands destroyed. Whether a brave new world will be born in Bangladesh is an open question. But it is not exactly our concern, nor can we materially influence the shape of things to come in that region. We could only wish them well. Admittedly, things are far from stable in Bangladesh. There is the possibility too that the Indian army may still be there in the Chittagong Hill Tracts. There is evidence to suggest that the art and practice of persecution is on the increase in Bangladesh. Some of these developments are a natural consequence of what Bangladesh has gone through, some pose questions of a more intractable, fundamental nature. Let Bangladesh pose its own questions and find its own answers. West Pakistan itself faces questions no less ticklish and no less fundamental in import. It is said that the recognition of Bangladesh will encourage secessionism here as well. If so, the issue to be pondered is not that of recognition but the tenuous nature of the framework known as West Pakistan.

The only sensible course to follow is to accord recognition to Bangladesh—at the proper time. A few issues must be probed and settled first. This presupposes talks under any cover. They must be held.

Simla and After

26 August 1972

Our correspondent writes:

WHAT India expects from the Simla agreement is becoming clearer with the passage of time. Since the signing of the agreement, the only talks which have been held between India and Pakistan related to the delineation of the line of actual control in Kashmir as it obtained on 17 December 1971, the day of the ceasefire. The delineation has been completed and actual withdrawals from the positions occupied after 17 December 1971 have started. Under the agreement, Pakistan will give up two outposts in the Lipa Valley while India will give up some area in the Kargil sector. India will, however, continue to be in occupation of important Pakistani outposts in the Kargil area which had been occupied before the ceasefire came into effect. This ensures that the Indian strategic road connecting Srinagar with Leh in Ladakh will henceforward be safe against the possibilities of sniping from Pakistani outposts.

The Indian objective of delineating the line of actual control in Kashmir before discussing withdrawals from areas in Punjab and Sind has therefore been effectively achieved. The Indian Defence Minister, Mr Jagjivan Ram, according to a report published in the *Patriot* of New Delhi dated 6 August 1972, said that no date had been fixed for the withdrawal of troops from the occupied areas in Punjab and Sind. The Simla agreement, it may be recalled, had provided that the withdrawal of troops from the international frontiers should be completed within 30 days of the ratification of the agreement. The ratification formalities were completed on 4 August 1972 with the handing over of the Indian instrument of ratification to the authorities in Islamabad. The Indian Minister's statement raises a shadow of doubt on the timetable of withdrawal of troops. The actual words used by him were: 'The Simla agreement will become effective after the exchange of instruments of ratification. Thereafter, sector commanders of both sides would meet to discuss the details of pull-out from different sectors. As such I cannot give the probable date of pull-out.'

Mr Jagjivan Ram also made it plain that India will claim from Pakistan the expenditure incurred on the prisoners of war now being held in India. He said that such expenditure on the POWs could be recovered under the Geneva conventions. According to him an average sum of Rs. 60/- was spent on a POW per month.

There has been some public outcry in India against the Simla agreement. The protest is led by the Jan Sangh which is not a very effective political group in India. Expert opinion in India continues to support the agreement for the simple reason that India's main objectives in relation to Pakistan seem to have been achieved.

Dilip Mukerji wrote in *The Times of India* of 12 August 1972, that President Bhutto had given 'a clear indication' at Simla that he would recognize Bangladesh to facilitate tripartite discussions on the prisoners of war issue. 'The reasons he has advanced for the sudden shift of posture do not bear scrutiny; it is plain that he has had to defer the debate on the question in the National Assembly because his ability to make its members fall in line has been seriously impaired by the language riots in Sind and other domestic developments … his back tracking on the recognition of Bangladesh is a poor augury towards implementing the Simla accord both in letter and spirit,' he wrote.

A despatch from Dacca carried in *The Times of India* the same day ascribed to Government of India officials the statement that the Security Council resolutions of December 1971 'have now been superseded by the Simla agreement which has been ratified by the Governments of Pakistan and India.' 'Official circles emphasized that insistence at this stage on the implementation of the December resolutions will create obstacles in the way of implementation of the Simla accord,' the newspaper's Dacca correspondent, Kirit Bhaumik, wrote in the context of the Chinese veto on the admission of Bangladesh into United Nations.

The Indian Government also seems to have taken exception to the statements made by the Pakistan Foreign Office that the purpose of the Suchetgarh talks was to determine the line of actual control in 'areas of Jammu and Kashmir where the old ceasefire line was disturbed by the December war'. This, according to *The Times of India* of 12 August 1972, was considered wide off the mark by Indian Government officials. 'They think that what the Pakistan Government spokesman said yesterday was probably for domestic consumption.'

According to *The Times of India* version, the Simla agreement had unambiguously described the line resulting from the ceasefire of 17 December 1971, as the 'new line of actual control'. 'While it is a fact that the entire ceasefire line of 1949 was not altered by the course of the war, the line of actual control that emerged from the truce on 17 December 1971 is not a *modified* ceasefire line of 1949 but a *new* line which has to be delineated all along its zigzag course,' the newspaper said.

The purpose behind all these fine distinctions which are now being hammered by India and which, in the absence of a denial from Islamabad may be presumed to have been accepted by Pakistan, is clear enough. The idea is to shake the United Nations out of the Kashmir dispute for good. Mrs Gandhi reminded Pakistan at the time when the National Assembly was debating the Simla accord that Pakistan should withdraw the Kashmir case from the United Nations. Pakistan has accepted the principle of bilateralism at Simla which, according to the Indian interpretation, means that neither the United Nations nor its observers on the ceasefire line have any more role to play. The Indian insistence on what it claims to be the new line of actual control also must be seen in view of her insistence that the new line should form the permanent international boundary between India and Pakistan.

As a bargaining counter, Indian ministers have also put in the claim that the whole of Azad Kashmir territory belongs to India and that they would also claim the territory which has been ceded to China as a result of the Pakistan-China Boundary Agreement. As for the return of territories in Sind and Punjab, the Indian Defence experts seem to be of the view that Indian withdrawals will not jeopardize their security.

Lt. Gen. M. M. Khanna, former commandant of the National Defence College, and Maj. Gen. D. Som Dutta made the assessment while addressing a public meeting at India International Centre.

Former Defence Secretary V. Shankar presided

Rebutting the criticizm [*sic*] of 'some political parties in the country' against the return of certain captured areas to Pakistan under the Simla agreement, Lt. Gen. Khanna said the fears were based on a wrong premise.

If the country had to go in for another war with Pakistan, it was not necessary to capture the same areas again. One of the principles of war was to surprise the enemy, and if the country tried to take the same areas again, it would be like the 'stupid attacks on Chhamb', he said.

Return of the captured areas and the troop pull-out, he said, was also correct militarily. The country could not keep the territories for long and would have been required to return them. But while doing so, the security aspects had not been ignored.

He pointed out that in returning 'Chicken's neck' and Shakargarh bulge, the country was not losing anything strategically. In either area, it had not captured any military assets of Pakistan.

While returning Dera Baba Nanak, the country was gaining Fazilka and was also retaining all the *strategic posts* in the Kargil sector. Under the provisions of the agreement, the country will also get back two Tithwal posts taken by Pakistan 'by treachery'.

The Rajasthan areas were mainly desert areas and a troop pull-out from them would have a good morale-boosting effect on the *jawans,* since the areas have no military value and their retention meant idling the troops, he said.

Rebutting the criticizm [*sic*] against the return of the captured territories, he said the idea of conquest and loot through wars was an outdated concept and no country could hold on to the areas forcibly taken permanently.

Ford Foundation and Bangladesh

2 September 1972

Our correspondent writes:

TO what extent the emergence of Bangladesh is the result of foreign encouragement has been the subject of an intense debate in Pakistan. Below is published a facsimile of a memorandum written on behalf of the Yale University Pakistan Project, financed by the Ford Foundation, which throws some light on the thinking of the American experts working in Pakistan before the crisis blewup. The memorandum is dated 17 March 1971, and was despatched on 20 March 1971. This was a week before the government of ex-President Yahya Khan started its military action in the eastern wing on 25 March 1971. The memorandum speaks of the emergency conditions under which the project was functioning at the time and, intriguingly enough, mentions the mode of payment—'most likely to be made in Bangladesh piasters.'

The document seems to be genuine. Since there was no Bangladesh at the time the possible nomenclature of its currency was not known. The use of the term *piasters* need not be taken too literally. What is important is that the emergence of Bangladesh as a separate country with its own currency had been visualized as an immediate possibility by the international powers well before the military action was started. Incidentally, PIDE stands for the Pakistan Institute of Development Economics which had been transferred to Dacca some time earlier. It was also at this Institute that most of the economic studies highlighting the growing disparity between the two wings had been compiled. Use of these studies in promoting estrangement between the two wings is now well known.

A few weeks back, this journal had published the Mason Report which was compiled in April 1971. It has since been represented that it was undertaken by a private group and that it was not a secret report. Both these points need not be contested. The more important aspect of the matter is the thinking represented by the authors of the report. It needs no emphasis that such reports go a long way towards influencing private and official opinion in USA. Two of the three authors of the Mason Report were connected with Ford Foundation projects in Pakistan.

For the purpose of clarity, the highlights of the Mason Report are being reproduced here once again:

1. 'The longer the independence of Bangladesh is delayed, the more likely it is that the leadership of the movement will pass from the moderate Shaikh Mujibur Rahman to the more leftist NAP.'
2. 'The new Bangladesh will set up friendly relations with India.'
3. 'A major role of US foreign policy in this area has been to seek a reduction of tensions in South East Asia, West Pakistan is bound to tone down its policy of confrontation with India.'
4. 'The Kashmir issue will also subside in importance not because of any reduction in tension but because West Pakistan, without the economic support of the East; will be unable to sustain the level of pressure it has been mounting until now.'
5. 'An independent Bangladesh will, if at all have only marginal economic contacts with China. It is unlikely that it will become a satellite of China.'
6. 'In the past the USSR has not been sensitive to the aspirations of East Pakistan and it is unlikely to make the new Bangladesh an area for a super power competition for influence.'

It is incontrovertible that the US policy goals are supported by the work of private American foundations. Diplomacy has varied arms to pursue its objectives. In any case, would the Ford Foundation please explain the memorandum under review? Historically, it would fit into a neat pattern.

The Awami League's pro-American attitude is something which cannot be contested by any serious political observer. Right from the time of Mr H. S. Suhrawardy, the Awami League has had a pro-American orientation. It, therefore, stands to reason that the Awami League in its policy calculations could well have relied upon American support. When the unfortunate military action was launched on 25 March 1971, the US consulate in Dacca was publicizing to the world that tanks and other heavy equipment had been used in the operation. (Not that they were not used). BBC and the Voice of America spoke with one voice before and after the operation. The Soviet Union's involvement was open and blatant. For the Indians it was the chance of a century. The British never miss a chance to profit by any situation.

Shaikh Mujibur Rahman, when he visited London in the first week of November 1969, was received at the airport by the representative of the British Foreign Office. At that time elections had not been held, and Shaikh Mujibur Rahman was one of the many opposition leaders playing their bit on the political stage in the country. But obviously he was a man with a different potential and therefore the red carpet treatment to him at the London airport. The British in all this business acted as the front men of the US. It is a different matter that the fruits are being reaped by the Soviet Union. But for how long? Western powers are trying hard to oust the Russian influence in Bangladesh. The Indian presence in this area serves the western interests just as much as it is acceptable to the Russians. It is the outer super power crust which is in dispute.

A West Pakistani who travelled to London by the same plane in November 1969 as Sh. Mujib, was intrigued by the official reception given to the latter. During a meeting with ex-President Iskandar Mirza, he remarked on this rather intriguing show of cordiality on the part of the British towards Shaikh Mujibur Rahman. The ex-President said he was aware of the Anglo-American efforts to split Pakistan. He said he had been trying to convince the British and the Americans on his own that this would not only unsettle the prevailing balance of power in the subcontinent but that ultimately it might not be in the interest of the western powers themselves. He said his arguments did not seem to be carrying much weight either in London or Washington. Maj. Gen. Iskandar Mirza also remarked that this was one of the reasons why he wanted to revisit Pakistan. He was anxious to discuss the emerging situation with the Pakistan authorities. His application for permission to visit Pakistan was not granted.

The purpose here is not to suggest that the creation of Bangladesh is a result of Indian or foreign intervention alone. Discerning observers had foreseen the emergence of Bangladesh years before the crisis came to a head. The watershed in this regard seems to be the Indo-Pakistan war of 1965. Nationalist sentiments in Bangladesh had been maturing since well before 1965. It is known that the nucleus of a Bengali nationalist group within the armed forces of Pakistan was first established in 1962. The object was to prepare for an armed struggle. The first public clamour for two economies had been made much earlier. Since the ground was ripe, the nationalist-separatist movement gained momentum over the years.

The foreign powers had their eyes close to ground. Perhaps they could see the inevitable much more clearly than the rulers in Islamabad or even the politicians in the western wing. And they prepared for it. It is not correct to trace the separatist movement from the time of the elections in December 1970. As Shaikh Mujibur Rahman has said himself he had been working for separation ever since the time of partition. The Shaikh's hindsight may not be all that incisive as he claims today. But surely the seeds of a separatist-nationalist movement go far deeper than the election results of December 1970. They were inherent in the geopolitical situation which was aggravated by the western wing's refusal to share power with the east. Incidentally, the Awami League's sweeping victory was not in the nature of a windfall. The withdrawal of the National Awami Party and other political groups in the eastern wing was neither accidental nor the acceptance of the inevitable. It was the result of a calculated policy to leave the field clear to the Awami League to reap a massive majority in what was conceived as a confrontation between East and West Pakistan. The idea was to strengthen Shaikh Mujibur Rahman's hands by leaving the arena to the Awami League alone.

The foreign powers could see the writing on the wall and encouraged the Awami League's posture in an attempt to mark out an area of influence for themselves. It is always better to anticipate the shape of things to come rather than be left out in the cold. This is what the foreign powers did, India for its own reasons, Russia for its own game, and the Anglo-Americans for their own designs. This is not to say that the primary responsibility for what happened in the eastern Wing between December 1970 and December 1971 does not lie on the military and political elite of West Pakistan. Neither should this be construed to mean that either the military action or the subsequent orgy of blood should in any way be condoned. The record is all too clear on that. What is sometimes underrated is the foreign involvement in the game, it is better to keep the perspective right for whatever it may be worth.

Surrender at Sundown

2 September 1972

D. Shah Khan

THE confusion that exists about the surrender at Dacca on 16 December tends to overshadow a pathetic story of the last days of Pakistan in that ill-fated province and about the people—the pro-Pakistan Bengalis, the *mohajirs*, and the West Pakistanis who participated in the bloody drama of defeat and despair. It is an unhappy episode about people who lived courageously through circumstances that were clearly deteriorating day by day, but who sadly seemed to dwell in a euphoria brought about by 25 years of belief in our invincibility and the absurd news that was fed by the radio and the newspapers.

It was a bitter drama and its real bitterness only became apparent when arms were laid down at Dacca and the Pakistanis suddenly found themselves defeated, demoralized, and exposed to the mercies of those very people against whom they had rallied so enthusiastically earlier. And the tragedy of it all was that few were prepared mentally or materially for such an unexpected and disastrous solution to the national crisis.

The start of the India-Pakistan war formally on 3 December was received with a sigh of relief as the beginning of the salvation of the beleaguered province. The brief war was lived through with optimism and bravery and till the last day this hope was sustained.

In Chittagong city, which was occupied by the advancing Indian forces on 17 December—the last major stronghold of Pakistan to fall, this agony and hope lingered a day longer.

Most of the Pakistanis explicitly believed in Radio Pakistan's news about the war situation and discounted the wild broadcasts of the foreign stations. Those Bengalis who saw things in a different light, faithfully switched over to BBC, VOA, AIR, and the Calcutta-based 'Bangladesh Radio', and in the darkness of their homes heard the news with a growing sense of hope and happiness. The difference between the news emanating from these various sources was so immense that it was impossible to imagine that the broadcasts were about the same war.

In fact, Radio Pakistan broadcast[s] its news with such earnestness that the euphoria it created served as an opiate till the last day and only the arrival of the jungle-green clad Indian forces shattered the illusion. Few of those who lived in East Pakistan seriously thought the situation was going against the country. Even as late as 14 December, everyone tended to look forward to some miraculous happening which would bring victory and subsequent release. The successes of September 1965 were recalled and the news of the fail of major Indian cities was eagerly awaited. After all 'victory is with the just'. The continuous bombing by the Indians too did not break this indomitable spirit and the will to face the danger.

The declaration of 'no surrender' by Lt. Gen. A. A. K. Niazi in the last days too was received with satisfaction and the pro-Pakistan public became more resolute than ever to face the worsening situation. In fact it could be honestly said that never before have so many people lived so defiantly to the last moment on false hope, tragic optimism, and bravado.

Although a curfew from sunset to sunrise had been declared in all major cities and towns of East Pakistan since the beginning of the war and blackout and other civil defence measures were in force, life continued almost normally. The shops and markets remained crowded; business, whatever was possible, was conducted and government and private offices functioned as usual.

Even lunch parties and other such functions were held by some people as a way of getting together and talking about things pleasant. Among the affluent sections of the society a new form of entertainment became the vogue in which two or three families bedded together in a friend's house for the night and spent the dreary blackout hours playing bridge, canasta, scrabble, and other games.

It was perhaps the gentle winter of Bengal (it was an enchanting one last December) and the verdant countryside that seemed to keep sordid realizm [*sic*] away and encouraged the people to wallow in a make-believe world. It was interesting to see this sense of bravado and hope. Even the most cynical appeared to have faith in miracles and everyone 'felt' in his innermost mind that certainly something dramatic will happen which would change the whole complexion of the war.

The news of the movement of the United States Seventh Fleet in the Bay of Bengal was received with approval and the 'I told you so' looks. Then a later rumour about the arrival of Chinese warships and aircraft only added strength to this optimism.

But then the inexorable hand of fate continued to move against us and gradually even the most hopeful started conceding that possibly things were not going quite as well as imagined.

Probably one of the reasons for this hopeful attitude of the Pakistanis in that province was that they could think of nothing else. East Pakistan is like a trap. It is surrounded on three sides by belligerent India (except for a small strip of Burmese border) and by the sea in the south. When the war started in earnest and the PIA and shipping services were suspended, the trap was snapped shut. Those who lived there realized that now there could be only two possible conclusions. One—if the war was won by Pakistan, there was no problem. And the other—if the war was lost, it spelt doom. A third solution lay in escape through Burma which very few succeeded in achieving, or by sea which was almost impossible.

Thus, faced with such limited options, the people could either sit, worry, and whimper or adopt a devil-may-care attitude and wait for the outcome. The latter attitude everyone adopted, partly because they were sanguine that the war will go in Pakistan's favour and partly as it is healthier to expect the better rather than the worst.

The first piece of news that caused some discomfort was the report of the alleged appeal by Maj. General Rao Farman Ali Khan to the United Nations Secretary General to help in the evacuation of Pakistani forces from East Pakistan. The news was stunning but an immediate disclaimer by President Yahya Khan brought about a sense of cheer once more. Earlier, Radio Pakistan's Dacca station had permanently ceased broadcasting, but this too was explained away as some technical problem.

By 13 December certain hard facts started becoming apparent. A gradual exodus of the public to the villages began. Then there was a slight rush to buy essential commodities. Offices began closing down and the streets which normally remained busy till just before sunset now became deserted by late afternoon. Even the cycle rickshaws, which had plied during the worst of times now refused to be hired out.

But new hope was pumped into this seemingly unhappy situation by the disclosure that Chittagong city and its environs had enough men, materials, and arms to last out at least two months if things became worse. Among the more enthusiastic sections, there was even increasing talk of fighting with the forces on the battlefields, on the beaches, in the swamps, and in the streets. The ghost of Sir Winston Churchill hovered over Chittagong!

By 14 December, the word 'surrender' was heard more frequently and the concerned people were now ready to discuss the term academically. It was argued that 'surrender' was too harsh a word—perhaps a ceasefire through United Nations intervention.

The news of 15 December was, however, most confusing. As far as Radio Pakistan was concerned we were fighting resolutely on all fronts. Other radio stations spoke of impending talks between the Indian and Pakistani commanders for a 'ceasefire' (few wanted to believe in the possibility of surrender).

16 December dawned quietly. The air raids had ceased and a sense of expectance prevailed and thoughts were subdued. The general public, still oblivious of the actual position, waited patiently for a miracle to happen. Surely we will not be let down? Not after all those sacrifices? They asked searchingly.

The wiser among the Pakistanis, particularly among the government officials, the businessmen and industrialists who had access to official reports about the actual situation, had already sensed the direction of the wind. They started moving into neutral zones, places of safety and into houses of Bengali friends, and mercifully there were many Bengalis who willingly opened their doors to those who sought refuge.

The surrender did take place at Dacca on 16 December just before sundown and the province ceased to exist. The Indian and Bangladesh flags were hoisted and the sun set on East Pakistan for the last time.

In Chittagong, however, things remained more or less as usual. The Pakistan flag continued to fly in the city, the police and military were seen moving about on the roads and the *Razakars* and *Al Badr* and other locally raised paramilitary forces were very much in evidence. It was still Pakistan everywhere.

By sunset time everyone obediently went home as the curfew began. Even the complete blackout was observed dutifully and vehicles of the Civil Defence sped about in the stillness of the night on patrol duty.

Radio Pakistan, Chittagong, which had continued to function till the last day, began its third and last transmission in a strange manner. It started the transmission late and broadcast no talks or other usual programmes. There were no patriotic or fiery martial songs which it had been regularly broadcasting. Instead, the radio played tender Bengali melodies, about Bengal, about its villages, rivers and its people. The typical musical fare which is so popular among the sentimental people of that province.

The news from Radio Pakistan was relayed without explanation and later the tearful broadcast of President Yahya Khan came on the air. The radio station went off the air much earlier than usual, bringing to a final end Radio Pakistan's voice from East Pakistan. There was no national anthem, no rousing music, no comment. Merely a brief announcement that transmission had ended. Khuda Hafiz.

On 17 December, the Pakistan flag was still fluttering in Chittagong. Few people came out of their houses. Trucks and jeeps loaded with Pakistani forces and West Pakistani policemen and other paramilitary men were seen in the early hours speeding away as the Pakistan army started withdrawing from the city. Some private cars and other vehicles could also be seen rushing about, and it later became known that these were the pro-Pakistan Bengalis and other non-Bengalis including the *mohajirs* and West Pakistanis who, like many others, woke up on the morning of 17 December to find they were living in what was now clearly Bangladesh.' It was their last desperate bid to hide away before the massive search began for them on a variety of charges. But unfortunately some of them never reached the places of safety as they were caught by mobs on the wayside and slaughtered.

At the graceful double storeyed Government House in Chittagong, which was the martial law headquarters, the final act of surrender was witnessed. The West Pakistani policemen who were quartered there hurriedly packed their equipment and belongings into trucks and left the Government House. For the first time the historic building stood desolate, unguarded and without a flag fluttering on the top. A small crowd of Bengalis which was watching the scene from a respectable distance raised a few insulting slogans at the departing West Pakistanis, but they, misunderstanding them, cheerfully waved out their parting wishes.

The city of Chittagong which had remained strangely calm in the morning suddenly blossomed into life as thousands of hysterical and shouting people appeared on the roads dancing and singing. Flags of India and Bangladesh fluttered all over and garlanded portraits of Shaikh Mujibur Rahman were placed before houses and shops. Unending processions of people kept pouring into the city raising slogans, waving flags, and buntings and stoning any signboard they found with 'Pakistan' written on it. Pakistani flags wherever found were pulled down and torn up. Offices of political parties like the PDP, Muslim League, Jamaat-e-Islami, JUI etc., were ransacked and the furniture and documents burnt in huge bonfires. The Government House was raided by large crowds who planted a Bangladesh flag atop it. The takeover was complete.

The Indian forces entered Chittagong by 10.30 a.m. in an assortment of vehicles. Some were their own, some civilian trucks, a few EPRTC buses and a few Pakistani army vehicles. They received a massive welcome from the cheering crowds who garlanded and showered petals on them and shook hands with them. Even the Bengali women and girls came out on the roads, resplendent in colourful clothes to welcome the Indians.

As the festivity mounted in the city, behind closed doors and shuttered windows huddled the pro-Pakistan elements. They were caught unawares by the surrender and could not take the precaution of going into hiding. The wiser among them had already moved to places of safety, but many more were trapped hopelessly in flimsy houses surrounded outside by thousands of frenzied people. They now awaited their fate. Some of them were saved by the Red Cross, some by Bengali friends and others, while a few managed to escape. But many more were caught by the mobs and either marched to jails or massacred.

Many of the *Razakars* and *Al Badr* elements fared worse. Ignorant of the surrender, some had surprisingly reported for duty on the morning of 17 December and were actually seen on guard duty when furious crowds caught and slaughtered them. Members of the Muslim League, the Jamaat, JUI etc. also suffered a similar fate. Scores of them were methodically hunted down from 17 onwards as they tried to make desperate efforts to go underground or escape to Burma. The great inquisition had started.

The Biharis and other *mohajirs* who lived in the city moved into huge refugee colonies in the suburbs of Chittagong. Others who were stranded in isolated pockets became victims of the killings. Bangladesh was a reality and the days of miracles had gone.

The Guilt Syndrome: Who Wants to Know the Truth?

9 September 1972

Iqbal Khan

FACED with the self-righteous babble that is constantly pouring out in Pakistani press on the subject of the military action in Bengal and subsequent events, one's first reaction is to say nothing. For one knows that reason alone is powerless to combat irrationality of this kind, whose roots lie deep in our social structures and in the long spiritual deprivation of our people.

There must be few events in history which were so extensively and thoroughly reported in the world press and other media as were the last year's events in Bengal. Not only were they published in Britain, but *independently* in America, Canada, France, Japan, Hongkong, Australia to name only the principal countries; not only in papers that thrive on sensationalism, but in the world's most highly respected papers, like *New York Times, Washington Post, The Observer, The Sunday Times, The Times, Le Monde*, again to name only a few.

There were photographs, television films, personal accounts of people of various nationalities who at the time happened to be in East Pakistan. But above all, there were circumstantial and eye witness reports—not from any one source but from *many different* sources. All told the same tale, testifying to the unbelievable fanaticism, and arrogance of Pakistani personnel and the cold-blooded calculations with which the 'mopping up' in East Pakistan was carried out.

Then there was the report—a harrowing document that!—of the World Bank, which the American President of the Bank, McNamara, tried unsuccessfully to suppress. (It is a question that Pakistanis never ask, but it lies at the heart of the whole affair; who are the friends of Pakistan—those who in that tragedy supported and tried to whitewash the acts of men who suppressed our freedom and committed such heinous crimes, or those who helped to expose them and thwart their ugly designs?)

And then finally there was evidence in flesh and blood in the form of the exodus of millions of Bengali men, women, and children (strange, isn't it? that when people talk self-righteously about India's invasion of East Pakistan and her flouting the international law, no one seems to remember or think much of these millions of refugees who were deliberately pushed over the border into India to create for her a political, economic, and administrative crisis of the first magnitude!). If our men were not committing the atrocities they were accused of, what were these poor, destitute millions fleeing from? From what horror, what calamity were they trying to escape? Listen to this:

> Anyone who goes to the camps and hospitals along India's border with Pakistan comes away believing the atrocity stories. I have seen babies who have been shot, men who have had their backs whipped raw. I have seen people literally struck dumb by the horror of seeing their children murdered in front of them or their daughters dragged off into sexual slavery … My personal reaction is one of wonder more than anything else. I have seen too many bodies to be horrified by anything much any more…
> (*Newsweek*, 28 June).

And this is only a tiny fraction of what was reported. But all this—huge, palpable body of evidence—is put in doubt, not only for the illiterate fanatics that abound in Pakistan, but also for the liberals and the enlightened. By what? What are the grounds for suspicion? For such overwhelming evidence to be treated with reserve and scepticism, the grounds for suspicion will have to be very weighty indeed. So, in what impartial documents, reports and other concrete evidence is the scepticism of our Pakistani liberals founded? On reports and explanations emanating from Yahya and his government?—that would be too laughable for words! On the basis of 'news' published in the thoroughly controlled and servile Pakistan press?—that, too, would be no less ludicrous. Where then is the counter-evidence on the strength of which Miss Daskawie (*Outlook*, 24 June) and others are so sure that what appeared in the foreign press was largely anti-Pakistani propaganda.

('It is true', says Miss Daskawie, 'that foreign propaganda was definitely anti-Pakistani in bias.')

There really is no counter-evidence worth the name—only suspicions, surmises, prejudices and—here is the real reason, if 'reason' it can be called—an uncritical belief in the greatness and goodness of one's own country and nation that is typical of backward minds. Our liberals and socialists alike are underneath as fanatically 'patriotic' as any reactionary. They refuse to believe Pakistan can ever be or do anything wrong. It follows that if anybody criticizes Pakistan, he must be a liar, or an enemy of Pakistan; there must be some dishonourable, ulterior reason for his 'anti-Pakistani' attitude.

And lo and behold, a dishonourable reason is soon discovered. If the American press mentioned something about West Pakistanis being prejudicial against the darker skinned Bengalis, is it not because the Americans have a guilt complex about their own racial prejudice? If they gave so much attention to the massacre of unarmed people in East Pakistan, is it not because their conscience is troubled about their own atrocities in Vietnam? And the reason why the British press was so concerned about the plight of Bengalis is of course obvious: 'Britain is trying to relive its imperial past!' And also, of course, don't you know that the British press is controlled by the Jews, who have connections with Israel, who is the enemy of the Arabs, with whom we are related as Muslims? And frankly the whole of the Christian world is against us because it hasn't forgotten the crusades…

Thus have our 'patriots' clutched at every feeblest shadow of a straw to save the 'honour'—not the honour of the people—but the honour of a crassly stupid dictator and of a military-bureaucratic establishment which, like a predatory monster, has for a quarter of a century devoured the best part of our country's wealth, destroyed our independence, crushed our liberties, grossly distorted our values, and forced the majority of our people to live in grinding poverty, physically and mentally crippled by disease and ignorance. Such are our liberals, democrats, and socialists!

Those of us who believe the western press are not exactly fools. If anything we are more sensitive than Miss Daskawie and other liberals to the pressures of big business and the consumer society on the information media—how capitalist-imperialist ideologies can suppress and distort facts. But we also know that there are limits to such distortions and that if there is any press in the world that generally tells the truth and can and often does defy the pressures of governments and big business, it is the western press. We know that papers like *The Times, The Sunday Times, The New York Times*, etc. rarely carry 'propaganda' for their governments, even though they may be, and are, committed to upholding a particular system and its values. We know that when a reported fact is corroborated by other reports on such a scale as were the events in East Bengal, and not only in a general way but in specific detail, then this is really as much as can be expected in this imperfect world to establish its authenticity.

We also know that far from carrying government propaganda, many of the newspapers that reported events in Bengal have been pronouncedly anti-government and anti-establishment. Think, for example, of the relentless and continuing criticizing of the US Vietnam policies by *The New York Times*; think of the Pentagon papers and Anderson papers in *Washington Post*; think of the spontaneous and devastating criticizm [*sic*] in the British press of the Heath government's deal with Ian Smith, which did so much to ruin that ignominious deal; think of *The Sunday Times'* courageous exposure of the British army's brutalities in Ulster.

We also know that the fact that the British government's and British firms' interests are so intimately involved in Ceylon and with its establishment, did not cause the British press to suppress the accounts of the sordid massacre of thousands of communist youth and peasants by the Bandaranaike government roughly at the same time as the tragedy in Bengal was being enacted; that despite the close links British government and big business have with the Shah of Iran and the King of Jordan, British papers have not hesitated to report the summary killings and torture of the Marxist rebels in Iran, nor the massacre of the *fedayeens* by the Hussein government; that despite the intimate links with the Jewish capital and Israel, *The Times* and the *Observer* (whose board of governors includes a Rothschild) defiantly exposed the torture which the Israeli government was carrying out on Arab prisoners; nor did the British press hesitate to tell the world of the torture which the British army carried out on nationalist rebels in Aden.

We also know that the same *Times* and *Sunday Times* that were so prominent in reporting the horrors in East Pakistan also took the lead in highlighting the brutalities committed by Bengalis on

Biharis last year and the plight of the latter more recently. (*Outlook* has readily reproduced *Hazel-hursts'* report on Biharis; would it not be a good idea to reproduce also some of his despatches last year?).

To argue that this tendency of the western press towards objectivity and honesty gives way to one prejudice or another whenever it comes to Pakistan, is to give Pakistan a significance in the world and history which might (and does) exist in chauvinist Pakistanis' imagination, but has no relation to reality. There remains the question of the motive behind the military action in East Pakistan and the responsibility for it.

Naturally, the Yahya regime and the Punjabi-dominated military-cum-civil service establishment could not be expected to say that military action was taken basically to retain power. But could there be any doubt about it? Could anyone who knows the 25 years' history of the suppression of democracy in Pakistan have any doubt that this suppression was absolutely necessary. If power—and especially the power to appropriate the country's wealth and foreign aid—were to remain in West Pakistani hands; and that this suppression and this retention of power was carried out successfully *only* because the army (claiming as it did 60% share of the country's revenues and much, much else) had a big stake in it, and, in any case; since 1958 was the sole ruler of Pakistan?

It was equally natural, and entirely expected, that if the movement for democracy was to be suppressed by the Yahya regime it should be done in the name of 'national integrity'—in order 'to save Pakistan'. The strange thing is that this kind of balderdash was accepted not only by the reactionary sections of the society but also by the liberals (and 'socialists'.) How could the liberals so unhesitatingly give their assent to any nonsense that was put forward by way of explanation by a dictator? Why didn't they come out in the streets and tell the government: Whatever your reasons, you will not get our support because your whole existence is unconstitutional and you have not been given the right to take any action on our behalf? What's the worth of such liberals and democrats who kick aside their democratic ideas the moment they hear someone shout 'the country', 'the nation!'

But let us look at the explanations given by the junta for its military action. Now, actually, there wasn't just one but several explanations (yet another fact that should have aroused suspicion. But not for our liberals and socialists! They are only too ready to question the veracity of the enormous evidence produced by foreign press, but swallowed whole every nonsense, contradiction, and inconsistency put out by the Yahya government).

One story circulated by the government was that there was a conspiracy hatched by Awami League, with the support of India; to dismember Pakistan, and the Pakistan army had to act to forestall this. This is a story indeed. Ever since Pakistan came into existence we have been hearing of such conspiracies. Do we not know how every popular movement in East Pakistan was crushed on the pretext that it was a 'conspiracy' hatched with Indian support? Yet during the 25 long years not a tiny shred of evidence has ever been produced to support this accusation! Given this experience, only fools and lackeys of the junta could accept such an explanation.

The second story was that the Awami League had prepared an armed uprising for the morning of 26 March and that the army's was a pre-emptive action. Now, had there been any thought of a military uprising on the part of Awami League, is it conceivable that Mujibur Rahman would have been left totally unguarded, as he in fact was, on the night of 25? How could one explain the almost complete absence of serious resistance on the night of 25? That the military action did not take place in response to any immediate danger is proved by the fact that on Yahya's side military preparations were going on for *quite some time*. PIA planes had been taken off their normal routes and were being used to transport army personnel to Dacca; shiploads of personnel and weapons were arriving in East Pakistani ports (in fact the Bengali port workers had refused to unload these ships) and Governor Ahsan had been replaced by Tikka Khan early in March—is it not clear that it was the Pakistani army, not the Awami League, that was preparing to strike? Moreover, what need could there be for the Awami League to attempt an armed uprising since, so far as they knew, the last stages of talks with Yahya Khan had gone well; on 24 March the Awami League had accepted amendments proposed by the government party and Mr Bhutto and were waiting for the signing of the formal draft. The third and widely accepted story goes that the army action was taken to stop the killing of Biharis, and to restore law and order.

Now, first, it is impossible to believe that such killings could not have been stopped and the situation could not have been controlled by ordinary methods and that in order to deal with the situation, Mujib had to be arrested (why was he branded as a 'traitor' if the reason for military action was to stop communal massacre?), the whole of East Pakistan had to be put under military rule, and a reign of terror of unprecedented ferocity had to be unleashed.

Secondly, if the atrocities against Biharis did occur, the possibility cannot be ruled out that they were deliberately provoked and engineered by the government itself. Indeed, having been cornered as the military rulers were, this is just the kind of mischief they would have done. In any case, the violence against Biharis—was it not the direct consequence of the repeated deception of the Bengalis by the junta and West Pakistani politicians, and of the murder of Bengalis? It must not be forgotten that on 5 March, many hundred Bengalis had been killed when an unarmed crowd was fired upon in Dacca. If that was not provocation, what is it?

The real reason for military action was, however, quite different and arose, as has already been suggested, out of the Junta's reluctance to hand over power to the Bengalis. This had always been the stumbling block on the road to democracy. Yahya had perhaps genuinely tried to see if democracy could be restored without surrendering real power to the Bengalis. But the Bengalis' majority in the country and in the National Assembly were brute facts. While he wriggled this way and that the democratic movement and militancy in East Pakistan escalated to such a degree that the restoration of democracy, autonomy of East Pakistan, and therefore the loss of power of Punjabi-dominated army and bureaucracy became inevitable and could not have been stopped by the usual show of force.

So Yahya decided for the 'final solution'—to put an end to this problem once and for all. The method was (i) to kill off the whole section of the Bengali intellectuals who were the backbone of the

Awami League and the real force behind the demand for political and economic autonomy. That is why on the night of 25 March when the action started, its targets were the university and the middle class areas (not where the massacre of Biharis was alleged to have occurred!) Students, scholars, doctors, [and] lawyers were picked out (identified by Bihari informants) and shot in their homes. Even the last glorious act performed in East Bengal, before surrendering to Indian army, was to call out from their homes 250 Bengali intellectuals and shoot them *en masse*! (ii) to butcher as many as possible and push the rest out of Bengal so that East Pakistan could not claim a majority in any future democratic assembly. Crude and horrible? Yes—but it is true.

The Sunday Times reported:

The government's policy for East Bengal as spelled out to me at Dacca has three elements:

(1) The Bengalis have proved themselves 'unreliable' and must be ruled by West Pakistanis.

(2) The Bengalis will have to be re-educated along proper Islamic lines. The 'Islamization of the masses'—this is the official jargon—is intended to eliminate secessionist tendencies and provide a strong religious bond with West Pakistan.

(3) When the Hindus have been eliminated by death and flight, their property will be used as a golden carrot to win over the under-privileged Muslim middle class. This will provide the base for erecting administrative and political structures in the future.

Yes, this is the horrible truth. But what Parveen Daskawie and other liberals really want is not the truth—it is now hardly hidden—but reassurance, reassurance that their abject surrender to vulgar chauvinism and dictatorship in those dark days, when their voices of protest and defiance could have saved Pakistan such humiliation and catastrophe, was somehow justified. This reassurance they are never going to get.

Our Guilt

9 September 1972

A. A. Akmut

NATIONS which succeed in the fulfilment of their national aspirations seldom are accused of crimes. It is only they that fail which are put in the dock. Now that voices are being raised to talk of our guilt in Bangladesh, it is this well-known fact of history which comes into play.

Let us look at a few examples from harsh reality. The Belgians perpetrated monstrous crimes on the inhabitants of the Congo, so much so that the international community, in 1908, intervened. But Belgium kept her hold over the ravaged land, she was successful and there was no cry about guilt.

The bombings of German civilian targets during the Second World War, the nuclear devastation wrought in Japan, evoked a mild reaction: but they were the doings of the victors. And if now voices are being raised even in the United States of America against the involvement in Vietnam, it is for one reason: that the policy of intervention has been unsuccessful.

Guilty are those who sit at the losing end. No nation has willingly allowed itself to be dismembered. All have offered resistance to such attempts, have fought bloody wars to foil them, have shouldered great hardships on the march to the goal of national unity. The American civil war proves it. And nobody puts the northern states on trial for it. We read of great battles, of marches and of deployment of armies. And there is but little mention of the scorched earth tactics which General Sherman employed while invading the South to bring the Confederacy down. But, of course, he carried the victorious colours.

We must keep these things in mind while judging the army action of 1971 in East Pakistan, it was carried out to preserve national unity and integrity. And now the accusers are creeping forward, raising a little finger and even a hoarse whisper. They go on record condemning what they call atrocities committed on an unarmed civilian population.

There is no war without cruelty and destruction. They that condemn the action of 1971 because they hold very sincere convictions should then come forward and denounce war in principle. Let them raise the call for unilateral, unconditional disarmament. One may disagree with them about the reasonableness of such a view; one cannot but honour them for the courage of their convictions.

The condemnation now, after our failure, is sheer intellectual cowardice. It is an undeniable fact that Yahya Khan was a usurper. He had violated the constitution which he was sworn to protect. He misappropriated to his own use all the equipment of the armed forces which is public property. He misused the lawful powers vested in him for an unlawful purpose. By arrogating to himself supreme power at the point of gun, he committed the offence of waging war against Pakistan. He subverted the loyalty of the armed forces by leading them into waging war against Pakistan. He violated the Army Act when he failed to act against the enemy with all the means at his disposal and when he cowardly ordered a surrender. He is guilty of a string of crimes under the Pakistan Penal Code as well as under the Army Act, sufficient to put him on trial and to hang him. And that is in fact what ought to be done with the criminal.

But his order to the armed forces to crack down on the secessionist elements was not a criminal act. It was an act of patriotism. A belated one, no doubt, for he should have done all that and more much earlier. Hence we are faced with the failure. But it was not a criminal act. His guilt, as far as that goes, is not that he acted, but that he acted too late, too little.

Remember the French trials of 1940, after the fall of France. The French government of the day, despairing of the massive German onslaught handed power over to Marshal Petain. He, under duress, had to accept an armistice on harsh terms. And then he put on trial his predecessors in office. Not for having declared war on Germany, but for having prepared for it poorly. Not for taking the nation into the conflict, but for doing so without having assured it first of the means necessary for the purpose. Just for this, that they had failed to do what was their duty.

If you please, the crime which Yahya Khan committed in East Pakistan was that he did less than was necessary and possible. But not the principle of taking action. The decision was correct; the execution wrong. That is his crime.

Already in 1970 when political activities restarted in Pakistan, it was clear to thinking people that the six point programme of Shaikh Mujibur Rahman and his associates was merely a scheme for secession, it was not forthright, it was fraudulent: but it was that much all the same.

The six point programme was a clear violation of the Pakistan Penal Code and thus actionable in a court of law. It is Yahya Khan's fault that he did not take the secessionists there but let them flourish. He is guilty of abetment of sedition.

The programme was also a violation of the Legal Framework Order. True, this had been promulgated illegally, but the fact that the political parties had accepted it as a basis for further political progress in the country has clad it, if not in legality, then at least in factual validity.

It was, then, Yahya Khan's duty to take a firm stand against the six points, right from 1 January 1970. Had he brought before our courts the six pointers, the ugly situation which developed later on would not have arisen. But on trial before history, he failed miserably… That is his guilt.

And ours, too.

Individually and collectively we failed to press the point home. Even the political leaders tried to make deals with the Sheikh. While all the time the fact was that he was a secessionist.

This is our collective guilt, this one thing: that we did not take a firm stand immediately secessionism raised its head; that we tried an appeasement which was foredoomed to failure; that, when the chips were down, we left the job to the armed forces, expecting that they would be able to finish it all.

The assertion that our armed forces were let loose on an unarmed peaceful population is sheer moonshine. The Awami League had prepared for a showdown from a long time. It had used outright lies, knowing them to be lies, to subvert the people ('The streets of Karachi are paved with the gold taken from Sonar Bangla, and we will bring it back'). When it felt strong enough, it offered provocations to test strength and to demonstrate its power. It intimidated political opponents. It made preparations for racial genocide, organized slaughter houses for human beings. This was no more a legitimate political movement: it was organized terror, massacre.

It was no genuine liberation movement either, being purely based on racial hatred. This is where Yahya Khan failed, that he allowed things to go out of hand. When finally he ordered the troops into action, he did no more than discharge his duty. That is no crime.

For that matter, our troops, when they counter attacked, did no more and no less than the one thing for which we have them: they, defended the integrity of the country, the unity of the nation. It may have been painful it was no doubt a bloody duty: but duty all the same, and we owe them gratitude for it, not abuses.

Let me make one thing clear: I have my own grudge against our armed forces. They followed Yahya Khan into criminality when he usurped power, they waged war against Pakistan in March 1969. There are many officers who ought to by rights be tried for that crime. But the action against the secessionists was an act of patriotism for which we ought to hold the armed forces in esteem.

There is that outcry over the blood spilt, over the women raped, over the assets destroyed. None of those who have shouted out have cared to determine first how much of all this goes to the account of the secessionists. Is the blood of a Pakistan patriot, hunted down by a gang of the secesionists, not a thousand times more dear to us than that of a gangster? Is a man murdered in a slaughter house less dead than one killed in fighting? Is a Bihari girl less raped than a Bengali girl?

But our great humanitarian minds of the day are silent on the point. They have swallowed the beautiful Indian and western propaganda, hook, line, and sinker. They do not bethink themselves of the fact that this propaganda comes out of Zionist brains, conceived to weaken Pakistan so that she should not be able to offer support to the Arabs of Palestine.

And all that talk of a massive mandate for the Awami League ... Some 70 per cent of the voters went to polls; about 60 per cent of those cast their ballot papers in favour of Awami Leaguers. All in all, Shaikh Mujibur Rahman collared less than 42 per cent of the total registered electorate. And this, too, without having it made clear to them that he wanted secession.

It is not contended that the electorate was fully committed to one united Pakistan, but in its majority it was indifferent to the six-point programme to the extent that either it voted against it or it did not care to go and vote for it. The talk of a near-unanimous Bengali desire for national independence is thus poorly founded.

It is all fine and good for Shaikh Mujibur Rahman, for his ilk, for India, for the Zionist-dominated western press, to speak of genocide and murder and arson by our forces: but coming out of the mouth and the pen of our intellectuals it has frightening consequences. It is a virtual endorsement of Shaikh Mujib's intention to put our men on trial for war crimes, it is a notice served on our armed forces that they should not, should never, should not under any circumstances, take up arms to oppose secessionists: for, if those are successful, our men will be held to be criminals for having done their duty under the law of the land.

It also amounts to declare open season on Pakistan. If a man who preaches secession is not brought to trial then and there; if those who deal with him firmly are considered to be criminals; then, I am afraid, Pakistan ceases to be a place where a Pakistani can live and breathe and work in safety. For the sake of his life and property, he will have to make common cause with secessionists at the drop of the hat, or else. This goes for every one of us, whatever his station in life.

There is a conclusion to be drawn. We are now passing into a phase where secessionist forces are gathering. They talk of their democratic rights: they claim to have the welfare of a section of the people at heart: they put forth all sorts of demands. And when one looks at them closely, they all are trying to do a Mujib.

Parochialism must be dealt with severely, it is our right to demand this of the government. It is also our duty. Anything that now further threatens the unity and integrity of this, our beloved land, has to be stamped out. And anybody who promotes such activities is a traitor. We have been guilty once. Let us not repeat the same guilt again, or else there will be no Pakistan left.

Akbar Bugti speaks up—What Mujib told him

16 September 1972

Hamida Khuhro

Q. You must be aware of your reputation as an uncompromising and somewhat impractical nationalist. How would you describe yourself?

A. I am a nationalist, I hope, whether uncompromising or impractical I cannot say. Sometimes certain things appear impractical to some people and to others they are not impractical. It is a difference of opinion. I hope nevertheless that I am a nationalist.

Q. An idealist?

A. A touch of idealism too, perhaps. More idealism than expediency.

Q. What are the influences that have shaped your political views?

A. It has been a slow process over a period of years. In my schooldays I was attracted by the Congress programme of non-co-operation and 'Quit India' and although I could not fully grasp the implications of these movements I supported them through 1942–45. We were somehow more aware of the Congress movement than of the Muslim League.

I was under the guardianship of Allama I. I. Kazi in those years. My father had died when I was very young and Allama Sahib was like a father to me. Actually my youth was spent in the company of Sindhi intellectuals, Dr Daudpota and Mr Brohi were my tutors and I was greatly influenced by them.

At the time of independence a referendum was held in Baluchistan in which members of the Shahi Jirga and Quetta municipality participated. The overwhelming majority of the members voted for Pakistan. After independence there was agitation in Baluchistan for constitutional reform and eventually an Advisory Council consisting of two members was constituted to assist the A.G.G. The first advisors to be appointed for a term of one year were Qazi Isa and Noor Mahommed Gola. The next year, 1951, Arbab Karam Khan Kansi and myself were appointed advisors. Previous to this I had been to the C.S.P. Academy in Lahore for a year for training in administration. Soon however, plans were afoot for the formation of one unit and before that came into being, Advisory Councils etc. were all dissolved.

In the Constituent Assembly, Baluchistan had one seat. We decided that we should avoid conflict between Baluchis and Pathans and that the seat should be held alternately by Baluchis and Pathans. The electoral college consisted of the Shahi Jirga and the Quetta Municipality. For the first term we selected a Pathan, Nawab Jogezai. When his term ended, we naturally expected the seat to go to a Baluchi but Iskander Mirza put up Dr Khan Sahib. I opposed this scheme and appealed to Dr Khan Sahib to withdraw but the appeal had no effect and Dr Khan Sahib was elected with the support of the government. When he was unseated through an election petition, the government changed the composition of the electoral college and made the members of the National Assembly the new electoral college. Nevertheless I campaigned against Dr Khan Sahib and inspite of all the government pressures succeeded in getting 18 votes against his 20. Dr Khan Sahib remained the member from Baluchistan until his death. In 1958 I was elected to the National Assembly and was Minister for interior before the Ayub-Mirza coup of October 1958. Actually the day before the coup I had changed portfolios with your father—he was given Interior and I had got Defence. I remember I went to see him on the evening of 7 to talk about the situation and we decided not to go to office the next day but await the events. In the night the military takeover took place.

Q. Could you explain how the trouble began in Baluchistan that resulted in that long drawn struggle?
A. The Kalat business had been building up. The Khan wanted some recognition of status for the state and some autonomy. Mirza encouraged him and told the Khan that he was willing to recognize status and autonomy for Kalat but he had to convince the government and for this he had to have money and a show of force from Kalat. The Khan replied that he could not give money as he had none. Money would be provided by Bahawalpur but he could make a show of force—which he did. Mirza, however, had other plans and encouraging the Khan was a part of his scheme to give an appearance of chaos in the country. The newspapers played up to him in a vociferous campaign that Kalat was about to rebel. Mirza asked the Khan to come to Karachi but under secret instructions from Mirza himself, the Khan refused to come. I offered to go and fetch him in order to avoid further trouble, but Mirza would not let me go and said that in two days, it would be too late. I could see then that he had some ulterior plan, and sure enough two days later the Khan was arrested and two days after that martial law was declared.

The Khan was arrested but the trouble spread and Nawab Naoroze Khan gathered a huge *lashkar* in the mountains of Jhalawan. A whole army division was sent against him, the G.O.C. and Brigadier Riaz Hussain were put in charge. For six months a full scale campaign was conducted with aerial bombardment and many Baluch lives were lost. The discontent continued to spread and other tribes joined the resistance. The government answer was mass arrests. A concentration camp was set up in Quetta cantonment known as the *Coolie* camp where even tortures of the most inhuman kind were resorted to. After six months Naoroze Khan was induced to surrender under the oath of the Holy Quran that he and his followers would be given amnesty. Naoroze Khan was royally received in the army camp but as soon as all his followers had surrendered, they were put in irons and taken to the concentration camp, and repression continued. Bizenjo and Gul Khan were in the camp and many people not directly involved in the resistance. Incidents continued all over Baluchistan. I was arrested on a murder charge and taken to Coolie camp where I remained for four months. Naoroze Khan was tried along with his relatives and immediate followers and seven of them were sentenced to death and seven to life imprisonment including Naoroze Khan himself. Special military courts were set up and many people were tried and sentenced. A special military court was set up for me and a trial was held. I was given the death sentence and Rs. 5 lakhs fine confirmed by the chief martial law administrator. After reading out this sentence, the presiding judge looked at me and paused—I was told later that I had a smile on my face—and then continued that the chief martial law administrator had graciously reduced this to life imprisonment. I was taken to Hyderabad jail where some of Naoroze Khan's people were also taken, others having been taken to Sukkur. Altogether seven of Naoroze Khan's family, one son and seven others, were executed.

After about 20 months in jail (about mid '61), I was released on a suspended sentence and had to pay Rs. 50,000 fine. While in Hyderabad jail I met Hyder Baksh Jatoi. He had been put in for five years because he had written a poem which the regime did not like. We were together for about a year. This was the first time I had come in contact with real leftist thinking—again through a Sindhi—and I was considerably influenced by him politically.

Meanwhile, hatred and discontent against the Ayub regime was growing and most of Baluchistan was under military occupation. The militia had also been sent to our areas. For the first Ayub elections in 1962 I was under a ban. There were two seats for Baluchistan. Khairbaksh (Marri) was elected from Quetta and Ataullah (Mengal) from Kalat. In the first Assembly session in Rawalpindi, Ataullah spoke and related all that had happened in Baluchistan belying Ayub's claim that it had been a bloodless coup. This speech created a sensation as most of the members heard for the first time about the events in Baluchistan—many of them said they had no idea at all of all this. The world press too was totally unaware because of the tight censorship. Khairbaksh also spoke on the same lines and my younger brother spoke in the Provincial Assembly.

He had been warned by Kalabagh that I was still under a jail sentence and I was warned as well. After the Assembly I returned to Quetta where we were to hold public *jalsas,* around 5 August. We had invited Mir Rasul Baksh Talpur and others. Ayub was to address a meeting in Quetta on 6 August and we were to hold a second meeting on 7 August. The administration tried to cow us and told us not to hold meetings, but we went ahead. My friends would not let me speak but others made fiery speeches. Demands were made for a public enquiry into the Baluchistan happenings and other matters of concern. These were addressed to Ayub who was to speak the next day. The only reply Ayub made to us in his speech the next day was a reference to me:

یہاں ایک سابقہ سیاستدان ہے جس نے جرم کیا اور جس کو سزائے موت ملا پھر میں نے مہربانی کر کے عمر قید میں تبدیل کیا۔ پھر اس کو چھوڑ دیا۔ وہ میری مہربانیوں کو نہیں سمجھ رہا ہے۔ اس نے کرائے کے مقررین لاکر میرے اور میرے آئین کے خلاف جدوجہد کر رہا ہے۔ اسے معلوم ہونا چاہیے کہ اس کو میں پھر اندر کر سکتا ہوں۔

These were almost exactly his words. Every one expected I would be taken in immediately. The next day thousands turned up at our *jalsa* and Kalabagh came in a closed jeep and stood listening to our speeches from a school opposite the meeting ground. We were very angry, of course, and the speakers really let loose the fury in their hearts.

After that we were invited by Baluch groups in Karachi to hold a meeting. Meanwhile orders were issued by the government externing a number of leaders from Baluchistan. We gathered in Karachi but our *jalsa* was not allowed to be held and was broken up by the police. A new date was arranged—21 August, I think. On the morning of 21 August, I was arrested, my suspension having been set aside. The order was signed by the deputy martial law administrator, General Musa. The *jalsa* was held nevertheless, at Kakri ground in Karachi. Khairbaksh and my brother spoke without restraint—the police could not perhaps understand them because they spoke in Baluchi, otherwise they would certainly have been hauled up for sedition, I was taken to Lyallpur jail and a week later Ataullah and many others were arrested. Sher Mohammed Marri, who had been exiled from Baluchistan, had orders for arrest issued against him. He reappeared in Baluchistan hills and organized guerilla bases. Sher Mohammed is an old socialist and his methods were scientific. His organization spread through Jhalawan all through eastern Baluchistan. It was, however, very slow work and it took him about a year and a half to build it up. Sher Mohammed was the head of the eastern command and Ali Mohammed Mengal the head of western command.

The army operations against the Baluch were again on a very large scale. General Tikka was put in charge in the beginning of 1963. The army moved towards Jhalawan carrying through a 'pacification' policy—something like Vietnam—cutting off food and water supplies, burning villages, aerial bombardment and so on. We were a little slow in organizing ourselves. The fight started from Jhalawan somewhat haphazardly, but gradually Sher Mohammed moved to Marri areas proper[ly] and organized the Marri and the Bugti and all eastern Baluchistan. Kalabagh was bent on crushing Baluchistan. The Chiefs were deposed officially, Khairbaksh, Ataullah, and myself. The government appointees were all killed by their own tribesmen. The trouble spread to adjoining areas and there was general lawlessness, brigandry etc. The situation thus created was naturally favourable to us. An underground newspaper *Spark* (after Lenin's *Iskra*) was produced in Baluchi, English, and Urdu. Some copies of this paper were sent to East Pakistan where they were reproduced in Bengali and distributed widely.

By the beginning of 1967, the government decided that the policy of repression was becoming counter productive and reconciliation might be tried. Bizenjo was released and when Ayub and Kalabagh fell out, Bizenjo was supported by Kalabagh in the elections in Karachi and won against Ayub's candidate. Soon after that Musa came as governor and announced a general amnesty. Twelve or thirteen hundred people were released, Musa came to Quetta to meet us. The government wanted 'normalization' of its relationship with the Baluch people. They wanted to 'reinstate' us as Chiefs. We replied that we had been *Sardars* all along—there was no question of 'reinstatement'. The government wanted some kind of ceremonial laying down of arms which we refused to do. Our point was that arms were always normally carried by Baluch tribesmen and therefore they could not be given up— moreover we already had the experience of Naoroze Khan behind us. The result was that we were accused of not cooperating and harrassment began again. In Quetta, the military surrounded a student hostel on the pretext that they were expecting trouble between Baluchis and Punjabis and fired about 4,000 rounds on the building killing some Baluch and Pathan students. There was trouble in the Pat feeder area. In May 1968, I was arrested again and taken to Mianwali jail. Gul Khan Naseer was with me at the time. He was also held on the charge that he had a frown on his face when I was being arrested. For this offence he was given three years. Bizenjo was arrested because he had a currency note in his pocket with this slogan written on it:

ون یونٹ توڑ دو۔ بلوچستان کے حق دو۔

Once again there was fighting in the Bugti areas and in Upper Sind, canals were breached, trains were looted and so on. Abdul Samad Achakzai who had been released after serving his full sentence of 14 years was arrested again.

Meanwhile events were moving fast in the rest of the country. Agitation against Ayub gathered strength, Bhutto was arrested, and finally after widespread disturbances, Ayub called the Round Table Conference. Mujib, Bhutto, and all of us were released. A number of us from Baluchistan went to Rawalpindi. It was soon apparent, however, that nothing would come of it, and we returned to Baluchistan.

With the reimposition of martial law and the subsequent breakup of one unit administration, General Riaz Hussain was appointed governor of Baluchistan. Naturally there was resentment in Baluchistan. None of us would meet him. When the army was taking action in East Pakistan, we learnt that proposals had been made to the Yahya government by the Baluchistan authorities i.e. General Riaz Hussain, that 'pre-emptive' action should be taken in Baluchistan. A list was prepared of several leading figures of the province and it was suggested that all those on the list should be immediately executed and that the mistake of East Pakistan should not be repeated. I believe that I was on top of this list with Bizenjo as number two. There was apprehension in Baluchistan and the people prepared for defence—the government feared rebellion. It seems however that the government decided to wait until it was free of operations in the east. It did not want two civil wars going on at the same time. The rest is, of course, recent history.

Q. You have, of course, spent a long time in jail including long periods of solitary confinement, C class jail in some of the toughest jails of Pakistan. I believe you were on hunger strike once for over five months. Has jail had any important impact on your character or views?

A. I have spent seven and a half years in jail. Jail either makes or breaks a man. It has not broken me but it has probably steeled me.

Q. What made you join the NAP? What was it in its programme that attracted you?

A. I have never been a member of NAP. Ataullah, Khairbaksh, and myself had never been members of NAP, although Bizenjo is an old member. Ataullah and I had been in jail for long periods. Khairbaksh joined, I think, in 1963 or 1964. Then, when we were released finally in 1969 Ataullah joined. I have never formally joined. I was under a ban under Yahya's Legal Framework Order, as I had been in prison over two years. Achakzai was also under a similar ban but his ban was removed when he applied to the government. In the end I think I was the only man left in Pakistan under L.F.O. ban.

Q. What is your present relationship with the NAP leadership in Baluchistan?

A. I have always been a sympathiser and *dua-go* that is to say until very recently. Our close association came to an end sometime in February this year. We have some basic differences now which I think I had better leave unsaid.

Q. What is your relationship with Wali Khan?

A. I have no differences with Wali Khan. We are friends. I have great respect and admiration for him and his family.

Q. How well do you know Shaikh Mujibur Rahman? Do you think he was sincere in wanting Pakistan to survive or do you think his object was separation?

A. I have known Mujib for many years—from about 1956. I think he wanted very much that Pakistan should survive. He resisted until the end demands for declaration of independence from the extremists in his party. Naturally he wanted the fullest possible autonomy for the eastern wing.

Q. You have had several meetings with Mujib when he was in London recently. Could you say what is his general attitude to Pakistan and does he see any future relationship between the two countries?

A. Yes, I met Mujib three times when he was in London. We had fairly long discussions about various matters—our difficulties, his difficulties, and how they were to be resolved. He was somewhat unhappy about Pakistan's failure to recognize Bangladesh. As regards relationship between Pakistan and Bangladesh, his opinion was that things would have been very different if Pakistan had recognized Bangladesh with his release or soon after. Every day that passes anger and frustration grows in his people *vis a vis* West Pakistan. They feel that after all that has passed—the bloodbath, the tragic events following the army intervention—Pakistan has done nothing to mitigate the past—to make amends of any kind, and not recognizing only adds insult to injury. If Pakistan extends recognition, then there is a chance that the countries can come closer together.

Q. Is Mujib determined to hold the war trials?

A. Yes—he says that trials should and will be held of those responsible for the atrocities committed. He says that if the situation is looked at legally, his is the legitimate government as he is the leader of the overwhelming majority in the country—i.e., of both wings.

Q. What would be his attitude in case of China's vetoing Bangladesh entry into the UN?

A. He was expecting that China might use the veto. In that case he felt that the position of his people would harden further *vis a vis* Pakistan and there would be no question of the release of POWs. He would also consider what counter steps to take.

Q. Do you think democracy could have worked in Pakistan if the army had not intervened in March 1971?

A. I think so—with East Pakistan included in Pakistan, there was every possibility. If power had been transferred to the majority party, democracy would certainly have worked.

Q. What do you think are the basic problems facing Pakistan today—what do you think are the chances and conditions of its survival?

A. The basic problem is the question of nationalities, besides the economic and labour problems, etc. Actually political and economic exploitation is linked. If we can settle the problem of nationalities, then Pakistan is saved. It is not impossible if there is a will to solve it.

Q. How can the confidence of the smaller provinces be restored?

A. By the acceptance of the fact that Pakistan is a multinational state. There are four nationalities with their own language, tradition, culture, history etc. These nationalities should get together for their mutual benefit on the basis of equality and decide to live together as a federal state. The four nationalities would be the federating units. These federating units would then decide what powers they wish to keep and what they wish the centre to have, i.e. defence, foreign affairs and currency would be given to the central government and of course any other powers that the units decide should go to the centre. The rest should belong unquestionably to the units. There should be no overlapping of authority, no interference whatsoever from one area in another and with each other's powers. There should be two Houses—one House of Representatives on population basis and one House of Nationalities with equal representation for each federating unit. The House of Nationalities should have enough powers to ensure that the majority in the House of Representatives is not used to take any action or pass any legislation against the wishes or interests and constitutional rights of any federating unit. In fact there should be adequate checks and balances.

Q. What guarantee would Sind have, for instance, in the matter of a fair share of the Indus waters?

A. There will have to be guarantees in the constitution, and these will have to be practical and workable, not only on paper. The Upper House will have to act as a watchdog.

Q. Do you think that with the army being overwhelmingly from one province, such guarantees can be realistic?

A. If 'confrontation' with our neighbours ends, the armed forces can be reduced to suit our needs, and also greater representation can be given to different regions in the armed forces. These steps will reduce mistrust of the forces in the country.

Q. If there is another army coup, do you think the country would break up or survive?

A. The danger would be there that the country might break up. People in the smaller provinces are fearful of such a development especially in view of what has happened in Baluchistan in the past and in Bangladesh more recently. There would be no trust on either side.

Q. If Pakistan disintegrates what shape do you think is likely to emerge in this region?

A. God forbid—if Pakistan breaks up we in Baluchistan would be the worst off because we would be the centre of big power pulls and pressures as indeed all of Pakistan will be too. Baluchistan might even lose its identity.

Q. What do you think of a possible confederation with India?

A. If we manage to normalize relations with India, remove mutual fear and distrust, and remove sources of friction there is no reason why ourselves, India, and Bangladesh should not come very close for mutual benefit. Actual forms of cooperation can be decided as the situation arises. I do not much care for labels of any kind.

Q. What do you think is the future of socialism in our part of the world?

A. It seems that socialism is going ahead with leaps and bounds all over the east—the third world. Eventually India, Pakistan, and Bangladesh and surrounding states are likely to become socialist. It's only a matter of time I think.

Q. Can you see a Maoist type revolutionary movement in which non-urban areas like Baluchistan and the countryside of Sind will give a lead and even achieve revolution regardless of the isolated faction-ridden bourgeoisie-dominated urban areas of the country?

A. I think so. We are not really an industrial country and a Maoist type of popular mass movement composed of the peasantry, shepherds, and tribesmen and so on will have to be the backbone of any movement if it has to be a really revolutionary movement and if it is to succeed. There are already forces at work in this direction—they don't have proper organization at the moment but progressively such movements will become better organized.

Q. Would you say that regional autonomy and emancipation of backward nationalities is a basic prerequisite before any countrywide movement for socialism?

A. Yes—it is at least a first step, if objective conditions are ripe then some steps can be eliminated—but again the nationalities question is interlinked with socialism. If you want to achieve socialism, you have to cater to the rights and needs of the nationalities.

Q. What lead can Baluchistan give us with its history of struggle against dictatorship and centralism?

A. I think we have been giving a lead for some years inspite of our 'backwardness', lack of education, small numbers, and other disadvantages. There is political awakening even in the mind of a shepherd in Baluchistan. He does not know the details and the complicated aspects of the question but he knows he is not free and master in his own home. He feels that he is exploited and that he must get rid of the exploiter.

Q. Whom does he see as his enemy—does he see the *Sardar* as his enemy or some outside force?

A. Perhaps that cannot be easily defined. To begin with, the *Sardar* or Chief is certainly the tool of the exploiter, but it is from that very class that people have arisen, people who have broken away from the traditional role as agents of exploiters and have brought about this awakening among the people. That is our experience.

Q. How do you see the relationship between Sind and Baluchistan?

A. Sind and Baluchistan have always been very close. A very large part of the population in Sind is Baluch—that is those who have migrated from Baluchistan and settled in Sind. This movement of people goes on to this day. Whenever there is a famine or drought and a 100 families move to Sind, 70 or 75 families out of these may return, the rest are likely to settle down in Sind. They consider themselves one with the people and there is no friction. Majority of the Baluch are bilingual; they speak Sindhi as well as Baluchi. Linguistically and culturally we are very close. In fact we could really be one country and one people.

Q. What is your opinion of the language troubles in Sind recently?

A. As I said before I believe there are four nationalities in Pakistan and some sub-groups too. So far as Sind is concerned in the recent troubles, no efforts were made on either side to come close to each other. Urdu speakers, since they have settled in Sind, should make efforts to become one with the people—which they have not done so far. Even now if both sides make efforts, harmony can be restored. Settlers should merge as Baluchis have done. They will then lead a happier life and there will be no friction.

Q. What do you think of the reported split in the NAP?

A. I am looking at it from an independent point of view and from outside Pakistan. I have not been in touch with events very closely for some months. The split would be bad for the party and it would be weakened. But then again if the party is not along the right lines, then this action would expose any deviation. The situation is still confused and I don't know all the details. The NAP had built up some kind of image before the people which seems to be crumbling now.

Q. You are perhaps aware of the press propaganda against you and the accusations of being anti-Pakistan etc. Would you like to say anything in clarification or add anything to what you have said?

A. I have been continually misrepresented by the Punjabi chauvinistic press or the Punjabi chauvinistic mind that does not wish to see or accept another's point of view or feelings. Either you accept their line or you are anti-state or subversive or foreign agent or what have you. They like to keep this contradiction or division alive all the time so that people are distracted from struggling for their emancipation and that different nationalities do not come together for this objective.

They have been saying that I want *Azad* Baluchistan or Greater Baluchistan but in fact I want *Azad* Pakistan where Baluchis are as *azad* as Punjabis or anyone else, and where they have equal representation and equal freedom.

Bangladesh: What Premise for a Settlement?

16 September 1972

Dr Parvez Hassan

MASSIVE national public attention has appropriately been focused on the pros and cons of the recognition of Bangladesh. Moral, political, and sometimes legal considerations are advanced to induce or explain governmental action in this regard. But overlooked, or discreetly underplayed, are the various economic factors that are undoubtedly being taken into account in the overall decision making.

Some leaders of public opinion have argued that immediate recognition would help cleanse the anti-West Pakistan venom in Bangladesh and that it would trigger off a rapprochement. To them, it could be pointed out that after recognition, Pakistan would have to address itself to questions of state succession—that is, of apportioning between West Pakistan and Bangladesh the various assets, rights, and liabilities of the Government of Pakistan. Even if both sides were then to approach these issues with good faith and in a spirit of magnanimity, a great deal of acrimony may well become unavoidable in the negotiations. The polarization of the East and West Pakistani economists on the question of economic exploitation of East Pakistan is a matter of recent record. The point is not that Pakistan will, or should, take a niggardly attitude in such negotiations. Indeed, the professional differences on merely the exploitative domination by West Pakistan may prove to be irreconcilable.

An additional factor that the government may be considering in the context of recognition may be its present inability to pass on to Bangladesh what may be found to be due to Bangladesh. Here, the *bona fides* of our government to equitably share the assets with Bangladesh may be incontestable; what may presently be inducing it to hold back recognition may be the near bankruptcy in which we find ourselves after the military adventurism in East Pakistan and the war with India. This would call for a deferring of recognition until after we are in a position to meet some of the liabilities determined or agreed to be ours.

Our staggering national debt is a matter of public knowledge. These loans were used for the various needs of both West and East Pakistan. Who is now responsible for its repayment—Pakistan or Bangladesh or both? On what basis, if any, is its apportionment to be done? Is international law on this point settled? These are some of the questions that would have to be sorted out after the recognition of Bangladesh. And it is on these points that it is feared that the venom will spread instead of being eradicated.

A preliminary point needs to be made at this stage. While dealing with the subject of state succession, it must be kept in mind that an approach that may now advantageously be taken towards the denial of certain debt liabilities may eventually compromise the government's position on a more fundamental matter. Additionally, what may at the moment seem economically expedient may indirectly open the door to economic demands against the Government of Pakistan can successfully deny its liability to repay certain debts, this may entail the following consequences:

(1) An indirect recognition of the *fait accompli* in East Pakistan because the denial would, in all likelihood, be premised on the international law principles of state succession. A necessary implication would be the recognition by the Government of Pakistan that a new 'state' has come into existence.

(2) The successful denial of a debt liability would, under international law, hinge on passing the liability in question to Bangladesh. As the liability of Bangladesh is established or agreed to, there could be invoked the 'benefits with the burdens' theory. Under this theory of state succession, one cannot be selective about the passing of rights and liabilities on changes of sovereignty. It allows a new state that accepts certain liabilities to, in turn, claim certain assets. In the present context, admission of certain debt liabilities by Bangladesh would entitle it to claim its share in the assets of the Government of Pakistan.

Concerning the general principles of state succession, international law distinguishes between various kinds of public debts. Thus it would point to a transfer of a debt liability to Bangladesh if the concerned loan had been solely or primarily used for a development project in East Pakistan. On the other hand, a loan contracted to assist the military effort against East Pakistan would hardly be expected to be owned or shared by Bangladesh. The difficulty here, of course, is deciding which public debts have been beneficially applied in or for East Pakistan. Equally loaded is status of such loans as have been 'invisibly' but beneficially applied in or for East Pakistan.

Another crucial factor in the determination of state succession questions is the fundamental distinction, between total succession and partial succession. A total succession is deemed to come about when as a result of the state succession, the debtor state ceases to exist as an international person. The debtor state, however, survives in the case of partial succession. Federations and dismemberments are examples of total successions while cessions and secessions illustrate partial succession.

Because the debtor state survives in partial succession, it is deemed to continue to be liable for the debt. This basic principle notwithstanding, there are precedents where repartition was accepted, But although such practice cannot be established to have changed the traditional international law principle of the continued liability of the debtor state, it could advantageously be cited by Pakistan.

Pakistan's case could be additionally supported by the unprecedented form of secession it has faced. The principle of the continued liability of the debtor state may be defensible when only a relatively small portion of the debtor state secedes—and indeed much of the traditional international law on the subject is founded on such cases—but where a substantial part of the territory and population secede, the rigours of international law principles can be expected to be relaxed.

Indeed, in view of the unique nature of the events that Pakistan has experienced, Pakistan could even take the position that there was in December 1971 not a 'secession' but a 'dismemberment' of Pakistan. The practice in cases of dismemberment would seem to be more favourable to our government.

While state succession doctrines may assist Pakistan's efforts to seek repartition, the working out of the basis of repartition is left entirely to the agreement between the concerned parties.

Professor D. P. O'Connell, the leading international law scholar on this subject, records a general consensus among jurists that the taxation ratio should be the basis upon which to divide the national debt. Others, he indicates, have adopted the tests of extent of territory, population, nationality of creditors, taxable value as distinct from actual revenue contributions, value of assets, contributions of the seceded area to the central administration, and any one or more combinations of these. A similar divergency of tests is to be found in treaties dealing with the subject. In some cases revenue has been the important element, but this is not a universally satisfactory test because the allocation of charges and revenue between the central treasury and the organs of local government differ from territory to territory. Since the contributions of a territory might be disproportionate to the allocations of the budget, the source, nature and locality of the revenue must all be taken into consideration. Moreover, to secure an equitable partition, the average over several years must be taken.

Professor O'Connell is also of the opinion that the extent of territory in itself is not a test, because it bears no relationship to population, wealth or revenues. Population is an important factor but it is not decisive because of a possible differentiation in prosperity between one part of a State and another. The Supreme Court of the United States, in a case concerning the division of the debt of dismembered Virginia, held that the repartition which approached nearest to justice was one based on the capital value of assets apportioned on the separation, and not on that of land or population.

The only principle, concludes Professor O'Connell, that emerges from a consideration of all the possible tests is that the distributive key must be related to the 'contributive force' of each part of dismembered territory, and this contributive force can only be realized by a consideration of all the possible influential factors. An analysis of the factors enables one to arrive at the amount of the revenue which the territory can furnish to the government for the purpose of servicing its appropriate part of the debt, after deduction of normal administrative expenses.

Notwithstanding the above, international law would seem to permit a successor state to completely deny its liability for certain 'odious debts' of the debtor state. A debt intrinsically hostile to the interests of a territory is considered 'odious'. Two types of debts have been distinguished as 'odious', those imposed on a community without its consent and contrary to its true interests, and those intended to finance the preparation or prosecution of war against the successor state, or even against other states.

But who determines whether a debt is contrary to the true interests of the successor state? If left to the successor state, objectivity cannot be assured. Sack, another international authority on this subject, has, therefore, persuasively argued that a successor state, in order to justify the invocation of the doctrine of odious debts, be required to prove, first, that the debt was contrary to the interests of the population of all or part of the seceding territory, and secondly, that the creditors were aware of this. Once these two things have been proved, the onus is upon the creditors to show that the funds have in fact been utilized for the benefit of the territory.

Thus, provided it can effectively meet the onus of proof, it may appear possible for Bangladesh to deny complete liability for certain debts on the ground that the concerned debts were contrary to its interest or furthered the military action against it.

The principles discussed above relate to the national debt. Where debts are contracted by a fiscally autonomous region, such a region, on secession, will continue to be liable for that debt. The Central Government should, accordingly, not ordinarily be held responsible for such debts as may have been contracted by the Government of East Pakistan.

It is also well established that a successor state like Bangladesh is under an obligation to respect those debts incurred in the ordinary routine of governmental administration in the territory acquired by it.

Invoking the principles of the state succession, Pakistan could develop a good case for diminishing or denying its liability for debt repayment. Although there are legion precedents that may suggest that in cases of secession, the parent state retains its duty to service its national debt, these could be distinguished on the ground that in these instances, the cession or secession related to a small part of the territory of the parent state. The extent of the loss of the territory and population of East Pakistan could well be emphasized to highlight the peculiar and unprecedented hardships in the present case.

Arguments could also be built on the premise that what we have recently experienced is 'dismemberment'. International practice and law on dismemberments point to more favourable principles that would assist the Pakistan Government in reducing its liability to repay the national debt.

Bangladesh and India: An Uneasy Alliance

23 September 1972

Dennis Walker

THE first signs of Bengali Muslim resistance to Indian ambitions broke out as early as the Pakistan 'civil war' period, when Pakistani troops still occupied Bangladesh soil. Early in August 1971, Shaikh Abu Nasser, younger brother of Shaikh Mujibur Rahman, told newsmen in New Delhi that we do not want the Indian Army marching into our territory because that will mean the end of our struggle (Radiance, New Delhi, 22 August 1971 p. 14).

The Indian response was to increase the regimentation of the Bangladesh exile government. The Indians particularly aimed to undermine the position of Khondkar Mushtaq Ahmad, Vice-President of the Awami League and Foreign Minister of the Bangladesh government—and the strong-willed Bengali nationalist around whom the resistance to India focused. Indian government pressure forced Awami League to share power with a 'broadly based consultative committee' stacked especially with such pro-Soviet East Bengali leaders as Professor Muzaffar Ahmad ... Indian supervision, however, even extended to excluding Mushtaq Ahmad, because of his politics, from heading a vital Bangladesh delegation to the United Nations. (Peter Hazelhurst 'India lures exiles for Russia' *The Times*, 7 October 1971 p. 6).

On the very eve of the Indian army's 'liberating mission' in East Pakistan, Mushtaq Ahmed, as Bangladesh Foreign Minister, continued to very clearly state that the Bangladesh people wanted to fight their own battles—they did not want an Indian invasion. (*Le Monde*: Selection Hebdomadaire, 18 November 1971 p. 4) After the formation of Bangladesh Mushtaq Ahmad was shunted away from foreign affairs to a minor portfolio in Bangladesh's first post-independence cabinet.

Invaders

Although a large section of the Bangladesh masses gave a sincere welcome to the Indian army as 'liberators', from the first a substantial minority of Bangladeshis regarded them as foreign invaders... Bengali peasants in Jessore refused to help or guide the invading Indian forces... (*Melbourne Age*, 18 December 1971, p. 6).

The Indian papers feared that the pro-Peking leftists discredited by China's support for 'the unity and integrity of Pakistan', might seek to regain lost popularity by playing on the Muslim, anti-Hindu identification of the Bangladesh masses. In other words, Indian withdrawal of troops was inspired by rising local Bengali feeling that the Indian army in Bangladesh was becoming a threat to the independence it claimed to have brought.

The increased independence and self-confidence the Indian troop withdrawals promised Mujib and his fledgling government have failed to materialize. For one thing, Indian troops almost immediately 're-entered' Bangladesh and began to operate once more against dissidents in the countryside. But another reason why the withdrawals did not give Mujib the independence he wanted was that they were quickly followed (19 March 1972) by the signing of the Indo-Bangladesh Friendship Treaty. This pact bound Bangladesh to closely coordinate all aspects of its defence, its foreign policy its economy—even its culture and literature—with Indian policies for the next 25 years.

More Discontent

The alliance with India, while temporarily strengthening Mujib's capacity to impose law-and-order, has heightened the violence of armed rebellion and public discontent in Bangladesh. For the leftists in Bangladesh, the alliance with Hindu India was a useful focus with which to rouse peasant discontent. For India the leftist opposition was almost the raison d'etre of her own overwhelming presence in post-liberation Bangladesh, the most powerful lever she had to impose her political and economic interests on Mujib.

Bangladesh's jute factories had been wrecked in the civil war or carried away by the withdrawing Indian army; so West Bengal's factories could take Bangladesh's jute crops if not by official trade then exploitatively through smuggling. In the New Delhi negotiations between the Central India and Bangladesh government for a trade agreement between the two countries, the West Bengal government especially despatched Mr Arun Moitra its Fisheries Minister to participate. His demand: Bangladesh's fish for highly urbanized West Bengal. (*The Statesman Weekly*, 1 April 1972 p. 5). By May, due to smuggling the prices of rice and fish had reached a level in Bangladesh far beyond anything the common people had known under Pakistani rule.

West Bengal's stability is so important for any Indian government and the economic advantages that the 'free-trade border' with ex-East Pakistan brings to Calcutta have acquired such self-momentum that New Delhi may not wish to stop the trend even at the price of alienating many Bangladeshis. The resentment aroused in Bangladesh had moreover made Shaikh Mujib more dependent politically (not to say economically) on India.

The situation has enabled Shaikh Mujib's foes in Bangladesh—Islamic fundamentalists or revolutionary socialists—to manoeuvre him into a position where he appears to some as the instrument of India, the last thing he wanted to be.

In his 1 April rally at Khulna he (Mujib) ordered his police to 'shoot the Naxalites down on sight' (*The Statesman Weekly*, 8 April 1972).

There lurks...

The reply to Mujib came quickly, Maulana Bhashani openly and publicly named India as the prime source of the country's post-independence problems... 'Seventy-five million people' he solemnly warned, 'who recently achieved independence from the clutches of Pakistan would not allow themselves to be dominated by India or any other power.'

By June, anti-Indian feeling in Bangladesh had reached a new height. Bangladesh papers openly branded the Indian army for the murder of innocent Bengali Muslim civilians in its operations against 'dissidents'. One paper said that 'India took more out of Bangladesh in five months than Pakistan took in 25 years.' Bernard Joseph, A.B.C. correspondent, reported from New Delhi that an alarmed Indian government had asked Shaikh Mujib to protect the Hindu minority in Bangladesh from terrorization—presumably because the minority was regarded as being primarily loyal to India. Shaikh Mujib promptly arrested four hundred Bangladeshis on charges of 'anti-Indian activities' (*The Statesman Weekly*, 24 June 1972).

The Future

The future appears gloomy, whether for Bangladesh, or for Bangladesh's relations with India. The precarious peace Pakistan and India patched up at Simla could well be endangered by anti-Indian sentiment in Bangladesh ... (And) unless the alliance with India brings tangible benefits to Bangladesh's Muslim masses, negative anti-Pakistan feeling may not long postpone a clash of culture, or interest, with the Indians.

Bangladesh is strategically too important to India for her to give more than half-hearted assent to the notion that it is an independent state. On this point India may one day clash with Bangladesh's proud nationalists. But the weight of reality falls on India's side, for after years of economic plunder by Pakistan, Bangladesh no longer has the resources, perhaps, to sustain the structure of a viable and independent nation-state ... If something happens, if the Hindu minority is not integrated successfully... then anti-Muslim identification will be excited again in West Bengal. Muslim-Hindu relations in Bangladesh will determine relations with India. But Shaikh Mujib (sensing public feeling) has failed to stop the anti-Indian campaign in his land's Bengali press. If hard-pressed by economic difficulties or his domestic foes, he might even be forced to encourage the search for a scapegoat and the Hindus would be logical with the Biharis gone.

Whatever the objective truth of Bangladeshi accusation against India, they are significant in that they indicate the profound gulf of history and sentiment that divides the Muslim Bangladeshis from Hindu West Bengal/India.

The memories of Pakistan's atrocities are still fresh. Daily the state of Bangladesh celebrates, under the official ideology of Mujib's secular Bengali nationalism the bond of common language and shared literature that links East to West. Yet on the morrow of Bangladesh's liberation by India, officials of Bhashani's NAP declared with engaging candour that 'the Bengali peasant is a Muslim first and Communist only second.' Bangladesh may not be able to pay its way, its people may be desperately poor, ignorant, and diseased; but their state is here to stay. Hundreds of years of Muslim quest for identity in Bengal legitimize its existence, it is founded on enduring realities. *(Courtesy, Farrago, Australia)*

ICOJ on the East Pakistan Crisis

30 September 1972

IRRESPECTIVE of the de facto political pressures it exercises, the International Commission of Jurists influences a very large segment of civilized public opinion in the world. It acts as an advisory body to the UN. In 1971 it decided to set up a Commission of Enquiry to survey the events in East Pakistan, but due to the outbreak of hostilities between India and Pakistan it could not fulfil its task, and hence, what has been published in the shape of the document entitled 'The Events in East Pakistan,' 1971, is a legal study by the Secretariat of the ICOJ. In their words 'the discussion of legal issues deals with some highly controversial subjects, but whenever we have formed a view on these issues we have thought it better to state our view clearly without equivocation. In doing so we wish to stress that this is a staff study, for which the Secretariat alone is responsible. It does not commit the individual members of the ICOJ.'

The evidence collected by the Secretariat on which it has based its findings consists of 'published books, newspaper accounts, sworn depositions by the refugees, and written statements of evidence given to the ICOJ between Oct. '72 and March '72 and statements made by European and American nationals who were in East Pakistan at the time.'

It would be pertinent to mention here that the Indian Govt. and the provisional Govt. of Bangladesh agreed to cooperate fully with the Commission, but unfortunately the former Pakistan Govt. refused their cooperation, contending that the subject of the enquiry was a purely internal matter. Below is a summary of the findings of the Commission of Enquiry.—Editor.

The introductory chapter of the Study gives a brief account of the genesis of Pakistan and the political developments in the country which led to the situation as it obtained before the military action in E.P. In its recapitulation of the events the study points out: 'There is some evidence to suggest that by 15 February the military leaders in the West had already taken a decision that the Bengalis should, if necessary, be frustrated by force of arms from achieving the autonomy on which they were so plainly bent'.

Part 2 of the Study gives a detailed account of the tripartite negotiations which took place between the military junta and the two contending political parties, leading to the final breakdown of talks and the resultant military action. On the basis of the evidence before it, and in which it is supported by the White Paper published by the Govt. of Pakistan on the E.P. crisis, the study concludes that the provocation for the military action was minimal if not altogether absent. 'The Awami League leaders knew that they had nothing to gain and everything to lose from violence as it could only lead to severe repression by the army. There is no doubt that they were remarkably successful.' The study, however, does not fail to mention: 'there is substantial reason to believe that acts of violence were committed, by the local population within this period. There is evidence to show that attacks were made on non-Bengalis in Rangpur during the week ending 13 March and in Saidpur on 24 March, during which shops and properties were burnt and a number of people killed. But considering the state of tension which prevailed, the extent of the violence was surprisingly restricted.'

Regarding the constitutional casuistry that went on at Dacca about the revoking of martial law, the Study points out in an ironical aside, 'considering the number of constitutional irregularities which had already occurred in the short history of the state of Pakistan, this objection showed a surprising degree of constitutional sensitivity.' What finally sealed the deadlock in the talks and led to the putting of the proverbial last nail in the coffin will perhaps never be known. However, the compilers of the Study have the following to say: 'When by 20 March a fair amount of agreement seemed to have been reached on an interim constitution, the A.L. representatives urged President Yahya Khan to bring over a statutory draftsman to draw up the necessary proclamation. President Yahya Khan kept pressing the A.L. to produce their own draft. Unwisely perhaps, they eventually agreed to do so. In the circumstances, and with no agreement secured from Mr Bhutto the A.L. could hardly have been expected to draft a compromise proposal. Their draft (which appears to have been based on their draft constitution prepared for submission to the Constituent Assembly) expresses their negotiating position. They claim that they put it forward not in the belief that it would be accepted in full, but expecting it to lead to more specific negotiations. However, they contend that at no stage were their proposals rejected by Yahya Khan who kept referring matters for decision by the expert advisers on both sides. The A.L. leaders are now convinced that President Yahya never had any intention of reaching an agreement with the A.L, and was merely playing for time.'

The sub-chapters of this part of the Study give a harrowing account of what happened in East Pakistan during the military crackdown. Not failing to mention that the A.L. leadership, never totally oblivious of Yahya Khan's intentions, might have prepared a plan for armed rebellion, it recounts atrocities committed by both the sides. Nevertheless, it differentiates between the atrocities committed against the population of East Pakistan as a deliberate policy by a disciplined force and the mob violence committed at times by Bengalis against Biharis.

The report of a World Bank mission which visited East Pakistan dated 8 July 1971, described Dacca and other towns in early June 1971 as follows: 'The first thing which strikes one—whether in Dacca or travelling in the country-side—is that there seem to be very few people about.—People fear to venture forth and, as a result, commerce has virtually ceased and economic activity is generally at a very low ebb.' The Report went on to describe the army destructions 'with a trail of devastation running from Khulna to Jessore to Kushtia to Pabna, Bogra, Rangpur, and Dinajpur'.

Part 3 of the Study examines the legal position of the actions taken by either side under the domestic law of Pakistan. In assessing the legal validity of the actions taken, the study relies on the ruling of the former Chief Justice, M. Muneer, in the famous Dosso case, which during the period in which the events took place was still operative. The Study emphasizes the ambivalence of the legal position, finding juridical support for actions of both sides: 'The general strike and the directives issued by Shaikh Mujib which had the effect of setting up a provisional A.L. government *were clearly illegal in terms of President Yahya Khan's martial law regime and under that law justified the use of such force as was necessary to restore the authority of the military govt.* On the other hand, if the army authorities had not intervened, it is clear that all the organs of government in E.P., including the judiciary, the civil service and the E.P. units of the armed forces *were prepared to accept the authority and directions of the A.L.* Applying the test of Chief Justice M. Muneer, if the legality of the new regime were to be judged not by reference to the old constitution but by reference to *its own success,* it had a powerful claim to be recognized, at least in E.P. as a validly constituted government. Moreover, unlike General Yahya's access to power, it had added authority of an overwhelming victory at a fair and free election. If the usurpation of power by Gen. Yahya Khan is accepted to be illegal, in the constitutional vacuum which resulted, Shaikh Mujib and the A.L., following their electoral victory, would seem to have a better title to constitute a provisional govt. of Pakistan than any one else.'

Part 4 of the Study examines the events in E.P. from the point of view of international penal law. While partly condoning the Pakistan army on the grounds that all repressive forces when unleashed act similarly, it holds the Govt. of Pakistan guilty on all counts. Condemning both the side[s] for commission of crimes cognizable under international penal law, it particularly indicts Pakistan for violating all the clauses of the International Bill of Human Rights which comprises the Universal Declaration of Human Rights, the Covenant on Economic, Social and Cultural Rights, the Covenant on Civil and Political Rights, and the Optional Protocol. To quote, 'the action taken by the law and order agencies may fairly be said to have been out of all proportion to the professed aim of maintaining law and order and the authority of the Pakistan Govt. Moreover, the killing and arbitrary arrest, detention and torture, were in clear violation of these principles.'

On the question of the violation of the Convention on the Elimination of Racial Discrimination, the Study holds both the Bengalis and the Biharis equally guilty. It holds that the Geneva Conventions, which also relate to conflicts 'not of an international character' were violated. Article 3 which is regarded as the basic text in the field prohibits amongst other stipulations: (a) violence to life and person, in particular murder of all kinds, mutilation, cruel treatment and torture; (b) taking of hostages; (c) outrages upon personal dignity, in particular humiliating and degrading treatment; (d) the passing of sentences and the carrying out of executions without previous judgement pronounced by a regularly constituted court, affording all the judicial guarantees which are recognized as indispensable by all the civilized peoples. 'There is hardly a phrase of this article which does not seem to have been violated on a massive scale—the evidence indicates that breaches of these provisions also occurred, though on a lesser scale, in the attacks made by some Bengalis against Biharis and other non-Bengali civilians.'

Ironically enough, since Pakistan had ratified the Genocide Convention but had not yet undertaken to enact the necessary legislation to give effect to the provisions of the Convention under internal law, therefore, genocide did not constitute a crime under the domestic law of Pakistan. However, the jurists opine that as soon as Pakistan ratified the Convention, genocide became an international crime, applicable to all persons within the territory of Pakistan.

The Study declares that it will be difficult to establish in a court of law the widely believed proposition that the Pakistan army indulged in genocide in E.P.

To prevent a nation from attaining autonomy does not constitute genocide.—It can hardly be suggested that the intention was to destroy the Bengali people. We find it quite impossible to assess the total number and we cannot place great confidence in the various estimates that have been made. However, it appears to be indubitable that the killed are to be numbered in tens of thousands and probably in hundreds of thousands. But this in itself is not sufficient to establish that the intent was to kill them simply because they belonged to the Bengali people as such.

But the study does go on to state: 'there is a strong prima facie case that the crime of genocide was committed against a group comprising a particular community'.

The study also holds the then Govt. of Pakistan guilty of crimes against humanity on the basis of the Convention of the Non-Applicability of Statutory Limitations to War Crimes and Crimes against Humanity, 1970, and the Nuremberg Principles which have by now become a part of the International Customary Law as these have been incorporated in various international treaties and conventions and made applicable to civil war situations. Since Pakistan voted for the above mentioned convention which entered into force in November '70, her vote in favour of it involves an acceptance of the principle that crimes against humanity are not limited to international war situations. 'Therefore, if it be accepted that the concept of war crimes and crimes against humanity are applicable to the hostilities in E.P. there is abundant evidence that war crimes were committed by the Pakistan administrative military machine and that many crimes against humanity were also committed.'

Coming to the question of individual responsibility the study again bases its findings on the Nuremberg Principles.

Those who carried out the "kill and burn" missions are liable to be prosecuted and punished unless there was no moral choice open to them. Those who ordered the commission of crimes are liable to prosecution. Equally those who passed on the orders or who knowing of these crimes or the orders for them failed to prevent their being carried out when they had the opportunity to do so are themselves guilty of complicity in the commission of crimes.

Regarding the trial of persons accused of having committed the above mentioned crimes the study suggests that an international tribunal constituted under the authority of the UN be set up.

Part 5 of the study examines the right of self-determination of a people in international law as applicable to the B.D. situation. While dealing with this question in the light of the UN Charter, the Study attempts to define the term 'people' and the term self-determination as distinct from the term 'Independence'. With respect to the question whether the population of E.P. constituted a people the study, on the basis of historical, social, ethnic, cultural, ideological, geographical, economic, and quantitative factors (with the sole exception of the religious factor) comes to the conclusion that there existed a Bengali people. In its words 'a people begins to exist only when it becomes conscious of its own identity and asserts its will to exist.' And, 'by 1970 the population of E.P. constituted a separate people within the "whole people" of the state of Pakistan.'

As regards the question: 'were the people of E.P. entitled to a right of independence under the principle of self-determination,' the study is of the view that they were not. Basing its view on the Declaration of Principles of International Law concerning friendly relations and cooperation amongst states in accordance with the charter of the UN and the opinions of international jurists, the study finds that the *right of self-determination is a right which can be exercised once only.'* According to this view if a people or their representatives have once chosen to join with others within either a unit or any federal state, that choice is a final exercise of their right to self-determination. They cannot afterwards claim the right to secede under the principle of the right to self-determination. It was on this principle that the claim to independence of the southern states in the American civil war was resisted. However, this principle is subject to the requirement that the government does comply with the principle of equal rights and does represent the whole population without distinction. The case built up by the A.L. leadership that E.P. was being denied equal rights had largely disappeared after the elections. The conflict falls within the purview of the domestic law of Pakistan. As established by Dosso's case the presidency of Yahya Khan and his martial law regime were legally valid and were recognized internationally as the Govt. of Pakistan.

It may also be remembered that the A.L. had no mandate for independence, nor did they claim to have one. They had fought the elections on the basis of the six points programme of autonomy, it was only when the army made it clear by their crackdown that they were not prepared to entertain a constitution on this basis that the A.L. leaders proclaimed the independence of B.D. and called for armed resistance. Therefore, if the Declaration of the Principles of International Law is accepted as laying down the proper criteria, it is difficult to see how it can be contended that in March 1971 *the people of E.P. and the leaders of A.L, on their behalf, were entitled to proclaim the independence of B.D. under the principle of self-determination.*

The study does find enough justification for the armed resistance organized by the A.L. against the actions of the Pakistan army.

'In our view it was not in accordance with the charter of the UN for a self-appointed and illegal military regime to arrogate to itself the right to impose a different form of constitution upon the country which was contrary to the expressed will of the majority. As the army had resorted to force to impose their will, the leaders of the majority party were entitled to call for armed resistance to defeat this action by an illegal regime.'

Part 7, and perhaps the most significant part of the study, concerns itself with the role of India. It is entitled, 'The Rules of Good Neighbourliness.' It holds India *guilty of providing military assistance* to the insurgents in E.P.

> According to the principles of Customary international law, India was under a duty to observe neutrality by refraining from supplying either of the belligerents with any military supplies or allowing them to use her neutral territory for the transit of military forces or for the preparation or launching of military operations. It appears that these *obligations under customary law of neutrality were not respected by India.*

As already pointed out in the study it cannot be established that the principle of self-determination of a people applied to this situation, India's assistance to the insurgents cannot be justified on this ground either.

The declaration on Principles of International Law approved in the UN Resolution 2625 states, 'Every state has the duty to refrain from organizing, instigating, assisting or participating in acts of civil strife or terrorist acts in another state or acquiescing in organized activity within its territory directed towards the commission of such acts, when the acts involve a threat or use of force.' On the face of it certain of India's acts fall within the terms of this condemnation. 'India's involvement seems to have gone further than this. There can be no doubt that India *did take military action against Pakistan before the outbreak of open war.* Apart from shelling across the frontier which had gone on for some time on both sides, more serious operations occured before the end of November Indian army penetrated several miles into Pakistan's territory with tank forces, and indeed captured and brought back to India some tanks.'

Coming to the outbreak of the December war the study declares that the pre-emptive air-strike by Pakistan against Indian air-bases on 3 December exceeded the exercise of the right of self-defence which the border situation in E.P. warranted. In its view the air strike did constitutes *casus belli.* 'The circumstances justified a declaration of war and India's claim that she was acting in self defence in accordance with the UN charter was legally valid. It does not follow, however, that all of India's subsequent actions can be justified on ground of self-defence. We find it difficult to accept that the scale of India's armed action was motivated solely by military considerations alone based on the need to protect her national frontiers and territory.

'India of course, also argues that as from 6 December when she recognized the govt. of B.D. her action was justified as legitimate support for her new ally in its struggle for independence. This is a *dangerous* doctrine and would set at naught all principles of international law enjoining neutrality on a third party in a civil war situation. All that a neighbouring country would need to do would be to grant recognition to the rebel forces in order to justify her intervention in their support. While the study disbelieves the allegation that India wanted to take advantage of the situation in order to settle its outstanding disputes with Pakistan on the western frontier, it holds that India did intend to use military action to free B.D. and enable it to become a sovereign state independent of Pakistan.

The compilers of the study conclude that India's intervention in E.P. could have been justified on humanitarian grounds. They point out that the 1950 treaty between India and Pakistan gave both the states a direct interest in the protection of religious minorities living in either country. Since the study holds that the army action in E.P. did take on a communal-religious colour, and this is (according to the authors) borne out by the composition of the refugee population which migrated to India, 'the problem in terms of the treaty did become an international affair.' Not precluding the possibility that the radio programmes from India might have 'served to increase the flow of refugees, by increasing their fear of the Pakistan army and by making it known that the India Government was prepared to allow them to cross the frontier and to provide for them in refugee camps' the study holds: 'indeed, it is in the realm of humanitarian law in the widest sense of the term that Pakistan was most vulnerable.' However, India did not even profess that it acted on humanitarian grounds. 'It must be emphasized that humanitarian intervention is not the ground or the justification that India has herself put forward. As we have seen India claims to have acted first in self-defence and secondly in giving support to the new Govt. of B.D. which she recognized when the hostilities began. If India had wished to justify her action on the principle of humanitarian intervention she should have first made a 'peremptory demand' to Pakistan insisting that positive action be taken to rectify the violations of human rights. As far as we are aware, no such demand was made.

A Letter from the Camps of India

7 October 1972

Jamil Ahmed

I HOPE you have received my earlier letters. This one I am writing with a purpose. I think the people outside the camps of India should know how we live.

We, the Pakistani civilians, have been housed in different cantonments encircled with barbed wires. The camp is of typical shape of war camps shown in war movies, with armed guards moving in the special passage made for them. On each corner they have watch-towers where the sentry is posted with LMG. In some camps trained dogs are put to help the armed guards.

Civilians get Rs. 30 per person which has been recently enhanced from Rs. 10. Sweepers and mill-owners are treated at par, we get rotten vegetables and dals to eat. No meat in all these eight months we have been here. The families live in separate barracks with at least four barbed wires in between the male and rest of the members of the family. They are allowed to meet three or four times in a week, but this is again subject to their willingness to do fatigue and all odd jobs, including cleaning the toilets … If one person out of the whole camp refuses to work, the authorities punish everyone by stopping meetings between families.

Sometimes people have been beaten mercilessly for not cooperating with the authorities. From 120 to 250 persons are housed in one barrack. During our stay here, there have been various diseases—including chickenpox. No proper medicine is available. There was no arrangement for sending these cases to hospital or segregating them so almost all the children went through its agony.

For the first few months, there were no medical facilities available. Now they have posted Pakistani army doctors in the camps to look after the civilians but they are handicapped by the limited medicines available.

After the Simla agreement the authorities have put more restrictions on the civilians. Now they have started handcuffing the people when they are taken outside the camp. Even the sick who are sent to hospital are handcuffed.

They also try hard to cultivate people among civilians to work as their agents in Pakistan. They have established interrogation centres where people are taken, asked about their personal life, and then offered handsome amounts if they agree to work. They say 'we shall establish contact with you there'. They say that not only should India and Pakistan live in peace but it should be one country once again—THE INDIA OF COURSE. And they say that we people can help them in making India and Pakistan one country again.

Please type this. Don't disclose my name or profession till I reach home … if ever …

The Russian Role

I was quite surprised by a letter in *Outlook* of 2 September by Tahira Mazhar, President of what she calls a 'Women's Democratic Association', an organization I didn't know existed.

Miss Mazhar's letter reminds me of another person, Vladimir Smirnov, APN commentator, who wrote in Karachi's *Sun* more than six months ago to 'explain' the Soviet role in the subcontinent. Smirnov believes that the criticizm [*sic*] on the Soviet Union—that it has destroyed Pakistan—is wrong, because:

(a) Russia has diplomatic relations with Pakistan;
(b) Russia has helped Pakistan strengthen its economy;
(c) Russia has helped Pakistan prospect for its natural resources;
(d) Russia has trained Pakistani specialists and
(e) Russia has played host to Pakistani statesmen, businessmen and doctors.

Vladimir Smirnov says that if the Russians wanted to exploit the people of Pakistan 'it was hardly necessary to develop relations of assistance and mutual cooperation'. This 'defence' is as naive as Tahira Mazhar's support for the Russians. In the process of 'helping' Pakistan, the Russians have helped themselves: for instance, the Russians have sent 'fishing experts' equipped with the most sophisticated devices for espionage, not to develop our natural resources but to fish out information of strategic importance.

'Mukti Bahini' Refuted

28 October 1972

I READ with interest and amusement the letter from 'Mukti Bahini' published in the issue of 29 July. The letter and the 'facts' as contained therein are of greater interest to me than to an ordinary Pakistani because I have only recently come from Bangladesh. How and why is anybody's guess.

It was a pleasure to learn through the 'Mukti Bahini' who has just listened to Radio Bangladesh and therefore accepted it as God's truth, that the people are happy with their newly found independence. More so because till the time I was there, people in my own circle were apt to say with a sigh *kee chaichelum, kee paichee* (what we wanted and what we got).

Of course, the Biharis are well looked after. As the right honourable Edward Kennedy very correctly remarked on his visit to Bangladesh and on being shown the Bihari concentration camps, the condition of the camps was much better than what he saw last year in Indian camps for the refugees from East Pakistan. The only difference is that if these Biharis are killed, tortured, raped or done away with in other ways, all is done quietly so that the peace of the world is not disturbed. There is no Indira Gandhi who will fight for the cause, there will be no Kosygin who will ask the government of the state to solve the problem on human grounds. There is no Ted Kennedy to see their plight. They have all started wearing dark glasses, so that they may not see what they do not like to see.

'Soldier of misfortune'
Karachi

The Charge-Sheet against Yahya Khan

18 November 1972

ON 21 December 1971, one day after General A. M. Yahya Khan had handed over power to Mr Z. A. Bhutto, a rally was held at Karachi, and forceful demands were made for a public trial of all those responsible for the dismemberment of Pakistan. This was followed by other rallies and demonstrations at Lahore, Pindi, and Lyallpur giving vent to the people's chagrin at the undoing of the country under Yahya's regime. And soon the voices of 'try and hang the culprits' became so strident that Mr Bhutto had to concede: 'If the people want a trial, I do not want to be a party to non-accountability'. In one of his speeches President Bhutto branded Yahya as a 'traitor'. If only to silence the voices, Mr Bhutto ordered the setting up of an Enquiry Commission under the chairmanship of Mr Justice Hamoodur Rahman, Chief Justice of the Supreme Court. The terms of reference of the Commission were defined as 'an enquiry into the circumstances leading to the military debacle in East Pakistan and the ceasefire in the West.' As Mr Bhutto had hoped, the furies were silenced.

The Government's original decision to impose secrecy upon the proceedings of the Hamoodur Rahman Commission was misconceived. The terms of reference related to a national disaster which had resulted in the dismemberment of the country, the loss of 56 per cent of its population, and the surrender of nearly a third of its armed forces on the land. It had also put the survival of the remaining half in grave jeopardy. It was both the right and the duty of the people to know exactly and in full detail what had happened, and how, and what the various witnesses had to say about the tragedy. The argument that public hearings would not be compatible with the requirements of national security was plain eyewash. In any event, all conceivable demands of national security would have been easily satisfied by leaving the commission free to conduct any part of the proceedings *in camera*.

The Hamoodur Rahman Commission (HRC) has completed its work, and its report has been handed over to the President. But no action has so far been taken, and it is believed, none is contemplated. What is worse, the HRC report remains shrouded in a veil of official secrecy. Obviously, the HRC has procured its desired effect. The public resentment against Yahya has cooled down, and, though individual voices of 'try and hang' may rend the air, the chief malefactors are safe and sound. So much so that a report appearing in the newspapers sometime back said Yahya Khan had requested that since things had now normalized, the house arrest under which he had been placed, ostensibly for his own protection, should be removed.

In the face of all this, we are left with two explanations and both unacceptable: Yahya and his clique, in the opinion of the HRC report cannot be held accountable for what happened in Pakistan between 25 March 1969 and 20 December 1971; the findings of the Commission do in fact call for a trial of Yahya and his clique, but the President, at the present juncture, doesn't think it fit to hold such a trial.

Both these explanations (and perhaps, there are others) for not holding the trial of Yahya and his clique would be unacceptable to anyone in Pakistan. The first: it is outright specious; the second: because *sufficient* reasons, or for that matter any reason whatsoever, has not been communicated for that stand.

However, Mr Bhutto's appointment of the HRC, under whatever pressure, was a tacit concession to the general feeling that Pakistan had been dismembered by grossly inefficient policies and that therefore the behaviour of the men who had been responsible for these policies was suspect. It may be noted that the President himself considered the alleged charges to be of serious dimension: for why else would he constitute such a high powered commission? And, it is precisely because this commendable beginning was not followed up to its natural conclusion, that we feel it all the more necessary to ask, why?

That Yahya and his clique should be tried is incontrovertible. In fact, the charges that may be framed against him are so many, and each so serious, that it astonishes every private citizen in this country that the matter has not as yet been taken up.

We may, at the very outset, enumerate the charges that may be levelled against Yahya and his clique; illegal seizure of power; misconduct in action while in command and with the intent to assist the enemy; wilful neglect of duty; surrender of East Pakistan; responsibility for crimes committed against Pakistani citizens during the civil war, both under Pakistani law and international laws; unofficer-like behaviour, etc.

Mr Justice Hamoodur Rahman, Chief Justice of the Supreme Court of Pakistan, while delivering judgement in the case, Asma Jilani vs Govt of Punjab, recorded, '(Therefore), *there can be no question that the military rule sought to be imposed upon the country by General A. M. Yahya Khan was entirely illegal.*'

Another part of the same judgment also reversed the earlier verdict of Justice Muhammad Munir (State vs Dosso case) which held that '(…) a victorious revolution or successful coup d'etat is an internationally recognized legal method of changing a constitution.'

Thus, both Yahya and Ayub were usurpers. It may not be an entirely futile exercise to put Yahya's illegal seizure of power and his attempt to impose military rule on the country into perspective.

Ayub Khan, when he 'relinquished' office on 24 March 1969, in a letter addressed to General Yahya exhorted him in the following words. 'It is your *legal and constitutional* responsibility to defend the country not only against external aggression but also to save it from internal disorder and chaos. The nation expects you to discharge this responsibility to preserve the security and integrity of the country and to restore normal social, economic, and administrative life.'

However, General Yahya, on 25 March 1969, on his own proclaimed martial law throughout the length and breadth of Pakistan and assumed the powers of Chief Martial Law Administrator. He also abrogated the constitution, dissolved the NA and PAs. By another proclamation of 31 March 1969, the CMLA purported to assume the office of President with retrospective effect from 25 March 1969. (It may be mentioned here that Yahya wrote a similar letter when he handed over power to Bhutto in December 1971. The contents of this letter remain a secret to this day.)

Thus, it is clear that Ayub Khan had not transferred power to Yahya; he had merely called upon him to fulfil his *'legal and constitutional responsibility'* as envisaged in the 1962 Constitution and to 'restore (…) normal life.' And therefore, following the relinquishment of office by Ayub Khan, the then Speaker of the National Assembly, Khan Abdul Jabbar Khan, should have assumed office as President of Pakistan.

It is therefore demonstrably manifest that General Yahya, in abrogating the Constitution which he as an officer of the Pakistan Army was under oath to defend, in dissolving the NA and PAs, and in assuming the office of President, was taking illegal and unconstitutional steps to seize power. Hence, the Supreme Court verdict that General A. M. Yahya Khan's seizure of power was entirely illegal.

Now, if Pakistan will allow military adventurers to abrogate the national constitution, dissolve the legislature, illegally seize power, in short play hell with the country, and go free, then it seems that the doors of government will always remain wide open to such *Bonapartism*.

However, if on the basis of the Supreme Court verdict in State vs Dossa case, vis., … 'a victorious revolution or successful coup d'etat is an internationally recognized method of changing a constitution, Yahya's regime is accepted as possessing a valid legal basis, then, by the same token, as a matter of fact, with much greater effect, the Provincial Government of Shaikh Mujib, in so far as it was accepted by the people, the administration, the judiciary, the police, and the militia as the only law-creating body, had a greater claim to constitute itself as the Government of Pakistan than the regime of Yahya since the latter did not have the approval of the entire people.

One of the gravest charges, punishable with death, against Yahya Khan is that he, through acts of commission and omission, caused half of Pakistan to be lost. Specific charges could be framed against him for wilful neglect of duty, obstruction of operations, misconduct in action while in command, and with the intent to assist the enemy. Section 24 of the Pakistan Army Act says:

Any person who shamefully abandons or delivers up any garrison, fortress or air field of which it is his duty to defend, or uses any means to induce or compel any commanding officer to do so, shall on conviction of court martial be punished with death or such less punishment… This is in fact high treason and he should specifically be tried for it.

Yahya never really intended to fight, his attitude throughout was defeatist. In West Pakistan Tikka Khan's division was inactive throughout the war, despite the fact that it was a crack division. It was evident for quite some time that a war would be inevitable but inspite of this fact no concrete plan of offence or defence was prepared as is obvious from the army's poor showing during the war. The result was a loss of 5,000 square miles in West Pakistan and an abject ceasefire. It is crime under the Pakistan Army Act for a commander to fail to urge the men under his command to fight courageously.

According to Air Marshal Nur Khan (*Outlook,* 24 June): 'Contrary to popular notions, the increase in the strength of the armed forces there (East Pakistan) was not geared to meet the possible threat of Indian intervention but was purely conceived as a measure of internal security.' The Air Marshal goes on to say: 'By declaring the emergency we actually warned India that we were about to escalate the conflict. The purpose of all this exercise was not to save East Pakistan, but only to get the Indians involved directly. What was sought to be achieved through this desperate gamble was to concede the loss of East Pakistan and later to internationalize the problem with a view to securing a ceasefire. It was also hoped that our marooned divisions in East Pakistan would be able to surrender to the Indian Army and not to the Mukti Bahini.'

This shows that Yahya Khan followed a policy of calculated surrender. By neglecting his duties as the C-in-C of the Pakistan Army as the Supreme Commander, he is guilty of specific offences, as mentioned above, which are all punishable under the Pakistan Army Act. Under the same military law, Yahya Khan should be made to answer for the excesses committed by the Pakistan Army pushed in East Pakistan from 25 March to 17 December 1971. There is enough *prima facie* evidence of atrocities committed in East Pakistan by the armed forces under his supreme command. For instance, mass killings in town and country; the sacking of whole villages and the destruction of slum habitations; the eviction of vast numbers of working people from the cities; the uprooting of millions of Pakistanis and their expulsion into Indian territory; the cold-blooded murder of twelve teachers of Dacca University on the night of 25 March; the torture and execution of countless students during the long months of the military action; and the last minute outbursts of vengeance in which groups of intellectuals were massacred all over East Pakistan. These excesses were within his knowledge as C-in-C. It was his moral, legal, and professional duty to see that these excesses were halted and the guilty personnel punished. Nothing of the kind was done.

In its report on the East Pakistan crisis, the International Commission of Jurists has indicted Pakistan for having violated all the clauses of the International Bill of Human Rights, comprising the Universal Declaration of Human Rights, the Covenant on Civil Rights, the Covenant on Economic, Social and Cultural Rights, and the Optional Protocol. To quote:

> …the action taken by the law and order agencies may fairly be said to have been out of all proportion
> to the professed aim of maintaining law and order and the authority of the Government of Pakistan.
> Moreover, the killing and arbitrary arrests, detention and torture, were in clear violation of these principles.

The Pakistan that now remains owes it to herself as much as to the part that is now separated to try and punish the culprits, particularly the head of the gang. If nothing is done, the guilt will smear the whole nation for all time to come. We might take a leaf out of the book of Albert Speer, a member of Hitler's cabinet and one of the accused persons at Nuremberg, who was so staggered by the revelations about the concentration camps that he wrote thus to the chairman of the ministerial cabinet: 'The previous leadership of the German nation bears a collective guilt for the fate that now hangs over the German people. Each member of that leadership must personally assume his responsibility in such a way that the guilt which might otherwise descend upon the whole German people is expiated.'

The prosecution of the principal individuals responsible did in fact help to expiate the sin of the German nation, and the chief prosecutor himself, while arraigning the Nazi leadership, conceded that the people as a whole did not bear any responsibility for the crimes.

Yahya Khan's actions and his licentiousness alone were more than sufficient to dismiss him from the army. His much talked about episodes read like a page from Casanova's diary, and were known generally. Hundreds of officers have been cashiered for unofficer-like behaviour. Section 52 of the Army Act reads:

Unbecoming behaviour: Any officer, junior commissioned officer or warrant officer, who behaves in a manner unbecoming his position and the character expected of him shall, on conviction by courtmartial, be liable to be dismissed or to suffer such less punishment, as is in this Act mentioned. Note 1: Unbecoming behaviour may be of military/social character. The criterion is whether or not the accused's behaviour is likely to bring *grave scandal to the army.*

It is quite obvious from Yahya Khan's history that he was eminently qualified for a court martial. That this was not held reflects his total control of the army and the 'forgiving' eye with which those in power were looked at. There is no reason why he should have been an exception, and be allowed to get away with such blatant flouting of the rules.

The corinthian baseness and wild drunkenness that plagued Yahya Khan's court, and remained undiminished even during the worst days of last year's catastrophe, travelled far beyond our frontiers and made mud of the country's name and image all over the world. For instance, the noted Indian journalist, Dilip Mukerji, who has visited Pakistan twice during the past few months, and written a lot about our country, has referred to Yahya Khan's enjoyment of blue films 'in agreeable company' and his usual pre-occupations after dusk, even during the darkest days of the East Pakistan tragedy. And all this while he was a serving general, the commander in chief of the army, and the supreme commander of the defence forces.

Some appointments and promotions made by him, or under his orders, civil as well as military side, are known to have been motivated by grossly unworthy considerations, in flagrant violation of the relevant rules and regulations. He is believed to have played fast and loose with the rules to benefit his stooges and touts, punish those who cared for their conscience, or please the countless women of easy virtue and common whores who used to dominate his court. Permits and licences and foreign exchange quotas are also said to have been liberally dispensed for the benefit of these women or their relatives, in utter disregard of the rules. The PICIC chief, Mr Said Ahmad who was said to have refused to oblige one of Yahya's favourite women with financial assistance for an industrial project, was summarily sacked and later prevented from proceeding abroad to take up an international assignment. On the other hand, Yahya is believed to have been privy to most of the dubious activities of a couple of management bosses against whom cases have already been registered on various charges of corruption, maladministration, and abuse of authority.

And all this time Yahya Khan has been held under protective detention at public expense—in considerable comfort if not in luxury. During the same period, hundreds of political workers including some belonging to the President's own party, labour leaders, journalists, and students have been put behind bars under one or another arbitrary law, on *ex cathedra* charges of subversive activity. An unknown number of them are still languishing in prison. Also during the troubled year since the fall of Yahya, over 1,800 public servants of various classes and grades have been capriciously thrown out of employment, even without a formal chargesheet, by means of a cruel martial law regulation specifically protected against challenge in any court of law, including the Supreme Court of Pakistan. For almost eight months, they were left out in the cold without any means of living or any inkling of what the future had in store for them. Only now have they been granted small mercies like pensions and permission to draw upon the provident fund deposits, or seek employment in the private sector.

And yet we claim to be living under the benign rule of an Islamic constitution which proclaims that 'all citizens are equal before law and are entitled to equal protection of law'.

So long as this dark catalogue of crime and misconduct is kept under the carpet and the culprit goes scot-free, the credentials of the new regime will continue to be under a cloud. And its title to prosecute and punish lesser men for less grievous offences will remain open to question. It is clear that unless Yahya Khan is tried the name and reputation of the whole of the armed forces of Pakistan will remain besmirched forever. And with them the spectre of guilt will hang on the people as a whole.

It goes without saying that Yahya Khan should be given a fair trial. It is for him to disprove the charges of willful neglect of duty and of assisting the enemy and that the surrender in East Pakistan and the cessation of territory in West Pakistan was not the direct result of his action and policies. Although he has been retired from the army he could perhaps still be tried under a court martial. Otherwise special legislation should be framed to constitute a special tribunal to judge the indictment.

Indian Expansionism: Culture and Self-interest

18 November 1972

Philippe Gavi

(The following is a verbatim translation of a section from Philippe Gavi's recent book, 'Le Triangle Indien de Bandoeng a Bangladesh')

16 December 1971: the Indian government is triumphant. The revanchists exult. The bourgeoisie struts. General Niazi, Commander of the Pakistani Forces, has surrendered in Dacca. Pakistan is defeated. What balm for those who had suffered a thrashing in the aggression against China in 1962! Neither a single newspaper, nor a weekly of the left or right, communist or non-communist, with the exception of the weekly *'Frontier'* from Calcutta, and of the *'Economic and Political Weekly'* from Bombay, questions the role played by India. The Indian *jawans* have defended the cause of justice, of civilization against barbarism, of morality against immorality. They have done their 'duty'. India has done her 'duty'. Certain reservations in the foreign press are of little importance. Foreigners can't understand; or else, they have been manipulated. It's a plot. Whoever doesn't agree risks immediate lynching. It is necessary to have read the Indian press of those days, assisted by the demonstrations of joy in the streets, to be able to assess the chauvinism, the militarism, the arrogance, and the ambitions of the Indian bourgeoisie.

Indian expansionism. Those who were accustomed to identifying India with non-violence, the dove of peace, and meditation, suddenly discovered that under the veneer of Gandhism lay a harsh, elated and dangerous state; all the more dangerous for being innately expansionist. The Maoists were wrong, and continue to be wrong when they consider the Indian Government to be a puppet government manipulated by the imperialist super-powers, USA and USSR, and, to a lesser extent, by Great Britain. When one governs one seventh of the world's population, one is not a puppet; the bourgeoisie exists, but not as a puppet. There is colonization, but it is only relative. India is neither a colony, nor a quasi-colony. Her economy is certainly dependent on Soviet and American aid but her rulers don't take any orders. They have the arrogance of auctioneers. British colonization, Soviet MIGs, American wheat, and foreign capital have not broken an imperialist mentality rooted in tradition.

The Indian bourgeoisie in power, that of Gandhi, Nehru, and Indira Gandhi, has not produced the equivalent of a 'Mein Kampf'; nor has it declared itself to assume the brown man's burden. Nevertheless, the concept of domination is innate in the Hindu Brahmins. Hindu philosophy is not the same for the upper and lower—castes and classes. For the former, it is a philosophy of power, of authority, of the preservation of social privileges, and of conquest. For the latter, it is a philosophy of passiveness, of acceptance, and of obedience. To each his fate and his duty. The philosophy of the upper bourgeoisie and of princes is found in the sacred books such as the 'Ramayana' and the 'Mahabharata', the rulers make repeated allusions to such texts, and the foreigner can understand only with difficulty the implications of the metaphors and evocations which are constantly repeated in the speeches of the ruling classes.

In the bookshops at railway stations, the Hindu past is always present in the form of collections of drawings which sell for a rupee, and tell the story of Rama, Krishna, and all the gods and goddesses of the Hindu pantheon. These albums do not contain a trace of pacifism. To the contrary, they are full of battles, duels, military epics, alliances, and massacres. The Brahmin family inculcates in children the concept of the 'dharma yuddha', the religious war, the just war. If you are convinced that you are fulfilling your spiritual duty, your 'dharma', you can throw yourself into any war, kill as many enemies as required for triumph of the cause of justice. The 'Mahabharata' tells the story of five brothers, the Pandavas, dispossessed of their heritage by their cousins, the Kauravas. The Pandavas hesitate; should they attack their own family? Krishna, a friend of the Pandava family, arrives and advises them to declare war and to kill all who cross their path, even their nearest and dearest ones, for they have moral right on their side. A proverb in current usage has been passed down from this story:

'Vina yuddhe nahi
diva suchyagra medini'

(We will not give up any of our territory, even the tip of a needle, without war.)

The Brahmin learns also that an enlightened monarch is justified in conquering neighbouring territory by force if it is with the intention of eradicating evil and ruling wisely. Did not Rama establish an empire by this method, in the name of virtue and morality?

At the end of the 19th century, a Bengali book called 'Anandamath' by Bankim Chatterjee was published, and remains a bestseller to this day. Kali reappeared in the guise of a new goddess, Anandamayee, the godmother of nationalism. It was becoming to have English and Muslim heads placed at her feet.

Later, the heads of Pakistanis and Naxalites would be cut off. Decapitation retains its symbolic force, and it is not unusual to discover the beheaded body of a 'miscreant' or an 'antisocial element' lying in a Calcutta bylane in the early hours of the morning: India's bourgeois society basks in this culture of the exercise of moral right by violence. Hindus massacre Muslims in the name of the same 'religious war' with which the Muslims, when the ratio of numbers is in their favour, massacre Hindus. If Gandhi advocated non-violence, no doubt wishing to save the bourgeoisie from retaliation, he also referred frequently to 'Rama Rajya'—literally the kingdom of Rama, and, by extension, the age of Rama.

Nehru's arrogance was that of the superior castes. Chou En-lai, the Chinese Prime Minister, was struck by his first meeting with Nehru at the time of the Bandung Conference in 1955. Ten years later, he commented on the patronizing attitude of the Indian Prime Minister before a group of Pakistani journalists, and later declared to some Ceylonese politicians: 'I have never met a more arrogant man than Nehru.'

On 19 April 1960, three planes landed at New Delhi airport. Marshal Chen Yi, the Chinese Foreign Minister, and Chou En-lai heard, with smiles fixed on their lips, the only welcoming cry voiced during their brief stay in Delhi: a timid *Hindee Chinee Bhai Bhai* which was covered by the polite applause of diplomats who had come to welcome them. The welcome was frigid. The Chinese team had come to negotiate the problem of frontiers. They were prepared to make all possible concessions and said that they did not want war. 'Our people need peace, our countries need friends', said Chou En-lai, evoking the five principles of peaceful coexistence: 'There is no reason why we cannot resolve peaceably and within these five principles all problems which can divide us.'

The border map was open to discussion by the Chinese. Not so by the Indian leaders, however, supported by a nationalistic press which whipped up the masses and castigated the land-grabbers and agressors. The kingdom of Rama does not negotiate, it takes; and in 1950, Nehru had already declared before the Lok Sabha:

'Our maps show that the MacMohan Line is our frontier, and it is our frontier, map or no map. This fact remains; we will hold this frontier and we will not permit anyone to cross it.'

Eleven years later, after Chou En-lai's vain visit, an amendment in the Indian Penal Code was approved:

Any person who, by written or spoken words, by signs, or by any visible manifestation, or by any other way, questions the territorial integrity of India, in a manner which is or which could be prejudicial to the interests, safety or the security of India, is punishable by a term of imprisonment which can go up to three years, or by a fine, or by both.

Purely economic and political reasons cannot explain the intransigence of Indian leaders, or the ill-will of an entire bourgeoisie which pretended to exercise a moral right over a territory which it had in fact wrongly annexed. The then correspondent of the *London Times* in the region, Mr Neville Maxwell, produced, in his extremely well-documented book, 'India's China War', arguments which coincided with the Chinese thesis and illuminated the expansionist mentality of Indian Brahmins. In effect, the latter were clinging to the terms of a treaty signed by Great Britain and Tibet, which had never been signed by the Chinese who had never accepted this Anglo-Tibetan treaty of 1914. They now proposed a line of demarcation which was a little more to the south, and which was perfectly justified by the geographic and ethnic configuration. Despite all offers of discussions, Indian patrols advanced into the zone defended by the Chinese and provoked a war, a 'dharma yuddha'. The bourgeoisie of the cities broke loose. All the militarism latent in Indian society was exposed. The press printed photographs of school boys and girls, as well as members of Parliament, brandishing guns. Ministers of East Punjab wore uniforms to make fiery utterances against China in the State Assembly. The Birlas offered the nation a miniature rifle, so that the people of New Delhi could be trained. Several thousand Indians of Chinese origin were first interned in camps in Rajasthan, and later deported. Students signed patriotic declarations with their blood. The Finance Minister, Morarji Desai, opened a national defence fund which received silver, gold, and jewellery. 'Ornaments for armaments', was a popular slogan. And Nehru thanked China: by her 'aggression', she had 'suddenly raised the curtain which had hidden the face of India, a serene face, energetic, yet calm and determined; an ancient face which stays always young and vibrant'. What shame when, on 21 November 1962, China announced a unilateral ceasefire—a China which, during the entire conflict, had avoided representing her troops' advance in military terms, and pulled them back to their point of departure without conditions, calling once again for negotiations!

Actually, China was not alone in being troubled by Indian arrogance. The Americans did not understand very well those whom they wanted as allies against China. President Kennedy suffered an indefinable ill-ease when the Indian Prime Minister visited him in Washington in November 1961. He confessed later to his adviser, Schlesinger, that this had been the 'worst visit ever paid on him by any leader.' He described his conversation with Nehru thus: 'it was like having the impression of catching something in one's hands, and finding it to be mist.'

The Indian bourgeoisie is thus difficult to fix, fluid and yet extremely coherent. Apparently, it has been broken culturally by colonization: certain layers may even seem 'westernized.' And yet, its craving for power, its sense of social hierarchy, its exaltation of authority, its rigid concept of the power-structure castes, bosses, fathers—moulds its attitudes, even if these are not translated into its speeches in English for foreign consumption; however, in the latter case it becomes only a question of justice, peace, non-violence, and respect for the individual.

During the months which preceded the unleashing of war against Pakistan in December 1971, the call for the holy war, the moral war, the war against the aggressor, in brief, 'the war against war', reverberated from newspaper to newspaper, in meetings of the Parliament, in street demonstrations, and in high-society receptions. Civil defence was made ready. Alarm sirens were tried out. The armed forces were alerted. The accounting of the refugees took place first 5, then 6, 7, and finally 10 million, as if they constituted aggression committed by Pakistan against Indian soil, the soil of the people; of an aggression against the Hindu nation. After victory, Mrs Indira Gandhi received from the hands of the President of the Indian Union the 'Bharat Ratna,' the highest award the nation can confer on its heroes. The Prime Minister was raised to a pedestal. She became 'Anandamayee'. In the press, one read that she was the 'shakti', the 'Yahya Mardini' of the 20th century, the goddess who killed the evil embodied by Yahya Khan, the President of Pakistan. This was a metaphor for the hero who chopped off the demon's head and placed it at the feet of the goddess Kali. Mrs Gandhi became both Kali, and Kali's servant.

If the dominant class in India is by nature expansionist, it is so by self-interest also. First, there is the concern for covering up its poor administration. What does bankruptcy matter if the people are proud? The sacred union against enemies of the nation and of Hindu culture helps the people in forgetting their daily suffering, and in diverting a latent potential for violence to outside the national boundaries. During the war with China—Nehru declared before the Lok Sabha: 'We can convert this challenge into a chance of developing ourselves, transforming the dark cloud over our frontiers into a bright sun, a sun not only of liberty but also of the well-being of our country'.

The attitude of the Indian Government during its conflict with Pakistan in 1971 was exactly the same. The war followed a difficult and troubled year. It diverted the people's attention for a time, silenced critics of the regime, and forced the communists of the right and left to support Mrs Gandhi's crusade and the foundation of Bangladesh. Only the Naxalites denounced the swindle. They denounced Indian expansionism, and the game of Russian social imperialism, and of American imperialism.

India's territorial expansionism is nothing new. After the 1948 war with Pakistan, India absorbed *de facto* and *de jure* the part of Kashmir occupied by her forces. To justify the annexation of a territory whose population was largely Muslim and which, both by the measure of communications and topography, was nearer to Pakistan than to its new rulers, New Delhi advanced the argument that the feudal Hindu Maharaja, who was little loved by the Kashmiris, had opted for union with India. The Maharaja had promised a plebiscite, but despite a resolution of the Security Council, India refused to implement it unless Pakistan withdrew her forces from the part of Kashmir occupied by them. Any tourist who has visited Srinagar can bear witness to the intensity of hostility of the population against Indian domination. The Indians behave like actual colonists, forcing the sale of their goods at prohibitive prices, and maintaining order with the help of strong garrisons manned by Punjabi soldiers. There is extreme poverty and the supporters of union with Pakistan, as well as those who advocate autonomy are systematically jailed. These imprisonments always multiply before an election, thus allowing New Delhi to claim to the world that the Kashmiris are satisfied with their lot. In August 1971, the Plebiscite Front, one of whose principal personalities is the extremely popular Sheikh Abdullah, a long-time guest of Indian jails called for a general strike. The entire state was paralyzed. However, one read in New Delhi newspapers that the strike call had not been followed. The Indo-Pakistan war of 1965 was a result of the Indian refusal to follow democratic principles (in Kashmir). In effect, India defends a colony by the same logic with which West Pakistan tried to preserve its eastern colony.

Kashmir is not the only territory which India annexed or 'protects'. In 1949, the Indian army intervened in Sikkim, an old vassal state of Tibet, and occupied by the British since the end of the

19th century. The operation consisted of inciting popular feelings against a backward dictator, the King of Gangtok. Sikkim passed under the protection of her powerful neighbor. India also manoeuvred in Tibet and openly supported the revolt unleashed by the Dalai Lama in 1956. She also exercises her tutelage over Bhutan, and behaves like a colonial power in Assam, in Nagaland, and in Tripura. In 1962, she annexed the small Portugese colony of Goa after the intervention of her troops. The scenario is always the same. The Indian Government claims repeated provocations by enemy troops. Demonstrations occur in the streets of the colonized area. The opposing army suppresses the movement brutally, and openly attacks the Indian forces which answer with a lightning intervention and occupation of the territory with the accolades of the population.

To this territorial expansionism, of which the invasion of Bangladesh is the brightest example, is added an expansionism of Indian capital; this is less well-known; doubtless because the government, wishing to retain capital in India limits its extent. Major industrialists like the Birlas have set up a number of textile factories, metallurgical complexes, etc, abroad. Rather than raising demand by enhancing salaries in India, the monopolists prefer capturing more secure markets in countries like Burma, the Philippines, Malaysia, and above all, in Africa. The increase of Indian capital abroad is little known. Hundreds of millions of rupees must have gone abroad on the black market. Apart from this 143 million rupees have been officially invested abroad since 1960. This rise is relatively modest, but the very existence of this outflow gives an indication of the turn of mind of the Indian capitalists. Never was the stock market as high as when Indian troops marched into Dacca. Since then the interest with which these capitalists view the new state of Bangladesh the multiplication of missions, and delegations, the visits of surveyors, commercial attaches, big operators, [and] advertising and marketing specialists shows what a godsend this new and vast market represents for Indian capital.

(Translated by Irfan Hussain)

Recognition Now or…?

25 November 1972

PRESIDENT Bhutto's pleas for the timely recognition of Bangladesh now border on the frantic and the desperate. It is a trifle strange for a man who flourishes his unflappability as an artist flaunts his ego. The image of invincibility is now frayed all over. For, it is clear that it is not self-induced wisdom, or the compulsion of realities by itself, which has evoked a change of attitude. It is rather the result of a tightening of screws on the part of international powers.

Regardless of the merits of recognition, Mr Bhutto's record on the issue is perforated with inconsistencies and contradictions. He opened his innings on 20 December last claiming Bangladesh to be an indivisible part of Pakistan and talked of a settlement within the 'framework of one Pakistan'. On 30 December, he was prepared for a dialogue with India but 'it must be based on the principle on which Pakistan was created' and that 'Pakistan's integrity is not negotiable'. Incidentally, on 31 December, Mrs Indira Gandhi sought direct peace talks between India and Pakistan 'and these have to be based on the recognition of Bangladesh'. Nearly a year later Mr Bhutto is endorsing the same position. In the meantime he negotiated many a new twists and turns. As an ingredient of new frontier politics, he once larded the recognition issue with the assurance that 'I must talk with my people. They have been deceived too much *in the past*'.

The month of January saw Pakistan severing diplomatic relations with a number of states which had accorded timely recognition to Bangladesh without Mr Bhutto's permission. Subsequent weeks witnessed the untiring President descend on a number of state capitals counselling patience to obliging friends and well-wishers. In the month of August he rediscovered the Muslim character of Bengal although Bangladesh had by then committed itself to a secular formulation and 'communal' parties there had been iced for good.

When China vetoed the admission of Bangladesh into the United Nations, Mr Bhutto collected the credit and brandished the veto as a sword or Damocles permanently hanging over the recognition issue, at least till such time as the 'Dacca authorities' implemented the UN resolutions. The resolutions in question still remain unimplemented.

Another constant in the picture has been Mr Bhutto's insistence that there must be a meeting with Sh. Mujib prior to recognition. On his part Sh. Mujib has always insisted on *prior* recognition and sovereign equality. A meeting, it would seem, was being sought by President Bhutto not to thrash out the outstanding issues but for its own bare sake, a mere formality, a face-saving device. Since the Shaikh would not oblige, even this pretence is now being dropped.

The President's latest pronouncements on the subject have the ring of sheer desperation. 'If the people do not take the correct decision now, they will have to live in economic backwardness', he says. It begs the question if the resumption of economic aid by America, Russia, and other powers is dependent on the issue of recognition? The question is significant only because Mr Bhutto's socialism is aid-oriented, if at all there can be such a phenomenon. Even otherwise the stance of the world powers is clear enough as is being reflected, additionally, in the corridors of the UN. India has taken the position from the beginning that the withdrawal of troops is connected (mysteriously, as some would put it) with the recognition of Bangladesh. Despite verbal denials this is the prevailing reality.

The point arises: why have the people been *deceived* so long? There is some skin and bones to the argument that Pakistan cannot live in isolation from its neighbour and that sealed borders and the lack of trade and commerce would inhibit economic growth. The real meat in the business, though, lies elsewhere. These compulsions and consequences could have been foreseen in December–January last and the walls of isolation need not have been raised on the foundations of mere rhetoric.

The fact of the matter is that Bangladesh has come to stay, not as a reincarnation of Muslim Bengal but as a shaky, secular, socialistic state with the only permanent feature being that the *status quo ante* 1971 cannot be envisaged at all for the foreseeable future. The President is again misrepresenting the existing realities when he suggests that the recognition of Bangladesh 'is the only alternative for Pakistan to *resume* its ties with the eastern wing'. There is no eastern wing any more and there will be no resumption of *ties* as such. What will evolve is a new relationship in which material and mundane factors like trade will form the dominant motivation.

The urgency behind the recognition issue is not provided by any benefits to Pakistan unless there is some reasonable ground to believe that her legitimate interests will be respected in the post recognition era. It is not that hard and fast guarantees must necessarily be obtained in advance. It is more a question of pinning reasonable hopes on reasonable assumptions. Is the ground ripe for these assumptions? Available evidence would not warrant such a conclusion. The urgency, therefore, could come to rest on other factors including the emerging interests of Bangladesh. For one, the position of Shaikh Mujib would be strengthened in the coming elections if the recognition issue is out of the way. There is no alternative to Sh. Mujib in Bangladesh and various powers, for different reasons, would like to see him secure in the saddle for a good long time. The issue has to be closed now, once and for all. Quite unexceptionable, this consensus of interest. The alternative could be chaos.

The crux of the matter is that recognition inevitable on principle and as an admission of reality, should usher in an era of tolerably harmonious relations. Therefore, if Bangladesh has made up its mind to go through a war crimes trial, it might as well go through the exercise before it dons the mantle of legitimacy which recognition by the mother country alone can confer on a seceding state.

It does not seem to make sense to nurse recognition on the blistering food of a war crimes trial. It might as well be held and done away with so that recognition (to follow) may set the pace for a new relationship. It will be equally practical to get the division of assets and liabilities and related questions out of the way. As Sh. Mujib said that given a sincerity of purpose, solutions could be found to these questions. His insistence on sovereign equality is a valid consideration. A *de facto* recognition could perhaps meet this objection. Pakistan could make no demands on Bangladesh now; it could perhaps only atone for the past. But Bangladesh perhaps has a few demands on Pakistan. What are they? It may be realistic to know what they are to concede what deserves to be conceded. Recognition can be valid only as a beginning towards a working relationship. Not otherwise.

Silver Lining

2 December 1972

THE acceptance by Bangladesh of the compromise version of the UN resolution opens the way to a welcome adjustment of relationships in the subcontinent. Unlike Simla, this could be a real opening for peace and harmony in the area. The difference could be one of intent. The Simla agreement relied on a few unstated assumptions and what seemed to be private understandings. These were shielded from public view. What has happened at the UN is a public commitment to the principle of interdependence between the issue of recognition and the release of the POWs now held in India.

It is possible to suggest that this may not be the end of the affair. United Nations decisions and recommendations have been ignored and flouted in the past with impunity. It would, however, appear to be unlikely that either Bangladesh or India would back out of the commitment which they have now made before the bar of world opinion. The assumption is that both countries have a stake in cooling the cauldron.

The situation had been made complicated by the overweening confidence of India as a necessary corollary of what appeared to be a decisive victory. Bangladesh, understandably, had its own scores to settle with Pakistan. The tide of international opinion in the past had been running against Pakistan. What is more the fruits of victory were being dangled from an olive branch. When the real intentions and the deeper objectives are sought to be camouflaged under seemingly harmless but unintended verbiage, complications are the predictable result. When it comes to relations between India and Pakistan, it may well be that this was what was actually intended. Attrition, as a matter of strategy, could be the only alternative to instant 'durable peace'. The pressure cooker of time, put on the head, could possibly accomplish what conventional diplomacy would shy away from. However, this technique had its own risks. A return to open and sane diplomacy is, therefore, doubly welcome.

What has happened at the UN seems to be more the result of the unflinching stand taken by China and the support extended to Pakistan by the smaller countries, notably Argentine and the Muslim countries. Russia and the western powers had kept up their pressure tactics. Till the last moment, Bangladesh had the vocal backing of Canada and Australia, and in the background of other major powers, in seeking to delink the recognition issue from the fate of the POWs. The matter

186

elicited a mention in the House of Commons on Tuesday last when Prime Minister Edward Heath declined to oblige a fellow member who wanted him to apprise India of Britain's humanitarian concern at the detention of 90,000 prisoners of war. Nor did Mr Heath go along when the member suggested that political trials in Bangladesh might hinder the way of reconciliation. Mr Heath contented himself with the pregnant remark that the return of prisoners and the exchange of nationals was part of a *wider* agreement between the countries. This has been precisely India's stance. A package deal is what India has always wanted. Simla in fact had all the undisclosed ingredients of a package arrangement. If President Bhutto represented it for a time as a piece by piece approach to peace, subsequent events did not corroborate him. And, precisely because much of the iceberg did not surface, the Simla agreement has not so far come to fruition.

The wrangle at the UN served to justify the stand that the recognition of Bangladesh, a step valid in itself; should be deferred till a more mellow mood comes to prevail in Dacca. If sovereign equality was all that Bangladesh wanted before it would agree to establish contact with Pakistan, it need not have balked at a commitment to simultaneously release the prisoners. The situation, as it existed, did permit the possibility that the prisoners could be used as a pawn in the game of political and financial pressurization. At no time has Bangladesh offered to drop the war crimes trials which, even if legally and morally justified, could now only serve as a political provocation. The proceedings at the UN open up the possibility that the trials may now be dropped. This would greatly facilitate the normalization of relations all round.

There have been a few other steps in the right direction. The exchange of prisoners captured on the western sector and the mutual repatriation of families will help mitigate human problems. This aspect of the residual problems had all the makings of a tragedy in itself. Human problems, to begin with, should not have been viewed as if it was a balance sheet with the debits and credits necessarily evened out at the end. There can be no trade in human misery. It may be a good idea to let the Bengalis take off for Bangladesh without let or hindrance and without waiting for reciprocity. Reciprocity in this matter is bound to come. The chances of peace and harmony in the area would be better if the victors were to learn to be content with what they have already achieved. Which is not insignificant. Pakistan being a defeated and a divided country, has nothing much more to concede. What it has to learn is to live with the realities as they exist. Pakistan cannot afford to live in or with the past. But neither can it afford to accept with a smile the cloak of subservience which is sought to be wrapped around her as a price of defeat. There are obvious limitations to how much Pakistan can bend to please or appease its neighbours. The events of 1971 spelled the end of confrontation. It does not mean that it has forfeited its right to defend its sovereign, national interests. President Bhutto was right in having played for time to improve the cards that he holds.

It goes without saying that the international powers will always have a dubious role to play in a situation like the one prevailing now in the subcontinent. Their friendly noises must be assessed with a degree of wariness. The pity of it is that bilateralism in this context may be a euphemism for domination. Peace is very desirable indeed. So is the feeling that one is the master in one's own backyard, or whatever is left of it. Unrealistic? The alternative is less than acceptable. For the time being though it may be in order to be a little more optimistic.

A Matter of Interpretation

9 December 1972

Nuzhat Amin

RAJA Tridev Roy, leader of the Pakistan delegation to the United Nations will, according to reports appearing in the local press, be accorded a hero's welcome by the President and the people of Pakistan when he returns from New York after scoring a 'diplomatic triumph' for the country. The UN General Assembly passed two separate resolutions—one on the desirability of Bangladesh admission and the other on the mandatory necessity of the release of Pakistani POWs—and the Assembly President, expressing the consensus on the issue, characterized them in his speech as 'interdependent.'

An official spokesman at Islamabad welcomed the compromise. 'A complete vindication of our standpoint,' as the President himself put it in his congratulatory message to Tridev Roy.

Pakistan had good reasons to feel satisfied. At the same time Bangladesh, too, is not unhappy about the two resolutions either. For, the interpretation Bangladesh gives to the UN resolutions differs widely from Pakistan's. To the extent that the Bangladesh Foreign Minister, Mr Abdus Samad Azad has rejected the interdependence of the two resolutions, and indicated that Bangladesh would not—could not—accept the move to link the entry of Bangladesh into the UN with the release of the Pakistani POWs in India.

Mr Bhutto too said as recently as 1 December last at a mammoth public meeting in Rawalpindi that he did not want to bargain on the issue of the POWs and recognition. The President, it is obvious, believes in leaving all his options open. The first resolution moved by Yugoslavia and cosponsored by 22 countries—most of them friends of the Soviet Union or India—which was adopted by the General Assembly 'expresses the desire that the People's Republic of Bangladesh ... (be) admitted to membership in the United Nations at an early date.' The second resolution moved by Argentina and co-sponsored by eight Muslim states expresses the desire that the parties concerned make all possible efforts, in a spirit of cooperation and mutual respect, to reach a fair settlement of the issues that are still pending and ask for the return of the prisoners of war in accordance with the Geneva Conventions of 1949 and the relevant provisions of Security Council Resolution 307 (1971). Regarding the resolutions which were adopted after extensive consultations—without debate and a vote—the United Nations General Assembly President said that 'it is essential to view this simultaneous adoption of these two draft resolutions as constituting an interdependence between these two viewpoints'. The word 'interdependence' was not part of the resolution but expressed the consensus of the General Assembly in this regard. The press and the government in Pakistan have interpreted this to mean that although the General Assembly thought the admission of Bangladesh desirable, it has been made quite clear that this was only a recommendation to the United Nations Security Council. But the United Nations resolution on the release of prisoners of war, the local press would have it, was of a mandatory character as it was in line with the Security Council Resolution 307 calling for withdrawal of troops and release of the prisoners of war; it was also in conformity with the provisions of the Geneva Conventions. According to an official spokesman of the government, even Mr S. A. Karim, leader of the Bangladesh observer team at the United Nations, admitted that by making the two resolutions interdependent 'what comes out is exactly the position taken by Pakistan.'

Radio Bangladesh, however, stated categorically on 30 November that as far as Bangladesh was concerned the resolutions have not been made interdependent: 'indeed the questions involved in the second resolution depend on the entry of Bangladesh into the UN'.

The two completely opposed viewpoints, or interpretations, might surprise the common man as the text of the resolutions are far from being ambiguous. But those who have ever tuned in to Radio Bangladesh, and listened to Radio Pakistan or, for that matter read the local papers on the same subject will have been startled by the varied, if not completely different accounts and interpretations of various events, of great import to both countries.

Take for instance Shaikh Mujibur Rahman's statements at public meetings, in interviews with foreign journalists, about the 3 million Bengalis killed, the 4 lakh women raped and the 23 lakh houses destroyed by the Pakistan Army during the Liberation War. Mr Bhutto, however, put the number of those killed at 30,000 and said there were (less than 20) cases of rape. Foreign journalists and international organizations like the International Committee of Red Cross pooh-pooh the Shaikh's wild cries and say his figures are greatly exaggerated. But they do not agree with the figures given by Pakistan either.

Ever since secession, and specially so in the last few months, Radio Bangladesh has devoted much broadcasting time to the plight of Bengalis stranded in Pakistan. Both the Shaikh and Abdus Samad Azad have appealed over and over again to the UN and the world in general to save these 4 lakh Bengalis 'living in captivity in Pakistan' from 'death and starvation.' According to Radio Bangladesh again, thousands of Bengali women are being kept in camps by Pakistanis and being forced to lead an immoral life. Mention is also often made of the 'concentration camps' where Bengali military personnel are kept and 'ill treated.' The plight of those Bengalis who have tried to flee from Pakistan and are consequently in jail is often told. These descriptions, says Radio Bangladesh, are given by Bengalis who have escaped from Pakistan. These reports are pure exaggerations.

The press in Pakistan is quiet on the subject of the fate of these Bengalis—except for occasional inconspicuously placed news items which appeared when the services of all Bengalis working in government and semi-government organizations who opted for B.D. were terminated and these personnel promised subsistence allowance. Bengalis in Pakistan make news only when they are trying to leave the country illegally. An occasional appeal by the various Bengali welfare organizations in the country appears in the dailies. These give readers an idea that Bengalis here are not exactly living in luxury. But the general public is unaware—because the press is quiet on the subject—that many Bengalis are not even receiving their subsistence allowance and even once well-to-do Bengali government servants with large families are living in tiny, overcrowded houses and have had to switch to cheaper food, while the lower middle class and poor Bengalis are living partly, and even wholly, on charity.

On the question of the repatriation of these Bengalis to Bangladesh, Mr Samad remarked as early as July that he had accepted Pakistan's proposal sent to the ICRC for the exchange of the Bengali and Bihari population. According to Samad, Pakistan had later backed out on some pretext. The correct position would seem to be that Pakistan would like the Biharis to remain in Bangladesh under conditions of security and firm treatment. Officially Pakistan has never offered to accept the Biharis in wholesale exchange.

While Pakistan is almost silent on the subject of Bengalis in the country, the fate of the Biharis in Bangladesh is given due coverage. These reports, written by foreign journalists, should be authentic. They tell of the condition of the Bihari population which is confined to ghettoes where hunger and disease are rampant. Radio Bangladesh denies this categorically and says that the camps made for the Biharis in the suburbs of Dacca have been inspected and approved by international relief organizations.

However vacillating Shaikh Mujibur Rahman may have been on any other matters, his stance on the recognition of Bangladesh by the mother country has remained unchanged. He has stated categorically that there will be no talks, no parleys with Pakistan till recognition. The Bangladesh Government is also adamant to try about 1,500 men of the Pakistan Army who she says committed various atrocities and genocide. The War Trial Commission set up by the B.D. Government, reports Radio Bangladesh, has been collecting evidence against these personnel, and will announce the date of trials as soon as the preliminaries have been completed. And even after the two resolutions were passed in the UN, the Bangladesh Minister for Communications told newsmen in Dacca that the trial of Pakistani prisoners of war would be held; that there was no change in Bangladesh's policy in this regard; that the UN Assembly resolutions had nothing to do with it. The *Evening Post* of Dacca reported on 1 December that 250 prisoners would be transferred to Dacca on 16 December for trial later. This was resented in Islamabad where it was said that it would hamper reconciliation.

Recognition, according to these reports, would then mean only a starting point for negotiations about pressing issues like the POWs and later on the assets which the Dacca Government is bound to claim, although no mention of these assets and liabilities have been made either by Dacca or

Islamabad. The Shaikh has certainly not promised that the POWs will be returned safely to Pakistan after the much sought after recognition. Yet Mr Bhutto seeks to give the vague impression that once we extend recognition, the POWs will automatically return—including those personnel accused of war crimes. He also makes it sound that the Biharis and the pro-Pakistani elements now languishing in prisons and camps on charges of collaborating with the East Pakistan Government will then be saved. In a recent speech in which he argued for recognition, he referred to the sentence of life imprisonment given to Dr A. M. Malik, former Governor of East Pakistan. He inferred that this would not have happened if Pakistan had recognized B.D. earlier.

Meanwhile the two UN General Assembly resolutions which were supposed to break the deadlock between the two countries have only managed to create further confusion.

Impressions of Bangladesh

16 December 1972

Sancho Panza

(This is the first part of an article by Syed Najiullah, one of the two Pakistani journalists who recently visited Bangladesh. He says he will henceforward use the pen name 'Sancho Panza which was recently conferred on me by Mr Nasim Ahmad, Secretary Information, etc.)

MY first contact with Bangladesh at Delhi was with Ataus Samad, a Dacca journalist, on our arrival at Palam on the morning of 13 October. He tried very hard to show coldness tempered with courtesy. But the next man I met before dawn that day was talking in the language of affection, though behind closed doors. And the third broke down as soon as we embraced each other and both of us wept. He even complained that the Indians were sore at his keenness to visit 10 Aurangzeb Road (Quaid's Delhi residence, now Netherlands' Embassy). What is more surprising, he gave me the theoretical justification for owning both the Pakistan movement and the liberation struggle of 1971 by Bengal, now Bangladesh.

According to my friend the one is the continuation of the other and liberation is not complete until friendly relations are restored between the two wings of former Pakistan. 'We may not be one country again ever, but there is nothing wrong in people-to-people relations between the two newly created entities', is very nearly the summing up of his conversation which was partly in Urdu and partly in English. Even Shaikh Mujibur Rahman told me there could be relations of the type we (Pakistan) have with Saudi Arabia which is the holiest land for all Muslims. My friend who re-entered Dacca from Calcutta with the ministers and other government leaders, was quite sure that we threw them out of Pakistan; that is what he and many others think about the whole process of the separatist movement of 1971. Even Tajuddin Ahmed told us they waited until November for a political settlement or an overture to that end.

But to the question whether they would like to revive the old structural ties, the most pro-Pakistan statements that we got was that it was for Pakistan to join Bangladesh and accept its writ because that was the majority area. In jest though, even the Shaikh told me that if we go on at this rate he would declare Bangladesh to be Pakistan and that we would be welcome to rejoin. Polemics apart,

193

and quite frankly at the level of the common people, there is no denying the fact that the atrocities of 1971 are perhaps the only obstacle and at present ineffaceable barrier against reunion. The one question that repeatedly came up for an answer by us was: why did you have to do it all? Obviously the thinking behind the question is that without all this they would not have gone out of Pakistan, and what West Pakistanis wanted was that they should go out permanently.

I saw a ballet in three acts produced at the Asian Fair in New Delhi on 18 November by a cultural troupe from Bangladesh sponsored and organized by the Bangladesh Ministry of Education. It was written by Mohammad Moniruzzaman. Choreography and dance direction was by G. A. Mannan, Gauhar Jamil, and Altamash Ahmed. It was produced by Syed Hasan Imam. It was a very moving piece of art quite inimitably done—'Bangladesh'. The story was of a typical village in Bangladesh with the boatmen, the fishermen, the fields, the ploughing, the sowing, the harvest, the vendors, and the *hat* and so on. Suddenly the evil in the shape of a monster takes over one day, and the people are in chains. They are oppressed and exploited. A revolt is organized and the people get back confidence in themselves. Then comes the crack-down. And in the village comes a wounded man who tells the story of horror of the black night and the brutal killings thereafter. Hundreds of thousands of bewildered refugees come and pass by the village in an aimless and endless procession. Many have lost their dear and near ones. Everyone is leaving his home and hearth. The villagers give whatever help they can offer. The younger people take a vow to do whatever is in their power to avenge the atrocities. News comes of the arrests and execution of the leaders of the revolt. The village organizes for the coming holocaust. Then come the *dalals* from the town with money and instructions from the oppressors and describe the occupying personnel as *firishtas*. And while one of them is still talking, units raid the village. Without any warning or provocation, they start burning down the houses and killing people. And then they go on looting, torturing, raping, and herding away the women of the village.

The village struggles hard to recover. The youth organize a Mukti Bahini training camp. Matlabali Dalal threatens one and all with dire consequences and sets up a peace committee. He is disowned and thrown out of the village. Then he returns with an armed unit and there is a fight. The invading unit is overpowered and destroyed and the village celebrates victory. The story itself either as given in the booklet or as depicted in the ballet, with all the mannerisms known to the art, is so simple and yet it is so very moving. Even the Indian audience which was not concerned directly was moved. The only Pakistani there in the gathering, the present writer, could not help crying. The shame and the remorse of it all!

What surprised me was that of all persons, even Ataus Samad jeeringly asked me which part I enjoyed—'the crackdown by Yahya'? That obviously showed how every Bengali holds everyone of us responsible for the crackdown and also for the atrocities of 1971. In our discussions with friends from the profession, we found that we could not convince them that West Pakistan and West Pakistanis could do nothing more than what we did—which was to approve of the action and gloat over the way the rebels were being dealt with. Let us not blame the army personnel alone for what happened there.

The civilians too talked about how the people of Bengal, had to be punished for challenging the right of the regime, a purely West Pakistani junta which was determined to perpetuate itself, to rule over the country. Most people we met seem to think that in our own interest we should have, and could have, stood up for democracy and fought the junta for a democratic dispensation in which we could live together. The six points, according to these friends with whom we discussed this, ensured the autonomy of West Pakistan: under an East Pakistani majority rule. Even if there was an improbable failure of the political process, the balance of interests could somehow still be maintained. Looking back one feels they are right. At any rate there was no justification for either the crackdown or the refusal to come to terms in a political dialogue. The madness that had taken over those in high office corresponded with the belief at the lower levels that what the junta wanted was the land, and just the land, without the people there, so that they could colonize it with West Pakistanis.

No wonder that at the level of the common people there is an indescribable hatred for Pakistan, West Pakistanis and anything that reminds them of 1971. But there is no denying that, as before, the leaders are more accommodating and will listen to anything reasonable. They have their political difficulties as indeed President Bhutto has. Bangladesh has come to stay. And no amount of kidding will wish that away.

The questions that are of absorbing interest to us are not so important to them. They are concerned with their independence and want to consolidate it even at the cost of their friendship with India. And currently the feeling is there among thinking Bangladeshis that India is not playing the game too considerately. Those who fought so valiantly against domination by Muslims will not compromise their independence in favour of India. Their secularism being only skin-deep, they are willing to rebuild links with Pakistan, but on their own terms.

Why Mujib won't talk?

23 December 1972

DACCA: Why has Shaikh Mujibur Rahman been refusing to meet President Bhutto? The question has been asked both in India and Bangladesh, leave alone Pakistan and the rest of the world. A well-meaning Indian politician had also come out with the suggestion that the Shaikh should meet Mr Bhutto.

The Dacca foreign office circles point out that the Sheikh has reasons far more deeper and important than merely a question of prestige. It was explained at some length by Mr Abdus Samad Azad, the Bangladesh Foreign Minister, to the two visiting Pakistani journalists that instead of serving any useful purpose the proposed meeting can actually complicate matters. After the visit of the two unofficial emissaries of Mr Bhutto, Mr Mazhar Ali Khan and Mr Najiullah, an impression has been strengthened that the Pakistan[i] President was trying to create a smoke screen of talks before the recognition, merely with a view to stall it. It was significantly noted by foreign office officials that Islamabad has already started talking about the question of assets and liabilities which have to be settled before the recognition.

In fact, one of the reasons given by Mr Mazhar Ali Khan for Mr Bhutto's insistence to have talks before the recognition, was that the Pakistan[i] President wants some settlement on the principles which would govern the division of assets and liabilities between Pakistan and Bangladesh. As Shaikh Mujibur Rahman had told the two Pakistani journalists in an interview, 'Bangladesh was willing to settle the problem after the recognition.' Pakistan on the other hand would like a prior commitment over the issue. If one goes by the Pakistan calculation, Bangladesh will have to foot something like Rs. 650 crores in terms of total Pakistani foreign debt amounting to over Rs. 1,100 crores.

Dacca is also believed to have received an idea from some of the South East Asian diplomats, particularly the Indonesians that Pakistan is also insisting for the 'compensation' to West Pakistani industrialists whose properties have been taken over by the Bangladesh Government. The figure generally traded by Islamabad to foreign diplomats about the West Pakistani properties left in Bangladesh amount to over Rs. 200 crores. It would be beyond the capacity of Bangladesh to pay even a fraction of such an amount.

Mr Bhutto's two journalist emissaries had also briefly touched on some of the other 'complications'

196

which have to be solved before the recognition. From their talks it appeared that Pakistan would like the Bangladesh recognition to be preceded by a joint declaration by Shaikh Mujibur Rahman and Mr Bhutto that 'the leaders of the elected representatives of the two wings of Pakistan have decided to separate from each other as independent and sovereign states'. This would, it was argued, help Mr Bhutto in telling his people that he had recognized Bangladesh not under pressure of duress of the Indian army, but according to the will of the elected representatives of the people of East Pakistan.

Since both Mr Mazhar Ali Khan and Mr Najiullah have enjoyed some confidence of Shaikh Mujibur Rahman in the past, because both had advocated the Bangladesh recognition, it was understandable that they carried greater weight in Bangladesh than any other visiting Pakistani could have done. Yet knowledgable circles in Dacca were rather perturbed over the extreme sophistication with which Mr Mazhar Ali Khan had pleaded Mr Bhutto's case. Reports of his talks in New Delhi had already given the impression to Dacca that the two Pakistani journalists, one of whom, Mr Najiullah, is a sort of an unofficial Press Adviser to President Bhutto, were coming to Dacca as mere apologists for Islamabad. This impression was confirmed by the talking the two visitors did during their brief stay in the Bangladesh capital.

Shaikh Mujibur Rahman, is reluctant to accede to the seemingly innocuous idea of meeting Mr Bhutto before the recognition, because he knows that it is not a simple affair. Mr Bhutto would like this summit for two reasons. Firstly, he wants to give the impression that Bangladesh has been 'weaned away' from India. This would be disastrous not only for Indo-Bangladesh relations but also for the growth of democratic forces inside Bangladesh. Secondly, this is a trap laid out by Mr Bhutto to confuse and complicate the issue. Knowing Mr Bhutto's present difficulties vis-a-vis the military leaders and the Chinese lobby in Pakistan, it seems most unlikely that he can accord recognition. What he wants is some sort of an excuse to tell his own people and the world outside, that 'however hard I had tried to come to terms with Shaikh Mujibur Rahman for settlement of some basic issues, before the Bangladesh recognition,

Dacca has been totally uncooperative in the matter. He can tell the Pakistanis, who are now agitating for the Bangladesh recognition because that appears to them the first step for the return of prisoners of war, that Shaikh Mujibur Rahman had put such unreasonable demands about 'assets and liabilities' that he broke negotiations, since that would have meant underwriting the bankruptcy of the country.

Mr Bhutto is likely to bring up the question of prisoners of war as well as the stranded Bengalis in West Pakistan. Bangladesh is naturally eager to solve these problems. But it is understood that no commitment could be made prior to the recognition. Falling to the temptation of talking to Mr Bhutto on any such issues would mean endless negotiations, and the most unseemly spectacle of political horse trading. What the Pakistan[i] President wants is not merely 'a chit chat over a cup of tea', but an excuse to drag his feet, just as he is doing on the delineation issue with India, enabling him to withstand pressures from inside his country over the recognition question. Dacca is in no mood to accommodate him over the issue.

(Courtesy: *The New Herald*, Kathmandu)

Bangladesh: Genesis and After—The Premeditated Push

30 December 1972

Sancho Panza

(The third and last of a series of articles written after a trip to Dacca).

MUCH of what happened during our visit is now the property of the public. We had an off-the-record interview in three parts—both of us together with the Shaikh, Mr Mazhar Ali Khan alone with him for about half an hour, and then a similar duration alone with me. We met the Foreign Minister twice, the Industries Minister, Sayed Nazrul Islam, the Finance Minister, Mr Tajuddin Ahmed, and the Law Minister, Dr Kamal Hussain, once each. I met the Commerce Minister, Mr Siddiqi at Delhi very briefly. I had a few minutes also with Dr Rahman Sobhan, one of the members of the Planning Commission and the Information Secretary, Mr Khurshid Alam. We met the Bangladesh High Commissioner in New Delhi more than once and his second-in-command too. In Dacca we met K. G. Mustafa and Abul Hashem quite often. On my return journey I met A. B. M. Musa on the plane. I met a few other journalists in Delhi who had been visiting India or passing through India on their way to London or other places abroad. Since they were all good personal friends, we could not help talking generally as well as about ourselves and our friends. I met quite a large number of Bengalis in Delhi especially during the week before I returned to Pakistan. My journalist friends in common with others were generally quite critical about the role of the West Pakistani intelligentsia during 1971. Many of them had the feeling that if we had risen up against the military regime in support of the people of East Pakistan, Pakistan would not merely have been saved but strengthened. But they had their doubts that we did not want to live with them any longer. My own opinion has changed as a result; or should I say I have been confirmed in my suspicions.

In my opinion, we have thrown East Pakistan out by force; after killing a few thousands (if not a few hundred thousands, as my Bengali friends would like us to believe) we have ensured that they do not come back to us to sit on our backs like the cannibals in Greek mythology. Secondly, I can see that we would have had a gleeful state celebration with illuminations and all if East Pakistan had gone out without 90,000 of our soldiers being held as prisoners of war in hostile India where they are being held as the price for our agreeing to sign away Kashmir in terms of a division on the line of control as the international frontier. And thirdly, we have no real objection to recognizing Bangladesh *de jure* etc. if we can be assured that the Bangladeshis will talk to us after withdrawing their veto over the prisoners of war and leaving us to deal with India bilaterally on that question and demand nothing from us in a division of assets and liabilities.

As to the first, I can recall that by 1970, we had made study after study to find out how long we would take to become viable and reach the take-off stage of development in our own right as West Pakistan so that we could shake off East Pakistan for good. Let us not forget that we succeeded in bulldozing all political objections to the Fourth Plan and launched it despite the fact that the panel of economists had submitted two separate reports by members from the two wings respectively split, in a vertical division. That is to say we tried deliberately to provide as much ammunition to the separationists (on both sides) as we could for the election slogans and were surprised (at least apparently) that these worked. Even as early as 1948, the bureaucracy used to talk about East Bengal's ultimate separation and argue against investment there in key projects. When Rooppur was put off towards the end of Ayub Khan's days, no secret was made of the fact that such a project could not be located in East Pakistan where it might any day go to India. There were so many secrets of this type that in 25 years there never was a finance minister or a finance secretary from that wing and the first and last Deputy Chairman of the Planning Commission was Mr M. Raschid, now Chairman PICIC.

When we saw that even then Shaikh Mujibur Rahman was willing to talk turkey, we went on negotiating with him until all arrangements for the crackdown of 25 March 1971 had been completed. And the first hint of the crackdown came from the side of Shaikh Mujibur Rahman to his West Pakistani friends minutes before President Yahya left for the airport to return to West Pakistan. The Assembly was not allowed to assemble. And quite intriguing is the fact that the formula of 22 March by President Yahya was acceptable to both Mr Zulfikar Ali Bhutto and Shaikh Mujibur Rahman. But that was the last encounter and there was nothing thereafter except the crackdown without any provocation. At least that is what we were told in Dacca.

The crackdown itself was quite senseless. If it had come on or about 1 March, it might have worked. But coming after the Awami League had taken over the whole administration for close to four weeks, there was no point in going for terrorizing the population with bombs, tanks, and the booming of guns. There was apparently no realization that a mutiny was only to be expected. The West Pakistanis could not possibly kill all the population of East Pakistan and the more we would kill, the more desperate the people would become. That being too naive a position for a regime which had all that technical and expert assistance including political advice of all the known sections and parties available to it, it can only be inferred that the decision had been taken long before the elections that East Pakistan should be jettisoned. What beats one is that the army which is an employment-intensive institution with a budget of over Rs. 400 crore could have agreed to the dismemberment of the country which would naturally reduce to zero the possibility and potential for a standing army even of half its present size. We had always believed that in its own interest, the army dictatorship would at least keep the country intact. To say that President Yahya was a drunkard and a stupid fool is only half the story. The army as an institution was in full command of the situation and its officers are as sensible and patriotic as any in this country. And at least the top brass knew what was happening. How could they be forced to do all that they are believed to have done or omitted to do including giving a serious thought to the risks involved? True, the rank and file was an obedient and unquestioning lot and could come into action only when they forced Yahya and Hameed out which brought us back to civilian rule.

Or was it a waiting game that the generals were playing, waiting for the miracle which did not come? Why did we have to embroil India into it? Did we seriously believe that while we went on throwing lakhs upon lakhs of refugees into India, it would do nothing to use the god-sent opportunity to embarrass us and dismember us? In the words of my Bengali friends, the commanders had orders to be as senseless and merciless as possible and there was no check except that of a mutiny from within in disgust. And there are wild stories circulating outside how such mutinies were the order of the day, though in isolated pockets. The Bangobandhu himself told me that our soldiers did refuse to kill and some were court-martialled while others were executed on the spot. Again, according to him, they are going to raise a memorial to those of the West Pakistani soldiers and officers who disobeyed their superiors in the field and either fought on their side or were punished for having so disobeyed. There are some junior officers too in this category, it is said. Shaikh Mujib's version suggests that there were literally hundreds of men in the list. He told me we could be proud of their humanistic and Islamic fervour in making the supreme sacrifice of their life in many cases and of the job in every case.

Nobody from among my Bengali friends knew any good reason why we could not agree to internal advice and external pressures to negotiate with the government in exile—at least the acceptance of the Polish Resolution in the Security Council which would have ensured that we get out of East Pakistan with all our soldiers and their equipment, their dependants and the civilians including other government servants. A natural whipping boy should be India. Obviously, it would not have liked our negotiations with Tajuddin Ahmed & Co. and could have physically prevented them though there is no evidence it did. But we had in our own captivity Shaikh Mujibur Rahman who could have delivered the goods. The only evidence is that India did not like the finale to the struggle without the intervention of Indian armed forces for rehabilitating its armies after the defeat of 1962 at the hands of the Chinese and for obtaining a special relationship with the newly emerging states which it did in terms of the Indo-Bangladesh Friendship Treaty of 19 March 1972, and otherwise. But that is not quite the explanation. What appears more plausible is that we needed a situation of complete and undeniable defeat and a humiliating surrender to justify the separation of East Pakistan from us. And then to ensure permanence to the state of separation and a state of complete absence of relations between us, we had to have atrocity stories and real or imagined rapes and killings of lakhs of women and men and children to boot. And these we managed with great effort. Tajuddin Ahmed told us they waited until the end of October 1971 for an overture or gesture of a compromise on the basis of one Pakistan. That perhaps is the reason why we could not negotiate with them.

There can be no doubt that behind all this opposition to recognition there is the desire to make things difficult for the present government and then, if this is replaced, what is good for the gander will not be good for the goose. But even so there is common agreement on both sides of the fence that the time for recognition was January 1972 immediately after Shaikh Mujibur Rahman had been released and had returned to Dacca. There are others who should be scared of the demands from Bangladesh for the division of assets and liabilities—as if there are only assets and no liabilities or the solvency of the state to be dissolved is so good and the assets are located all of them in West Pakistan. In the third category are those who have been working for the dissolution of the partnership between East and West Pakistan and they are quite a legion. Otherwise, why could we have our first election only when West Pakistan's viability had been certified and guaranteed by the top economic experts of this region?

For people of my way of thinking, the launching of the Fourth Plan in July 1970 was the end of Quaid's Pakistan. It is today another Pakistan that Mr Bhutto is trying to build. Pakistan Paindabad.

The Bangladesh Story: Denial of a Fair Share

6 January 1973

Sayeed Hasan Khan

PAKISTAN has taken the first steps towards normalization of its relations with India. But the question of evolving a modus vivendi with Bangladesh remains unresolved. President Bhutto has given a fair indication of the line he wishes to pursue, but his task has been made difficult by unhelpful public opinion. It seems that the people are still reluctant to grow out of old myths and fantasies. They have yet to rid themselves of many illusions and clear their hearts of anger against the people of Bangladesh.

Bitterness in Pakistan towards Bangladesh stems from beliefs assiduously promoted by the vested interest such as that Hindus constituted 85 per cent of the total number of teachers in Muslim Bengal and that they subverted the younger generation of Bengalis and turned them against the ideology of Pakistan; that the Indian armed forces conquered East Pakistan for the Mukti Bahini; and that but for India's intervention, Pakistan's armed forces would have succeeded in purging East Bengal of secessionist elements. Unless the people in Pakistan are told that these presumptions are incorrect and that the people of Bangladesh tried their best to stay with Pakistan, a rational assessment of the reality will not be possible. Recent history has not been examined critically and objectively.

First of all it is incorrect that 85 per cent of teachers in East Pakistan were Hindus. However, even if we assume this to be true how can we forget that a greater percentage of Hindu teachers had failed to wean the Bengali Muslims away from the Muslim League platform when the crucial battles for Pakistan were fought in 1946? False notions prevented West Pakistanis appreciating the real conflict in the minds of the people of Bengal. The allegation that they were puppets in the hands of Hindu manipulators angered Muslim Bengalis and alienated them from us.

The decisive role of the Indian army in helping the secession of East Bengal cannot be denied nor underrated. But one should recognize the factors that made it possible for the Indians to become the liberators of Muslim Bengal.

A look into the past may help us to understand events in a different perspective. The All-India Muslim League which led the Pakistan Movement was formed in 1906 in Dacca. Bengali Muslims were from the very beginning in the forefront of the fight for independence because they had suffered most from ruthless exploitation at the hands of the British and the Hindus. In 1930, Dr Sir Mohammad Iqbal, whom we rightly credit with conceiving Pakistan, totally omitted the Bengali Muslims from his historic speech at the session of the All-India Muslim League at Allahabad. There is no answer to the Bengalis' charge about this absence of their demands in the session.

Dr Iqbal had suggested a Muslim state for North Western India only, excluding the Ambala Division. An Indian historian, Professor Mujib, has written that in a private conversation Dr Iqbal had told him that originally he had only the Punjab Muslims in mind. Today's Pakistan more or less conforms to the Allama's concept. At a later stage, when the Bengali leadership acquired some influence in the All India Muslim League, the late Mr Fazl-ul-Haq's move in the open session gave decisive strength to the Pakistan struggle at a time when Punjab's Premier, Sir Sikandar Hayat Khan, was merely lukewarm.

In this resolution, sovereign independent states were demanded. Bengal was to become a sovereign Muslim state. This resolution was later amended at the Convention of the All-India Muslim Legislators held in Delhi in April 1946. There was opposition to the amendment from various speakers including Maulana Abul Hasham, an important leader from Bengal. But it was another Bengali, Mr H. S. Suhrawardy who averted a conflict and piloted the resolution in favour of a single state.

At the time of independence, Suhrawardy was riding on a crest of popularity. Coming from Bengal, which was the highest province to join Pakistan, he expected to become its first prime minister. This was also the feeling among other Bengalis. Mr Suhrawardy himself mentioned to this writer during his last visit to London that he had been given such an impression by the Muslim League leadership of the time. Yet we all know how he was hounded out of politics.

There is a background to this. After the Calcutta riots, Mr Gandhi decided to go to the disturbed areas. Mr Suhrawardy invited him to stay with him and offered to tour Bengal with him in order to ensure communal peace. This gesture was not liked by the Quaid-i-Azam, and Mr Liaquat Ali Khan perhaps made political capital out of it. Mr Suhrawardy was not only discouraged from coming to Pakistan, he was also thrown out of the Constituent Assembly. One of the interesting questions of history is: what would have happened if a Bengali had been made the first Prime Minister of Pakistan?

Even when Pakistan had a Bengali in that position, in the person of Khwaja Nazimuddin, he was summarily dismissed on the flimsiest of pretexts. When the Bengali leadership tried to use its majority in the Constituent Assembly, the Assembly was dissolved. The late Mr Ghulam Muhammad, the leader of Pakistan's bureaucracy and a representative of high finance, committed both these unconstitutional acts with impunity and with the active connivance of the then army chief, Ayub Khan. The Bengalis were obviously not a part of the establishment in Pakistan. And this establishment has played a great part, an ignoble one, in the disintegration of the state.

Suhrawardy, who by then had been able to build the nucleus of an opposition, tried to avoid the inevitable East-West Pakistan conflict by offering to cooperate with the establishment. He piloted the One Unit bill which made parity possible. But it also was used and dropped. Mr Fazl-ul-Haq later picked up the threads and helped in framing the first constitution of Pakistan. This was torn up by Ayub Khan. The late Mr Feroze Khan Noon, the last prime minister before Ayub's dictatorship was genuinely keen to hold general elections in the country, which would have brought an effective Bengali leadership to share power in the central government. The attempt was frustrated by Iskandar Mirza and Ayub Khan in 1958.

For over a decade, Ayub Khan presided over the fate of Pakistan; he was like an albatross round its neck. During his tenure, the 1965 war with India further convinced the East Pakistanis that they were being used as mere pawns in the power game with India. The Bengali leadership was not even consulted before Ayub took the plunge in Kashmir. By this time all the old leaders such as Suhrawardy, Fazl-ul-Haq, and Nazim-ud-Din were dead or eclipsed. The new generation in Muslim Bengal was very bitter against West Pakistan because it felt it would never have a say in the state. No wonder, it started thinking vaguely of an independent existence.

Sh. Mujibur Rahman who had worked with Suhrawardy and who had been in the Pakistan movement made a last attempt through his six points (first announced ironically in Lahore) to live with us. Whether these six points were separatist or confederal or anti-Pakistan, is now an academic issue. But they provided the last chance of our living together. But the Bengali offer was rejected.

The army moved into action in March 1971 against the biggest political party of the country in order to cheat it out of its legitimate political victory. The Indians who had never taken kindly to the loss of the hinterland of Calcutta, made common cause with the Bengalis and aided and encouraged the Mukti Bahini. Later the Indian army openly entered and took part in the invasion of East Pakistan. Thus the Pakistan army and the Indian army together created Bangladesh and brought about its emergence possibly sooner than expected: the motives of both armies were of course different but the end result was the same.

The fate of East Pakistan had really begun to be sealed during the Ayub regime which had thought that a dictatorship could solve all problems. Not only did his behavior debase and dehumanize the people of Bengal, the economic and political superiority of the West Pakistani ruling class made the Bengalis realize that the control of their resources should be in their own hands. These wishes were expressed in the form of the six points. The scandalous opulence of 22 families who were all based in West Pakistan, alienated the Bengalis more and more. The way things were manipulated by our rulers and the press and intellectuals who were sold to the regime involved West Pakistani masses in the regime's opposition to Bengali political leadership.

Responsibility of the people of West Pakistan is not inconsiderable. Except for a short period during the anti-Ayub agitation, the people in West Pakistan never supported the Bengalis in their flight against dictatorship. It was the same case when Yahya Khan unleashed his policy of blood and terror. Yahya Khan tore to shreds the democratic concept of the sovereignty of the people.

The whole world condemned Yahya Khan's actions. But the people in West Pakistan gave him full support. There are reports that sweets were distributed in Lahore and Karachi when Yahya Khan's forces cracked down on the Bengalis. West Pakistani support to Yahya Khan, the despot, and the Bengali masses' support to Mujibur Rahman, the bourgeois leader, gave the conflict between East and West Pakistan the character of a colonial war.

It is thus not entirely evilmindedness if some people insist on seeing the events in Bangladesh in the context of a colonial conflict. In the heat of unbridled passions, terrible atrocities were committed on the innocent Bengali masses in the name of restoration of the 'authority of the government'. The Bengalis retaliated as they had done in 1857 when the first mutiny against British soldiers took place in Bengal. Bengali soldiers had then raped and killed the women and children of their European officers. The same crimes appear to have been committed by the Bengalis against the families of West Pakistanis. Some of the Muslims from West Pakistan raped Bengali Muslim girls while the Bengali Muslims behaved in the same manner towards their compatriots from West Pakistan.

The chauvinistic parts of Bengali nationalism may be condemned. But its understandability cannot be ignored. This nationalism was based on the integrity and uniqueness of the indigenous 'national culture' in which the Hindu minority of East Bengal was an integral part. This was, however, distinct from the cultural outlook of the Urdu-speaking settlers, amongst whom the Biharis were predominant. Since the ideas and poetry of Tagore were an important part of this culture, he became the national poet. One of his poems has become the national anthem.

The question is: whither Bangladesh? Frantz Fanon, the ideologue of the Algerian revolution, distinguishes two rough-hewn, yet clearly distinct facets of the ideological and organizational evolution of a colonial revolution. First, there is a period of guerilla warfare, during which there must arise a unified nationalist programme. Next, there is the period following the achievement of national independence when organizational and conceptual energies are channelled into the chores of a socialist state.

In the case of Bangladesh the Indian Army's intervention shortened the period of guerilla war. Thus the Bengalis could neither purify their ideology, nor were they able to plan for the future along the right lines. A long, hard struggle would have enabled them to give a completely new bearing and orientation to their struggle. In the absence of a real revolutionary ideology, the liberation movement has degenerated. The social cohesion and common organization of the armed struggle disintegrated with the surrender of the West Pakistani forces.

Independent Bangladesh is faced with economic chaos, physical destruction, social divisions, and class conflicts. The new administration consists of a corrupt bureaucracy which is a hangover of the past. During the short span of the liberation struggle, jails were broken open and social outcasts were accepted as comrades-in-arms in the fight for independence. After independence, the criminals have gone back to their old profession, and are responsible for the deterioration in the law and order situation.

Social interests coincided during the liberation struggle and formed the basis of a common fight and organization. But the unity was temporary and contingent. It disappeared with the victory. The chaos and destruction of the last two years has resulted in a disintegration of the traditions of Bengali society.

In today's Bangladesh the interests of the peasants, the proletariat, and petit bourgeois are trying to get complete control of the resources in the new state. The Russians and the Indians, even the Americans and the whole capitalist world are trying their best to save the bourgeois leadership of Bangladesh from defeat at the hands of mass revolutionary forces. Whether they will succeed only time will show. The time at the disposal of the Awami League leadership is very short. It will need all its resources, energy, and effort for the purification of its soul to save Bengal and itself from further destruction.

A Stooge: The New Left on Record

6 January 1973

Izzat Majeed

THE social opportunism of quite a few 'elders of the left' is once again showing its wrinkled face over the question of Bangladesh. This time the scapegoat is the 'new new generation' and all the summersaults, distortions and outright lies possible are being used to justify the prevailing myopic theoretical hysteria and, of course, the age old business of selling the right quotations to the right regime—from feudal reaction to feudal 'socialism'.

Let us analyse the characteristic arguments of this 'socialism-pasand elite' in connection with the question of Bangladesh. The letters of General 'Tiger' Niazi are now being quoted as proof of the fact that the entire East Pakistani people desired secession and were fully endorsing the anti-people, counter revolutionary designs of the pro-Indian imperialist stooge Mujibur Rahman. This is indeed a pathetic attempt to conveniently whitewash the whole-hearted support these same 'socialists' gave to the fascist regime of Yahya Khan and its 'military action' in East Bengal. What were a 'few anti Pakistan elements' in March 1971, have today become the 'genuine representatives' of the entire East Bengali people! At the same time we, of the 'new new generation', are being patronizingly rebuked for having supported Mujib's movement as a national liberation struggle. This, of course, is a lie. These 'elders' are blind to the distinction between the national liberation struggle of the East Bengali people and Mujib's conspiracy with the expansionist ruling classes of India and world imperialism to replace the West Pakistani ruling classes with those of India. To equate the glorious, continuing struggle of the East Bengali people with the phenomenon of Mujibur Rahman is an insult to Marxism-Leninism. Dialectical analysis teaches us that what appears to be durable, gigantic, stagnant has no future while that which is emerging is the future.

We, of the 'new, new generation,' (through pamphleteering and discussions in democratic forums like *Halqai Arbabi Zauq* etc) had from the very beginning, come out in the open and in wholehearted support of the revolutionary people of East Bengal who were waging a momentous armed struggle simultaneously against the fascism of Yahya Khan and the Indian-Russian supported Mukti Bahini. We recognized and respected the genuine national liberation movement in East Bengal. At the same time we also struggled to expose the counter revolutionary machinations of Mujibur Rahman, US imperialism and Russian social imperialism. Our elder 'socialists' tremble at the name of Mohammad Toha and the Communist Party (Marxist-Leninist) and for good reason—for their slogan has always been: 'Death to revolution, victory to counter revolution'. And these Bengali people under the leadership of Mohammad Toha and the Communist Party (Marxist-Leninist) are the vanguard of the South Asian revolution.

Another argument put forward by this 'socialist elite' would be truly hilarious, but for the fact that it emanates from the platform of what is regarded as the left. It is argued that the recognition of Bangladesh would really help the revolutionary forces in East Bengal, as it would take the wind out of the anti-Pakistan phobia which Mujib is constantly whipping up in order to restore his flagging 'Bangabandhu-ness'. As a consequence the people of East Bengal would no longer be fooled through 'the diversion of their attention from the revolutionary tasks' and, voila, we would have a red East Bengal!

This is either sophistry at its best or plain dishonesty. Have they ever wondered why the expansionist ruling classes of India, US imperialism, Russian social imperialism, that bathtub of imperialism, Britain—and the pro-Russian 'left' here at home—in short all the reactionary forces of the world, are desperately clamouring for the recognition of Bangladesh? Presumably they do not want the attention of the East Bengali people to be devoted to Pakistan hatred, but to the fulfilment of their 'revolutionary tasks'! If this is so, then Marxism-Leninism is moonshine and the brutality of world imperialism the greatest of revolutionary forces. In any case the 'Pakistan hatred', is the last straw which Mujibur Rahman is frantically clinging to in the East Bengal ocean of revolutionary turmoil. Recognition or no recognition, he is not going to stop exploiting this emotion, at least till the election in March 1973.

Today, three full divisions of the Indian occupying army are sustaining the virtually non-existent state machinery of Bangladesh and hunting down the revolutionary forces of the people. The Russian navy is busy 'clearing' Chittagong and the US imperialists have been awarded the contract to 'clear' another port. A news item in the *Pakistan Times* (13 December 1972) stated that the Karnaphuli paper mills, the largest in Asia, will be forced to close down, not as much as for the loss of the West Pakistani market, but because of the breakdown of a steady flow of supply of raw materials:

> The mill was consuming entirely local material, mainly bamboo and firewood, which was procured from the vast resources of the Chittagong Hill Tracts. Dacca authorities are finding difficulty in procuring raw material now as the bulk of the source of supply has fallen in the Chittagong Hill Tracts where Shaikh Mujib's administration has not been able to extend their control. Despite help (sic) from the Indian army, these reports stated, stiff resistance posed by people in that area could not be broken down ... (APP).

It does not require much intelligence for any socialist to read between the lines and conceive of the background of this report—which is only one of many that punctuate the development of events during the past year.

Apart from strengthening the puppet government, especially in the international sphere, the recognition of Bangladesh would mean the immediate release of 28,000 Bengali armed forces personnel held prisoner here and of 15,000 people concerned with civil administration—all of whom are desperately needed by the panic-stricken regime of Mujib to consolidate its state machinery and attempt to crush the revolutionary forces. The Indian army, while waging a counter revolutionary, anti-people war against the revolutionary people of East Bengal, remains just as alien to the terrain as was the Pakistani army before them. This makes the immediate release of the Bengali armed forces personnel all the more urgent—for them.

In this connection another allegation flung at the 'new, new generation' by a self-styled oracle of the 'left' is that the revolutionary Pakistani youth and the moribund reactionaries of the Jamaat-i-Islami share the same platform on the question of Bangladesh. We find this charge particularly malicious. The Jamaat-i-lslami is being represented as a powerful manipulator of our destiny. Under the garb of attacking the fantasies of Maudoodi, this particular oracle supported every regime that came to power. And today all the right quotations are being used to support feudal socialism. Like all reactionaries, the Jamaat-i-Islami is a paper tiger—and more paper than tiger at that too. The recent 'student agitation' has clearly shown that the Jamaat's opposition to the recognition of Bangladesh is merely an attempt to exploit the national contradiction in order to settle scores with Mr Bhutto over the crushing electoral defeat, as well as to rehabilitate its own political position.

The recognition of Bangladesh when it comes, will not be an act of 'free choice' on the part of the present regime. As Mr Bhutto himself declared in his interview to Loren Jenkins (Newsweek 18 December), 'I did tell them that I would recognize 'Bangladesh' by taking the question to my National Assembly. But then I found the situation so explosive that I postponed the matter'. The mounting pressure of world imperialism and the 'vicious blackmail' of the Indian reactionaries via our POWs and the internment of even ordinary civilians is not to promote revolution but to assure the subcontinent's 'peace and tranquility' in the interests of all reactionary forces.

The East Bengali people are in the vanguard of the South Asian revolution. The expansionist ruling classes of India and their external masters, US imperialism and Russian social imperialism, fully appreciate the historical consequences of a 'socialist subcontinent'. As such they will cling on to this area—their last battlefield—with all the ferocity, ruthlessness, madness, and cunning at their command. Mohammad Toha and the communist party (Marxist-Leninist) face one of the most difficult class wars in history. The revolutionary forces will not be marching on to Dacca tomorrow. But then whoever heard of an overnight social change? A revolution is not a dinner party, nor is it subservient to the whims of theoretical myopics. The East Bengali revolutionaries are fully aware of their responsibilities and their tasks. As Toha told M. L. Choudhry (ibid):

'Bangladesh being a small country without any friendly rear area, we can not hope to create a base like Yenan. Only the masses of peasants over a vast stretch of territory can be our rear area.' He (Toha) envisages, M. L. Choudhry continues, quite a long period of grassroots work—of politicalization—and organization before mounting an armed challenge to the 'puppet government and its neo-colonial masters.' Toha thinks that 'revolution cannot succeed in Bangladesh alone. It will have to be in the whole subcontinent. We have to forego links and cooperate with other revolutionaries in the subcontinent.'

The question of Bangladesh, however, is not the only question which suffers from the dishonesty of social opportunists. Here are a few gems of scientific analysis:

'Both (i e., what is patronisingly termed as the new, new generation and the revisionists) support the "cultural autonomy" movements of nationalities in Pakistan'.

'Both regard Pakistan, or West Pakistan or Punjab as the case may be as an imperialist state and the rest as colonies.'

'Both believe that the first step in the direction of socialist revolution is to make independent states of nationalities'.

This is indeed a rare analysis in the annals of social opportunism. On the question of nationalities in Pakistan, we recognize the fact that the nationalities of Sind, Baluchistan, and N.W.F.P. have been oppressed by the exploiting classes of the Punjab, and Karachi. This has given rise to a contradiction between the people of the exploited nationalities on the one hand and the exploiting classes of Karachi and the Punjab: The law of uneven development, as Lenin elaborated, is an absolute law of capitalism; and wherever there is uneven development contradictions must exist. Furthermore, in a class society there must also be a contradiction between different nationalities.

If, today, the people of the Punjab hesitate to face the reality of these nationalities, then the unity of the oppressed people of Pakistan will perhaps be fatally damaged and the local agents of class oppression—the Wali Khans, the G. M. Syeds, the Bizenjos, the Mengals etc., etc. will find fertile ground for the intensification of their class tyranny.

Furthermore, another slander thrown at the revolutionary Pakistani youth is that it regards the creation of Pakistan as the imperialist conspiracy of 'divide and rule' or merely 'a fraudulent creation of Punjabi oppressors' and as such does not believe in its independence, territorial integrity, and sovereignty. The revolutionary Pakistani youth has always maintained that the contradiction between the people of Pakistan and the expansionist ruling classes of India is antagonistic, irreconcilable and has a definite historical background. As such, the (people's democratic) revolution in Pakistan is national in form and socialist in content. The pro-Moscow revisionist 'left' in Pakistan, has, for the past 25 years, criminally and deliberately ignored this contradiction.

The vulgar, revisionist pro-Moscow 'left' has always highlighted the class struggle (i.e., class struggle in the abstract.)

At the same time, the reactionary ruling classes always exploited the national contradiction to intensify their tyranny of class oppression and to link Pakistan even more ruthlessly with the dictates and needs of US imperialism.

We, of the 'new, new generation', maintain that at the present historical juncture in the third world—and especially in Pakistan—the national and class contradictions are interlinked, integrated and have to be resolved simultaneously. The independence, territorial integrity and sovereignty of Pakistan can be achieved ONLY by destroying the present day semi-colonial system of barbaric class oppression. Much as it would amaze our 'socialist elite', ONLY the masses are the true guardians of Pakistan's independence. As such any attempt to seek external 'help' from Russian social imperialists or US imperialists is criminal daydreaming. It is playing into the hands of the anti-people, anti-revolution, anti-China, Russian collective Asian security scheme or the US imperialist plan to revive, expand and consolidate CENTO in order to contain the revolutionary struggle in these countries as well as to protect the US oil interest.

Today a year has passed since the 'fall' of Dacca. Our social opportunists are trying to convince the people the 'reality' of puppet Mujibur Rahman's 'Bangladesh', They have not heard of Marx's profound words that national shame is the foster mother of revolution. On the contrary, to them the emotion of national shame provides a good opportunity for getting rid of the nation itself!

The revolutionary Pakistani youth believes in revolutionary patriotism based on Marxism-Leninism. To them the 'fall' of Dacca is not the end of the story but only the beginning. The beginning of a protracted struggle for a socialist society. A beginning which will sweep all social opportunists right into the sewer of history.

A Trial of Conscience

20 January 1973

INEVITABLY, the demand for a trial of the ex-President, General Mohammad Yahya Khan, has been gaining ground. Equally understandably, the regime has been skirting the issue on one spurious plea or the other. The latest addition to the patchwork is Khan Wali Khan's charge that the now famous confrontation in the National Assembly, with its ominous echoes still reverberating, was really sparked off by a call for Yahya Khan's trial voiced inside the House. Since it touched a raw nerve, the Treasury's spokesmen, according to him, injected an element of heat into the exchange which ultimately led to the Opposition's continuing boycott.

The case for the ex-President's trial rests on its own logic. The supreme consideration is to expose the national conscience to a probe in daylight. The failure of Yahya Khan was not the failure of an individual or the military establishment. It also reflected a paralysis of the national will for which all of us as individuals must share the blame. Yahya Khan or the military establishment were part of a larger state structure and a social-political environment whose one characteristic was to live in a world insulated against reality. The military establishment has never been so large as to have always ruled the roost without the tacit consent of a significant segment of the people. The same goes for the era of civilian despots in our history. Yahya Khan behaved the way he did because he felt he was at one with the patriotic values of the day. He also correctly presumed that there would be no reckoning. Not only the military establishment but the civil service, the mass media, the majority of the politicians and, by inference, the people at large gave him direct and indirect support. There were a few honourable exceptions. Their voice was choked.

A trial is necessary because this nation as a whole will be on trial. It deserves to be. Since it accepts tyranny, any tyranny—political, social or economic—resignation or narrow chauvinism, it needs to be confronted with its own moral cowardice. Yahya Khan represented more than the elite of the day. He represented an attitude of mind. He also represented the spirit and the actuality of non-accountability. Neither that attitude of mind nor the folly of non-accountability has yet been laid by the heel. This is precisely why this trial must be held. To suggest that unless Yahya Khan is brought to book, the people as a whole will continue to suffer from a sense of collective guilt is only part of the truth. By and large they have no sense of guilt. The trial may help them to discover themselves. It

213

is this collective opportunism which is shared equally by the left and the right, by the military brass and the civilians, by the old and the young, by the leadership and the people, this national pastime as such which should be exposed. The mechanism will be the defence put forward by Yahya Khan. The cupboard will be open.

Only secondarily Yahya Khan as the President and the commander-in-chief at the time will be facing the consequences of his actions. Less so the issues of military doctrine, strategy, preparedness, and performance plus the related issues of excesses etc. The responsibility of individual politicians, the only aspect which seems to be worrying Khan Wali Khan may also come to the surface.

The basic issues are collective and moral in the sense that no society, unless it is conscious of its obligations, will be able to exercise its rights either. There is a corelation between freedom and restraint. Without an anchor in human and ethical values, no society deserves to survive and possibly will not survive. This society of ours is aware of the deeper values, of course. Beyond that, however, there is no working relationship. All performance at nearly all levels is reduced to the yellow, vapoury non-substance of expediency and opportunism. The worst part is the process of rationalization which converts opportunism into commitment, self-interest into collective interest and expediency into a sense of purpose.

When the motion for a trial was moved in the National Assembly, it was ruled out by the venerated chair on the specious plea that the question was not of recent occurrence nor did it relate to an issue of *public importance*. It is obvious that nothing has changed in this hall of sooty mirrors. The events of 1971 were neither a catharsis nor a point of departure, not even an excuse for self-examination. If the dismemberment of a country and a military defeat are not questions of urgent public importance, what else could be?

As for the timeliness of the motion, the regime itself may share the blame. It started the day by sending generals, admirals, and air marshals back to the pavilion. It acted in swift anger against nearly 1,800 civil servants who were thought to have committed the petty crime of corruption, misconduct or inefficiency. It talked darkly of the black crime of treason. Action was in the air, only to be delayed and finally, shelved.

Incidentally, what has happened to the Hamoodur Rahman Commission's report? Who is sitting over it and why? Defence is now sought to be given a national and a popular dimension. The National Guards are about to make their appearance on the scene to provide new sinews to the defence potential. It may all be very fair and very much needed. What is needed more is a sense of confidence in the institutional infrastructure itself. No institution can be above the law or above the basic human values. A national defence consciousness must also be extended to the frontiers of knowledge. One way to build for the future is to assess the mistakes of the past in an open debate. There are misgivings in the public mind that the Commission itself did a scrappy job in assessing the reasons for the military debacle. The withholding of the report, under whatever pretext, will only serve to heighten misgivings in the matter.

As for the trial itself, the provision in the draft constitution that the legislature will be empowered to make a law for trials of offences of treason and subversion by persons in public services or holding public offices, will not suffice. This is merely a device to further bury the issue under the dust of procrastination. To enable the legislature to make a law under a constitution which is yet in the making is no substitute for action—here and now. The inference is obvious. This is one more matter of urgent public importance which the regime is dead set on pushing under the carpet. Counter-charges and threats to try other leaders who 'collaborated' with Yahya Khan are mere pettyfogging. After all, a trial, judiciously conducted, will pinpoint individual political leaders as to their advice and consent in the fateful days that led to the climactic 17 December 1971. Mr Khursheed Hasan Meer, in taking this line of argument, seems to be invoking a mutual immunity. This is not a matter for horse-trading. This is one issue on which the dictum applies: let right be done.

Mukti Bahini—an Assessment

20 January 1973

D. Shah Khan

THE world wide publicity given to the Mukti Bahini (liberation army) of the Bangladesh movement has invested the organization with an image that brackets it with some of the greatest guerrilla fighters that have emerged yet. Its exploits have been blown up to such proportions and its success in confronting the Pakistani armed forces has been acclaimed so highly that it appears it was the Mukti Bahini alone who 'liberated' Bangladesh, with the Indians relegated to mopping up operations only. All this provides a confusing picture of the situation and tends to paint the performance of Pakistani forces in humiliating colours, in that they were defeated by an ill-trained and lightly armed body of men. In the absence of any reports by unbiased observers it is difficult to decide whether the Bahini was truly all that it was made out to be, or whether it was in reality something much less—at best some sort of a minor appendage to the Indian action.

The foreign press had, from the very beginning, drawn an unfair analogy between East Pakistan and South Vietnam, with the Mukti Bahini like the Viet Cong lurking in the marshes to inflict the coup de grace on the retreating Pakistani soldiers. All the actions of the Bahini were viewed through Vietnam-tinted spectacles by the circus of foreign reporters based at Calcutta and fed to an audience that sought such colourful news. Little interest was shown in Pakistani clarifications, although we have little cause for a grouse here for it must be conceded that our propagandists, with their archaic methods, could hardly prove equal to the task.

The Indians, who fathered the crisis, went even further to present the Mukti Bahini as the latest in the lone line of liberation fighters. Che Guevara was hopelessly eclipsed by these warriors who had set precedents that would be unequalled in history. The 'faceless ones' who appeared from nowhere and after dealing death blows on the enemy again melted into space. The unknown heroes who had wrested control of much of the countryside. Almost like a serialized thriller, AIR and the Bangladesh Radio solemnly broadcast a nightly feast of their hair-raising adventures.

Some of the more classic achievements of the Mukti Bahini besides their daily output of 'heroic exploits' was the 'assassination' of General Tikka Khan, the then Governor of East Pakistan, the killing of 2,000 Pakistani officers and the liberation of the entire Sylhet district. The 'assassination' of Gen. Tikka was a particularly colourful story which was first broadcast by AIR and later played up by the foreign press. According to the tale the General was shot dead by one Col. Shahabuddin at Dacca. A later version said the General had been killed by Mukti Bahini men who made a suicidal attack on the Government House in Dacca on 26/27 March. This story persisted in Bangladesh for a long time and the '*People's View*', a daily of Chittagong, published in April 1972 a scholarly article on the 'assassination' and how the General's nephew (sister's son) masqueraded in his place till 'he' was transferred to West Pakistan.

Another interesting story that received much international currency was the monsoon offensive 'launched' by the Mukti Bahini. The foreign press had come to the conclusion that since communication and transportation in East Pakistan become paralyzed due to the monsoons, the Pakistan army would be hopelessly trapped in the far-flung areas, and the Mukti Bahini, infiltrated in large numbers, would easily wipe out the isolated outposts, and the major cantonments would fall, due to lack of supplies. Much good ink was wasted on this weird story before the press admitted by October that the offensive had not even started, much less done any harm.

Such jaundiced publicity led the world to believe that East Pakistan would eventually fall, and the Bangladesh Radio happily provided the date as Eid time! But, inspite of such bright write-ups, the strategic situation in East Pakistan after months of 'determined struggle' by the nearly one lakh (Indian figures) liberation fighters remained largely unchanged. The main achievements of the Mukti Bahini during this period were essentially civil targets like assassinating Bengali loyalist leaders, sinking ships and foodgrain barges, blowing up power lines and transformers and destroying road and rail bridges. Though the list was somewhat formidable, yet, compared to the wild claims that much of the Pakistani 'occupation' force was eliminated and the rest trapped in cantonments, it was almost nothing. The fact that the Indians fought the Pakistani forces from late November to mid-December before they surrendered totally belied these exaggerated boasts of military success.

The Indians and probably the Russians had already realized the worth of these 'successes' when it became clear to them that the Mukti Bahini had hardly dented the Pakistani army defences and that it was fully in control of the province. This reason compelled New Delhi and Moscow to adopt a new strategy which meant concerted attacks on Pakistani border posts by Indians under the guise of Mukti Bahini. This started in November and continued till the war broke out.

In fact, from the very beginning the Mukti Bahini had received such excellent treatment in the Indian press, that it had even misled the Indian planners. An Indian author Major General D. K. Palit in his book 'The Lightning Campaign' which appeared in February this year, held the Mukti Bahini guilty of exaggerating their performance. He discloses how the Indian planners had in the early days of the crisis overestimated the role of the freedom fighters when he writes, 'Consequently, when reports were received of the blowing up of bridges, the disruption of road and rail communications and highly exaggerated accounts of guerrilla successes, a completely wrong appreciation of their military potential was made. There were expectations that Dacca and Comilla having been isolated from the main port, Chittagong, Pakistani garrisons in the capital, in the interior and in the border outposts would be logistically hamstrung—and that their predicament would grow worse with the onset of the monsoons.'

The Mukti Bahini was originally formed sometime in the second week of March 1971 after the historic 7 March speech of Shaikh Mujibur Rahman in which he came perilously close to declaring freedom. The organization was then set up by the Awami League and its students wing, the Student's League. A hall of the Dacca University was sequestrated to become the HQ and a large number of arms were procured. Training in arms was provided by some Bengali ex-servicemen. Other parties like the Muzaffar NAP and its student body also set up their own groups. These bodies, though civilian in nature had, it was later learnt, made a working contact with the EBR, the EPR, and the police force. The members of these Mukti Bahini groups were in those days the real force behind the extremist Bengali nationalists favouring freedom. Besides pressurizing the Awami League to declare independence, the Mukti Bahini members and Awami Leaguers went about enforcing the edicts of Shaikh Mujibur Rahman, harassing people and commandeering vehicles and arms. They were also responsible for much of the bloodshed of non-Bengalis in those tense days and the acts of provocation against the army. But the fate of this Mukti Bahini, given over more to hooliganism than serious planning, was short lived, as much of its main body at Dacca was either captured or disbanded by the Pakistan army in the very beginning of its operations on 25 March night.

But, while the civil Mukti Bahini was strutting about, the Awami League had initiated contacts with some Bengali officers of the armed forces through Col. (Retd.) M. A. G. Osmany, an Awami League MNA. Col. Osmany sent one Major Khalid Musharraf, a regular officer, on a tour of the province instructing the Bengali officers and men to get ready for action. Special secret cells were set up in the cantonments and the nucleus of the military Mukti Bahini formed. When the Pakistan force made its pre-emptive strike on 25 March, these elements were fully prepared to assume the role of freedom fighters and take up the fight for secession. The alleged message of Shaikh Mujibur Rahman declaring independence was passed on to them and the 'go-ahead' signal given through the EPR wireless system. The army's swift action did much to nullify their plans, and Chittagong was the only major city which fell to them. The rebel officers and men of the EBR, EPR, and the police immediately set up the Bangladesh liberation force wherever possible and began large scale insurgency. Major Ziaur Rahman, an officer of the EBR, broadcasting from the captured Chittagong station of Radio Pakistan, assumed the command of the force temporarily, as Pakistan army action had somehow deprived them of the leadership of many of their senior Bengali officers. This force provided resistance to the army before it was either captured or disbanded and the rest crossed the border. By the end of April 1971, East Pakistan had been cleared of such rebellious elements.

In India the rebel officers and men of the various forces regrouped, and were refurbished with arms by the Indians. Other Bengali ex-servicemen also joined them and a fairly crack corp was formed under the command of Col. Osmany. These were later referred to as the BDF (Bangladesh Forces) and were largely used for attacks across the border and occasionally for subversive activities.

The Indians also set up another Mukti Bahini drawn largely from the Bengali refugees who had swarmed to India. This was a strange mixture of various elements and included seedy students, idealists, political workers, adventurists, in fact anyone who cared to join. This Bahini was organized in camps and given six weeks training by Indian instructors in the use of firearms, subversion and other such activities.

It was true that the Mukti Bahini had great nuisance value, but their use as a force to confront the Pakistani army did not succeed to the extent that it was imagined by the Indians and the foreign press. Any neutral observer would have assumed that one lakh trained men, operating in a highly favourable terrain, with the entire population behind them would be more than a match for any army, much less for Pakistan which hardly had the wherewithal to manage such a situation. But the facts show clearly otherwise, and the result after the long crisis hardly lends credence to the stories of the Mukti Bahini's achievements.

The Indians too in the beginning had thought on similar lines, and while training and arming the Mukti Bahini, had overestimated their ability and assumed that such a force would be adequate not only to contain but also to overwhelm the Pakistani forces. Maj. Gen. Palit, in his book mentioned earlier, relates the failure of this initial thinking of New Delhi when he writes: 'It was felt at one time that somehow guerrilla warfare conducted by the Mukti Bahini, given a modicum of support from India in the way of border sanctuaries, arms and ammunition, coordination and training, would be sufficient eventually to defeat the Pakistan army and liberate Bangladesh. This kind of optimistic appraisal was further encouraged both by glowing press reports regarding 'liberated areas' occupied by the Mukti Bahini forces and propaganda reports and statements issued by Bangladesh leaders in exile. For examples a delegate to the International Conference on Bangladesh held at New Delhi in early September claimed that the guerrillas were taking a monthly toll of 5,000 Pakistani casualties and that the Pakistan government was being forced to spend upto 150 crores per month on the insurgency operations: the actual figures in each case were about one-tenth of these claims.'

But the inability of the Mukti Bahini to act as an armed force to defeat the Pakistan Army does not mean that the organization was devoid of any real purpose. Its actual merit, though largely unintentional, was its political role in the struggle besides providing excellent propaganda material. It became before long a rallying point for the large number of people who were getting dissatisfied with the situation in the province and becoming increasingly hostile to Pakistan. For them the liberation army's name became almost synonymous with their aspirations for eventual freedom from the 'tyranny' of the West Pakistanis. For them it could be compared to the resistance of the French and other Europeans to the Nazi occupation and the struggle that went with it. The Mukti Bahini symbolized the participation of the normally gentle and peace-loving Bengalis in the violent movement and forged their hatred into a powerful weapon. This political role was again largely provided by the short-sighted and stupid policies of some Pakistani officials whose conduct of the whole affair was deplorable and was one of the causes of the loss of the province.

The Mukti Bahini operated mostly in the villages where it was humanly impossible to post troops in strength. Thus much of the security of the rural areas was left to some hastily raised para-military forces like the Razakars, Al-Badr, and Al-Shams. These elements not only proved wholly unequal to the task but in due course became a source of provocation to the public. Whenever the Mukti Bahini struck, and their handiwork meant an attack on a lone police post or the killing of a loyalist Bengali leader, the Razakars retaliated the next day. They rarely managed to round up the culprits, but harassed the population, arrested a few innocent people and even made summary executions. Their disgraceful behaviour did much to alienate the people and if they did not support the Mukti Bahini, they had no love for the Pakistanis either. Such activities of the para forces, together with the regrettable acts of a few armymen, did much to contribute to the growing hatred of the village Bengalis towards Pakistan and the increasing popularity of the Mukti Bahini. It was not long before the countryside was politically lost to Pakistan and became a safe haven for the liberation army. These insurgent forces found this an excellent situation to operate in and it was with impunity that they started disrupting the lines of communication and troubling the local security forces. The Mukti Bahini even collected a form of a voluntary tax in cash and kind and issued edicts, one of which required farmers to cultivate the lands of those people who had fled to India and to give them a half portion of the yield when they returned. The Bahini also had many opportunities to play the role of local Robin Hoods, as some of the leaders who had professed their support for Pakistan had done it merely to enable them to grab the lands and houses of Hindus and those who had fled to India. The Bahini went about killing such usurpers and restoring the properties to the victims.

The true worth of the legendary force became evident after the surrender when the participants in the drama started distributing the laurels among themselves. The biggest share went to the Indians, and rightly too, because it was their show from the beginning to the end. In scores of articles and news stories appearing in the Indian press after the war, the Indian armed forces were given the entire credit for the victory and except for some perfunctory references to the Mukti Bahini as 'good guides' they received no further adulatory mention. Even the BDF, who are reported to have acquitted themselves well, were ignored by the Indians. At no place in the flood of stories was there much of a mention of the Mukti Bahini's boast of having 'liberated' most of the countryside. Had this been done, the entire task of the Indian forces would have amounted to nothing more than the capture of a few Pakistani fortifications, which in any case, according to Bangladesh Radio, were on the verge of collapse. This would have made the 15,000 or so Indian casualties in East Pakistan appear redundant.

The Indians actually spoke of pushing back the enemy inch by inch and far from fighting a 'desperate and demoralised' opponent had the good grace of admitting that Pakistanis fought ferociously and bravely to the end. Many of the Indian writers admitted that their forces succeeded because they were better equipped, and larger in number, and that Pakistani strategy had failed. Such admissions only contradicted the wild claims of the Mukti Bahini that they had reduced the Pakistanis to a mass of quivering jelly which any force could have easily captured.

The references to the Mukti Bahini as 'good guides' caused no end of bitterness among the Bengalis and it was left to the Bangladesh press to fill the void with elaborate tales of heroism, almost like textbook fables. Soon, almost anyone who died in the nine-month-long struggle had been suitably rehabilitated and many of the living crowned with golden laurels. The Dacca government, sensing the unhappy results of the tendency, immediately set up special boards to record the tales of valour with proper proof.

The task of depriving the Bahini of the citations they claimed again unwittingly fell to the Indians. Sometime after the war the Indian Government released a statement of Pakistani losses in the way of men and material. These details were nothing more than the usual procedure to reckon the profit and loss after a war. But most surprisingly, the statement had entirely ignored the Bangladesh forces, although India claimed that those forces fought under its command. This raised a controversy in Dacca and no less a person than Col. Osmany found it necessary to issue something in the nature of a rejoinder. He said he owed it to his colleagues to put the record straight about the good work done by the BDF and Mukti Bahini in the struggle, and presented figures which were almost double those of the Indians. This parallel claim of success by Col. Osmany seemed to show that either the Indians did not consider the Bangladesh forces a part of their campaign or that the Bengalis thought they did not fight under Indian sponsorship.

The Mukti Bahini, who were painted as idealists fighting for a sacred cause by the foreign press, soon destroyed this happy image too. With the surrender in East Pakistan, the time came to surface from the safety of marshes and jungles and bask in the sun of public approbation. The Bahini emerged, but not in the large numbers that had been forecast. But they were enough to prove a grave embarrassment to the Bangladesh government, which discovered that for all their character and prowess in battle, they were actually a well-armed but an undisciplined band of adventurists. The leftists, who had proved to be the best fighters of the lot, soon regrouped under their party flags and, after a little triumphant strutting about, again withdrew from the limelight. The Awami Leaguers also largely returned to their party fold and later became the strong arm of their organization. All this left a third group, fairly large in number, which owed allegiance to no one. They were the real and pseudo-liberation fighters, the soldiers of fortune, the adventurists, or anyone who saw an opportunity to benefit by the chaos prevailing in Bangladesh. Their number became legion as they won new recruits by the simple expedient of any youngmen growing long hair and sporting a beard. These elements, under the handy label of freedom-fighters soon embarked on a career of loot, rape, killing, and kidnapping. Under the claim of being Mukti Bahini, and armed with modern automatics to emphasise their identity, they occupied huge abandoned properties, looted shops and godowns in broad daylight, executed people on charges of collaboration and held others to ransom. Their initial targets were the non-Bengalis and the pro-Pakistan Bengalis; but later they started harassing other Bengalis, and even

Awami Leaguers. The police feared them as they ran a powerful parallel organization almost like the elite S.S. of the Nazis. Their present performance was indeed vastly different from their earlier image as dedicated young men who underwent much privation and suffering for the cause of the motherland.

At first the Awami League government contrived to contain the Mukti Bahini by creating another armed group called the 'Mujib Bahini', whose task was to play down the reputation of the Mukti Bahini and enforce law and order. But this plan fell through due to the ineffectiveness of the force, which was little better in character than those whom it was out to control. The Mukti Bahini bitterly resented the Mujib Bahini and called them opportunists who never participated in the struggle but were now out to grab the loot.

The next move of the government was to disarm the Mukti Bahini, specially the leftists, many of whom had again gone underground. This drive too was unsuccessful as foreign press reports disclosed that the arms surrendered fell far short of the estimates. After this the government set up a militia and asked the Mukti Bahini members to report to the training camps. Other venues of employment were opened and lucrative offers of business and scholarship were made to the recalcitrant warriors of yesterday to wean them away from their, path of violence. This programme too did not succeed. The third attempt caked for strengthening the BDF and the police to counter these elements, and this drive is still continuing.

The Bangladesh leaders who had, in the days of exile, done much to project the image of the Mukti Bahini as a mighty force fighting for justice and other cherished causes, are today saddled with the task of undoing all this mythology before it boomerangs against them. The threats that the one-time guerrilla, A. S. M. Rab, recently held out to Shaikh Mujibur Rahman, only stress the need for the government to neutralize the fighters, at the earliest. Shaikh Mujibur Rahman realized this danger in the early days when he tried to control the Bahini. His harshest step so far has been an ultimatum to the Bahini members to respond to the government's efforts to rehabilitate them, or they would be termed as miscreants and Razakars, and treated accordingly. But the question remains whether the men in power at Dacca can control the monster they created, or whether the government will become its first victim in a not too distant future? With elections in the offing in Bangladesh this question becomes all the more important.

Towards a Cultural Revolution

27 January 1973

Kausar Usman

THE loss of East Pakistan is indeed a great national tragedy. And people in West Pakistan generally blame various things and various people for this tragedy. Some blame Ayub, some Yahya, some Mujibur Rahman, some even Bhutto, while petty politicians of the old school put the blame on the loss of democracy, without realizing, of course, that they themselves did everything to destroy any vestiges of democracy that we might have had in the beginning. Yet there is hardly anyone who has tried to arrive at the crux of the matter.

The loss of East Pakistan can, in all fairness, be attributed to all the things that have been mentioned above to a small measure, but the fact is that the unity of Pakistan was doomed to extinction when the government of Pakistan failed to evolve a national language in the very beginning, inspite of the Quaid-i-Azam's declaration to this effect. It is ironic that it was Mujib who walked out of the Quaid's historic speech in Paltan Maidan in 1948 and it was Mujib who, twenty four years later, declared an independent Bangladesh in the same Paltan Maidan.

This particular incident symbolizes the inaction of the successive governments to give the nation a cultural basis for unity. Instead, throughout our short history everyone talked of some insubstantial ideology of Pakistan, which they considered the only basis for the unity of its people. Indeed this ideology of Pakistan, which apparently refers to Islam, was the basis for the creation of Pakistan. But as soon as the object of this struggle, that is, Pakistan, was achieved, people had to be given something else to unite them. Islam, in the pre-partition era might have been a tremendous uniting force, but there is no gainsaying the fact that its appeal was effective only in as much as it was directed towards the hatred of Hindus and all they stood for. Once this centre of hatred was removed by the creation of Pakistan, Islam ceased to be the uniting factor. As a result a vacuum was created and in it were nursed the parochial feelings of various nationalities that constituted Pakistan. It is by no means an isolated incident in history. In fact history bears a testimony to the fact that whenever any political entity is created on the basis of hatred, it in itself, by its very constitution, gives rise to more germs of hatred, once the original centre of hatred is removed.

The makers of Pakistan created the country after a tremendous struggle but they did not think ahead, they did not look into the future, as to how this nation with diverse nationalities was to be united into a single Pakistani nation. The only thing which could have united the nation would have been the development of a common culture, even the use of a certain amount of coercion to achieve it would not have been unjustified. But no attention was paid to this and parochial feelings kept on being fanned while our political stalwarts and *ulema* kept on talking of a euphemistic 'ideology' as if it was a magic wand, which could keep the nation united by magic.

Thus the differences kept on being widened, particularly after the political blunder of the creation of parity between east and west. By this act began a serious confrontation between east and west. For while the west had some sort of a loose cultural unity, the east was indeed very different. Taking advantage of this, some political leaders, for personal aggrandizement, built up these differences to the extent that finally we had to see this day of shame.

No single individual was responsible for this catastrophe. Neither Mujib, nor Yahya, nor Indira. It was merely a process of history which had to culminate in this regardless of who was at the helm of affairs. One has to view this event in this perspective to understand that east and west were destined to separate now or later, not because of an individual's incompetence or revelry but because of the social, cultural, and historical developments that preceded it. Whoever was at the helm of affairs then could not have averted it and would have ended up as the scapegoat for all the ills accumulated over a period of twenty-five years. And whoever succeeded him, would come in with a clean slate and would have the added benefit of having a convenient scapegoat to blame and a more homogeneous Pakistan to rule. It is just Yahya's misfortune that he had to be the one to lose East Pakistan, and Bhutto's good fortune that he had to succeed him.

But before Mr Bhutto gloats over his good fortune he must understand the historical development which led to the separation of East Pakistan and realize that confrontation being over between east and west, there is every likelihood that hitherto dormant parochial feelings in West Pakistan might come out in the open and pit one province against the other. The fact that, before the dust had settled on the debacle of last December, such tendencies had already begun to raise their ugly heads in three out of four provinces is a pointer towards the shape of things to come. There is no denying the fact that in this moth-eaten Pakistan of today there is no one, other than Mr Bhutto, who has the drive, energy, and the ability to steer the ship of state to calm waters. But Mr Bhutto might, because of his preoccupation with foreign affairs, overlook the root cause of the debacle, namely the absence of cultural unity.

It is a matter of good fortune for us that the problem is not as acute today as it was when Pakistan was divided into two parts. In spite of whatever efforts the rulers of Pakistan could have made (which they did not) in the past twenty-five years towards cultural unity between east and west, they would invariably have to contend with serious ethnic differences between the two people. Whatever synthesis might have emerged from this would have had a strong bias towards Hindu culture because of its strong influence on the Bengali culture. Such a culture could hardly be termed as Muslim culture (I use the word Muslim rather than Islamic) which we aspire for and think we belong to. Fortunately, by the loss of East Pakistan we have, whether we realize it or not, lost complete physical contact with the east. We have now nowhere to look but the west. We, the Muslims of West Pakistan, at last do not have to associate ourselves with that somnolent part of the world called the Indian subcontinent. We have at last become what we are, the children of Central Asia, the Middle East, and Asia Minor. Even historically we have gone round in a full circle. Just as the Turks emerged from the steppes of Asia Minor to conquer half of the western world and then began to recede till finally they settled in Anatolia, a foreign land. Similarly we, from the same family, moved east, conquered an empire, then began to recede and finally settled in West Pakistan, a foreign land. The reason why I am emphasizing this circle is to drive home the point that we are historically a people of Central Asia. The culture that we *claim* today to be ours is basically a culture of India. One has only to dissect the way of life of our people and view the different aspects of the culture such as art, architecture, language, dress, music, songs, dances etc. to verify the truth of the statement, to verify that beneath the superficial mould of Hindu culture lies buried an infinitely superior culture because it is truly our own.

The various parts of Pakistan have various degrees of a veneer of Hindu culture according to their distance from the seat of Hindu culture according to their distance from the seat of Hindu culture. Perhaps Baluchistan, only, and to some extent the *Frontier* also, preserve a certain amount of cultural purity. But the fact is that there is a marked similarity between the culture of all the four provinces. Nowhere is the cultural similarity more apparent than in the folk dress, songs and dances, which apart from being similar amongst themselves, are also similar to that of Afghanistan, Iran, and Turkey and at the same time diametrically opposed to that of India. For instance, what connection is there between the lovely melodious tunes of Baluchi, or Pushto songs to that of the chanting Lata Mangeshkar style, copied by our singers. What relation is there between the manly Khattak dance and the effeminate Ghanshyam ballet, reminiscent of Devis dancing in a temple, during a lingam worship ceremony?

So here we have an unprecedented cultural unity, all we need is a cultural revolution side by side with the economic and social revolution which should merge all the four so-called nationalities of Pakistan into one indivisible whole. But since we have an opportunity given to us to institute a cultural revolution one must not forget that ours is a scientific world, where any nation which tries to bury itself in the past is left behind. We must, therefore, begin a cultural revolution which, while it obliterates the traces of an archaic Hindu culture in its original pure form, also attempts to assimilate all that is good in the western world, because to ignore the western culture in the modern world is to go around with one's eyes closed.

But how is one to begin, how does one lay the first brick? To answer this question one has to investigate the basis, the foundation upon which all cultures are based. This basis, without doubt, is a common language. Institute, or even impose a common language, and everything else would follow. Literature and poetry would soon flower out of it. And thus we would have the flowering of a new dynamic culture. As regards the choice of language to be introduced, the old stalwarts must give up their insistence that the classical Urdu which progressed and thus is associated with our period of slavery under the British, is the language of Pakistan. For choosing the language we have again to go back to the masses and see what language they commonly understand. The language of Pakistan today is a curious mixture of English and a very simplified Urdu. Very seldom can one, for that matter even the ardent supporters of Urdu, speak one whole sentence without a few English words interjected in it. What we have, therefore, to do is to evolve a synthesis, just as Urdu was evolved as a synthesis between Persian and Hindi. Just as Urdu adopted the Persian script, to follow in the same vein, let the new language, the synthesis of English and Urdu, adopt the Roman script. By this simple act we shall not only give ourselves a common colloquial language which will be understood by all, but also open to ourselves the wealth of knowledge and scientific developments that are available through a knowledge of the English language.

To sum up, it is only through a cultural revolution (which looks outward rather than inward) even if it has to be imposed, that a semblance of unity can be given to our broken nation. It is only through this that the mistakes of the past can be averted and the nation unified. Need it be said that there is no better juncture than this to institute it, when everything is in a process of change, and no better person than Mr Bhutto to introduce it, because he today is the symbol of revolution to come.

Home via Kathmandu

17 February 1973

Jabran Omar Abidi

THEY arrive in every conceivable way and in every conceivable condition. Some come in buses, some perched on trucks, some on carts and animals, still others use their own two feet to reach the gateway to home—Kathmandu.

Pregnant women who had walked barefoot for the past few days without food, women carrying babies who had been born 'rastey main'. Men staggering and hobbling. Cripples crippled by their former countrymen. Hungry, thirsty, tortured, and marked for life, they all come to Kathmandu.

Somehow or the other, they make their way to the Pakistan Embassy. Here, they learn their first lesson in Kathmandu. The Embassy is not only reluctant to acknowledge them as Pakistanis, it also refuses to help them.

'They' are Pakistanis. These Pakistanis were left stranded when the Pakistan army surrendered to the Indian army and the Mukti Bahini. Being pro-Pakistan, they were discriminated against in every way. Their life, their property or their womenfolk: none was safe. Many were rounded up and put in concentration camps which have been described as 'hell'. Others were given food and shelter by friends.

Food went first to the Bengalis. Even food parcels from the Red Cross for the camps were taken by the Bengalis. Prisoners in the camps were continuously tortured and starved. Thousands were 'executed' as 'collaborators'.

Security of life did not exist. Those in the camps lived in constant fear of death and those in hiding in fear of discovery. Anybody caught hiding a 'Pakistani' is fair game for the Mukti Bahini or any other Bengalis.

For them, there is only one home—Pakistan. Being Pakistanis, there is no other place for them to go to. Unfortunately, the powers that be at home do not want them. So these Pakistanis cannot be repatriated back to Pakistan—their homeland.

Prisoners break out of camps or bribe their way out. Those in hiding get their friends to get them permits for India. Whether the Pakistani is a prisoner or he has been in hiding, he usually gets a permit thanks to some go between. The permit is almost always forged and costs Rs. 100/-. The next thing to do is to get a Rs. 500/- guide to the Indian border.

Being abandoned at the border, the Pakistani must spend another Rs. 1000/- for a guide till Calcutta. Indian guides are motivated by the same factor and that is money. 'If they think that you are rich or have more money than you say you have, they will kill you'. All too many of these Pakistanis die at the border.

Once in India, they search for relatives or friends who can help them or give them shelter for a few days. Having found them, they leave their families with them and start on the long trek to Kathmandu. For those who have no relatives in India, Calcutta is just a stopping place to gather strength for the trip to Kathmandu.

Few of these homeless people can afford to travel by train or bus. For the majority, the journey is accomplished on their own two feet.

With famine conditions in Bihar and a generally poor food situation throughout India, the most important thing for travel is food. No matter what it is or in what shape or where it is found, food must be obtained. A lucky few can buy it with money they have or have been given.

Roots, berries, plants or animals—they all are food. Even garbage dumps yield food to the hungry travellers. Those who cannot steal or scavenge food soon become experts. Water is often drunk from stagnant pools.

It is relatively easy to cross into Nepal. The number of Pakistanis in Kathmandu bears witness to this fact. Either they cross the border in the night or by their wits and ingenuity enter Nepal at a border checkpost. Getting through a checkpost depends on the Pakistani's ability to bluff his way through.

Kathmandu is full of Pakistanis and hippies. The way things are going, soon there will be more Pakistanis in Kathmandu than the Nepalese themselves. With the denial of help from the embassy, these Pakistanis must live till they can leave Kathmandu as well as they can.

Before they can leave Kathmandu, they must establish their identity as Pakistanis. To do this they must write to a father, a mother or a wife who is in Pakistan. An affidavit by one of these three attested by a magistrate, must be sent to the relative in Kathmandu proving his or her relationship to the sender of the affidavit and his or Pakistan citizenship. An affidavit from any other relation is unacceptable to the embassy.

Otherwise, the Pakistani in Kathmandu must get an affidavit from a firm which has its head office in West Pakistan stating that he is an employee of the firm and had been sent to East Pakistan on the firm's business. When the affidavit is presented to the embassy, they make out a Pakistani passport in the name of the presenter. The making of the passport is usually the end of the embassy's help. If the Pakistani can be sent a ticket by the relatives or by his firm or else, he can afford to buy one (Royal Nepal Airlines is the cheapest—less than Rs. 3,500/-), he can fly home. If the money for the ticket is unavailable, then they have to forget about going home, if even a hundred rupees are needed, the embassy will not help.

Pakistanis unable to come home swarm Kathmandu. The majority live in slums which have sprung up overnight. Pakistanis work as common labourers or as vendors—usually fruit vendors. Their earnings are barely enough to keep body and soul together, let alone save money to come back to Pakistan. Those who cannot find work, steal or beg. Life in Kathmandu is hard enough for men. As for women, life is best summed up in extracts from a letter which a woman, widowed by the Mukti Bahini, wrote to a friend of her late husband: 'I don't know what to do… I cannot tell you how I am living here … For God's sake, I beg you to do something to get me out of here'. She not only has herself to support, she also must support her two small children.

The lucky ones who do leave Kathmandu for home must make sure that they can reach the airport in time. They either walk, or if they can find it, go by some form of transport or the other. One person, Afzal H., needed one US dollar with which to buy food and travel to the airport by the airline bus. His flight was leaving the next day and he did not have any money left. It took him four hours of pleading before the embassy fellows gave him the dollar. They gave the dollar only when he promised to pay the government back when he reached Karachi. As he is as yet unemployed, he sees no way by which he can repay the debt.

On landing at Karachi, it is clear that they are homeless. Shabbily dressed with hardly any luggage worth the name, they pass through customs to cling weeping to their relatives who have come to meet them. For the unmet, their first introduction to Karachi is usually a taxi-driver who offers to take them anywhere they wish—provided that they pay him when they get there.

Thousands start the long hazardous journey home. Thousands die on the way. Hundreds are refused the permission and facilities to come to their homeland. Only a few make it. Most of them end up in Karachi's newest and fastest growing slum—Orangi. Unwanted, unacknowledged, and unsung, they live their lives in filth, misery, and apathy.

What kind of a country is Pakistan? It was born in blood at the time of partition. Originally conceived as a homeland for the 'Mussulmans' of India, it closed its doors on immigration from India. This was a necessity, of course. The trouble in East Pakistan saw brother killing brother, a two-way carnage which seemed to chill nobody's spine. Now it repudiates its own citizens stranded in Bangladesh. Can a society like this flourish?

A New Move on the Board

17 March 1973

THE resumption of US arms aid to Pakistan may prove to be the beginning of new relationships in a region which has seen two wars in the last seven years but no reduction of tension. To the extent that it may give Pakistan the much needed sense of security, it may be welcome. Past experience would, however, project its own sceptical rider. Treaty commitments or the inflow of arms in the past saved Pakistan neither from invasion nor from dismemberment.

The resumption, nevertheless, comes at a time of great psychological anxiety. Mounting internal and external pressures in the wake of dismemberment have heightened a sense of vulnerability which can hardly be assuaged by the disclosure that barring six divisions the entire, enlarged Indian army remains concentrated on West Pakistan's borders. This looks after the Simla spirit if ever there was any and if at all it survived the gun-point negotiations over the demarcation of the line of actual control. The Simla agreement, conceived in mutual deceit, has lived up to its promise. It was not designed to succeed. *Realpolitik* has displaced the invisible ink with which parts of the agreement were written. The continued detention of POWs, the spectre of war crimes, the unnecessary wrangle over the recognition of Bangladesh and related issues have all contributed to the renewed emergence of a hardened, crusty suspicion. The prevailing reality is the line-up on the border. This is a repetition of 1950, 1951, 1965, and 1971. In fairness, this is not a situation for which President Bhutto, or Pakistan alone can be blamed. If they look for support elsewhere, it is understandable.

The desirable normalization of relations with Bangladesh, obviously on the basis of recognition is proving to be an elusive exercise. Recent elections in Bangladesh add another weighty brick to the logic of recognition. Whatever the future of Bangladesh, Pakistan is in no position to influence the course of events there. It is neither possible nor desirable. Yet, there is room for the suspicion that Sh. Mujib's regime is really not interested in lowering the temperature vis a vis Islamabad. The memories of 1971 were his main election armament. The plight of Bengalis in Pakistan, admittedly not enviable on any count, provides the missiles for his propaganda machines. It is strange, therefore, to find that the proposed first mass transfer of Bengalis from Pakistan has been held up due to an objection by Bangladesh. The facile argument has been advanced that nearly all the 15,000 Bengalis on the list are indigent persons and some are even criminals. When Bangladesh clamours that *all* of the 400,000 Bengalis should be freed from the rigours which they are supposed to be undergoing in Pakistan, this pick and choose procedure is hard to understand. Does a poor Bengali suffer any less than an ex-civil servant? Does he have any less claim on the promised land? Must human beings, like cattle, be appraised in terms of their milk/meat yield per head?

As for the criminals, if any, surely there is no dearth of jails in Bangladesh. If they are wide enough to hold 40,000 collaborators, there can be room for a few dozen exported 'with compliments' from Pakistan. Even a criminal may find the air sweeter in his own country. As far back as 1965, the Dacca papers often used to carry despatches highlighting what they thought was a planned exodus of criminals from the West into East Pakistan. The criminals are still there. They have merely changed their nationality. It is peculiar how old prejudices survive in new garbs. When politics blocks the alleviation of human suffering, it is insufferable. This, despite the possible retort that no West Pakistani has a right to preach humanitarianism to the rulers in Bangladesh.

The POWs and the war crimes issue should be treated on the same plane. A declaration of intent by Pakistan on the issue of recognition should clear the last hurdle in the way of bilateral or triangular talks. The objective should be reconciliation and normalization and all issues should be subservient to this basic requirement. Whatever the ethical and juridical justification for a war crimes trial, it should be viewed in the context of the long, pernicious shadows it will cast on the process of normalization. Over the last 14 months, India and Bangladesh had it within their power to hold a war crimes trial and be done with it. The mere fact that it has been delayed so long gives rise to the impression that it is intended as a continuing instrument of blackmail, ready for use whenever it may be needed. A relationship of goodwill can hardly be built on a foundation of blackmail or intimidation through power.

And this is precisely the point and the lesson of the past 25 years. Once again it seems that the logic of history and of geography is being side-tracked by a narrow-minded interpretation of national interests. If Pakistan errs on the side of short-sightedness, India's image of its own interests is vitiated by an aggressive combination of nationalism, chauvinism, and power consciousness. Bangladesh, understandably, has its sights misty with the apparitions of vindictiveness. In this welter of disguised intentions, the international powers naturally have free play.

Even since 1971, foreign presence in one shape or another has loomed larger not only over the subcontinent but over neighbouring areas. Not only the residual state of Pakistan but Iran and Afghanistan too have felt the rustle of insecurity. The entire area appears soft to those who know that a change in any one country will affect the others. Pakistan shares a common frontier with two countries which have close military and economic ties with Soviet Russia. A third, Iraq, lies close by and has shown a vivid interest in the internal affairs of Pakistan. Anyone who thinks that the pot is not boiling, internally and externally, must be in love with the cup of complacency. Not unexpected, therefore, are Pakistan's overtures to the United States. Although a beggar cannot be a chooser, its desirability from Pakistan's point of view cannot be taken for granted.

A relationship between two wholly unequal powers generates its own social, political and economic distortions. President Bhutto may secure his flanks both internally and externally but these alignments, inevitable to some, may not necessarily serve national interests in the long run. For one thing, it is a setback to the slow and unimpressive process of self-reliance. For another, it necessarily generates undemocratic tendencies which are already throttling this polity. It may also exacerbate regional tensions already on the boil. A more rational arrangement would have been a purely regional grouping for peace. That option, however, has been foreclosed because India is not a generous neighbour and because regional peace cannot be really savoured if it is merely a disguised extension of the Indo-Soviet alliance. This is alignment without even a fig leaf.

Prevarications on Recognition

7 July 1973

THE issue of the recognition of Bangladesh is being messed around as much by the ruling party as by the opposition. Mr Bhutto has been running with the hares and hunting with the hounds in an unnecessary display of his proven nimble-footedness while the opposition, unrealistic as ever, nurses the issue as if it has discovered a time bomb.

The opposition seems to have taken a leaf out of Mr Bhutto's Tashkent book except that it is playing it out to an empty gallery. The last act having been staged before a traumatized, hypnotized audience in 1971, this continuing rehearsal is nothing more than an extended farce.

It is true that had Mr Bhutto been in the opposition, he would have raised the same kind of hocus pocus. In fact, even as the President of Pakistan and unmindful of the chastening responsibilities of his office, he has continued to sentimentalize on the prospects and possibilities flowing out of the concept of Muslim Bengal. In his very first address to the nation on 20 December 1971, he made the untenable assertion that 'East Pakistan is an inseparable and indissoluble part of Pakistan'. On a latter occasion he offered to discuss the modalities for future arrangements on the condition that 'this should be within the framework of one Pakistan'.

The PPP-dominated National Assembly, aided and abetted by the wooly-minded opposition, has enshrined Bangladesh as a province of Pakistan in the new constitution. To quote: 'The constitution shall be appropriately amended so as to enable the people of the *province* of East Pakistan, as and when foreign aggression in that province and its effects are eliminated, to be represented in the affairs of the federation'. Hence the reference to the Supreme Court.

When the ruling party itself chooses to trade in blinkers for the sake of temporary political advantage, the opposition, free of the constraints of office, naturally kicks the ball around with abandon. Air Marshal Asghar Khan is now talking of reunification. It is to be hoped that he has done his calculations better when he gives only a six-month lease of life to the present regime.

The fact of the matter is that our leadership on either side of the fence is a prisoner of that original sin, namely, the Pakistan ideology or Islamic ideology, which has a destructive dialectics of its own. It has to be preserved so that it can be flouted. It must be reaffirmed if only to be slighted and ignored. Every holder of an office of state and every legislator is committed under oath to 'preserve the Islamic ideology which is the basis of the creation of Pakistan'. Here the matter ends for the simple reason that a modern state cannot be run as a truly Islamic polity. And when it comes to choosing between the dictates of Islamic brotherhood and petty gain, the choice, is obvious. This gigantic dichotomy between a formal, oral commitment and the compulsions of mundane necessity lead to labyrinthine contradictions. A self-proclaimed ideological state now has to run the mocking gauntlet of repudiating its own nationals stranded in Bangladesh. And nobody is the worse for mouthing this errant ideological hypocrisy.

The reluctance to recognize Bangladesh flows partly out of this ideological abracadabra. The rest flourishes on pure political opportunism. The present rulers who gleefully endorsed the military action on 25 March 1971, now plead for the option to recognize Bangladesh at their discretion which, not unexpectedly, stops short of actual recognition. Because Mr Bhutto must squeeze some personal political advantage out of every issue. Most of the opposition which raised not its voice against the excesses then committed in the name of Islam and the country, would not condescend to recognize the ailing reality of Bangladesh because they prefer to abide by a non-existent unity.

The point which needs a real searching of hearts is, do we really want Bangladesh back in the fold? A discussion of the factors, legitimate and illegitimate, which led to the creation of Bangladesh is no longer relevant. Residual Pakistan, now sporting a fighting chance for economic viability, has not been able to contend with the sharpened aspirations and demands of the different segments of its population. What chance for a workable aggregate of interests if the underprivileged but aggressive majority from Bangladesh once again invades the emaciated circle? Emotionalism apart, the hard facts are that Bangladesh, in sheer economic terms, is a liability which Pakistan cannot carry on its wobbly shoulders. Now that the choice is no longer with us, let us be content with the realities as they are. A combination of factors—Indian viciousness, strident Bengali nationalism, international intrigue and, not the least, the mindless policies of our political and military elite—created a given set of conditions in 1971, which has since crystallized. The inherent geopolitical tension which marked the erstwhile state of Pakistan has now been resolved. *That is if we can save the rest.* The irrevocable process of history demands that we encourage Bangladesh to chart out its not so manifest destiny with the help of the good samaritans, international and subcontinental, whose conscience for once pricked in good time and for the right cause. Paradoxically, it is a situation where nobody should, in the last analysis, have any cause for complaint except those in Pakistan who would still shy away from the recognition of Bangladesh. Possibly they know not what they are saying or doing. They never did.

It is possible to argue that a country is not a conglomeration of mere loaves and fishes. Granted. A more pertinent answer, of course, has to be sought from the people of Bangladesh. In 1970 the verdict of Muslim Bengal was clear enough. In 1971 it was cemented with a lot of warm, innocent blood. Even if there is a backlash now and which, as a matter of habit, is overplayed by the press in Pakistan, there is no chance that the two streams can meet as of old. Other barriers of steel will block the way. Prospects of renewed cooperation for mutual good, even a special relationship, need not be thwarted by the formal deed of recognition. In fact, recognition may speed up the necessary readjustment process which is overdue.

The overriding consideration is that recognition will set into motion the processes to untangle the humanitarian issues which seem to bother the ruling party and the opposition stalwarts the least. The POWs have become a pawn in a farcical political harangue. Even their wives and relatives rekindle their chant only when it suits the regime's political strategy. And those around here who hero-worship the 'freedom fighters in Muslim Bengal' hardly mention the segregated/incarcerated Bengalis nearer home. They too are Muslims. The Biharis in Bangladesh are already the forgotten casualties of history. All this does not make much sense, does it?

Student Excitement

7 July 1973

Our correspondent writes:

CRIES of 'recognize Bangladesh and bring back the POWs' by women and children in Islamabad contrasted strangely with the slogans of Karachi students: '*bacha bacha kat marae ga, Bangladesh nahi banae ga*'. The country-wide uproar by Opposition parties against recognition of Bangladesh, in Karachi took the form of a mobilization of students who spearheaded the movement here. The results were predictable: several students were arrested, all polytechnic institutions were closed till 17 August, all University examinations before 20 July were postponed indefinitely, section 144 once more came into prominence as meetings were broken up. And the Karachi Muslim League set up a Legal Aid Committee for providing help to students arrested in the demonstrations.

A meeting at the Karachi University campus last week, organized by the Jamiat-dominated union, was an indication of the prevailing mood. 'Break me up in two parts and then ask me to make a new myself, just as we are asked to make a new Pakistan' was a comment passed by one of the speakers. At the University, with its predominance of Jamiat supporters, one can always hear disparaging remarks being bandied about. 'My hands are not coloured by the blood of the innocent so I am not an *awami* president'—one of the milder sayings.

The students alleged that the government 'had sold the blood of our martyrs on the heights of Simla'. A pamphlet circulated at the meeting made the request to Bhutto: 'Please don't dance to the tune of Aunty Indira and Uncle Kosygin'. The logic advanced was that a man who threatened to fight for a thousand years, and later bowed his head before Mrs Gandhi, was quite capable of turning into a puppet for somebody else.

The Jamiat workers were dressed in a ghostly white. The badges they had on consisted of a red band, representing the sacrifices the Jamiat offered in the Punjab, and a pledge that they would not hesitate to do so in Karachi. The badge was accompanied by strips boldly proclaiming *Bangladesh na manzoor*. The meeting was very successful and well organized, marked by a crusading zeal and fervour that only the Jamiat can introduce in its meetings.

In his speech the union president warned that as long as the UDF supported the *Bangladesh na manzoor* movement it would get unqualified support from the Jamiat, but even if one member of the UDF withdrew his support it would alienate the students. Another speaker, with true Jamiat fanaticism said: 'The blood in our veins is not there to circulate within our bodies but it is there to flow in our cause.' Mr Bhutto's unfortunate habit of going back on his word was thoroughly condemned at the meeting. Referring to his January speech in which he had said that if 'Bangladesh is *na manzoor* to you it is *na manzoor* to me' the students demanded why he was raising the issue again when it was settled at that time.

Later, the procession by University students in Nazimabad could hardly be called a procession. There were only a handful of students guarded by an army of policemen. Here again the speeches were in the same vein as in the University meeting.

The movement, it is to be hoped, will not assume serious proportions. One can only be thankful to the good lord for sparing Karachi the likes of Mr Khar at the helm of affairs. Mr Khar's reaction to a similar movement by Lahore students last year was a masterpiece of suppression and brutality in which students were hauled off wholescale to the dreaded Lahore Fort. The administration's reaction in Karachi so far has been extremely civil, judging by Khar's standards. There is not much logic to the *na manzoor* movement but it should better be left to peter out of its own accord.

What really happened in '71?

7 July 1973

G. W. Choudhury

The following is a revealing personal account of the events leading to the military action in Bangladesh on 25 March 1971. The author, G. W. Choudhury, was a confidante of Ayub Khan and later served as a minister under Yahya Khan. He was a member of Yahya's 'inner' cabinet and was associated with the negotiations with Sh. Mujibur Rahman except in the final round. This account was published in the International Affairs, London, in its April issue.—Editor

AFTER a decade of 'political stability' and 'good' economic progress under Ayub Khan, when it used to be cited as a 'model' for developing countries, Pakistan faced one of its worst political crises during the winter of 1968–69. The outcome was the fall of Ayub Khan but not the restoration of democracy which had been the original aim of the political agitation. On the contrary, in March 1969, Pakistan began a second period of martial law under General Yahya Khan. The fall of Ayub has been extensively analysed, but two vitally important factors behind it have not been discussed: the Pakistani generals' loss of confidence in him and the secret deal between Z. A. Bhutto (now President of a truncated Pakistan) and Lieutenant-General Peerzada, the chief architect of the army coup against Ayub. The understanding between Bhutto and Peerzada also played an important part in the developments leading up to the disintegration of Pakistan in December 1971. Both men had been sacked by Ayub—one as Foreign Minister and the other as his Military Secretary—and they were drawn together by their common hostility to him.

The agitation against Ayub was started by a trifling incident in Rawalpindi—a scuffle between students and local police over some allegedly smuggled goods. The unrest spread rapidly all over the country, first in West Pakistan and then in the East. The leadership of the 'revolutionary movement' was assumed by Bhutto—the most well-dressed and aristocratic of revolutionary leaders. Many, including myself, wondered how he had managed to become a 'revolutionary hero' overnight. Later, after I had joined the Pakistan Cabinet (in November 1969) and had been able to talk to both Ayub and Yahya as well as to the other generals, it became clear to me that Bhutto had had a signal to go ahead from the generals before he launched the movement. Significantly, the army remained a passive

238

spectator of the disturbances, and when Ayub turned to it for support he was told to find a political, not a military, solution. But when he arranged round-table conferences with the political leaders, Bhutto was conspicuous by his absence. On the other hand, Ayub was able to negotiate with Mujibur Rahman (now Prime Minister of Bangladesh), and they very nearly agreed on a settlement. But Mujib was tantalized by the prospect presented by Ayub's opponents in the army, of getting power through the 'front door' (i. e. through elections) rather than by the 'back door' which was what Ayub offered him. Whether or not he let himself be fooled by the generals is a matter of interpretation.

On 25 March 1969, martial law was imposed in Pakistan for the second time in a decade. But the situations in which Ayub and Yahya took this step were entirely different. When Ayub came to power Pakistan's democratic institutions had been perverted and its politicians discredited. On the other hand, when Yahya became President, there was great resentment against authoritarian rule and lively agitation in favour of democracy. So, in his first broadcast on 26 March, Yahya gave a pledge that there would be a 'smooth transfer of power to the representatives of the people elected freely on the basis of an adult franchise.' This pledge was at first greeted with considerable scepticism; it was the sort of declaration that had only too often accompanied the emergence of military regimes in the Third World. Yahya, however, soon began a real dialogue with the leaders of the various parties; he toured the country from end to end and the politicians gradually became impressed by his sincerity.

I myself was involved in this political dialogue as a member of the three-man planning cell which was the first civilian body to be associated with Yahya's military regime. Ayub's downfall was believed to have been due to his exclusive dependence on senior civil servants, most of whom had served in the old Indian Civil Service under the British Raj. General Peerzada, who was the most powerful man in the Yahya government, wanted to avoid a similar 'mistake' and there made sure that no senior bureaucrats were able to get near Yahya. But when he came to realize that he and his military colleagues were not competent to run the machinery of government, he had to look for help from outside. This was how the planning cell came into existence. As a member of it, I had lengthy discussions with all the political leaders, including Mujib and Bhutto. I was also able to observe the straightforwardness of Yahya's dealings with the politicians. He devoted most attention to Mujib—rightly so, since he was the leader of the Bengalis and was very suspicious about the military regime's intentions. Mujib had never forgotten the arbitrary removal in 1957 of the Prime Minister, H. S. Suhrawardy, his political mentor and the founder of the Awami League by President Iskander Mirza, who a year later presided over the establishment of a military regime. He showed the greatest anxiety to secure every possible safeguard against similar treatment being meted out to him if—as was bound to happen—he lost some of his popularity after coming to power. Eventually, Yahya began to win his confidence and a good personal relationship gradually developed between them.

But Yahya was never master in his own house, as Ayub had been. He never had more than a limited hold over the army generals, who in fact constituted the ruling junta between March 1969 and December 1971, nor did he seem either anxious or able to acquire a position of complete dominance. Consequently what he did, or intended to do, was often torpedoed by other members of the ruling clique. Yet so far as it was possible to perceive what was really going on, things did appear to be moving in the right direction; Pakistan seemed about to show that it could carry out a peaceful transfer of power from a military to a democratic regime. Moreover, after joining Yahya's cabinet early in November 1969, I became convinced that he intended to have a genuine political settlement between the two parts of Pakistan by giving the Bengalis, who formed a majority of the population, a real share in the decision-making process within a loose federal or confederal system. On numerous occasions Yahya told me that the East Pakistanis had not had their proper share in any sphere of national life and that this must be rectified. I was greatly encouraged and hopefully began to work out the details of the scheme for the transfer of power. I also drafted the speech of 28 November 1969, in which Yahya announced his proposals for the future of the country.

Yahya's plan conceded all the demands put forward by Mujib; elections on the basis of one man one vote; a single-chamber central legislature; and the abolition of the amalgamation of West Pakistan into 'one unit'. Although the Bengalis of the East 'wing' formed a majority in undivided Pakistan, their representation in the federal legislature had always been equal to that of the West 'wing'. They accepted this parity of representation in 1955 on condition that the principle of parity should also apply in the allocation of funds for economic development, representation in the armed services and in every other sphere. But since in practice there had been no parity except in the electoral representation of the two 'wings', the Bengalis felt justified in demanding to be released from their side of the bargain. They were also opposed to a bicameral system for the central legislature because they feared that what they gained by being represented on a 'one man, one vote' basis in one chamber would be lost if a second chamber, constituted on a territorial basis had a majority of West Pakistan seats.

Yahya, however, was prepared to accept a—unicameral system in which all matters—even constitutional issues—were decided by a simple majority vote; in his speech he merely expressed a pious hope that on constitutional matters there would be a consensus of opinion from the various parts of the proposed federation. He was also prepared to break up the amalgamation of West Pakistan into 'one unit', which the (primarily Punjab) ruling elite had carried out in 1955 because they felt it was the best way to protect West Pakistan's economic interest vis-a-vis the East. It also strengthened the arguments for parity of representation in the central assembly on the grounds that the two 'wings' of the country must have equal representation. The Bengalis did not like the 'one unit' arrangement because it weakened their bargaining position; the smaller provinces of West Pakistan shared the Bengalis' fears of Punjabi domination, but under the 'one unit' system had no separate voice with which to express their feelings. Mujib could not openly demand the break-up of the 'one unit', but he made it clear to Yahya that it would be most welcome.

The most important constitutional issue of all, however, was the relationship between the centre and the provinces. Paradoxically, the Bengalis, who since they were in a majority should have had no fear of domination, were anxious to secure the maximum degree of autonomy for their province, particularly in economic and financial matters. Yahya made no attempt to tackle this crucial issue. Instead he left it to the decision of the new national assembly, which was to draw up a constitution, at the same time strongly supporting the Bengali claim for maximum autonomy. Naturally, Mujib had no objection to leaving this issue to the new assembly in which there would be a clear Bengali majority.

Outside Pakistan, the World press welcomed Yahya's 'bold' and 'sincere' proposals for restoring democratic processes in Pakistan. Yahya was described as a shy and reluctant dictator. President Nixon was reported to have advised the Greek ambassador in Washington to follow the example of Yahya. All those whether inside or outside the country, who wanted to see Pakistan united and stable, welcomed his proposals for the transfer of power. In the past, the ruling elite in West Pakistan had always looked at Bengal's problems from the angle of 'law and order'. This was the first—and last—attempt to put the complicated relationship between East and West Pakistan on a sound political basis.

Many questions can be asked about a plan which aroused such strong expectations. Did the army really want to hand over power at all? Did Mujib want settlement on the basis of a united Pakistan or did he only intend to use the elections to establish his credentials as the sole leader of emerging Bangladesh? And what were the aims of Bhutto?

One thing that was soon apparent was that the army generals and the West Pakistani political leaders thought that Yahya had gone too far in trying to placate the Bengalis at the cost of the 'national interest' as they interpreted it. In order to protect the country against a Bengali-dominated assembly, they put forward two particular demands. First, the constitutional document, which—since the country had no constitution—had to be promulgated before elections could be legally held, must contain a definition of the limits of provincial autonomy; and secondly, in the new assembly, constitutional matters must be decided, not by a simple majority, but by a two-thirds vote or at least 60 per cent of the total membership. It was argued that there was no reason why Yahya should not take a definite decision on the extent of provincial autonomy, just as he had decided on the basis of representation and the break-up of 'one-unit'. The non-Awami League leaders from East Pakistan took this line as well as the West Pakistani leaders and the military junta.

Yahya between the generals and Mujib

The matter was thrashed out at a series of meetings of the 'inner cabinet' which was composed of Yahya; his principal staff officer, General Peerzada; the Chief of Staff, General Hamid, who began to entertain hopes of succeeding Yahya as the country's third military president; two military provincial governors and the two deputy (provincial) martial law administrators of East and West Pakistan. I myself was the only civilian present and I attended not as a cabinet minister but as a constitutional expert. Eventually, it was almost decided to accept the demand for a two-thirds majority on constitutional matters and to define the extent of provincial autonomy in the constitutional document or 'Legal Framework Order 1970' (popularly known as LFO). But Mujib made it clear through the Governor of East Pakistan, Admiral Ahsan, that to do so would mean the end of negotiations and the beginning of an armed confrontation.

Yahya was in a real dilemma. The generals seemed to prefer to have a confrontation before elections—i.e. before Mujib could consolidate his position in East Pakistan. But Ahsan, the only member of the junta who understood the political realities in the East 'wing', assured the President that a united Pakistan would not survive a confrontation with Mujib. In an attempt to find a way out of the impasse, I proposed at a meeting of the inner cabinet in January 1970 that instead of trying to define the extent of provincial autonomy, the LFO should define the minimum requirements that were essential for the existence of *one* Pakistan. This proposal surprised Yahya and angered the hawks among the generals. But it was strongly supported by Ahsan, and I was allowed to elaborate it. Surprisingly, and to the great relief of Yahya, Ahsan and myself, it was eventually accepted by the generals. But although the crisis seemed to be over, subsequent events showed that it had only been postponed for a year.

The LFO, which was at last published on 31 March 1970, contained five points or principles which were regarded as the minimum requirements for a united Pakistan. (1) Pakistan must be based on Islamic ideology—Mujib was neutral on this issue. (2) The country must have a democratic constitution providing for free and fair elections—no one could object to that. (3) Pakistan's territorial integrity must be upheld in the constitution—Mujib could not object to this because, whatever his ultimate goal, he could not openly challenge the 'oneness' of the country. (4) The disparity between the 'wings', particularly in economic development, must be eliminated by statutory provisions to be guaranteed in the constitution—again Mujib could have no objection. (5) The distribution of power must be made in such a way that the provinces enjoyed the maximum degree of autonomy consistent with giving the central government sufficient power to discharge its federal responsibilities, including the maintenance of the country's territorial integrity. No doubt the intention was to set up a conventional federal system. But since the working of this stipulation was deliberately vague, it was capable of more than one interpretation; it allowed Mujib to base his election campaign on his Six Points while those who wanted a united, federal Pakistan could still hope that they had got it. The LFO was criticized particularly in East Pakistan as a retreat from the plan put forward, by Yahya in November 1969. In a sense this was true. But those who knew the inside story of how the document had been drawn up realized that some compromise was essential and were not dissatisfied with the outcome. Mujib, who learned what had gone on from Ahsan, accepted the outcome, and when the Awami League council demanded that he should boycott the elections because of the 'new restrictions' in the LFO, he refused to agree. He was reported to have told his 'inner cabinet' that his sole aim was to win the elections by capturing 99 per cent of the Bengali seats. Who could then—he was said to have argued—ignore his plan for Bangladesh? He was also reported to have predicted support from 'outside sources'.

The elections were originally fixed for October 1970. But after disastrous floods in East Pakistan in August, they were postponed for two months. In November East Bengal was devastated by a cyclone and there were demands for a further postponement of the elections. Mujib, however, threatened to revolt if the elections were delayed any longer, and Yahya agreed that they should go ahead. This decision finally destroyed Mujib's doubts about Yahya's sincerity and made the relationship between them even more cordial; in November 1970 they had three secret meetings and Yahya cheerfully told me that the new Pakistani constitution would combine Mujib's Six Points and the five principles laid down in the LFO. He had just completed his triangular tour of Moscow (June), Washington (October), and Peking (November), and it was widely believed that he had already reached an understanding with Mujib that he should continue as President while Mujib became Prime Minister.

Meanwhile in West Pakistan, where right-wing parties had always been strong, Bhutto was winning more and more support. The main theme of his election campaign was a 'thousand years' war with India to restore the national honour which Ayub was alleged to have sacrificed at the Tashkent conference in 1966 under pressure from the Soviet Union. More significant—and ominous—were Bhutto's growing links with the generals. They turned to him to protect the so-called 'national interests' because they realized that they had been deprived of their confrontation with Mujib. Far from rejecting the LFO, he now seemed to have a better understanding than ever with Yahya on constitutional issues. Moreover, it was clear that Mujib was going to win at the polls and that his victory would be all the greater because the highly emotional Bengalis were furiously angry with the central government for its alleged failure to deal adequately with the cyclone disaster.

The elections, held on 7 December 1970, were by any standard completely free and fair. As expected, Mujib had a landslide victory in East Pakistan, gaining an absolute majority in the national assembly by capturing 167 out of the 169 seats allotted to the East 'wing'. He enjoyed a similar success in the provincial assembly at Dacca. What was surprising about the election results was the total defeat of the right-wing and orthodox parties in the West 'wing' and the emergence of a non-Punjabi, Bhutto, as the leader of West Pakistan, or, more precisely, of the Punjab.

Bhutto's success boded ill for the future of a united Pakistan. There was no love lost between him and Mujib; on the contrary, they shared a mutual distrust and dislike, if not hatred. More important, neither possessed any broad perspective or vision. Unlike such Congress leaders as Gandhi and Nehru, or Muslim League leaders like Jinnah, neither Mujib nor Bhutto possessed any of the qualities of a leader whose aim is to achieve his objectives at a minimum cost in terms of human suffering and loss to society. In a sense both were products of Ayub Khan's authoritarian regime; both flourished on negative appeals to the illiterate voters of Pakistan—one by whipping up regional feeling against Punjabi domination and the other by whipping up militant national feeling against India. Neither had any constructive or positive approach. The third party in the political equation, the army, unlike the British authorities in 1946–47, also seems to have been insincere, bent on retaining the absolute power which it had enjoyed for the past eleven years. Only Yahya, Ahsan and a few other generals;

particularly among the younger group in the Pakistan army, really seemed to want a genuine political settlement. But their hand was weakened after the election when the country began to drift inexorably towards confrontation.

Drift towards confrontation

In the LFO Yahya had provided that the new national assembly must complete its task of framing a new constitution within 120 days. This time limit was accepted by all the political leaders. It had taken two constituent assemblies nine years to frame a constitution for Pakistan between 1947 and 1956, and everyone wanted to prevent a repetition of this tragic delay. It was also agreed that the majority group or groups responsible for producing a constitution would show the draft to the President before formally presenting it to the assembly. Mujib had already solemnly promised Yahya, during their secret talks in November, to show him the Awami League's draft.

Yahya, who was anxious to begin talks with the newly elected leaders as soon as possible invited Mujib to come to Rawalpindi. Mujib declined but invited the President to come to Dacca instead. Yahya, accepted and asked me to go with him so that he could have expert advice on Mujib's draft constitution. The two leaders met on 12 January and talked for more than three hours. But Yahya emerged from the meeting a bitter and frustrated man. Mujib, he complained, had gone back on his word and refused to show him his draft constitution on the grounds that, as leader of the majority party, he and he alone was responsible for the new constitution. Mujib also demanded the immediate summoning of the assembly otherwise the consequences would be dire. It seemed plain that the confrontation, which had been avoided with such difficulty in 1970 could no longer be prevented.

Yahya went on from Dacca to hold talks with Bhutto in his home town of larkana. Bhutto had also begun to show signs of intransigence. He started to issue press statements declaring that the 'Punjab was the bastion of power' and could not be ignored in any future government or in the making of the constitution. He also made it clear that he would 'not play the role of a loyal opposition leader'; and that since the Awami League victory was confined to one region (East Pakistan), 'two majority groups, must be recognized and two prime ministers might be necessary'. An impartial reading of Bhutto's utterances, together with his active lobbying of the hawks in the Pakistan army, would lead one to conclude that if he had to make a choice between two 'Ps'—Power or Pakistan—he would choose the former.

At Larkana Yahya and prominent members of the junta, including General Peerzada and General Hamid, enjoyed Bhutto's hospitality and held long conferences with him. I myself was not present at these talks but I learned about them afterwards from reliable sources. It seems that they were fatal for the prospects of a united Pakistan. Bhutto exploited to the full the sense of frustration left in Yahya's mind by his meeting with Mujib in Dacca. He was strongly supported by his old friend, Peerzada, who enjoyed Yahya's unlimited trust and confidence. The result was that while still at Larkana the junta, ignoring Bhutto's provocative utterances, decided to prepare a contingency plan. In case Mujib persisted 'in his uncompromising attitude'. At a meeting on 14 February it also decided to dissolve the Pakistan cabinet; apparently because the Bengali ministers and one non-Bengali minister (who was a close friend of Mujib) were working hard to find a compromise. At the same meeting it was also decided that Admiral Ahsan (who had in fact expressed a wish to resign) should be replaced as Governor of East Pakistan by a hawk, General Tikka Khan.

In the meantime India had stopped all flights between East and West Pakistan because of the alleged hijacking of an Indian plane by Pakistanis at Lahore. While negotiations over the incident were still going on between the Indian and Pakistani governments, Mujib publicly described it as a 'conspiracy' to postpone the transfer of power, while Bhutto declared that the so-called hijackers were 'national heroes,' Mujib's remarks were resented by the generals, who, began to describe him as an 'Indian agent'. At a farewell party given for members of the cabinet, General Hamid told me that his 'boys' (*i.e.* soldiers) were 'getting restless for action'. When I pointed out the dangers of such a course of action; he retorted: I could fix it up in 72 hours'.

On 1 March the national assembly, which was due to meet on the 3rd, was indefinitely postponed after Bhutto had threatened that he would boycott it unless Mujib came to terms with him. But by now their mutual suspicion and hatred made this impossible. In East Pakistan there was a violent reaction to the postponement. Mujib described it as non-cooperation, but it was not the Gandhian type of non-violent, non-cooperation, it was an open revolt which virtually amounted to a unilateral declaration of independence for Bangladesh. Cries of Joy Bangla (victory for Bengal) were heard everywhere, and what was almost a parallel government began to function under Mujib's instructions. Between 3 and 25 March the central government's writ did not run in East Pakistan.

This explosive situation was mainly created by Bhutto's boycott of the assembly. Many people still feel that if it had not been postponed, Mujib might still have been able to produce an agreed constitution with the help of West Pakistani deputies who did not belong to Bhutto's party and who had already arrived in Dacca for the opening of the assembly. But Bhutto was now the junta's most influential adviser; he was even reported to have prepared Yahya's various statements including the decision to postpone the assembly.

Even at this late stage, however, Yahya and Mujib were still talking to each other on the telephone and still seemed anxious to negotiate. Mujib appeared to be getting nervous about the activities of his own extremists while Yahya still hoped to go down in history as the man responsible for a voluntary transfer of power from a military to a civilian regime. On 15 March, he went to Dacca and next day began a crucial series of talks with Mujib. The negotiations were carried on at two levels; at a summit level between Yahya and Mujib, with Bhutto joining in later; and at an expert level between three teams—Yahya's advisers, led by his former Law Minister (now law adviser), Justice Cornelius and General Peerzada; the Awami League team, led by Tajuddin (who subsequently acted as Prime Minister of Bangladesh before Mujib's return from detention in West Pakistan) and Dr Kamal Hossain (now Bangladesh's Law Minister); and Bhutto's team, consisting of members of his party secretly advised by senior Punjabi bureaucrats.

By 20 March the press was reporting that a compromise constitutional formula, incorporating most of the fundamentals of Mujib's Six Points, had been agreed. The reports turned out to be too good to be true. Next day Mujib rejected the compromise formula and on 23 a new formula, drawn up by the Awami League team, was presented by Dr Hossain. There was in fact—as Dr Hossain himself was reported to have said—very little difference between the two drafts. Both preserved the unity of Pakistan; both restricted the powers of the centre, as far as East Pakistan was concerned, as much as possible. All the same the Dacca talks broke down, and on 25 March the Pakistan army took matters into its own hands. The resort to force was bound to destroy a united Pakistan and the end came with the entry of a triumphant Indian army into Dacca on 16 December 1971.

Since both drafts envisaged one Pakistan, why did not the army and Bhutto accept the Awami League's constitution? And since both conceded the Bengalis' demand for autonomy on the basis of the Six Points, why did not Mujib and the Awami League accept Yahya's draft. During two visits to Pakistan in 1971 I sought the answers to those two crucial questions, but failed to find any satisfactory or definite explanation. Perhaps the break-up of Pakistan was made inevitable by the growing tension, suspicion and even hatred between the ruling elite of West Pakistan and the Bengali intelligentsia—although it came as a great shock to many, like myself, who had cherished the ideals behind the Muslims' demand for a separate state in the 1940s. But could not the terrible bloodshed connected with the emergence of Bangladesh have been avoided? Gandhi and Nehru committed themselves to full independence for India, yet they showed great statesmanship in accepting Dominion Status and even a British Governor-General so that a smooth and quick transfer of power could take place. Unlike Subash Bose who invited Japan's help during the Second World War, they stuck to the path of negotiation. Could not Mujib have shown the same wisdom and prevented the killing of (according to his estimate) three million Bengalis? Could he not have avoided a situation which led inevitably to the introduction of foreign (Indian) troops and the destruction not only of the country's economic infrastructure but also of the social fabric?

I cannot vouch for what happened at the final Dacca talks in March 1971, but I can certainly state that when Yahya went to Dacca in January he was prepared to accept Mujib's Six Points without reservation. I may further disclose that he asked me to prepare a formula on the relationship between the centre and the provinces. I drafted a plan for a confederal solution on the basis of the Six Points, which after the election I knew was the only way to preserve a united Pakistan, Yahya wrote on my draft: 'What is the difference between your scheme and the Six Points?' Yet he accepted it and took it with him to Dacca in January. Mujib's fatal mistake was his refusal at that meeting to honour his pledge to show Yahya his draft constitution. But the story is incomplete without a reference to Bhutto and his friends in the army like Peerzada and Hamid. When the full story of Pakistan's dismemberment can be told, they may well be found to have the prime responsibility for the failure of the final Dacca talks and the tragic consequences.

The Man to Watch

7 July 1973

Roger Moody

UP on the top of the hill, in a bungalow which overlooks the lush green Kaghan valley, sits the man who first brought the army into politics in Pakistan. A little lower down on the same hill path, surrounded by barbed wire, and guarded by a whole platoon, the man who effectively broke the country in two, drinks and slums out his days and nights under house arrest. At the bottom of the road where it meets the town of Abbottabad, working from stables converted into a party office and living quarters, resides the man who—quite possibly—will be the next President of Pakistan.

They are all three Khans—tenuous descendants of the Mongol chiefs who first opened up this part of the subcontinent and closed off many avenues of progress. Ayub Khan... Yahya Khan... and Asghar Khan. Two former army Supremos and a retired Air Marshal, living within a stones throw and a bullets bite of each other. In almost any other part of the world, such proximity of the failed and future leaders would spark off gossip columns in the press, a few hearty national jokes, if not the odd pilgrimage or two.

But in Pakistan today, such sentiments seem wildly out of place. Incongruity has become the essence of the political game, and the bizarre seems commonplace. Yahya Khan is girded round with a hundred soldiers, in case he is tempted to tell the truth about what happened in East Pakistan during the 'crackdown' of March 1971. And Asghar Khan has had his house burned to the ground, his public meetings broken up by thugs, his workers shot at, and almost weekly threats to 'get rid of him', made by some government minister or official because he has, in large measure, told the truth about the disaster which struck the country at that time and is affecting it now.

Asghar Khan is a quiet, imposing, infinitely self-restrained man, whose only indications of a military history are his neat moustache and near-perfect English accent. When he refers to President Zulfikar Ali Bhutto as a 'fascist' you realize it is not mere name-calling, but derives from a long and bitter experience of the ruin of democratic processes in Pakistan. Asghar Khan opposed Ayub Khan's regime. It is a matter of cold record that he supported Shaikh Mujib, called Yahya Khan a 'traitor' at the height of the confrontation in Bangladesh, when no other leader in the country hardly dared speak his name. Within days of Bhutto coming to power, the former Air Marshal accused him directly of engineering the army's action in East Pakistan 'either to crush the Bengalis as a political opposition, or to force them to secede and leave him a free hand in West Pakistan.'

There is a certain amount of evidence to support Asghar Khan's view. Back in May 1971, Peter Hazlehurst of *The Times* (London) drew up a 'charge sheet' of responsibility for the genocide let loose on the Bengalis that year. It was his own firm view, on first hand observation and talks with Pakistani leaders that the major obstacle to a negotiated settlement with Shaikh Mujibur Rahman and the Awami League (which, after all, had won the majority of seats in the previous year's election) was Mr Bhutto. He simply refused to negotiate. Last week a former close associate of Mr Bhutto's admitted to a colleague of mine, in private, the same thing. But, as Asghar Khan pointed out to me, perhaps the most damning evidence comes from a recent move of the President's own making. Just after the 'Bangladesh affair', Mr Bhutto set up a high-powered judicial committee to apportion responsibility for the break-up of Pakistan. The findings of that committee have never been made public. And no one is allowed to visit Yahya Khan.

The Air Marshal and his party (Tehrik-i-Istiqlal, literally 'Movement for Strength') have not confined their attacks on the present government to fanning the flames of the past. But the fact remains that, in contrast to the main opposition force—the United Democratic Front—their central *raison d'etre* is to deny the legitimacy of the Bhutto regime. The UDF (a perplexing conglomerate of parties, headed by the militantly Muslim Jamaat-i-Islami and the left-wing National Awami Party) fights its battles in the National Assembly, and in abortive public meetings which are broken up by People's Party youths, and the police (I saw this for myself last Sunday in Lahore). On the other hand, the Tehrik-i-Istiqlal will have no truck whatever with the government. Its style of politics is a mixture of the hustings (Asghar Khan has made 37 'whistle- stops' in one region alone in the last few months) and the stream-lined press conference. The Tehrik's workers are intent, lacking any of the flamboyance of the PPP, or the high-pressure salesmanship the UDF occasionally smacks of.

Such respectable, but undramatic activity prompted me to ask him how he saw the 'collapse of Bhutto' which he had predicted several months ago, as happening 'within the year', and his own emergence as the people's choice (which he unabashedly expects). He could not be more specific than to hope for the resignation of the present government, under manifold pressures from inside Pakistan, and the installation of a 'neutral administration' by the Chief Justice, which will arrange another general election.

It is here perhaps that the major weakness not only of the Tehrik's position—but that of the UDF—breaks surface. Few observers of Pakistani affairs will doubt that the President's installation of two tame governors above the heads of the elected governments in Baluchistan and North West Frontier Province; the current army action in Baluchistan—which smacks distinctly of the military interference in Bangladesh; the blanket imposition of Section 144 (which prohibits public gatherings) against the opposition parties; the daily hooliganism of the People's Party workers, and literally weekly arrests of prominent journalists and editors bears the stamp of dictatorship. ('Martial law all over again', comments Asghar Khan.)

However, the opposition's programme seems limited to calling for new elections or a return to democracy. Inevitably ordinary people ask: 'why would they do any better than the PPP?' They lack the patronage and flare of PPP leaders; the NAP already has a none too auspicious history of coalition governing in North West Frontier Province and Baluchistan. Above all, perhaps, the unwieldy nature of the UDF, with its attempt to combine right and left wing is hardly a convincing weapon against the fissiparous tendencies which, rightly or wrongly, President Bhutto professes to see in every opposition nook and cranny.

Asghar Khan certainly has one thing which the UDF lacks—a personal history of courage in the face of totalitarianism. But the gap between his present position as a leader without a visible large power base, a crusader with a cause, rather than a politician with a programme—and the sheer numerical strength—in universities, factories and in the villages—required to confront the present regime, seems huge.

Possibly the sheer crudity of the methods used by the PPP to stifle the opposition, and the weakness of the President's own position ('He cannot speak publicly without a thousand police' appropriately commented Asghar Khan. 'And we can't speak with them!') will lead to countrywide disorders sooner than now seems likely.

But it is questionable whether, when Bhutto falls, people like Asghar Khan will still be around to take up the reins of power. Or whether in the meantime, he and those of his ilk, will not have fallen under police bullets, PPP brickbats, or an 'unknown assassin's' bomb.

The Logic of Recognition

14 July 1973

Khurshid Hyder

THE current campaign against the recognition of Bangladesh is a purposeless and dangerous exercise. It fails to appreciate the issues involved and completely overlooks the changed political situation which has been created in the subcontinent as a result of the events of 1971.

Most of the arguments being put forth for non-recognition are tenuous and misleading. They are not based on factual analysis but on emotional guesses. For instance, it is affirmed that the recognition of Bangladesh will destroy or undermine the ideology of Pakistan. While saying so none of the opponents of recognition have taken the trouble of either defining the said ideology, or how within the framework of their definition it will get subverted. Pakistan was demanded by the Muslims of the subcontinent when the Hindus refused them the constitutional safeguards for the protection of their religion, language, and culture and give them adequate representation in the political institutions. The Lahore resolution of 1940 which first adumbrated the demand for a Muslim homeland envisaged *two* and not *one*, states. Iqbal's Muslim state was limited to the Muslim majority areas of the north-west. Chaudhri Rahmat Ali's Pakistan was confined to the territories which comprise Pakistan now. For the Muslims of Bengal he had suggested a separate state to be known as Bang-i-Islam.

The second reason extensively aired against recognition is that it will spark off separatist tendencies in the various constituent provinces of West Pakistan. This is totally erroneous. The nature of relationship between the various provinces of West Pakistan on the one hand, and East and West Pakistan on the other, is not in the least analogous. The union between East and West Pakistan had been incongruous from the very start. The fact of geographical separation is the most crucial single factor which accounted for all the other differences—be they linguistic and cultural, or economic and strategic. But for geographical division, separatist tendencies would not have taken root, thrived and ultimately found fulfilment in the emergence of Bangladesh.

The case of West Pakistan is vastly different. None of the four provinces can be a viable independent entity. There is an underlying cultural and ethnic harmony between the people of the various regions; their economic and commercial interests are complementary. The analogy thus does

251

not hold. Moreover, if people want to live together as a nation, nothing can thwart their will; but if this will is not there, no one can keep them together as a nation.

Furthermore, the contention that by withholding recognition we will be able to bring about a reunion of the two erstwhile wings is chimerical and fails to take into account the political trends in Bangladesh. Bengali Muslims may be disenchanted with the present state of affairs in Bangladesh, anti-Indian sentiment may be widely prevalent, but there is not even a faint hint of a pro-Pakistan backlash. Instead of striving for an *anschluss* we should aim towards greater understanding of each other's point of view and close economic and commercial links which may help Bangladesh to lessen her growing dependence on India. The history of twenty-four years of union was anything but happy and starkly counsels against the re-enactment of the past arrangement in any form.

The Muslims of Bengal have suffered enormously in the past two centuries. Ever since the decline of the Moghul power in the eighteenth century and its supersession by British rule, Muslims have been the victims of endless exploitation and oppression. William Hunter in his famous book *The Indian Muslims* has vividly portrayed the plight of the Muslims under the British Raj in the nineteenth century. Later, with the emergence of western educated business and professional Hindu community, the Muslims of Bengal had to bear the brunt of multiple domination. Curzon's partition of Bengal may have helped somewhat to correct the imbalance between the rich industrialized West Bengal and the impoverished eastern section of the province. But unfortunately it was not allowed to function and had to be rescinded under Hindu pressure.

Without going into the genesis of the 1971 crisis, let it not be forgotten that it were the Bengalis who suffered the most as a result of it. They had to live through the anguished months of civil strife and violence; it were their territory, homes and hearths which were devastated in the war. The establishment of Bangladesh has not brought their woes to an end. It is morally incumbent on us to extend them whatever help we can. It is not piety to shout religious slogans and harangues on Islamic ideology to serve narrow political ends. But it will be piety if we extend a helping hand to the Bengali Muslims when they are passing through a very difficult time. It can only be possible if the lines of communications are re-established after the recognition of Bangladesh.

The recognition issue is inextricably linked with the question of the repatriation of the POWs. New Delhi has made this abundantly clear. The fiction of surrender to the joint command was launched for this very reason. By indefinitely postponing the question of recognition, we shall be condemning 90,000 Pakistanis to languish in Indian detention camps *ad infinitum*.

Viewed historically, the doctrine of non-recognition has never been an effective instrument of diplomacy. West Germany, after years of adamant resistance, has been forced to acknowledge the reality of East Germany. America's non-recognition of the Soviet Union for fourteen long years—1919–1933—was devoid of any results. The same can be said of the policy of non-recognition of China which was adopted by most of the members of the Atlantic Alliance. After two decades of futile diplomacy, the policy of non-recognition has had to be discarded in favour of recognition.

It should also be stressed in this context that non-recognition of Bangladesh will put our friends and allies in a very difficult position. An overwhelming majority of states, including four of the five permanent members of the Security Council, have recognized the new state. China has steadfastly stood behind us and has helped us prevent the entry of Bangladesh into the United Nations. But it may be difficult and awkward for her to do it indefinitely.

A number of Muslim countries, who initially upheld our policies towards Dacca, have since extended *de jure* or *de facto* recognition to Bangladesh. Besides Malaysia and Indonesia, a number of other countries Iraq, Afghanistan, and Yemen have also recognized Bangladesh. It is quite likely that in the course of time, many others may feel compelled to follow suit. Such a possibility should be foreclosed by taking a timely decision on recognition. Otherwise it may adversely affect our negotiating position both with regard to India and Bangladesh.

However, recognition of Bangladesh *should by no means be unconditional.* There *must* be prior or simultaneous agreement on the repatriation of POWs, on the rights of the non-Bengali minority there and all other economic and financial issues flowing out of the break-up of the country. It does make sense to say that till there is mutually satisfactory agreement on all these points in dispute, Bangladesh should not be recognized. But to clamour that it should not be recognized *per se* makes no sense at all.

Once Bangladesh is recognized, it may be possible for the two countries to gradually shake off the legacy of bitterness and hatred left by the war of 1971 and make a fresh start towards friendlier relations.

The Lingering Talks

11 August 1973

Sancho Panza

O N Sunday before last when Mr Haksar was still chanting 'good talks',' useful discussions', 'satisfied', 'optimistic', and so on, a British journalist told me he could foresee that the talks would fail. His main reason for saying so was that sooner or later issues would come up which would require some clear and open concessions to be made by the Bangladesh government and Mr Haksar would feel the pinch of communicating with Shaikh Mujibur Rahman through Delhi and Belgrade. The adjournment seems to have resulted from something very close to this reason as the main and final consideration for the adjournment which was obviously sought by New Delhi.

Our own side seems to have readily agreed to a small two-week adjournment for domestic reasons of a changeover from the interim to the permanent constitution. I cannot entirely agree with the suggestion made by certain Indian correspondents that we did not want a settlement except on our terms. But this could be true to an extent because Pakistan was in no position to agree to a take-it-or-leave-it proposition of a package deal. What we could do was to phase out the package deal into elements of a process of settlement bringing it into line with a step-by-step approach with the compensatory mechanism to see that each step by one side was accompanied by the reciprocal measure on the other, and the next initiative by the first party was ensured. Instead, the approach now seems to be that certain aspects of the Delhi Declaration have been isolated and will await action at a later stage. For instance, the issue of trials has been simplified by its isolation and the understanding that we will hold 203 against India's 195 until President Bhutto and Prime Minister Shaikh Mujibur Rahman can meet and come to a settlement on the question. Until then, we continue to hold the 203 and the Indians hold the 195; the guarantee is that the 195 will not be handed over to Bangladesh.

The two sides did try during the talks to cover the whole gamut of the relations between the two countries, India and Pakistan. There was a review also of the working of the Simla accord. From what Mr Haksar said to Pakistani correspondents, one could notice that the reluctance to proceed towards the issues covered by Article 3 of the agreement and to convene a summit was shared by both sides. Pakistan was equally unwilling to have Mrs Gandhi on a state visit to Pakistan while the

254

most important matters bedevilling the relations between the two countries were still not out of the way. With 90,000 prisoners in India, how could she be received in Pakistan as the head of a friendly country should be?

The most important aspect of the talks, however, was the doggedness with which the two sides persisted in their efforts to narrow down their differences. Eight days of talks, two sittings with the President, and consultations with Delhi and Belgrade/Brioni did show that both sides meant business. But it is sad that the Indian side had come here with a publicly committed position which could not have been welcomed by Pakistan. Pakistan's concession to the Delhi Declaration was that it sought clarifications instead of rejecting it outright. The approach to the ICJ would suggest that the mood was one of rejection. That Bangladesh had given up the pre-condition of recognition by Pakistan was not quite correct; towards the end of the Rawalpindi negotiations, the issue was back, evidently at the instance of Dacca, possibly as a result of the general review of the subcontinental situation, as Mr Aziz Ahmed classifies it. Obviously that was the cause of the annoyance of Mr Haksar and the breakdown which he so admirably converted into an adjournment after his meeting with President Bhutto.

The question of recognition by Pakistan has now become more complicated. Bangladesh now wants, perhaps that Pakistan should ensure to it the membership of the United Nations. That is appropriately a function of the Security Council and for Pakistan to make a promise of making a gift of it to Dacca, there should be the backing at least of Peking if not of all those who have been supporting Pakistan so far in its stance of not recognizing the breakaway state at the request of the mother-country. More than that, Pakistan and the others are committed to the stand that the resolutions of the United Nations must be obeyed by the applicant before it can be given membership of the international body. If Dacca continues to drag its feet and yet wants to be seated in the General Assembly in September, it should find some face-saving device for Pakistan to be able to tell its friends not only to recognize Dacca but also to have Bangladesh seated in the United Nations. Quite understandably, this was the issue that limited the prospects of Mr Haksar's mission to Pakistan.

It was said by Indian sources that the issue arose out of a suggestion made by Pakistan on the issue of Biharis and their option to Pakistan which takes the figure of those to be repatriated to 260,000. Our side evidently suggested that when recognition comes and normal relations between Pakistan and Bangladesh are resumed, many of those who now want to migrate to Pakistan or vice versa to Bangladesh, may change their mind. We would, therefore accept at this stage only those who belong here in any case or such of them as are otherwise committed because of federal jobs. In the context of these arguments, the other side obviously strayed out of the humanitarian problem to the political problem of recognition with the rider of membership of the United Nations. It is true that the Indian side could have accepted our suggestion to put off the issue of Biharis until normal relations are restored between the two countries. But obviously they needed the consent of Bangladesh on such an important and cardinal issue which forms part of the Delhi Declaration. It became a new issue when it came back from Belgrade in the form of a demand for recognition here and now, and a demarche to all our friends to give instant recognition to Bangladesh and propose to have it seated in the United Nations. The thinking of Shaikh Mujibur Rahman can be read in every comma of this suggestion.

Mr Aziz Ahmed's press statement, however, takes the discussion on the 'new' issues to be a part of the general review and dismisses the suggestion that 'new' issues were at all raised which might well be the case literally. 'The merit of the Delhi Declaration lies in that it delinked these humanitarian issues from political matter', he says. The larger subject of promoting subcontinental reconciliation was part of the general review.

Otherwise, the mission of Haksar and Co., was quite a success. The issue of 195 accused is out of the way, if only by defering a decision on the issue. The question of assets and liabilities has been left to be negotiated at the proper time and opportunity in a bilateral setting. That is to say that only the humanitarian issues have come to the negotiation table and the two sides have very nearly succeeded in solving them. A delay of two weeks and a fouling-up because of the confusion possibly introduced by Dacca does not matter.

There could have been a temptation to get something out of talks—something to show to the Indian public. And possibly our side would not mind a concession or two on the overflights issue. Similarly, the Indians could have opened up communications, both telegraphic and postal—again on humanitarian grounds. One can understand India's reluctance to resume diplomatic relations with us although the reasons do not apply any longer. But no one can insist that there is any justification for not resuming normal telegraphic and postal communications and exchange of correspondents.

Pakistan at the ICJ

11 August 1973

Aziz Kurtha

THE specialized study of international law, and particularly the international laws of war, is as esoteric as it is paradoxical. Its esoteric nature emanates from the lamentable fact that its study is limited to all too few specialists the majority of whom are professors to western universities. In a sense this is understandable because the occasions for invoking and applying the laws of war are necessarily as calamitous as they are rare. International hostilities of almost global proportions and treachery beyond the pale of normal human behaviour are curiously the usual occasions for invoking this area of law.

International law, moreover, exists in an uneasy twilight zone between power politics and law where the bark of international laws and regulations are often much worse than their bite. It's a well-known fact that despite the explicit prohibitions in the United Nations Charter and a score of other treaties restraining states from resorting to the use of force there are nevertheless at least a dozen areas of the world where serious international hostilities are currently in progress. Here emerges the paradox of the laws of war which regulate the conduct of hostilities when in fact those very hostilities are prescribed by international law.

In the context of this depressing scenario the International Court of Justice (ICJ) established in 1945 can hope to achieve only basic minimum in bringing about the pacific settlement of disputes as is evidenced by the fact that only some 50 cases have been referred to it in the 28 years of its existence.

Pakistan's application filed on 11 May before the ICJ under, inter alia, the Genocide Convention of 1948 is the second occasion on which the Genocide Convention has come up for hearing before the World Court. It is also the third occasion on which the Government of India has appeared before this tribunal. In 1955 the Government of India was locked in dispute with Portugal before the ICJ in convention with Portugese claims of certain rights of passage over Indian territory near Goa. In 1972 India lost its case with Pakistan before the Court relating to the jurisdiction of the International Civil Aviation Organization consequent upon India's refusal to grant rights of passage to Pakistani aircraft over Indian territory in the 1970s.

Pakistan's present application relating to the Genocide Convention emanates from Indian decision to hand over some 195 Pakistani nationals to Bangladesh for trial on alleged charges of genocide and other war crimes. Basically Pakistan put forward two pleas before the Court namely (1) that it had exclusive jurisdiction to try the alleged war criminals, if any, and (2) that the Government of India should be restrained from handing over the 195 persons to Bangladesh. The question of the prolonged detention of the 90,000 prisoners of war in apparent violation of the Geneva Conventions of 1949 is only a peripheral and not the central issue before the Court.

The hurried circumstances in which the application was filed before the Court is emphasized by the fact that Pakistan's Attorney General, Mr Yahya Bakhtiar, had to abruptly cut short his visit to Iran with President Bhutto in May this year and immediately proceed to The Hague. Contrary to expectations the application could not be entertained or acted upon promptly in a few days. This was due not only because the Court was already seized of the controversial problem of French nuclear tests in the Pacific near Australia as well as the British-Icelandic dispute of fishing rights near Iceland but also because the Government of India refused to appear before the ICJ and be a party to the Court proceedings. Those who have cared to follow this case closely in the newspapers will note that Pakistan's application also contained a request for what are termed 'interim measures' which may require a brief explanation. 'Interim measures' are basically the equivalent of an application for an injunction or a stay order under local domestic law. The unusual feature of an interim measures application is that the ICJ under its status and the Court's rules is able to issue orders on such an application, in this case for restraining the handing over of 195 persons to Bangladesh, before it even decides whether it has jurisdiction in the case as a whole. In the light of the Court's precedents Pakistan was justified in expecting an early decision, on the matter. For instance in a famous case relating to Iranian oil nationalization measures the British Government had requested interim measures in late June 1951 and the order of the Court indicating such measures was made on 5 July 1951. Similarly in a Swiss-American dispute (the Interhandel Case 1957) Switzerland requested interim measures of protection on 3 October 1957 and the Court order refusing such measures was made on 24 October.

However, the complicating factor in Pakistan's application was India's refusal to appear before the Court. India did so principally on the grounds that its consent to being impleaded before the Court under the Genocide Convention was not sought as was required under its reservation, dated 27 August 1959, to that Convention. This contention was not sufficiently anticipated by Pakistan given the necessarily urgent circumstances in which the application was made. However, India's position in this respect has been vacillating, to say the least. As Mr Kuldip Nayar noted in an article in the Statesman of India dated 14 June 1973,

'At one stage, the Political Affairs Committee of the Cabinet, which discussed the matter at length came to the conclusion that "a limited appearance" would be in order. To challenge the jurisdiction of the International Court, on the one hand, and to agree to make a "limited appearance", on the other, was typical of the Delhi's policy. But then our Ambassador to Holland, the Maharaja of Patiala, was pushing New Delhi not to boycott the court and at least two members of the Political Affairs Committee felt that non-appearance might annoy some "non-committed" judges.'

India's final decision to stay away from the Court was taken by Mr Niren De, the Indian Attorney General, who was leading India's delegation at The Hague. Nevertheless India has continued to submit detailed written memorandums to the Court challenging the various pleas of Pakistan. This unprecedented attempt by India to both have its cake and eat it too led Pakistan's Attorney General Mr Yahya Bakhtiar to make the following comment in the court on 5 June 1973:

> Mr President, in our view the course being followed by India amounts to an abuse of the process of the Court. India, while declining to appear and professing to disregard these proceedings, is in fact arguing her case virtually as fully as is she were appearing, by means of a series of communications which the Court cannot well avoid receiving …

Then a little belatedly Pakistan fired another legal broadside by invoking an old but important Treaty, the 'General Act for Pacific Settlement of International Disputes, 1928' as an additional basis for the Court's jurisdiction. The resuscitation of this Act was an interesting move particularly as it was also being cited in the court by Australia against France to stop the nuclear tests in the Pacific, and by Britain against Iceland in support of its claim of fishing rights. The viability of this move in the case of Pakistan is yet uncertain because it appears that this Act was omitted in the approximately 600 treaties which India and Pakistan agreed at the time of partition, as applicable to both countries.

While India claims that this omission is fatal to Pakistan's case, Pakistan's counter-argument is that the list was never intented to be exhaustive and that 'the General Act for Pacific Settlement of International Disputes, 1928 devolved both upon the Dominions of India and Pakistan …' by virtue of the Indian Independence International Arrangements Order, 1947 and by the general law of state succession.

In the background of these legal labyrinths loomed the prospect of direct negotiations between India and Pakistan to settle the main bones of contention, namely repatriation of the POWs and recognition of Bangladesh. The first round of these negotiations in Islamabad have just been concluded and they are to be resumed in New Delhi this month. It was in context of these forthcoming talks that Pakistan requested the ICJ on 11 July 1973, to defer or postpone further consideration of its request for interim measures of protection. This move has erroneously and somewhat mischievously been constructed by the Indian press as withdrawal and rejection of Pakistan's request for interim measures.

However the Court's order dated 13 July 1973 granting Pakistan's request for a postponment, by a majority of 8 votes to 4, makes it quite clear that the request was for a postponment only and 'that a request for the indication of interim measures of protection may be made at any time during the proceedings in the case.' Moreover, the separate opinion of the Indian judge on the Court,

Mr Nagendra Singh, also makes it plain that Pakistan 'requested the Court to agree to *postpone* the entire case' in view of the forthcoming negotiations.

The Court has now gone into recess until January 1974 and has fixed dates in October and December 1973 to enable Pakistan and India respectively to file further written proceedings. Given the Court's limited powers of settling the tragic mutual pugnacity of the two countries, all parties must be hoping that direct negotiations may be fruitful enough to make the legal proceeding infructuous. The wisdom of instituting the proceedings may be challenged by some but it is clear, however, that despite the various pitfalls Pakistan's reference to the Court has in fact, at least temporarily, prevented the handing over of 195 persons to Bangladesh for trial.

Pakistan and US Strategy
(A Case in Consented Betrayal)

18 August 1973

Eqbal Ahmed

ON 18 September Z. A. Bhutto, President of Pakistan, will be the guest of President Nixon. They had last met on 18 December 1971, a day after Pakistan's defeat by India and emergence of East Pakistan as an independent state (Bangladesh). Mr Bhutto, then in New York for the UN meetings and designated to be President, had travelled to Key Biscayne to receive assurances of American support for the dismembered country.

Since then the most pressing problems arising out of the conflict in the subcontinent have remained unresolved. After a brief thaw following meetings in June–July 1972 between Mrs Gandhi and Mr Bhutto, our relations with India have been uncertain. Eighteen months after the cessation, of hostilities, 92,000 Pakistani soldiers and civilians remain prisoners of war in India.

This unprecedented fact, a clear violation of the Geneva Convention of 1949 (Article 118), has augmented the fear and distrust of India which has, since its inception, dominated and distorted Pakistan's internal and external policies. That some prisoners have been killed in the camps, allegedly attempting to escape, has further embittered feelings.

Then there are an estimated 250,000 Bengalis stranded in Pakistan, the military personnel among them being confined to guarded barracks—hostages for the release of Pakistani prisoners; victims also of Shaikh Mujib, the Bengali Prime Minister's demagogic insistence on war crimes trial of Pakistani POWs. The rich and influential among them have mostly bought their way out. The poor, now foreigners in the country that was theirs, have no wires to pull; they are progressively losing their jobs and live in fear. The majority are skilled people whose services Bangladesh desperately needs. Their return should not be impeded for the dubious emotional satisfaction of a legally questionable war crimes trial.

Finally, there are the luckless 'Biharis' in Bangladesh, a minority of about 500,000. As Muslim refugees from the 1946–47 communal massacres in India, they remained loyal to Pakistan, and were used and then abandoned by it in 1971. Now they are abused and persecuted in Bangladesh, barely surviving on meagre international charity, herded in squalid camps. It is a measure of our predicament that the subcontinent's three governments are united only in rejecting responsibility for this hapless people.

Their survival, literally at stake, will depend on the generosity of rich nations and on the willingness of Pakistan, India, and Bangladesh to see them as symbols of our collective inhumanity. The ultimate obligation rests with Pakistan, for a majority of them wish to remain its citizens. Some would undoubtedly stay in Bangladesh, and others want to return to India. All, including the US, might contribute to a planned scheme for their resettlement. That will conform to the proclaimed but rarely practised aims of international aid—encourage peaceful settlement of a violent situation, induce governments to meet their moral and political obligation, provide opportunity for regional cooperation, and alleviate human suffering.

If President Nixon were truly concerned with promoting a 'generation of peace', his discussions with Mr Bhutto would concentrate on a settlement of these problems as necessary first steps toward it in South Asia. Mr Bhutto can help by bringing with him a parliamentary mandate for the recognition of Bangladesh. But the White House effort is unlikely to go beyond the empty pieties of a joint communique. The logic of US-Pakistan relations appear to be against it.

To understand the parameters of US/Pakistan relations, one must re-examine the White House 'tilt' in Pakistan's favour during the conflict over Bangladesh; and its relevance to the Nixon-Kissinger global strategy.

Nixon incurred considerable congressional and public criticizm [sic] for supporting the Pakistani junta despite its brutal suppression of East Pakistan's regionalist movement. At the cost of betraying its loyal Bengali friends (Shaikh Mujibur Rahman and his associates), of alienating India where US aid had invested $10 billion, of enhancing the risk of an Indo-Pakistani war, and of permitting the expansion of Soviet influence in South Asia, Washington appeared to be supporting a sure loser in Pakistan.

No one saw any rationale for this policy. The White House hardly offered any. To the contrary, it reinforced the accusations of its favoritism by supplying Pakistan weapons worth $5 million—a contribution negligible to its military effort but significant for enhancing the intransigence of the junta, and for symbolizing US support for it.

The Anderson papers, accounts of the National Security Council meetings during the Indo-Pakistan war, compounded the confusion. They revealed Dr Kissinger's tactics without even hinting at his strategic calculations of US interests. Although he emphasized that the matter was of 'global significance', and the US must 'make clear our position in relation to our greater strategy' the secret memos yield no explanation of the conflict's 'global significance' or America's 'greater strategy'.

Yet the tactical considerations revealed in the memos make sense only in the context of the Nixon-Kissinger strategy of: (a) Stimulating the Sino-Soviet hostility by encouraging Soviet encirclement of China and augmenting Chinese fears of Russia. (b) Increasing Soviet stake in international stability by permitting it economic and political incentives in the form of favourable trade with the US, and partnership in countries of minor strategic value to the US (c) Promoting pro-American constellations of power in strategically important regions such as the Mediterranean and the Indian Ocean.

Before examining Pakistan's place in this strategy, it may be instructive to recall the tactical revelations of the Anderson papers. First, the White House 'tilted' deliberately in Pakistan's favor, and wanted this prejudice publicized. Second, the tilt was symbolic, lacking substance. Its aim was to create an impression of support for it rather than to actually aid Pakistan, or punish India. Hence, some not all aid to India was ordered cut off, and 'Dr Kissinger said to make sure…to emphasize what is cut off and not what is being continued.' Third, the outcome of the conflict, i.e. the dismemberment of Pakistan, *was expected, and Washington was not concerned with preventing it.* As Kissinger put it, 'Everyone knows how this will come out and everyone knows that India will ultimately occupy East Pakistan'. Fourth, the US regarded with equanimity the potential expansion of Indian and Soviet influence in Bangladesh which, said Kissinger, 'will not necessarily be our basket case.' Fifth, India's status as an independent, non-communist country was not perceived as threatened, Mrs Gandhi was expected to appreciate the symbolic character and limited objectives of American policy. 'The lady is cold blooded and tough and will not turn into a Soviet satellite merely because of pique', said Professor Kissinger.

Finally, the White House attitude of equanimity toward the potential expansion of Russian influence *did not extend to West Pakistan.* Its posture of symbolic support was obviously designed to assure America's dominant influence with the West Pakistani governing elite.

Also, it was not until after the collapse of Pakistani defense in the East, that the White House made its first substantive moves fearing an Indian push on West Pakistan. Iran and Jordan, until then kept on a 'close hold basis were encouraged to transfer arms to Pakistan. And the nuclear carrier USS Enterprise was ordered to show flag in the Bay of Bengal.

West Pakistan is strategically valuable as a state bounded by India, Iran, Afghanistan, China, and Russia. But even more important now is its location on the Indian Ocean, overlooking the Persian Gulf—the source of an estimated 60–75% of the world's oil reserves. The policy of perpetuating an American foothold in West Pakistan while welcoming a Soviet-US partnership in the rest of the subcontinent, seems related to the Nixon-Kissinger strategy of creating a dependable constellation of power in the Mediterranean and Indian Ocean regions. The goal is the creation of an informal yet cohesive military network to supercede the role in that region previously assigned to NATO, and to the ill-fated Baghdad Pact. With Spain and Portugal, Turkey and Greece, Iran and Israel as the primates of pax Americana in the Mediterranean and the Middle East, Pakistan is assigned the role of a secondary surrogate.

Dr Kissinger has advocated the policy of promoting regional military networks, to be supported in case of need by US air and naval power, since 1955. In an article entitled 'Military Policy and Defence of the "Grey Areas"' he had recommended the 'creation of strategic reserves', of 'nucleus defence forces in the three critical countries': Iran, Pakistan, and Indo-China. His evaluation of the critical countries changed. But the concept held; and in 1968 found this expression: 'Regional groupings supported by the US will have to take over major responsibilities for their immediate areas, with the US being concerned more with the overall framework of order than with the management of every regional enterprise.' In 1970 it acquired an official name: The Nixon Doctrine.

Nixon's 1970 visit to the Sixth Fleet, his first trip abroad as President, underscored the importance he attached to the Mediterranean, especially as the presidential visit concentrated on the aircraft carrier Saratoga which had been poised in a well-coordinated plan with Israel for possible intervention in Jordan. Meanwhile, Defence Secretary Laird was in Athens giving what he described as 'high priority' to the 'modernization' of Greek forces. Since then, US-Greek defence relations have grown closer: and the US navy has acquired home ports there. Similar developments have occurred in relation to Turkey, Spain, and Portugal with which the US reached in Azores one of its more comprehensive defence deals.

If these states are being readied to act as sentinels, Israel and Iran appear to have been allotted the role of chief marshals. Israel fits all the specifications of an ideal surrogate. Its military performance in 1967 has been a matter of unabashed envy to the Vietnam frustrated Chiefs of General Staff. Its air force is regarded as an effective deterrent against Syrian or Iraqi attacks on friends and allies in the oil rich kingdoms. Between France and India it is the only power to enjoy the nuclear option. Its technological sophistication reassures US officials who have deep faith in the decisive power of machines. Above all, its economic and military dependence on the US is viewed as being permanent; hence its permanence as an ally is presumed. The image is of Sparta in service of Rome. An irresistible opportunity.

As a result, on White House urging in September 1970, the Congress gave the executive authority what the *NEW YORK TIMES* described as, 'the most open-ended arms buying program in the world.' (*NEW YORK TIMES*, 29 September 1970) And the Honourable John McCormack, the Speaker of the House, said with an injured note of surprise: 'I have never seen in my 42 years as a member of this body language of this kind used in an authorization or in an appropriation bill.' Consequently, Israel armed with the most advanced offensive weapons in the conventional arsenal of the US, has become the great power of the Middle East. No other country in the world ever enjoyed so complete a commitment from the US. And no other state in history achieved status as a great power almost entirely on the basis of foreign support. It is only in this context that one can explain active Israeli campaigning for the re-election of Nixon, and Nixon's statement that there can be no viable security for Israel without US military alliance with Greece.

Iran is emerging swiftly, and is expected soon to equal Israel as a major military power in Southwest Asia. Since the CIA's overthrow of Mossadegh's nationalist government in August 1953, the Shah has been an exemplary ally. In the fifties and early sixties he used US military and security assistance effectively to consolidate power. Then, while remaining hospitable to international corporations, he combined totalitarian methods for maintaining stability with a successful program of economic development. Motivated by a strong sense of 'regional responsibility', he has developed excellent relations with Israel while maintaining close ties with Turkey and Pakistan. He has stepped into the vacuum created by the British withdrawal from the Gulf, and helps combat the revolutionary movements in the area. His defence budget soars annually: $833 million in 1970; a billion in 1971; an expected $1.8 billion in 1973. With annual oil earnings of $2 billion, he is able to pay for the weapons; and for the American advisors who teach how to use them. He has now on order from the US $2.5 billion worth of arms, and more advisors. For the US it is good diplomacy and excellent business. President Nixon paid a pointed visit to the Shah last summer before returning to Washington from Moscow, lest he misunderstand the flexible character and limited objectives of detente.

Pakistan cannot expect so exalted a place. With the stabilization of Iran's once shaky throne, reduction of tension with China, and the more sophisticated approach to Russia, the US views Pakistan's role now as being less critical than had Dr Kissinger in the fifties. It wishes Pakistan only to remain inhospitable to the Soviet Union, particularly to its navy. And to be allied with Iran and Turkey in a nativized CENTO. Expansion of naval facilities in Pakistan can be useful to the US navy. Hence, preparations are underway for their development in Pasni and Gawadar along the Mekran coast overlooking the Persian Gulf. As a Muslim nation, neither Persian nor Arab, and without territorial claims in the Gulf, Pakistan is also ideally situated to help in the counter-insurgency efforts, and administration of the disputed Emirates. Hence it has been encouraged to play an advisory role in Muscat, Oman, Abu-Dhabi, and Kuwait.

President Bhutto has difficulty accepting Pakistan's devaluation in US strategic planning. In Washington he will appeal for an even-handed application of the Nixon Doctrine, i.e., for sizeable armaments aid. He may also remind Nixon of the fact that by aligning again with a pro-American regional grouping, Pakistan has renewed the enmity of Afghanistan, Iraq, and USSR on its vulnerable western borders, while its defence against India remains weak. But in Washington hardly anyone takes seriously the possibility of India occupying Pakistan. It is viewed as paranoia worthy only of manipulation. The US has neither the interest nor the resources to redress the India-Pakistan military imbalance. Hence, Bhutto is unlikely to get what he wants. He may get enough: though, for him and his generals to hope for another dose, and remain regional groupees.

The assumptions which define US strategy may be briefly summarized: First, the US regards the national liberation movements as primary threats to its interests, particularly in areas strategic to the existing balance of power. To deal with it seeks what Dr Kissinger calls 'legitimizing principle of social repression.' The doctrine of limited war (i.e, localization of American intervention) and regional grouping of conservative regimes (to be backed by a capital-intensive US naval and air power) are designed as the means of discouraging and defeating revolutions.

Secondly, the USSR is still viewed suspiciously as an ambitious challenger of American paramountcy. Kissinger correctly perceives Russia also as potentially a *status quo* power, in need of incentives to act conservatively. International instability is viewed as disadvantageous to the US. Hence, US policy toward USSR combines elements of cooptation and selective rewards in some regions; of confrontation and containment in others.

In the Mediterranean, Red Sea, and the Persian Gulf the US perceives its hegemony threatened by the radical and revolutionary movements, and by Soviet 'intrusion'. Officials in the Nixon government believe that following the Johnson-Kosygin meeting in Glassboro, the US miscalculated the extent of Soviet ambition and its capability for penetration in the Middle East. As a result, they remained sanguine over growing Soviet influence in the area. Example was cited of Soviet military missions in UAR.

Lacking sizable aircraft carriers necessary for air-combat and deep inland penetration, the Russian navy was considered incapable of posing a challenge to the Sixth Fleet. American officials had felt sure that in an effort to overcome this disadvantage, the USSR shall not introduce Soviet personnel in the Middle East as it had not done so in North Vietnam. The news that Soviet pilots might be manning the advanced MIGs in UAR destroyed both assumptions and aroused American concern to the extent that the normally cool Dr Kissinger spoke of forcibly ejecting USSR from Egypt.

Third, the region in question is strategically and economically too critical to allow for a policy of 'coexistence'. The projected future shortage of energy supplies make Middle Eastern oil not only a major source of profit but the most strategic resource of modern times. For the US to control this resource is not only an economic but a military necessity. The maintenance of an American security umbrella over a bulk of the world's energy resources may even provide the US with a needed leverage over the increasingly autonomous Japan and Western Europe.

Fourth, the fear that American power is slipping from both Western Europe and the Mediterranean region is enhanced by the belief that France (for reasons of 'Gaulist chauvinism',) and Italy (because of 'instability and leftward swing') have become unreliable allies. In Great Britain, Washington retains a lingering hope and trust. But given its economic problems, and the isolationist mood of its people, the United Kingdom is expected to continue to 'abdicate its responsibilities' as a world power. As a result, officials envisage a gradual elimination of NATO activities at least in the Mediterranean, and wish to replace it with a new alliance of dependable states more or less dependent on US economic and military power.

Fifth, given the economic and social pressures at home, the US government foresees the impossibility of committing more military personnel abroad. In order to avoid serious opposition to an aggressive foreign policy, to reduce operational costs of deploying large numbers of American soldiers and to prevent the resurgence of 'neo- isolationist sentiments' in America, the government is seeking to minimize direct involvement of American 'boys' abroad by making maximum use not only of technology, but also of mercenaries and surrogates. Thus, the Mediterranean is witnessing not only the emergence of a 'Southern Strategy', the application of 'Nixon Doctrine' to the Mediterranean, but also a special brand of 'Vietnamization'.

Sixth, it appears clear that US policy under Nixon prefers the creation of regional constellations of pro-western allies based on bilateral ties with the US rather than on formal collective security pacts favoured under Truman and Eisenhower. This trend is based on Kissinger's correct assessment of the disadvantages which accrue to the leading member of formal collective security arrangements. A set of allies, each tied by separate bilateral agreements to the paramount power gives the latter manoeuverability and control unobtainable in collective arrangements. It is a tribute to the flexibility of this arrangement that countries such as Muslim Pakistan. Arab Jordan, fascist Greece, militarist Turkey can all fit in the same alliance without causing any embarrassment to themselves, each other, or the paramount power.

Lastly, it is noteworthy that, with the exception of Israel and Pakistan, all the primary agents in this configuration of power are fascist or proto-fascist governments. Close analysis of recent US role in the making and survival of regimes in Greece and Turkey indicates a conscious preference in Washington for what may be described as 'developmental fascism.' This preference is pragmatic and stems from the quest of stability. Alliance with the US is unlikely to be a popular posture in any country of the region except, Israel (whose population apparently believes such a relationship to be basic to their security). Hence no democratic government can sustain it for too long. Only a tyranny can keep the lid on popular demand for a neutralist or independent foreign policy. Spain and Portugal are viewed as examples of the success and suitability for underdeveloped nations of national fascism wedded to economic growth.

President Bhutto is apparently swallowing the US line—hook and sinker. Indicative of this fact were Mr Bhutto's statement in Key Biscayne on 18 December 1971 a day after the surrender of our army in East Bengal and following his meeting with Nixon, the unusual warming up of Pakistan-Iran relations, the attempt of Mr Aziz Ahmed in Tehran and of General Tikka Khan in Washington to peddle closer military ties with the West, the anti-Soviet thrust of official Pakistani rhetoric in the CENTO meetings, and the expansion of Pakistani advisory role in the Emirates of the Gulf.

It is understandable that a nation demoralized by defeat and dismemberment, bounded by a hungry, hostile India on the one hand, and on the other by a rich, ambitious and friendly Iran should seek security by becoming a satellite, in a regional constellation of power led by the latter. The psychology of dependence, the most debilitating in our colonial and feudal heritage, presents a surrogate position as a compelling choice. The alternative of an independent, neutralist policy of a sovereign, self-reliant nation must, on the other hand, appear unrealistic and risky to policy makers whose political minds remain rooted in the past. Yet the policy we are adopting poses serious risks to the interests and even the survival of Pakistan. I hope that at least Mr Bhutto, who unlike the bureaucrats and the generals, is not entirely a product of colonial ethos and institutions, will see the risks inherent in this policy and the better alternatives to it. For, at present only he is in a position to transcend traditional ties and withstand institutional pressures.

The Accord

1 September 1973

THE Delhi agreement must be given a hand without reserve. Primarily, it must be welcomed because it promises to end the agony of millions now trapped in India, Pakistan, and Bangladesh. Secondarily, it opens the possibility of a new era of sane relationships in the subcontinent. It partly vindicates Pakistan's stand on the issue of war crimes trials. Only the narrow-minded will seek to find fault with the terms of the agreement which, to our mind, is the best which could be obtained under the circumstances.

Politics implies the struggle for supremacy—whether among nations, political parties or individual leaders—and this involves the attempt to take unfair advantage, hoodwink or browbeat one another. It is doubly welcome that the present agreement appears to have been reached as a result of all three parties to the dispute realizing, in their own self-interest to be sure, the need for living together amicably.

Wars are fought, won and lost on the judgement of political and military leaders, who are usually good at taking all the credit if things go right and at palming off the blame on others if they do not. The real sufferers are the soldiers—and to an appreciable extent the civilians—who had no say in the matter and who were sacrificed, both literally and symbolically, on the altar of misguided political ambition. As should be inscribed on the tomb of every soldier or a nationalist guerilla who has died fighting for a cause he did not comprehend: 'I gave my life for freedom, this I know. Those who bade me fight told me so.'

The 93,000 POWs who after their long period of incarceration should be returning soon, according to the terms of the agreement, need to be absorbed, with compassion, into the fabric of a society against which they may well have a sense of grievance. They will have to adjust themselves to the new pattern while pondering over the question as to why it all happened and who really was responsible for the debacle.

Reunion with their families may bring a few days of euphoria, but it seems a fair assumption that a nagging doubt will persist in their minds, which can only be got rid of by publishing the Hamoodur Rahman Commission Report and by bringing Yahya Khan to trial before an open court.

As for the Bengalis in Pakistan, their cherished dream of repatriation should become a reality.

By and large, they have suffered less than the three other communities—the POWs in India and the Bengalis and Biharis in Bangladesh—who were the chief victims of the tragedy of 1971, whose genesis goes back as far as one's political convictions wish to take it.

The 80,000 Biharis that Pakistan has agreed to take in should not present an insoluble problem so far as their resettlement is concerned. The remaining 180,000 who are reported to have opted for Pakistan can feel reassured that the door has not been closed on them. Once there is a show of good faith from all the parties concerned, bilateral negotiations between Pakistan and Bangladesh will doubtless produce a solution for them. When so much has been borne by so many for so long, a little more patience and tolerance will hurt no one.

While credit must be given to the Indian and Pakistani negotiators for arriving at some form of understanding after eleven protracted, nerve-racking days, it may not be too easily apparent that the primary credit for the agreement should go to China. If in all the bleak days that followed the war, China had not stood steadfastly by Pakistan, even to the extent of vetoing the admission of Bangladesh into the United Nations, it is unlikely that Pakistan would have been in any position to bargain over the details of the settlement.

There are other reasons, of course, why the agreement had to come about. No political action is motivated by one simple aim. There are many complex strands woven into the political smokescreen and each plays its part in the final denouement. There can be no denying that India was finding the continued retention of the POWs counter-productive and the awareness that world opinion was slowly but inexorably turning against it must have influenced the timing of the event. Similarly, Bangladesh's understandable desire to be admitted into the United Nations could not be achieved unless it showed some flexibility and magnanimity in its hitherto rigid stand. The recognition of Bangladesh is implicit in the agreement. And here the regime's stand to face realities must be fully supported. Naturally, Pakistan too has had to make concessions. These are: a) Pakistan will use its good offices with its ally, China, to ensure that Bangladesh is admitted into the United Nations; b) Pakistan which had at one stage refused to accept the Biharis as its responsibility, is now prepared to take in as many as 80,000 on humanitarian grounds, and also to discuss the future of the 180,000 other Biharis who ostensibly wish to come here; c) Pakistan may recognize Bangladesh as soon as all 93,000 POWs from India—inclusive of the 195 whom Bangladesh wanted to try for war crimes—come back to the country.

The issue of the war crimes trials had stood in the way of any progress towards peace and friendship right from the time it was taken up by an embittered Shaikh Mujibur Rahman. If at last sense has prevailed, it is a cause for muted optimism. The possibility is wide open that the trials will be dropped. This is a major gain from Pakistan's viewpoint.

As has always been evident, the real problems faced by Pakistan, India, and Bangladesh are economic. The poverty-stricken people of the three countries, assailed virtually annually by natural calamities, cannot and should not allow their leaders to use them as pawns in an ultimately meaningless struggle for power and prestige. Cooperation and goodwill are required for best results.

A Penny for Your Sufferings

29 September 1973

THE recent freezing of the bank accounts of Bengalis who have chosen to be repatriated to Bangladesh strikes against the very principle of humanitarianism. Those affected by this measure have already suffered enough trials and tribulations in what was their own country. The need to subject them to more is, in our opinion, wholly unjustified and unlikely to help salvage the bilateral relations which is ostensibly the promise of the Delhi agreement. Repatriation will be a long-drawn-out process. How are the expatriates to survive in the mean time? How are the banks to determine who has chosen to call it a day and who has preferred to stay behind? What treasures does the government expect to recover from a harassed, disinherited minority? This morally bankrupt game may not be worth the wilting candle.

Politics is a dirty game, but it is not imperative to cast aside every shred of humanity to win at it. There are countless issues where political manouevring is necessary for the state as well as the people. What is so easily forgotten is that the two are not identical. Those who take the decisions glibly assume that they are acting for the benefit of the people, while their deeds only cause greater misery and resentment. What is happening in this subcontinent is that in the face of heart-rending mass poverty and colossal natural calamities, political leaders are—in the name of the people—making strenuous efforts to win the game of one upmanship.

The Delhi agreement is clearly dependent on the goodwill of all three parties, and if even one of them in any way tries to score a point or take advantage of some semantic loophole, more suffering for the people will be the result. In a world which is progressively being shorn of ethical values, politics cannot be excused for placing expediency above human needs. It is time that the Pakistani POWs in India, the Bengalis in Pakistan, and the Biharis in Bangladesh are given precedence in each of the three countries' political strategy. They are not puppets, and if they continue to be used as such, it reflects nothing but discredit on the leadership.

The trouble with every act that has a political connotation is that it is never an isolated one but one that is a ring in a chain of events. The past may be responsible for the present; the present is certainly responsible for the future. Thus, the freezing of bank accounts can only unleash a new term of unfairness and injustice for the desecrated multitude.

If those who were pro-Pakistan have suffered grievously at the hands of rabid Bengali nationalists, it is no reason for us to retaliate in kind. Retaliation in fact brings us down to a lower level than would magnanimity and compassion. India, as the largest power of the three, has the greatest responsibility for ensuring peace in the subcontinent. The uncalled for delay in the return of our POWs is a negative gesture, although no doubt reasons can be fabricated for misunderstanding the meaning of 'simultaneous'.

However, these are early days. Repatriation has just begun, and it would be naive to expect that there will be no hitch in the six months or so that it is scheduled to continue until it is completed. Complications are already evident. Without world response to the UN Secretary General's appeal for shipping facilities, the work of repatriation may be unavoidably held up. But this applies only to Pakistan and Bangladesh. India has no such excuse for delaying the return of the POWs.

Assuming that the process of repatriation continues without any major breakdown, the question of rehabilitation on will be of paramount importance. Here it is not so much the government as the people who will be required to show the compassion and selfless charity for the sufferings of their fellow human beings that mark the birth of collective maturity, which alone can prevent politicians from sacrificing land, lives and aspirations for the sake of an exalted ego.

Pakistan, at its very inception, was in a sense a haven for refugees. Today, although circumstances have changed and those homeless, uprooted, disinherited folk who will be taken in are the withered plants of the ravages of war, it is eminently possible to accommodate them in a befitting manner without regard to parochial and communal sentiments. Without this basic respect for other less fortunate human beings and an unforced humility, there is little prospect of a people ever creating a national character that can stand the scrutiny of time.

The pattern that is slowly emerging in the subcontinent is not a pleasant one. In India there is, according to President Giri, 'a crisis of character'. Pakistan has no time for introspection because it is beset with political problems, particularly in Baluchistan, and economic problems which, unless resolved, will break the back of the common man. Conditions in Bangladesh are even worse, and now that the euphoria of independence has worn off, lawlessness and anarchy seem to be the order of the day.

It is in the context of this sombre backdrop that the ramifications of any action that threatens reaction or reprisal from the other side must be viewed. Unnecessary hardship caused on a misguided notion can only breed more bitterness and resentment among the forsaken, who have reason enough to feel bitter already. Leaders may consider political bargaining to be a matter of numbers and figures, but even in our computer age, each figure and number represents an individual whose right to happiness is being bartered away. Those arriving and those departing carry precious little with them. Must the screws be turned tighter?

Dacca Diary I

17 November 1973

Dennis Walker

(The writer is an Australian scholar of Bengali who recently visited Bangladesh.)
Dacca, 25 September 1973, at 8:00 p.m.:

THE change from sunlit Hindu New Delhi to gloomy Muslim Dacca is more than a contrast of my landing times. There are two different worlds here and two different qualities of experience. Deceptively westernized, Delhi was the imperial capital not merely of the British in India but of Sultans and Mughal emperors before them; with its Hindi signs placed unobtrusively beside international English, it represents a tradition of people who have known how to win. In contrast, Dacca—capital of a Muslim Bengal that for hundreds of years has been generally but the colony of a colony—wears the emblems of its identity like a badge of pain. The blue Bengali neon sign flickers in the darkness as our bus bumps across from the plane: 'Dacca Biman Bander' (Dacca airport). There is no English. The airport workers in Dacca wear genuinely indigenous clothing, looking—with their bristling eyebrows, black Islamic beards, and ubiquitous grubby white prayer caps—almost Middle Eastern, whereas the New Delhi airport staff in Indian clothing look as though they had been dressed up in smart uniforms by officials with an eye peeled for encouraging the international tourist trade. The generally small and run down appearance of Dacca airport premises, tells its own story of West Pakistan's exploitation and neglect of the east 'wing' prior to 1971; and of the unachieved promise of independence thereafter.

Some old student friends meet me. Bumping away from the airport along the intolerable roads, through the dimly lit streets, I am struck by how little the people and the environment have visibly changed. 'Well, last time in 1969, I came to East Pakistan. Now it is Bangladesh!' I observe. My friend replies thoughtfully: 'Yes, but still we are not happy. Another great power is crushing us down.'

The next day I meet some sociology and economics lecturers at Dacca University and from them get some background on the tense relations between Bangladesh and its all powerful Indian 'liberators' that has dominated Bangladesh's post-independence existence. These men were militantly secularist and pro-Indian before independence and were among those who provided intellectual ballast and programmes for Shaikh Mujibur Rahman's Awami League that led Bangladesh's struggle for freedom. They were totally opposed to the whole idea of religion being used as a basis of nationalism to yoke Bangladesh in an unworkable union to a 1,100 miles distant West Pakistan. They were above all rational planners and modernisers with no axes to grind. Now in independent Bangladesh, they remain in outlook secular but have come to believe that this shared ideal of secular nationalism is an inadequate basis for an alliance with India, which they believe to be against all Bangladesh's material and moral interests. They are rapidly turning into 'Muslim Bengal' nationalists.

To their probing questions about Australian foreign policy (they seem to know more about it than I do), I answer that our Prime Minister, Whitlam, has hardly mentioned the name of Bangladesh at all and that his whole policy in the subcontinent seems almost wholly directed to closer and closer cooperation with India as one means to project Australia in Asia. 'Yes, we know this Mr Walker' says the economist with some bitterness. 'We know that the westerners and their governments associate us with the Indians. They infact make no special provision for us at all because they regard us as an extention of India. This is something we resent very much here in Bangladesh. We are not Hindus like the Indians, we are determined to be masters in our own house and we are determined to end this situation where India has dictated the foreign policy our country follows. You may know, Mr Walker, that a number of months back, our government made some signs that it would welcome any gesture of friendship from China and that the Chinese responded by offering to buy jute from us at premium prices. This is the usual method by which the Chinese people prepare the way for diplomatic relations. But because the Indians put so much pressure on us, diplomatic and economic, we could not take the Chinese offer. We were very angry with China because she supported Pakistan against us in our liberation war and because she will even now veto our admission into the UN until we release the last Pakistani prisoner of war that we hold. But for the sake of our own hope to become an independent country we cannot carry on this dispute with China. To be independent, we must get into the United Nations which we will never do with China as our enemy. What people in the Awami League also feel is that China would be a reliable friend to act as a balance to India should we establish diplomatic relations with it. Since the cultural revolution, China has been ruled by rational people with little interest in exporting their social revolution. They have a vested interest in strengthening small countries like our own that neighbour India, but want to be independent of her. If we could prove to them that we are independent, they will support us and not interfere in our internal affairs. The Chinese would be good friends for Bangladesh. But the problem is that the Indians do not like us to be friends with China. They and the Russians are even twisting our arms to force us to join the Asian collective security pact. We do not want to join the Asian collective security arrangement because we knew that it is directed against China, and if we join it, we will make China our bitter enemy forever—and then we will never get free of India. We want nothing to do with India's and Russians attempts to turn the Indian Ocean into their private reserve; but we specially do not want to join any pact that will make Bangladesh's territory a military supply route for India to attack China because in that case China will be forced to strike back at us and devastate our territory. We are neither pro-Indian nor pro-Chinese, Mr Walker. The only question forms is that we fought once for our independence and that we never again want to see our country trampled underfoot by any foreign soldier of any foreign country whatever. We want peace—but India is taking the fruits of independence from us.'

I turned to the sociologist and asked, 'Are you anti-India like the others?' He replied 'For God's sake, never ask that direct kind of a question. Whatever we may feel it is best sometimes that we be discreet about expressing it. You know that not a single foreign mission in Dacca—yes, ask all the foreign embassies and UN agencies here, they have all made very exhaustive and objective studies of us—agrees with our anti-Indian phobia. They have concluded our attitudes lack objective justification. And yes, whatever we feel, Mr Walker, it is best sometimes that we express it a bit discreetly. I will tell you a story. You know the American Negro in the 1950s. On a hot summer's night, he was walking down the street cursing the white man, what a bastard the white man is, how he will like to slit the white oppressor's throat etc. etc. Turning the corners he almost bumped into a white man. Instantaneously the Negro was completely transformed. He snapped quickly to attention, saluted the white man with alacrity, and began to call him 'master, boss, at your service.' Later walking down the street he started to curse the white man again, how he hated him, how he would like to run his knife through the white man etc., etc. If you can explain the Negro's behaviour in sociological terms, you will be well equipped to understand where we in Bangladesh stand with the Indians today. The time of showdown has not yet come. But one thing. Whatever the Indians may tell you about us, never forget this. We are something neither India nor Pakistan can ever be in their present frontiers—a true nation. 'Surely you mean Bangladesh would be a true nation if the Bengali-speaking Hindus of Indian-held West Bengal were added?'

'Some might say, but I as a sociologist say it is irrelevant, that we the Bengali Muslims of Bangladesh, sociologically, culturally, historically, economically, and even linguistically through our own dialect, have all the attributes of a self-sustaining and independent nation. Those who deny it will learn to their cost!'

The Talk of Disintegration

17 November 1973

S. M. Zafar

THE following are a few specimens from the statements of political leaders of Pakistan made about the future of Pakistan. These leaders belong to various parties. The statements are reproduced without mentioning the names:

1) If people do not rise to remove the PPP from power within twelve months, surely Pakistan shall disintegrate. Issue of *Jasarat* dated the 24 August 1973.
2) If Pakistan is further broken, Punjab and Sind shall be greater sufferers (as compared to N.W.F.P. and Baluchistan)—issue of *Pakistan Times* dated the 31 October 1973.
3) If Mr Zulfikar Ali Bhutto is removed from his office, Pakistan shall be destroyed (because of lack of cohesion—issue of Daily *Mashriq* dated the 3 July 1972.

None of these statements is factually correct, nor politically wise. None of these statements can be called patriotic. Besides being inter se contradictory, the unfortunate aspect is that none of these statements was necessary.

Neither the continuance of the PPP in power can adversely affect the territorial integrity of Pakistan, nor the removal of Mr Z. A. Bhutto from his office can make any difference to the ideological and geographical existence of the country; nor the misfortune of disintegration can be less disastrous and calamitous to any one province; it shall affect all the cities, all the towns and every individual now inhabiting Pakistan.

I have selected these three statements as models from amongst many other similar statements uttered in the recent past with the theme that if the named circumstance remains present or becomes absent, Pakistan shall come to an end. Existence of Pakistan has been equated with anything and its contrary. If there is no free economy, argues one champion, the country shall perish through financial crisis. Some other bright thinker forecasts that if the system of education is not immediately channelled in the indicated direction, there will be ideological death followed by disintegration of the country. Going down the line while reading these statements, one could imagine an expert saying—if we do not plant trees, Pakistan shall wither away. Out of the plethora of such like indiscreet and disgusting statements, these are a few to illustrate the standard of political awareness in our country.

One must analyse these statements and criticize them in strong terms. In fact, public opinion has not reacted appropriately and adequately to these statements. Time has come to express and exhibit intolerance and abhorrence towards these political prophesies and to manifest naked antipathy towards such chronicles. As I am not addressing any particular individual but am criticizing the type of statements, the criticizm [*sic*] has not been fettered with checks against being harsh and disrespectful.

I have tried to find out the reason or the rationale for such statements. Those who have argued with me and justified some of these statements have given their own reasons. One group tells me that if Pakistan experiences any more of fascism, the country shall not be able to withstand the evil consequences of the system. On this account they justify the statements where it is said that if people do not rise to remove the PPP from power, Pakistan shall disintegrate. I am not in a position to categorically enunciate the future of our political system. May be the democratic forces actually fail and one-party-rule or nearly one-party-rule becomes the order of the day. Yet I am confident that the people of Pakistan shall not bargain their liberty to get democracy from outside. Liberty is not in currency at all. I shall rather live as a Pakistani (even in jail) trying to resist fascism than to say 'to hell with this country'. In fact, by suggesting that if fascism succeeds, the country shall disintegrate, we encourage fascism indirectly. The fascist may believe the statement to be partially correct and will thus have no fear of retribution. On the contrary, let us all remain determined that a fascist shall ultimately have to give account to the people of Pakistan in the state of Pakistan which will outlive the sins of the fascist.

I am personally opposed to fascism. It is a curse. Yet it is unimaginable to equate the commencement or the duration of undemocratic government with the beginning of the end of the country. Fascism may bring misfortunes to the people of the country—to us, and to the future generation but not to the state. The regimentation and fascism must be resisted by criticizing, by opposing fascism, by educating public opinion against the system, and by putting political clogs on its advancement. It is not at all necessary to arouse public agitation against fascism by bringing in the question of the existence or the destruction of the country. In this regard, the nation must be nourished on optimism and our article of faith should be that the country shall live but fascism shall ultimately die.

In the next category comes the statement as to who would suffer more in case of disintegration of Pakistan. The only and the correct assessment is contained in the historic utterance of Quaid-i-Millat who said, 'If Pakistan dies, who lives?' The question of any one province suffering more than the other is not relevant.

The separation of East Pakistan from West Pakistan has already irreparably harmed the interests of Muslims in the subcontinent. The prestige of Muslims in this region can never be the same as it was on 20 December 1971. Our impact as a nation in world politics, even if Bangladesh and West

Pakistan become friendly can never reach the pre-disintegration position. We are two small countries now and gradually the world public opinion would become known to us. So far our public is not conscious of how the world is treating a small and reduced Pakistan. Say by the end of the next year, the people of both the wings would know the full reality. This loss should have been enough. Any further disintegration would almost suffocate the Muslim voice in the subcontinent. In that loss there would be no distinction of any one province from the other. The black paint brush shall blacken every face—be it Punjabi, Sindhi, Baluchi, or Pathan.

Some people opine that East Pakistan was an economic burden and that the separation has removed the stonemill off our neck. These are selfish utterances and lack farsightedness. How can they evaluate economics and the concept of state and liberty with the same measure? With that process of reasoning as valid, shall we advise other countries of the world to give up their backward areas? Has any other nation talked in these terms? Why? Because the very premise is false and they know it. Those who in Pakistan are justifying the separation of East Pakistan and West Pakistan on economic basis should at once know that their premise is false. In fact, it is they who followed on to compare the losses to the provinces in case of disintegration. If the separation of East Pakistan and West Pakistan can be assessed in terms of benefit to West Pakistan, a priori, it can be urged that in case of further disintegration one province will suffer less than the other. The entire gambit is wrong. The very perspective is distorted. Disintegration of Pakistan was a disaster and further disintegration shall spell misery on every individual Pakistani.

I am quite clear in my mind that Pakistan was created by men with better reason. They had studied history clearly. They tried to get a homeland because that was a question of survival. Any reversal shall lead towards our gradual disappearance as a nation.

Similarly, it is unpardonable to condone the sycophancy of those who wish to equate one man with the past, present and future of the country. The rationale for the supporters of such statements is identical to the rationale of those who supported the statement of the first category vis-à-vis fascism, although here the objection stated is to oppose political individualism and chaos.

History has recorded that those who thought that after them there would be the deluge, are buried deep down in their graves but their countries have continued to live thereafter as before and in some cases more prosperous and vigorous.

Even the Quaid-i-Azam has not been found to be indispensable for Pakistan. To me, he was the founder of Pakistan but not Pakistan himself. We owe so much to him as a nation, but it is wrong to conceive that Pakistan came into existence due to the exclusively personal volition of the Quaid-i-Azam. Muslim nationalism existed in the subcontinent long before the Quaid-i-Azam entered politics in the subcontinent. This nationalism showed its vigorous existence in the year 1857 when the Muslims rose in a war of independence, and later manifested its political far-sightedness under the leadership of Sir Syed Ahmed. Muslim nationalism remained determined and clear in its objective, which was taken over adroitly and moulded properly by the Quaid-i-Azam, resulting in the Pakistan resolution of 1940 and the achievement of the geographical Pakistan.

Quaid-i-Azam died but Pakistan lived. His lieutenant, Liaquat Ali Khan, took over the reins of the government and through hard and selfless work became Quaid-i-Millat. His death did not negate the existence of Pakistan. We lost many other veterans but Pakistan continued to exist. The separation of East Pakistan in the year 1971 took place when everyone then in politics and then important, was alive. The tragic event did not follow the death of any particular leader. In fact, the debacle was due to the living and not in consequence of a death. Mortals may come and mortals may go but Pakistan shall live. It is for the public to reject with disdain any statement made from any quarter asserting that the well-being of an individual or the continuation in power of someone is essential for the existence of Pakistan. Muslim nationalism is not dependent for its reflections on anyone of the leaders but is dependent on the collective will of the people of Pakistan.

Dacca Diary II: Then and now

24 November 1973

Dennis Walker

CONVERSATIONS with some students walking down the lush sylvan pathway at the rear of the University. In this green world the hatreds and passions of the party political violence that wracks independent Bangladesh, or the conflict with India, or the armed conflict between student factions in the Dacca University student elections in which four youths had been shot dead a few days before, seem all very remote. 'There don't seem to be very many autorickshaws in the streets now compared to when I was here in 1969'. I observe. 'Is it lack of fuel?' 'It is not lack of fuel. The Indian army loaded three-quarters of the autorickshaws onto their lorries and took them back with them to Calcutta when they left Bangladesh in 1972.'

I tell the student 'that would be a serious thing if you could prove it. Were you an eye witness?' 'Well, I did not see the autorickshaws taken but when I was a refugee in West Bengal, I saw train after train passing from Bangladesh packed with Pakistan tanks. Ah, only I had a camera with me then, to record it for the next generation in our land—the Indian army plundering from the country they said they would liberate, the tanks and artillery that our Bangladesh taxpayers sweated blood year after year to pay for. You know, India's plunder of military equipment that by right belongs to Bangladesh is a great grievance here even with the government. We heard on the BBC's Bengali commentary quoting Peter Gill of the Telegraph from Dacca that the Bangladesh government had asked India to return 81 of our tanks. We know where such mild requests lead with the Indians! India will never give any heavy or modern military equipment to Bangladesh. They removed the Chinese and American tanks and artillery the Paks left behind so that our army would not have the capacity to resist them should they invade our country again. Even the rifles and machine-guns the Pakistanis left they took—then sold to our government for expensive foreign exchange that we could not afford, a few light Russian weapons that will be just enough for 'internal security', for crushing the opposition parties resisting Indian imperialism. The students fume about smuggling across the Bangladesh-India border; e.g. (seemingly correct, according to the Bangladesh Observer in February 1972 the Bangladesh government had made a query to the West Bengal police that received a tongue-in-cheek reply of pretended non-information)

280

about cars with Dacca license plates that now cruised the streets of Calcutta. Initially carried off by the Indian army, these cars have since gone by the process of smuggling that India has lacked the means (or the will) to effectively stop, and which has been responsible for haemorrhage of resources from Bangladesh to India that Bangladeshis I spoke with compared to their former exploitation at the hands of West Pakistan, and which they believe stems from an Indian government programme to reduce Bangladesh to a 'subhuman level' where it will no longer have even the will to resist the 'neo-colonial rule' and 'exploitation' of its gigantic neighbour.

Appalled by the irrational intensity of their hatred of the Indians and of Shaikh Mujib's government, which they see as having sold out to 'the Indian imperialists,' I argue with them that in Bangladesh's own interests it would be best, perhaps, to avoid a head-on confrontation with a militarily powerful India. 'You might be right', one of them replies in a subdued voice. 'We also would like to avoid it and keep the present government since although it has not successfully defended our national interests and although it has some Indian agents in it, at least it has tried sometimes. If we overthrew it, the Indians would invade Bangladesh and merely replace it with a cabinet composed 100% of complete stooges who would have no other function than to execute the orders of the Indian occupation commander, and we would lose everything. But you know very well that we Bangladeshis are a mercurial people. Moreover, we have become expert from the Pakistan period in putting the blame on others, so you see India is the scapegoat for everything that has gone wrong since our independence. So it is almost inevitable that the Muslim masses here will rise up against the Indian kafirs ('infidels') in a year or two and that all the student groups except the Indian agents of the Muzaffar NAP will join the uprising. The Hindu minority here will be butchered or driven from our country as Indian spies. The Indian army will invade to try to save the government, or install a new government of their choice, in Dacca. Indian army will systematically exterminate the intelligentsia here as the Pakistanis sometimes tried to do—but the Indians will kill everyone who can even read or write to make sure that there is no educated leadership for the Bengali Muslims to rise again. Even their puppets in the Muzaffar NAP they will exterminate because in time of revolution it is impossible to distinguish agents from rebel Muslims and anyway they hate us intensely and they will be killing us indiscriminately for the pleasure of it. Yes, you are right, we should find some other way except face-to-face confrontation with the Indians but the problem has developed too far now for that. In this hopeless situation we all expect to die and we have accepted that will be our fate.'

Despite counsels from anti-Awami League friends to keep my eyes peeled for signs of deterioration in the living standards of the masses, I do not observe that the common people are suffering that much more now in comparison with their conditions when I first came in 1969, and as they were in former East Pakistan. It is true that the prices of essential commodities like soap and cloth is now outrageously high, yet for labourers and rickshaw drivers who have seen their earnings tripled or quadrupled since independence, survival has been possible. They are all dressed as well (or badly) under Shaikh Mujib and Bangladesh as they were under the military dictators of Pakistan. For the urban unemployed, old people, and unmarried working class women, the situation as regards food and clothing is of course grim, but even here there is resistance of family solidarity and the support it provides, and the possibility of cadging rice and clothing from the international relief agencies and government fair-price shops. Even so, the section of the urban poor lacking in jobs is suffering terribly. And it is here that one begins to hear mutterings of pro-Pakistan feelings and rejection of the whole Bangladesh venture. 'Shaikh Mujib told us wrong figures' the poor say. 'He has not bettered our lot as he promised' or 'things were better in the time of Pakistan.' Or 'Ayub Khan built many buildings, we had much work in the time of Ayub Khan' or 'we have brought the axe down on our own feet in leaving Pakistan.' It does not seem very serious yet there is little regret for the departure of the West Pakistanis who often hated the Bengali Muslims and were hated in return by them. But there is a sense that Bengali nationalism has failed and a growing conviction among this deeply religious people that a secular Bangladesh allied to India and the 'malon' (accursed) Hindus can never be their spiritual home. Among the lower middle class—petty clerks, for example, with their conservative Muslim background, and who because of their fixed incomes have been suffering terribly from the post independence price-rise—there is also this pro-Pakistan feeling. One finds clerks who never listen to radio except at news-time because they cannot tolerate the Hindu-centric songs the government radio broadcasts to promote secular nationalism. 'Ah, Bangladesh!' they exclaim 'what we were promised—and what we got!' Nonetheless, the element of regret for Pakistan is greatly and tendentiously inflated by the Indian press. It is actually less prominent, for instance, than regret for the Ottoman empire in Arab Asia following the First World War, or regret for the British empire in Bangladesh itself following the partition and birth of Pakistan in 1947 with all its quick disappointments.

Dacca Diary III: The City of Violence

1 December 1973

YET it is hard not to generally become overwhelmed by a sense of depression in touring Dacca. The city seems to have been touched by some magical wand that has arrested it at the stage of development it had reached when I felt it in December 1969—when the political crisis that was to explode into Bangladesh was well and truly getting underway. A great mosque near Ramna racecourse that was a framework of construction bamboos scaffolding then, is still only a skeleton of stone that grotesquely lacks roof or walls and whose worshippers therefore pray in the open air. At what had been developing into a feverish construction site in the sun-dappled quiescent green suburban street where I had lived, peasant Bengali Islam has wrested another triumph—the red construction bricks have metamorphasized into the handmade abode of a country family now settled in Dacca. Time and again I saw buildings I had known in 1969: one storey buildings that were to have new storeys added but which reverted to their original status when construction cement ran out and which now stand in the blistering sun with corroded iron construction rods spouting functionlessly from their roofs. It is not wholly the consequence of Bangladesh's birth since there is world-wide shortage of building cement now due to America buying up South Korea's stocks for her aggression in Indo-China; but in the old Pakistan, Bangladesh could have bought with soft local Pakistani rupees from West Pakistan atleast some of the cement she now must buy at exorbitant rates in precious international hard currency from the world markets. More than one Bangladesh economist told me that since independence Bangladeshis have come increasingly to understand that in old Pakistan, Bangladesh, while exploited by West Pakistan, had also obtained for soft Pakistani currency, important items like kerosene fuel, flour, grains, cotton, and its manufactured textiles which after independence, Bangladesh now has to buy in small quantities and at the cost of limited foreign exchange from 'these sharp businessmen in Delhi' or from other foreign sources—with the result that the country's development has slowed down badly.

Although the physical and spiritual scars of the war for independence and West Pakistanis' atrocities have mostly healed now, in many ways Bangladesh does not seem a normal society. Having passed through a baptism of fire and grown accustomed to bloodshed and the power that comes with carrying guns in hand, the Bangladesh common people are much less amenable to commands of their social betters now. Whereas in 1969, the rickshaw drivers looked hungrily, almost cunningly at prospective customers they now are openly abusive of their middle class customers. The land still in a sense lives in the tension left by war. Every day the hospitals are flooded with the mutilated or bullet-riddled bodies of the victims of the attacks of bandits or of the running sten gun vendetta that rages day and night between government and opposition parties. After 8.30 p.m., a chill visibly settles over the city and people shuffle off home, for it is then that the bandits and political para-military groups begin their night's work. There are police in strength stationed at every crossroads but when a shot is fired they quickly scuttle off to the nearest high building and fortify themselves there behind their sub-machine guns. As the common people sarcastically remark, in independent Bangladesh it is the rickshaw drivers who set the rules to their terrified passengers, wives who beat their husbands—and as regards the law and order crisis—the cats who are afraid of a mouse. Standing in the heart of Dacca at 8.45, I suddenly find no rickshaw wallah willing to drive me to the university close by because beyond the heart of the city they fear attack from bandits or the para-military political groups that are sometimes hard to distinguish from them. Whereas in 1969 in Dacca, one could catch a rickshaw and ride anywhere in the city to midnight and beyond.

A few conversations with representatives of the Bengali common people, leave me, however, in some doubt whether the masses of Bangladesh are ready to rise. The alarmist reporting in the western press in the first year after independence that an uprising against Mujib and political chaos were just around the corner, the hate propaganda in India's England, Hindi, and Bengali dailies that the Bangladeshis are thinly disguised Pakistanis straining at the leash to erupt, and slit the throat of every Hindu Indian in sight, the rhetoric of the now wholly alienated Dacca University intellectuals who now speak of launching a 'biplob' (revolution) against Mujib and his government all seems out of touch with the mood of the poor. The attitude of many people who fall into the category of workers or peasants seems to be that they want to get back once more to sane and normal living, coupled with a determination to physically rebuff and if need be liquidate those elements that for political reasons are trying to prevent a return to normality. While the war between the political parties has claimed many lives in post-independence Bangladesh, it is also true that many of the 1,000 Bangladesh Mukti Bahini liberation fighters murdered by 'secret killers' for instance were simply killed by peasants enraged at the political pretensions and strong-arm extortion that people claiming to be ex-freedom fighters have been furthering at their expense since the Pakistan army's departure. The ruling Awami League's para-military 'Rakhi Bahini' the Marxist-Leninist revolutionaries banded together in the Bhashani NAP or in the underground communist parties trying to launch an agrarian uprising in the countryside, the remnants of the pro-Pakistan para-military Razakars and the banned right-wing religious parties fighting Mujib, and the anti-India fanatics of the 'Muslim Bangla' Movement ('they hate Hindus more than they love Allah')—all have seen their cadres slyly clubbed to death or sometimes, openly torn to pieces by a population that has reached the limit of patience with political violence and slogans. Yet attempts by Maoist insurgents to involve the peasant masses in a revolution continue.

On 5 October 1973, a '60-strong band of the elements trying to start an agrarian uprising against Mujib raided the police station at Saturia near Dacca, wounding three policemen seriously and making off with guns and ammunition ... the bandits also looted a bank and broke open a food storage centre inviting the town people to help themselves to the stock of imported wheat. Police later recovered 20 tons of wheat from neighbouring villages out of 60 tons that were stolen.' (*Hongkong Standard*, 7 October 1973). Whether such strategems can successfully involve the peasantry in an uprising remains, however, to be seen, for the leftists have seriously misjudged the mood of the people before.

In the Bhashani NAP office, I am given a leaflet by its Secretary General Kazi Jafar Ahmed on the Bangladesh national elections of March 1973, ascribing the ruling Awami League's overwhelming victory to the systematic use of corruption, falsification, brazen and underhand activities, and above all terror (besides which) all the annals of West Bengal, Hitler's Germany, Mussolini's Italy, Batista's Cuba and the election, recently held in South Vietnam at direct gunpoint of American occupation troops, pale into insignificance. It is perfectly true that the elections were the occasion for another ugly exhibition of fascist strong-arm methods by the Awami League and its para-military Rakhi Bahini. As the NAP leader explained at his press conference, opposition candidates often faced the electorate literally under a hail of bullets from Rakhi Bahini; among those they later tried to kill, were NAP (Bhashani) Dacca candidate Abdul Hamid, and the popular, very anti-Indian chairman of the Jasad (National Socialist Party) Major Jalil. The state-controlled press, radio, and television were turned into a propaganda machine for the return of Mujib and his government during the election campaign, with no hearing given to opposition figures or views. Public transport and even the helicopters of international relief organizations, were blatantly commandeered for use by Awami Leaguers in their election campaign. The dead voted and Rakhi Bahini is said to have entered the polling booths and stuffed their boxes with fraudulent votes. (It may even be true, as the NAP Secretary charged, that Indian citizens, mostly 'Young Congress' party workers were brought across the international borders in busloads to vote for the Awami League in outlying districts where opposition party prospects were good.)

Certainly, Shaikh Mujib's statement in the flush of his elect on triumph that 'there were now no opposition parties left in the country' was not calculated to heal political division for the opposition parties interpreted it as indicative of budding Awami League totalitarianism. But does the Awami League's unstatesman like skullduggery at the polls mean that, as Kazi Jafar Ahmed (and leaders in all other opposition parties) put it, 'the people's views have in no sense found expression through this election' and 'rather through it the ruling class has silenced the people's voice.' Violence and corruption seem to have also marked the few elections the Pakistan military permitted their East Pakistani subjects to hold before Bangladesh's independence. Similarly, the contention of the Bhashani NAP, Rabb's National Socialist Party, and Ataur Rahman Khan's Bangladesh National League that the 45% of the electorate who did not vote were kept away by the Awami League terror rather than disinterest and would have voted for them, appears unrealistic. The truth is that, the political terrorization of the various parties aside, the opposition, groups caught the full weight of the peasant-worker law-and-order backlash. Although the electorate agreed with their anti-Indian tirade, it also intelligently realized that it was the only thing holding the motley united front of the opposition leaders together and that if they got in power their disunity would plunge the country in chaos. Although the workers and peasants abhorred the soaring cost of living, Shaikh Mujib's alliance with kafir India, and his government's corruption and incompetence, they still gave him an overwhelming mandate to lead again as 'our last hope.' Moreover, the common people still reveal a deep liking and trust in Mujib. 'Everyone around Mujib is rotten *(pocha)*' they say 'but he is still good. He is father of the nation. If we support him he can still save us from ruin?' This is the kind of thinking I heard time and time again.

Open Letter to Sh. Mujib

1 December 1973

Dear Shaikh Sahib,

THAT you were a Pakistani yourself from 14.8.47 to 20 December 1971 persuades me to address this letter to you.

As the issue in the letter is not personal and pertains to the public, and in which the people in West Pakistan and the people in your land are vitally interested, I am addressing an open letter.

Our first acquaintance was made when in the year 1951 you came to Lahore as a representative of East Pakistan students and I along with others met you as a representative of the Punjab Students Federation. We had meetings for undefined, inchoate but romantic objectives. We met as young Pakistanis looking for a great future. Then I suddenly saw you through the papers relating to the Agartala Conspiracy Case. I must confess that the papers convinced me that there was a case fit for trial and so a judicial tribunal was constituted to sift the truth from falsehood. What happened to the trial is a matter of the past. However, I do remember, when you were released from Dacca and you came to Islamabad to attend a round table conference, I came early in the morning to East Pakistan House and we discussed some possibilities of a viable solution so that 'Pakistan may stay'. These are the reminiscences which form the back drop for the contents of this letter.

On 20 December 1971 consequent upon the surrender of the Pakistan armed forces at Dacca, a new country of Bangladesh became a de facto reality. However, its de jure position is not recognized by the government here and the people of this wing are still keeping the chairs in the National Assembly vacant for the members of East Pakistan to come and occupy them. Many of us know that this is not going to happen.

You and your colleagues, on the other hand, are insisting that the people of Pakistan should recognize Bangladesh as a new state, but the wound has cut very deep. It is extremely hurting and constantly too. In this surrender, we as a nation have not only bled profusely but have lost our identity. This calls for time and demands superior vision by leaders on both sides.

In fact, you and your colleagues have satisfaction *in praesenti* in that you have achieved what you call your dream. We call it a nightmare. I do not intend to anger you by suggesting that your dream was faulty but I do consider it necessary to put on record that an opportunity is opening now before you by which you can reverse the tide and bring about a detente between the two people. In my estimation, the reversal is likely to happen on its own. There will be an open urge expressed by the people of the two wings to come to a closer contact notwithstanding the past, but you can help in quickening the process. The end of the process may not be a political unification of the two wings but it can be for a better understanding. The present generation earnestly requires this understanding. The *onus* of history is on you. Before separation it was possibly on the leaders of West Pakistan.

One of the crucial issues which will determine the future relationship of the two people is the question of the trial of 195 POWs. Never before has the fate of so many (120 million) been tied to the fate of the so few (195) and never before has, in psychological terms, been the time so short for a decision of such a high magnitude, particularly when the decision is to be taken entirely by one side, namely, yours.

Your claim is that you can try these 195 POWs for war crimes. We in Pakistan are confirmed in our belief that in the performance of their duties, these POWs did not commit any crime. Excesses, if any, are notable or actionable only in Pakistan and only by Pakistan tribunals. (In fact, even this is not conceded by a large section of public opinion in West Pakistan).

Obviously, the two claims are divergent and irreconcilable. Evidence in your possession for the trial of POWs has been noticed by most of us in various publications prepared in and issued by the Foreign Office of India and publications emanating from Dacca. The nature of evidence apart, the jurisprudence of trial on the basis of that evidence comes in conflict with the nature of duty imposed by history upon those who were responsible in East Pakistan to maintain and keep every inch of that part of the country 'safe and clean from the outsiders'. Even if the evidence in your possession is believed, the vital issue of the right to act cannot be denied to those who acted. Put yourself in their position and imagine that if the northern districts of your country were to seek separation, what will you do? You will use all the force that you can to stop it happening. Once the use of force is justified, the abuse of it is accountable only before the parent state.

But the issue is not merely moral or legal. It is essentially political. It is political in various senses. A decision on this issue is going to affect not only the present generation but many more generations to come. If you decide that you must try those POWs, your people will plunge into a hoary past. They will turn back instead of looking forward. There will be acrimony. There will be horrible memories exaggerated from evidence tailored for a trial. This will be matched by advocates raising the issue of patriotism and national duty. There shall be a world public to watch us washing our dirty linen before them.

If you try these POWs, the people in West Pakistan would be justified in demanding in the name of justice also a trial for the atrocities committed on pro-Pakistani elements domiciled in East Pakistan, upon Biharis and upon devoted workers of Al-Badar and Al-Fatah. There is also substance in the claim that those who indulged in espionage or leakage of essential information are triable in Pakistan according to the law of the realm. If they are tried, on the facts and the evidence, they may be liable to be convicted. But should all this happen? In both cases law and ethics cannot provide any answer. Please do not seek a legal rationale for the situation.

We need each other politically as well as commercially. You must have by this time realized that India is too big a power and 'Bangladesh' is too small. Big powers and their neighbours cannot go well for long unless there is a one-sided subjugation. You will require some sort of support from time to time and the best can be provided by those who are similarly situated.

You have many personal friends in West Pakistan. Please contact them and find out their views on this issue. You can write to them or meet them at some convenient international city. I am sure, on this issue, they will advise you to let the past bury its dead.

In case you decide to give up the trial of 195 POWs the vista for an understanding is immediately opened and the burden would be lighter on you and heavier on West Pakistan.

Yours sincerely,
S. M. Zafar.

Dacca Diary IV: How Secular or how Communal?

8 December 1973

Dennis Walker

MY stay in Bangladesh covered the first week of Ramadhan. The year before, Muslims and Hindus had clashed throughout Bangladesh during the Hindu festival of Durga Puja. Now, in 1973, Durga Puja and Ramadhan were coinciding and the Bengali press was full of exhortations to the government to take special precautions. Yet though the Bangladesh common people were obviously in a bitterly anti-Indian mood, their indifference to opposition agitation on the issue had led Maulana Bhashani to call off his threatened movement demanding a boycott of Indian goods and severance of Bangladesh's treaty relations with her great neighbour, due to be launched on 28 September with ritual burnings of Indian textiles in all towns of Bangladesh. Although disappointment with the failure of independence to bring either social justice or national independence (since 'India has replaced Pakistan as oppressor of Bangladesh' as even the most untutored say) runs deep among the Bengali Muslim masses, it is still very uncertain that they will accept the leadership the parliamentary or underground opposition offers. Despite appearances, Shaikh Mujib's position as the only possible leader therefore remains strong.

All discussions with Bangladeshis lead finally to one subject—India. India, Bangladesh's gigantic neighbour that surrounds her on three sides and whose mighty shadow falls over every inch of Bangladesh soil and every problem the new nation faces. The Indian press has a simple explanation for Bangladesh's unease: communalism'. If Bangladeshis are hostile the onus for that must rest with the Bangladeshis who are blinded by an exclusivist Islamic hatred of Hindus and hence 'ungrateful' to all that their Indian liberators and post-liberation benefactors have done for them. 'New Delhi', sermonized the Calcutta *Statesman Weekly* of 25 August 1973, 'has conducted its relations with Dacca with all the tact it could muster. But the possibility that it will never be forgiven by Bangladesh for liberating it is an unpalatable truth that New Delhi policy makers cannot now fail to take into account.' The Statesman denounced 'the insidious campaign (in Bangladesh) of destroying everything resembling a special relationship between the two countries. Maulana Bhashani apart, those described as Muslim Bangla activists are plainly very much in the picture ... heady nationalism, economic

290

frustrations, and a sense of Muslim identity against which nothing could be more feeble an antidote than secularism add up to an explosive mixture. Despite all that happened in the liberation war, the possibility of Dacca's restoring close ties with Pakistan, albeit on a basis of complete equality, is not something which New Delhi should be incredulous about.'

Arriving in Dacca, bearing cuttings from the Indian press's campaign against the 'anti-Hindu communalists' of Bangladesh, I wonder if it is the same country. In the Dacca University canteen I see Hindu and Muslim students chatting over cans of tea about Bengali literature with an inter-communal amiability probably unique in the Indian subcontinent. Certainly, Bangladesh is a paradise for minorities in comparison to neighbouring India where the systematic massacre of the country's Muslim minority has become almost the post-independence Indian way of life, where the large minority of untouchables are, when they request betterment of then sub-human status, 'burned alive or thrown down into wells… beaten up, their women raped by gangs of attackers. Frequently their miserable houses are destroyed and their meagre possessions stolen. The police, when not themselves the agents of persecution are often slow to take action.' (Michael Hornsby: 'Indian Harijans Struggling to Lose the Untouchability Tag', *The Times*, London, 20 August 1973). Yet, since Bangladesh's independence, rather than concentrating on problems of prejudice at home both the Indian press and the Indian government have repeatedly intervened to secure the interests of Bangladesh's ten million-strong minority of Hindus. Because Bangladeshis see their country's main post-independence problem as the struggle to maintain independence from India, this outside interest in Bangladesh Hindus has mainly succeeded in identifying them as a fifth column with an extra-territorial loyalty to India; it seems, indeed, hard to understand how the Indian attitude could have been calculated to help the minority it ostensibly aimed to protect.

And yet, much of the positive legacy of Bengali nationalist secularism still endures from the Pakistan period. There are Hindu members of the parliament and the cabinet, and since this latest general election mandate, Shaikh Mujib has shown more resolution in assuring Hindus their due place in the civil service; politically courageous in view of the rise in communal feeling that the alliance with India and Indian big-brotherism here caused. The understanding of the independence struggle period where Hindus and Muslims united without a thought for the religious differences to wrest freedom ('shadinata') from the Pakistan army may be more, but educated people of the two communities still communicate with honesty and fellow feeling.

It is indeed indicative of the extent to which India repeated all of West Pakistan's mistakes of cultural and political arrogance that her most determined enemies in Bangladesh today are drawn from the Mukti Bahini fighters who have seen her at closest hand and who are most predisposed to the secular and humanist ideals she professes. I spoke with a young Mukti Bahini who was trained in India in diving and took part in the Mukti Bahini sinking of several Pakistaniships in Chittagong harbour—which the Pakistan military spokesman, with characteristic racism, said 'could only have been the work of Indian navy frogmen.' He is militantly secular in his ideals of nationalism and opposed to making Muslim identity a basis for Bangladesh nationhood. He squarely blames his own community for communal ill feelings.

'This communalism is a great problem. Our government is in a very difficult position. To get some balance, they have started reading the Quran, the Hindu Gita, and the Bible together over the wireless, but still the masses resist the idea. I think the problem is basically the type of education we get in Bangladesh. Ask any child here who is the ideal of generosity—he will at once say Hatim Tayi, an Arab not a Bengsli. So you see, from our earliest days we are taught to identify with the Arabs and the Middle Easterners more than with our own Hindu neighbours, racially identical to us'

'Do you want a united Bengal of Bangladesh and Indian-occupied West Bengal?' I ask.

'With communal relations as they are, only after fifty years', he replies with a laugh.

Arms and the Subcontinent

15 December 1973

IN the wake of the unresolved Middle East conflict which continues to demand world attention as the winter grows colder for those western nations that side with criminal injustice, there has been a flurry of diplomatic activity in some of the states that are on the periphery of the central crisis. As the current battleground of superpower politics, the Middle East decidedly has a bearing on the affairs of the subcontinent.

Prime Minister Bhutto's visits to Kuwait and to the Gulf States of Abu Dhabi, Dubai, Bahrain, and Qatar are all the more significant because of their timing. Mr Brezhnev has been to India to further strengthen Russia's military and economic commitment to the one nation in the subcontinent which nurtures dreams of becoming a great power. M. Jean de Lipkowski, the French Secretary of State for Foreign Affairs, who has just left Pakistan for the Middle East, hinted at the imbalance likely to result from any arms embargo on Pakistan. Is the subcontinent once again to be the arena of opposed superpower interests?

In the past few months there has been a noticeable thaw in Pakistan's relationship with India and Bangladesh. The repatriation of prisoners-of-war from India and the shuttle service between Pakistan and Bangladesh, involving the repatriation from one to the other of Bengalis and Biharis respectively. The general amnesty granted by Shaikh Mujibur Rahman to the loyalists who were pro-Pakistan at the time of the break-up, and who have been in prison since, is another forward step towards closer relations. It is conceivable that left to themselves the three nations may work out an amicable *modus vivendi*. But will the two giants stand aside, or even work for amity?

Of all things, an arms race is least likely to promote prospects for peace and prosperity. The problem of mass poverty, which everyone recognizes as of primary importance, cannot be solved by producing or acquiring more guns. Bangladesh can for the present be excused from the argument. But there is precious little justification for Mrs Gandhi or Mr Bhutto to turn their backs on the election pledges made to suffering millions. The Russo-Indian alliance along with the support of Afghanistan does constitute a threat to Pakistan, a challenge to American interests in the area and a warning to China. Pakistan has thus to react, and is therefore less culpable, although not entirely blameless.

If the basic premise that India and Pakistan need to coexist is accepted, then it must be said that

293

their attitude and actions result from looking through the wrong end of the telescope. Instead of giving real substance to a possible detente by mutually agreeing to reduce their defence budgets, they are engaged both overtly and covertly in building up their military strength. Weapons unfortunately not only tend to get used but also to create conditions where their use becomes more likely. A show of outward military strength is often an effective smokescreen for internal political weakness. And it is precisely for this reason that the superpowers seek to increase their influence by aiding nations militarily irrespective of whether there is any imminent danger.

The assumption that Mr Bhutto's visits to the oil-rich Arab states are tied up with the need to procure arms to counterbalance Russian military aid to India is reasonable. The Islamic summit meeting at Lahore next month, in which the Arab nations will figure prominently, may give truth to the speculation that Pakistan is to set up its own armaments complex financed by the Arab states and with the help of French technology. Such a step can be held to be a necessity but it could also be both wasteful and provocative as well as irrelevant to the main issue, which is internal cohesion.

Mr Bhutto has now been firmly in the saddle for two years. In this time he has, despite his undoubted political acumen, been unable to win over the opposition and to unite the country behind him. Baluchistan and the N.W.F.P. remain in a state of ferment, partly at least because of Mr Bhutto's own unpopular and undemocratic political moves. Mr Bizenjo, Mr Mengal, and Mr Khairbux Mari are still in jail, while their followers reportedly continue to militate against the federal troops that have been policing the area. It is these divisions that Mr Bhutto must resolve before seeking to neutralize the external pressures.

India has its own problems, and the almost unconcealed desire to exercise hegemony over its smaller neighbours is one of them. Mrs Gandhi's abandonment of her father's policy of neutrality only put an official stamp on an existing reality. The cloak of 'neutrality' never quite hid India whenever her own self-interest was involved. The 1971 war is perhaps still too recent and harrowing to be looked at dispassionately. But whatever may be said of India's role, it cannot be denied that the vast majority of the Bengalis turned against Pakistan. The danger Pakistan faces is not so much the military might of India as the disaffection of sections of its own people. This can be exploited by enemies, but its existence is our own fault.

Mr Bhutto, as a student of history, probably senses the direction in which the country should move. The posture of confrontation can only be self-defeating in the long run. Too much dependence on a superpower—or even a great power—tends to embroil a country in troublesome situations and have unpleasant repercussions. Mr Bhutto can thus bide his time and work towards the desired goal in a manner designed to assure consensus rather than contrariness. But the essence of history is time, while that of politics is expedience.

These whistle-stop tours of Mr Bhutto, whether within or outside the country, are generally born of expedience, when they are not merely for razzle-dazzle display. The corroborating evidence offered by Mr Bhutto's spectacular somersaults on sensitive political issues and his evident lack of success in inspiring the trust of political opponents, leave alone their support, points to a potentially explosive situation. For the sake of this dismembered country, he must watch his steps carefully.

The Twins and their Promise

29 December 1973

TWO years after Pakistan split up, the twins are shaping up in a manner which shows remarkable political parallelism. But for its more favourable land-population ratio, the superior economic infrastructure and the far larger resources base, Pakistan, insofar as its political portrait is concerned looks more like a disconcerting replica of Bangladesh. It is only the inherited economic viability which makes the Pakistan of today beckon a different promise from that of Bangladesh. If the context was confined to the doings of the political leadership alone, the twins would be dozing in the same kind of slough.

Both countries, after the traumatic events of 1971, came under the disarming spell of a personality cult. The Bangabandhu emerged as a rather non-munificent father figure over there while residual Pakistan fell in the lap of the Quaid-i-Awam whose bounties are financed out of a mortgage on the future. A relentless, messiah-like aura was built around the two leaders, ignoring, as always, the lessons of history. Both run a highly centralized, personalized system of government which has eroded the prospects of an institutionalized democracy. The picture, with minor differences, is true of both the young states.

The word of either of the two leaders is a law unto itself. Both keep a heavy and firm grip on the apparatus of the party for whatever it is worth and, by deliberate design, on every lever of the state. Neither has a peer within the party or outside its ranks and neither of them seems to believe in the philosophy of the delegation of authority or anything remotely suggestive of a collective leadership. Both delight in carrying the burden of destiny on their rather unprepared shoulders. Fortunately or otherwise, the sense of mission which both had arrogated to themselves has turned from a vision into a reality. This has happened because both are ambitious, hard-driving individuals with a flair for politics and a capacity to galvanize the masses. Depending on how the people fare under the respective new dispensation, the end-cause the two leaders represented, as apart from the means employed, could be deemed to be just. Having gained the end, a dissimilarity between the two personalities becomes evident. Mr Bhutto is at home within the demanding precincts of statecraft; Mr Mujibur Rahman feels lost in the labyrinthine corridors of power. Agitational politics and statecraft are two different worlds. Still, living with power has created identical grooves on the two personalities. Their basic traits of egotism and intolerance and sensitivity to criticizm have been magnified. Both tend to equate the good of the country with their own grip on power. Naturally, both distrust each other. Neither of them could reach what they consider to be the present point of their unshared glory in an undivided Pakistan. In that context, the prize of any political office would have been constantly subjected to a wider set of constraints. Each, therefore is happy in his own self-demarcated plot.

It was the legitimate legacy of the 1970 elections that a single party emerged in either wing to dominate the political scene. Since then, however, this dominance has been sought to be perpetuated through less legitimate means. The opposition parties in both regions are yet in the shadows as much due to their own weaknesses as due to the unsophisticated tactics of the party in power. There is a streak of fascism surfacing in both countries although it is not going to work in either. In Bangladesh the volatile, emotion-swayed people have gone through a bout of blood and seem heading for a restless, uncertain future. In Pakistan, the political geography of the country precludes the emergence of a one-party state.

General elections have legitimized the exercise of power in Bangladesh although it has not necessarily thrown up a credible or viable democratic framework. Shaikh Mujib has had to arm himself with emergency powers, create a party-orientated para-military force like the Rakhi Bahni, use armed force to crush the dissidents in Chittagong and even compromise in the sensitive sphere of national sovereignty. Mr Bhutto, of course, revels in the steel armour of the DPR, relies on sinews like the hand-picked Federal Security Force and has had to use force in Baluchistan—without apparent result. Both have suppressed press freedom. A corrupt, and yet indispensable party hierarchy haunts the trail blazed by both leaders. The professional services have suffered an eclipse. Opportunists and hacks rule the roost, most of all in the propaganda ministries. Is it not symptomatic that the terminology of the endless harrangue is about the same? If Shaikh Mujib regales his interviewers with the 'I love my people and they love me' theme, Mr Bhutto speaks of two Bhuttos, one in the heart of the people and the other on the dais. If Sh. Mujib blames the ills of the earth on the devastation of the war of liberation, Mr Bhutto finds a ready excuse in the 12-year-long night of military despotism. If one of them raked up the hollow vision of a *sonar bangla*, the other sought to mesmerize his naive audiences with the heroic talk of a resurgent Germany and Japan. If there are Pakistani agents plaguing the recovery of Bangladesh, there are Indian and Soviet agents and the London Plan-wallas sabotaging the proliferating reforms in Pakistan.

And now for the silver lining. The jails in Bangladesh have been emptied of the 40,000 or so 'collaborators'. The amnesty recently granted is a step in the right direction although the debilitating process of blood-letting, political vendetta, and witchhunting has yet to run its course. In Pakistan, the politics of confrontation has yet to be reversed although there are desirable signs of a change of tactics in that direction.

A question mark shapes up. Here are two political leaders who command an absolute majority in their respective parliaments and who certainly moved the masses with their own message, who had the opportunity and the commitment to build a new system out of the ashes of the old, who had the better of the entrenched vested interests as an opening advantage and who, perhaps could deliver the goods. Why is it then that the promise is petering out in a sandstorm of suppression and oppression? Is it fated that the light will not burn in these parts?

Part II
Zulfikar Ali Bhutto

Tame Rendezvous at Sanghar

8 April 1972

Our correspondent writes:

PRESIDENT Bhutto likes to make good his public promises except, of course, for the famous Tashkent business—whatever it was. In his first nationwide broadcast as President of Pakistan, Mr Bhutto had vowed that he would maintain close links with the people, whom he acknowledged as the fountain head of power. Last week he chose Sanghar. Sanghar is a sleepy little town of some 10,000 souls which has few claims on history except as the stronghold of the Pir Sahib of Pagaro—regarded almost as the shadow of God by his fanatic Hur followers.

But, for Mr Bhutto, Sanghar is associated with a promise. As Morning News said 'when a marauding wave of blood thirsty, sharp shooting natives opened fire on Mr Bhutto's motorcade on 31 March 1970, and the local administration prevented him from addressing a public meeting in this town … Mr Bhutto promised that he would come one day and address a memorable public meeting here'. On 31 March, President Bhutto came to town in an Army Air Corps helicopter, wearing a Chinese cap, and literally jolted this ramshackle place into something like a carnival. The occasion was a presidential meeting.

Preparation had been afoot for days. Party dignitaries and workers from Karachi had been visiting Sanghar and, in collaboration with local officials, had set the stage for the President's triumphant visit. MNA Sattar Gabol, acknowledged by his associates as a peerless rostrum-expert, had been there for four days. According to Morning News, the rostrum was built by over a thousand persons—500 Peoples' Guards and as many workers imported from Karachi. Also lending a hand was the local administration led by the Deputy Commissioner.

Underestimating the good President's popularity perhaps, workers had put in thousands of man-hours in an effort to produce the carnival atmosphere. Banners, streamers, flags, ceremonial arches, and gates added to the carnival touch. On the arch leading to the delegates' enclosure, and rather unsuccessfully trying to explain its presence at a political meeting, was the blushing legend *'baharon phool barsao mera mehboob aya hai'*. Journalists, local and foreign, had been invited. Dusty buses plying from nearby, and equally dusty, townships and ferrying 'the people' were much in evidence.

The venue of the meeting was all colour, including an imposing posse of mounted police guards in resplendent uniform from a nearby police training centre. According to one estimate nearly 10,000 men in uniform, including a section of the Rangers, had been brought over for policing duties. Exaggerated? Maybe. But the journalists covering the show felt the security pinch all right.

Undeniably it was security at its tightest when Mr Bhutto flew into Karachi the same afternoon by helicopter and landed at the Polo Grounds. Every person working in the WPIDC and Dawood Centres had been asked to clear out by 3 p.m. Never before has security been taken to such extreme lengths. This contrasts strangely with Mr Bhutto's performance at his public meeting in Karachi on 5 January when he railed against the security precautions, dramatically caused the protection desk to be removed and asked the multitude to come nearer. 'I need no protection' as the peoples' beloved leader. At Sanghar, the yawning chasm of space between the people and the leader was screaming mutely.

The public meeting was apparently a bid by Mr Bhutto to establish the influence of his party in an area where it had little or no support. Astute politician that he is, Mr Bhutto puts great store by the power of the spoken word. (He leans equally on dramatic action too. At the meeting he grandiloquently announced a Rs. 10,000 gift for the family of the person who was killed in the attack on Mr Bhutto's party at Sanghar in 1970). Understandably so. The power of the spoken word is what has got him where he is. Add to it the ingredients of colour and spectacle, a tried and tested formula successfully employed elsewhere before. And one understands the weeks of planning for the Lahore meeting and a less grandiose effort at Sanghar. But, here, something seemed to misfire.

Contrary to the expressed expectations of a crowd of half a million, the crowd was around 40,000. It was not a boisterous, enthusiastic crowd, rather a silent, patient one. Even the faithful TV could not project much of the hand-waving dancing crowd. Foreign correspondents covering the meeting reported that a section of the crowd walked out and that Mr Bhutto had to curtail his speech because of a thinning crowd. Some say the walkout began when the President was speaking on the recent land reforms. Others were of the opinion that it was triggered off when the President said that he was about to end the speech in Urdu. Whatever the reason, this was promptly denied the next day by the official agencies concerned. Foreign correspondents also drew the inference that the President, unlike in the Punjab where the PPP tide is still running high, seems to be losing ground in his own home province. Not a wholly unfair assumption, judging from the look of things at Sanghar.

But, then, one must remember the lay of the land. This is traditional Pir of Pagaro territory and there has been no love lost between the President and the Pir Sahib. At election time, the one national assembly seat was bagged by a supporter of the Pir Sahib. Out of the four provincial assembly seats, only one was taken by a PPP-backed independent candidate.

It would be unfair to read too much into the tame rendezvous at Sanghar. Sind these days is having a taste of intense regional nationalism and Mr Bhutto, creditably, has been no regional chauvinist. At least, since he became President he has not been running with the local hare, although the provincial administration seems to have been sweeping with a pretty thick broom.

Mr Bhutto sounded the right notes at the public meeting except for the rather unfortunate references to the fate of the Red Indians on the American continent. An unjustified parallel, for whatever reasons he chose to make it. A little more ominous was his warning of a political strife in case of a breakdown of the PPP-NAP-JUI agreement. One was disagreeably reminded of Ayub Khan's speech in Dacca in which he said that 'if people don't understand the weapon of language then we will have to use the language of weapons' in reference to the six-points issue. The Urdu papers quoted Mr Bhutto as saying that there would be a 'siyasi jang' whereas the English papers referred to this as a 'political confrontation'. This 'siyasi jang' could mean anything from a civil war to a localized police action. However, credit must be given to Mr Bhutto for his eminently sensible approach to the language problem and the need for amity between 'old and new' Sindhis.

The meeting over, as the Evening Star put it, the buses departed and many of those who had been brought to the show from outlying townships were left stranded, feeling cheated. In politics, as in life itself, if you are not on the bandwagon in time, you are bound to miss the bus, no matter who the ruling president is.

On the Brink

15 April 1972

IN a crisis-ridden country like ours, one learns to live on the verge of hope and despair. Illusions come to be traded as facts of life. Lessons are learned only to be forgotten. Few seem to realize that we are living on the brink of disaster.

The not unexpected crumbling of the PPP-NAP-JUI accord is the latest in a series of misfortunes inflicted upon the country by its bankrupt political leadership. The discord, the arguments, and the counter-arguments, are in fact facetious. The root of the matter is that the leadership, without exception, devolves on small men whom the deepening crisis has failed to lift beyond the confines of petty inter-party intrigue and a lust for power.

A heavier share of the burden must fall on the shoulders of President Bhutto, not necessarily because he is in the wrong, but because he happens to be the head of the state and leader of the majority party. Nobody knows better than he does what the consequences of failure would be. The merciless pressures that are building up around us should be well within his knowledge. This time, as a consequence of failure, nothing will be left to merit sophistry, explanation, rationalization or plain afterthoughts. It will be the *great tragedy* of his own making without a reprint order. It will be curtains.

Mr Wali Khan's half-gallant, half-serious assertion of *de jure* authority over the Frontier and Baluchistan areas has an ominously familiar ring. It brings to mind the fateful days of February '71. Mr Bhutto then was still riding the high 'bastions of power' horse, galloping with a torch of fire between Karachi and Khyber and herding all MNAs elect, irrespective of their party affiliations, away from the 'slaughter house' precincts of the National Assembly in Dacca. The point to remember here is not Mr Bhutto's weakness for fiery words and gestures, but his remarkably consistent record of seeking to avoid negotiations in a properly constituted forum where they would otherwise normally and legitimately belong. In this regard, his consistency of behaviour and of motives is frightening because of the equally consistent likelihood of parallel results.

When Ayub Khan was tottering, Mr Bhutto would not deign to join the RTC to give him the proverbial *coup de grace*. The result was that Yahya Khan slid into the saddle, ultimately to drench this country with blood and dishonour. Sure, Mr Bhutto was one up on the 'discredited politicians' and prepared himself for the long wait. Then came the confrontation with Shaikh Mujib, which may or may not have been wholly of Mr Bhutto's making. That he had a finger deep in the gory pudding is not to be denied. He would neither go to the National Assembly nor would he concede the right of the majority party to form a government without his own participation. The story was not quite as simple but there can be no two opinions about the repercussions that inevitably followed. Sure, Mr Bhutto, in his single-minded pursuit of power, emerged one up on both Shaikh Mujib and Yahya Khan. At what cost though?

In the current confrontation, it is possible that Mr Bhutto may once again emerge with the upper hand. But, is the game worth the candle? The tripartite agreement and its wording are not the core of the dispute. Otherwise it could have been possible to agree on non-party governors for all the four provinces or to refer the disputed clause 3 to the Supreme Court. It is more a clash of personalities than of principles, more a squabbling for a share in power than a row over interpretation or broken promises. On Mr Bhutto's part this lapse is unforgivable: that he is playing with the fate of the country in relying on discredited instruments like martial law. It is not worth defending. Not a dog's chance that it could be preserved for long. Right from the moment he came into power, President Bhutto should have tried to rule through building up a national consensus. He chose, deliberately, to turn the other way. His choice of governors, his reliance on martial law, his reluctance to call the national assembly or to frame a constitution, interim or permanent, all of these appeared to be, and actually were, probes towards building a one-party state with a personalized base of power. That the plan does not seem to be working does not mean that it has been given up. The unsavoury alliance with Khan Qayyum Khan is a remorseless step in the same direction. As we go to the press, the first reports about the interim constitution justify our worst fears.

Not wholly edifying either is Mr Wali Khan's role in this sorry mess. (The third stranger in the corridor is hardly worth being brought to book). When the alliance was signed and sealed on 6 March, Mr Wali Khan and his working committee supported the continuation of martial law till 14 August in 'larger national interests', without causing a lump in the now sensitive party throats. Surely, nothing has happened in the meantime to warrant a drastic redefinition of national interests? What has certainly happened is that Mr Wali Khan sees more clearly than before the ripening chances of his being catapulted into a position of power through a mixture of internal and external pressurization. In this game, it is important to secure the Frontier and Baluchistan under the party colours. Neither the country nor President Bhutto is being given any quarter in this relentless race for power.

The NAP has certainly lost credibility over the last couple of months by a show of rare opportunism. It has sought to allay the fears of private enterprise on the one hand and talked of wholesale nationalization on the other. It seeks to protect the oppressed landless peasant and the well-to-do landowner all in the same breath. It espouses the concept of four nationalities and simultaneously drops its parental claim on Pakhtoonistan as 'no longer a relevant' issue. It talks of blood and guns; it also cooes like a dove. Its secularism finds a safe repose within the curvaceous folds of the JUI. It is all things to all manner of men at the same time.

The NAP offers a possible alternative to the present regime. To this extent it is welcome since it is of the essence of democracy to have a choice. But this is no time to press home the choice. This country, poised on the brink, cannot afford a confrontation, internal or external. President Bhutto must be given a fair chance to have his day, unless he chooses to advance the clock himself.

Wind out of Opposition's Sails

22 April 1972

IS it really Mr Bhutto's style? If so, of politics or of diplomacy? Was it really so dramatic as Mian Daultana made it out to be—so unexpected, that is? Why did he have to time it so? All such questions keep coming back to the mind and there are no ready answers.

The fact is that, as Khan Wali Khan admitted to a foreign correspondent, 'he has taken the wind off our sails' by announcing the end of martial law on 21 April, conditional to the acceptance of his draft of the interim constitution by the National Assembly. He has demonstrated in his election to the Presidentship of the Assembly that he has the brute majority with him. The resolution in support of the continuation of martial law upto 14 August was signed by 101 members; the names were not disclosed. So he should have had no doubt that he could bulldoze any draft through the House. Was he not being too reasonable to be believed?

About one thing there is convincing evidence: President Bhutto had made up his mind about the date of lifting of martial law before he held those meetings with NAP-JUI leaders at Peshawar. He had told Mr Mahmud Ali Kasuri at least two days before that meeting that he should work out the option of lifting martial law on 21 April. Mr Rafi Raza too, seems to have known that martial law would be lifted on 21 April, since about that time meetings with the NAP-JUI leaders were being held at a crisis tempo. The deadlock was a part of the tactics. Mrs Bhutto too seems to have been in the picture.

The belief is that there were at least two or three more who knew of the decision. There is no evidence why such a decision was taken; or was it forced on the President? One or two guesses would be relevant: It had begun to be seriously considered why martial law should be at all there when everything could be done through normal legislation and despite the writ jurisdiction of courts. It should have occurred to Mr Kasuri to tell the President that lawyers, even good lawyers like him, could not win certain types of cases with some specific types of legislations. It should have been found that the leadership need not distrust the PPP legislators to such an extent that even a two-thirds majority in the House did not give them the confidence which martial law otherwise gave. Mr Bhutto knows that some desertions from the party had occurred because at that time the party could not hope to come to power. When it had assumed power, the floor-crossings would be from the other side to his party. The QML unloaded itself on his side. Perhaps even more relevant was the growing feeling that instead of the PPP gaining ground in the N.W.F.P. and Baluchistan through the administration headed by its appointees as governors, the NAP was making a dent in the PPP strongholds in the Punjab and, to a less significant extent, in Sind also. And that because of the NAP's active campaigning against martial law's continuation.

But many here were of the view that Mr Bhutto's politics is usually an extension of his diplomacy. In fact, his dedication to international affairs is so overwhelming that he always looks at domestic politics through the coloured glasses of the foreign office. Be that as it may, the need for presenting a united front to Mrs Gandhi during the coming confrontation is not a matter of principle with the NAP alone; or rather it would be more valid for Mr Bhutto to think in terms of timing a complete rapprochement at the national level: for a united and single-minded leadership, in his person, facing the Indian Prime Minister resolutely, lest there should be any mistake on her part in assessing the strength and determination of this country in dealing with India and Bangladesh. Mr Bhutto always insists on timing his decisions and announcements for maximum effect, bordering sometimes on dramatics.

It could, however, be, that the experience of the last few months, with martial law as the main instrument of administration in the executive branch, was not all that successful. The courts had frowned too often. A confrontation with the judiciary was in the offing in some form or the other. The Supreme Court was still pondering over the question of legitimacy raised before it. If the executive lost, it would get no sympathy from the public. And if the judiciary went down again, it would attract all the public sympathy, and that of the coming generations too. Here again, Mr Kasuri must have been the main sobering influence on the President against some of the younger hot-heads who talked more of fixing people and things, than of living up to the expectations of the people.

I do not agree with the thesis which many observers propound that there was pressure from our friends abroad and such backers as we have, to democratise the politics quickly so that they could come forward to help us in kind and cash, by grants and loans. I would much rather consider the other theory that after three months of efforts at socialistic reforms which were both half-hearted and ill- planned, the administration could think of only democratisation as a popular measure which could secure some lasting public backing for the regime. But the last argument always was: Can martial law go beyond 14 August, if not why not take it off here and now? Let us admit the plain fact that Mr Bhutto now feels strong enough to permit democratic politics without any threat to himself.

—'Manju'

Oath in a Fish Bowl

29 April 1972

Our correspondent writes:

JUDGING by the traditions of state funerals, the requiem played for martial law at the racecourse here last week, was less of a dirge and more of a cacaphony. What was planned as an orderly state function turned out to be President Bhutto's public meetings *a la* Bungkarno's public rallies *sans* the better behaved listeners at Jakarta's Merdeka Stadium. It was not suprising that the organizers indulged in mutual recriminations leading to an official enquiry into their failure.

The justification for the public swearing-in under the interim constitution was provided by the President himself in his speech at the racecourse. He said that he could not have taken oath of office unless the people were there to witness it. Anticipating the criticizm [*sic*] of the extravaganza, he declared: Nobody raises a finger when the capitalist and the rich spend lavishly on their pleasures. However, even overlooking the obvious fact that no capitalist in Pakistan ever spent half as much on entertainment in a life time, the real worth of the returns on the considerable investment is disputable. Not many of those who were caught amidst the mindless mass at the racecourse would be cherishing the experience. All that they got for suffering the constant shoving around and choking dust, were some intelligible snatches of the President's speech and a PAF flypast that could not be obscured from anyone's view.

Although the bread is getting steadily dearer, still the public is entitled to its circus and it cannot be denied that a real effort had gone into making this a really big show. Special trains were run from such faraway points as Karachi, Quetta, and Bahawalpur. Fleets of buses, trucks, and motor wagons came from the Frontier, Azad Kashmir, and several towns around the capital. The tally does not include those who flew PIA, stayed at the plush Intercontinental or Shehrazad hotels and did not pay a paisa for either.

Political Affairs Minister Jatoi had declared at his televised press conference, two days before the big day that the journeys would have to be paid for. He had not said by whom. At least those who had come by air and trains admitted that they didn't. All the same, the Minister's statement was indicative of the regime's progress on the road to maturity, for the statement did not necessitate the inevitable retraction. On at least two occasions since assuming office, the new administration had to make spectacular somersaults. First, abolishing the public holiday on the Quaid-i-Azam's birthday, the new leaders had announced that a full-fledged working day would be a more befitting tribute to the memory of the father of the nation. Just twenty-four hours later, an official handout had restored the holiday and blamed the rotten order of the bad old days for the abolition. Next, Minister Hafeez Peerzada announced that the President was to pay all the expenses of a train-load of diplomats taken to Larkana. Once again, the next day it was declared that the President did not have that kind of money and that the state would have to pay its public relations bill.

Leaving aside the little known fact as to who paid for the transportation to the oath-taking ceremony, it is by now openly stated that the seats in the special trains were allocated to various political parties proportionately on the basis of their representation in the National Assembly. The same standard was applied to the party flags flown at the racecourse. For instance the Jamaat-e-Islami with its four MNAs had four and the PDP with only Mr Noorul Amin to represent it in the National Assembly, had a lone standard fluttering at the mast. However, the parade ground, dominated by huge red hoardings that proclaimed the virtues of democracy and the supremacy of the people, was flooded with the PPP's flags, outnumbering all others twenty to one. To give the final touch of democracy, the President, with his governors and ministers, shared the main dais with Mr Wali Khan, Sardar Shaukat Hayat, and Maulana Mufti Mahmood.

The occasion could have turned out to be a memorable one had the vast multitude been kept orderly. With all arrangements swept aside, the crowd had developed a will of its own and drove away half of the invitees, including a number of diplomats. Those who stayed on envied their colleagues who could not get in. Mrs Bhutto who had not been allotted a seat on the President's dais, had to be given shelter there. The repeated appeals of the brigadier commanding the armed forces' parade could create space only for the marching troops and mechanized columns to squeeze through. The end of the day saw the PPP and the police blaming each other for the *faux pas*.

The Peoples Guard alleged that the police had asked it to look after the crowd at one end of the ground and leave other jobs alone. According to them, they were asked to come in only when the collapse was complete. The police, on the other hand, asserted that it could not command obedience because various groups coming in processions with the PPP flags, ignored every request and did as they pleased. 'You do not expect me to take on the PPP, do you?' said a police officer to a protesting journalist.

The prevailing mood is best illustrated by what happened at the President's House two days later. A number of journalists were invited to a dinner. One of them, whose recent critical writings have been too strong for the bureaucracy's taste, was invited by a secretary to a bout of wrestling. The journalist, delicately, suggested boxing gloves instead.

The Singer Not the Song

29 April 1972

A correspondent writes:

DROVES of people were converging on the stadium from every direction, and it seemed impossible that they could all fit in. But they did, all 200,000 of them—packed so tight that I had trouble finding an exposed bit of ground to grind out my cigarette.

Outside, it had been like a carnival with thousands of little stalls doing a roaring trade in food and cold drinks. The buses and trucks which had helped fill the stadium now filled the air with discordant music from blaring speakers, while hawkers added to the din with their harsh and meaningless cries. Even if the rally wasn't going to give us anything new, it was certainly providing a great boost to small business.

Within the stadium, the crowd had the composition and consistency of a hick audience at a funfair: the performer had better deliver, or else. Squeezed in between them, I caught the smell of dirty bodies, and unwashed clothes: the whiff of old, soiled socks was in the air. This was the smell of the masses. And why not? If our politicians, generals, bureaucrats, journalists and businessmen could wallow happily in the filth of their corruption, did not the worker and the peasant have the right, in fact the need, to sprinkle a little natural dirt on himself? After all, not all of us have the opportunity to slip into the pond with the big-pigs and rub the soothing slime onto our bodies.

An hour-and-a-half before the President's arrival, a small Cessna buzzed the stadium at 30 feet: the pilot grinning and waving, and behind him, a cameraman busy filming this sea of upturned faces. The sound of the engine was drowned out by the crowd: when the little plane approached, there would be pin-drop silence—and as it came lower and lower, the tension would grow until it was suddenly released in a loud roar of approval (and disappointment?) as the pilot pulled out of his dive. And the pilot could sense this, for he played the crowd the way a matador plays a bull. Each time, he would come down from a different angle, just a little bit lower, and with every pass, the bloodlust grew. Luckily, the plane flew off before the humour and merriment dissipated entirely.

The carnival spirit was evident by the fact that despite the billing of the rally as a major policy speech, there was virtually no speculation among the crowd about the contents of the statement to

311

be made. People were here to enjoy themselves: they had come here. 200,000 strong, to see and hear the star of the show—it was a case of the singer, not the song.

The stage had been set for one of Mr Bhutto's instant referendums: earlier, too, he had whipped up crowds to a pitch where they would roar 'YES!' to anything he demanded of them, and then turn around and tell the nation that he was taking such-and-such step because the people wanted him to. However, not many people are familiar with the orator's simple trick of feeding his audience a string of rhetorical questions ('Are you for one Pakistan?' 'Are you for a strong Pakistan?' etc.), and then slipping in the loaded question when the crowd has caught the rhythm of this delightful game. So Mr Bhutto gets his show of hands primarily because he does not give his audience time to think about the issues involved.

All this is not to suggest that this is any new insight into crowd psychology: this technique has been effectively used before by Hitler, Sukarno, and Nkrumah, to name only a few. While the liberal may find such a blatant manipulation of public opinion revolting, it is my contention that the manipulation resorted to in developed countries is far more insidious and sinister than anything we have here today.

Back to Lahore stadium: the huge crowd waited patiently for the star—some of them had been waiting for over six hours, and yet it was a remarkably disciplined crowd. Every now and then, someone would stand up to catch a glimpse of some arriving dignitary, or just to stretch his legs, and would immediately become the target of a volley of orange peels, small clods of earth, and a volley of good-natured curses. Far to the right, a loud-speaker blared forth slogans in an attempt to warm up the crowd, but the crowd wasn't having any: the response to party slogans was restricted to a handful. And besides, in the centre of the stadium, where I was, and to the stands on my left, the loud speaker was barely audible. The other speakers, I thought, would be turned on when the President arrived.

As H-hour drew closer, the breath of tension touched the crowd. I had a sudden, apocalyptic vision: some mishap, the crowd, caught in the vortex of panic making frenzied attempts to flee in every direction, trampling thousands into bloody pulp. For always, violence is around the corner when large crowds gather.

Suddenly, these macabre images were shattered by loud cheers and thunderous applause: after a number of false starts, the President had arrived. Clapping his hands over his head, then extending them first in this direction, then in that, he gradually silenced the crowd which was now on its feet. And suddenly all the characters on the stage froze to attention, and I realized that the brief snatches of music were the national anthem. It was not until the recital of the Holy Quran started that I grasped the enormity of the failure of the sound-system: hardly a word could be understood where I was sitting. And all around me, and in the stands on my left, people were getting up, shouting and signalling their inability to hear the proceedings. This din, of course, drowned out the few loud-speakers that were functioning.

And in this hubbub, I thought wryly of our basic lack of professionalism in any area you care to think of: administration, business, defence, science—you name it, and I can prove that we are, at best, fumbling amateurs. This whole circus had been touted for days as the best-arranged rally ever. The National Arts College had assumed the role of official decorators, and had filled the stadium with indecipherable slogans. A fleet of trucks and buses had been laid on, and somebody had even thought of keeping baloons and pigeons ready for release when the President arrived. And despite all this meticulous planning, the most important element had been left to chance: in a rally of this size and importance, nobody had apparently taken the trouble of double—and triple—checking the speaker-system, and of keeping a back-up system in readiness.

So, wasn't the white man justified in his view that we have no staying power? For we start a job with a lot of bustling and promises, only to see the impetus and sense of purpose petering out before our eyes. And then the lethargy and don't-give-a-damn feeling sets in, and all is as before, only more so. To repeat the question in another way, is our national inferiority complex due to the fact that in our heart of hearts, we know ourselves to be inferior? And to prevent ourselves from admitting it, we resort to bluff and bluster, trying to hoodwink the world into believing that we are a viable and competent nation, until in the end we succeed in fooling only ourselves.

Once more, I returned to the here-now. Looking through a pair of high-powered binoculars, I could discern the nervousness on Khar's face—he looked like like a man in trouble: I'd hate to be in his shoes that day (or any other day, come to think of it). Kausar Niazi was making frantic gestures at the crowd on my left, and Mr Bhutto was struggling manfully with the speaker-system. He begged, cajoled, and threatened the sections of the crowd which could not hear—to either sit quietly, or leave. But the irony was that these threats and pleas could not reach the people for whom they were intended. And so it went on until Mr Bhutto finally lost his cool: at one point, he picked up a vase and hurled it at some people in the front-row. I could imagine the headlines in the foreign press ('Bhutto Beans Bloke'), and those in the local press ('President Showers Flowers on People').

All this while, there had been a constant outflow of people from the stands: the crowd was thinning fast. After an hour of trying to get the people to listen, Mr Bhutto decided to get on with the job regardless of the audience. What with the lousy sound and the constant murmur of a restless crowd, I could only catch a word now and then, so I concentrated on watching him instead. His hands and arms moved constantly: not in the abrupt, chopping motions of the hack politician, but the full, flowing movements of the orator. The pity of it was that he just could not grip the crowd; he was simply not getting the response that is the life-blood of the public performer.

And suddenly, I felt a surge of sympathy for the man: after all, he had to bear the humiliation of seeing an audience melt away before his eyes, probably for the first time in his career, simply because of the incompetence of his subordinates. And all this before the eyes of diplomats and journalists from a large number of countries. What had been intended as a demonstration of Mr Bhutto's popularity had degenerated into a demonstration of our ineptness and inefficiency.

Finally, half-an-hour before the end of the speech, I made my escape. As I stood up, I saw the extent of the fiasco—only a third of the crowd was left. And as I walked towards the exit, I caught a last glimpse of Mr Bhutto, arms flailing, high voice booming and echoing from the speaker near the gate, and, like anti-tank guns, TV cameras covering his every move.

And with this last glimpse, another gut-twisting vision filled my mind: the stadium finally empty of people, and the star going on, until the guests, stooges and hangers-on also creep away without daring to disturb the chairman. And all this while, he goes on in his strident, often cracking, but always hypnotic voice posing rhetoric questions to an empty stadium and getting back only fading echoes.

Author's note:

This is a highly subjective account of the President's public meeting at the Lahore (now Ghaddafi) Stadium on 19 March 1972

Raised Eyebrows in New Delhi

24 June 1972

Editor's note: Reproduced below are excerpts from Oriana Fallaci's interview with President Z. A. Bhutto. The remarks contained therein have raised eyebrows all over India and may cast a shadow on the summit talks. These extracts were published in the 'Times of India' of 1 and 2 June 1972. We received the cuttings of the same and comments thereon in the Indian papers from London. These are being published to provide a perspective to the summit talks.

IN a vituperative attack on Mrs Indira Gandhi, President Bhutto has described her as a woman without initiative and imagination. Mr Bhutto reportedly made the remark in an interview given to a woman journalist, Oriana Fallaci, and published in the Saturday issue of the Italian journal, *Europeo*, which has just become available here.

Mr Bhutto said he considered Mrs Gandhi a mediocre woman with mediocre intelligence and added: 'There is nothing great in her. Only the country she governs is great. I would like to say that it is the throne which makes her look high and also the name which she carries.'

Mr Bhutto said, 'Believe me, if it were the Prime Minister of Ceylon, there could be nothing more than a Bandarnaike. If it was the Prime Minister of Israel, then there is no comparison to Golda Meir. She is much superior. She has an acute mind, a clear judgement and she overcomes crises which are more difficult than those faced by Mrs Gandhi. Mrs Bandarnaike has reached that position by virtue of her being the widow of Mr S. W. R. D. Bandarnaike and Mrs Gandhi for the simple reason of being the daughter of Nehru without having his brilliance. With all her saris, her red mark on the forehead, her smile, Mrs Gandhi will never impress me. She has never impressed me from the day when I knew her in London.'

Mr Bhutto claimed that he and Mrs Gandhi had taken part in a conference in their London days and he found her taking notes in all seriousness. He asked her: 'Are you taking notes or writing a thesis?' He said he did not believe she could do a thesis 'otherwise she could have succeeded in taking that doctorate in Trinity at Oxford. In two years at Oxford, I did a course of three years. And in three years, she was not capable of finishing the course.'

The interviewer reported that she asked Mr Bhutto whether he was not exaggerating and being a little unjust. 'Do you really believe that she could rise to such a position and remain there if she was nothing. Or do you believe that it does not mean anything, because she is a woman.'

Mr Bhutto answered, 'No no, I have nothing against women being heads of states although I do not consider that women could be better heads of state than men. My judgement of Mrs Gandhi is impersonal, objective. It is not suggested, not even by the fact that she conducts herself in a deplorable manner by not releasing the prisoners of war and by not respecting the Geneva conventions. I have always seen her like this—a diligent and hardworking school girl, a woman without initiative or imagination. Today it is better than when she was studying at Oxford or taking notes at London. Power has created confidence in herself and she has achieved success. And this success is disproportionate to her merits. If India and Pakistan were to become partners of a confederation, I would take away the post from Mrs Gandhi without any effort.'

Mr Bhutto went on: 'I don't fear an intellectual confrontation with her. I am therefore, ready to meet her when she wants even in New Delhi. I am ready to go even to New Delhi as Talleyrand after the Vienna congress. The only idea which disturbs me is that of being escorted by a guard of honour by the Indian army and a physical contact with the madame. It irritates me. My God, I can't think of it. Rather please tell me what does Mrs Gandhi say about me?'

The interviewer then told Mr Bhutto that Mrs Gandhi had told her that he was a man without equilibrium, that he said one thing today and another tomorrow, and that she could not understand what he had in his head. Mr Bhutto said, 'I will reply immediately. The only thing which I accept of the John Locke philosophy is this affirmative. "Coherence is a virtue of small minds." In other words, I think that a fundamental concept must remain steady. But within that concept one should move forward. It blows hot and cold. An intellectual should not be rigid about a set idea. It should be elastic.'

Mr Bhutto said apparent incoherence was the first virtue of the intelligent mind and an astute politician. If Mrs Gandhi did not understand this, she did not understand the goodness of her job. Her father understood this.

When the interviewer said that Mrs Gandhi thought of her father not as a politician but as a saint, Mr Bhutto said, 'Mrs Gandhi has done her father a wrong. She should have had at least half of her father's talent. Although he was against the principle of Pakistan, I have always admired that man.'

Oriana Fallaci's report was based on six sessions with Mr Bhutto. It began with her asking Mr Bhutto about the soundness of creating a nation with two wings separated by 2,000 kilometres of alien territory. Mr Bhutto pointed out that the two wings had remained together for 25 years in spite of the errors that had been committed. When the flag and religion were the same, distance was not a problem.

The interviewer observed: 'I understand Mrs Gandhi better when she says that the partition of 1947 was unjust and that the communal wars of the 70s were ridiculous.'

Mr Bhutto said, 'Mrs Gandhi does not but dream of taking the whole subcontinent and of subjugating us. She would like to have a confederation to wipe out Pakistan from the face of the earth, and for this she says that we are brothers, etc.' Mr Bhutto asserted that Hindus and Muslims were never brothers. The two religious systems of living cultures and approaches were basically different.

'From the day of birth to the day of death, the Hindus and the Muslims are subjected to different ways of life and they do not have any meeting point. Even their methods of eating and drinking are different. They are two strong and irreconciliable faiths. This explains why the two have not succeeded in reaching a compromise so far.'

A part of the interview covered events leading to the India-Pakistan war. Mr Bhutto called Gen. Yahya Khan a 'disgusting drunkard' and Shaikh Mujibur Rahman a 'congenital liar'.

Asked whether he was aware that Dacca believed he was responsible for the massacre on the night of 25 March, he countered how one could discredit him with an episode 'so barbarous and stupid'. Only a disgusting drunkard like Gen. Yahya could do such a bad and bloody job.

About Shaikh Mujib he said he had never been intelligent and added, 'He is a congenital liar. He cannot do anything but lying. For example he says three million people were killed. He is mad and everybody is mad, including the press which went on publishing that three million were killed. The Indian version is one million. Then comes Mujib who doubles and then trebles it. This is characteristic of his personality. He did the same thing with the cyclone.'

The Times of India of 2 June had some vitriolic comments to offer on the interview. 'Bhutto's latest diatribe against Mrs Gandhi has raised in political circles fresh misgivings about his designs.

'Mr Bhutto's attack on Mrs Gandhi at a time when this country is taking special care to prepare the ground for holding the summit is considered particularly intriguing.

'The timing as well as the vocabulary used by Mr Bhutto only strengthens the widely held belief here and abroad that Mr Bhutto has been saying different things to different audiences'

It goes on to say that:

'In the past, Mr Bhutto has not failed when it suited him to speak eloquently on the prospects of a durable peace in the subcontinent but his latest statement goes only to revise the suspicion that his credibility cannot be taken for granted.

'A report from Islamabad published in a New York daily indicates that Pakistan might go as far as to walk out of the summit unless the Bangladesh Prime Minister, Shaikh Mujibur Rahman, participates without waiting for Pakistani recognition.

'This atrocious piece of news is not seen as totally unrelated to the main purpose of Mr Bhutto's current tour of some West Asian and African countries.

'At least this posture is consistent with Mr Bhutto's approach to India and Bangladesh. Even at this stage he appears to be reluctant to face the reality in the subcontinent following the emergence of a sovereign independent Bangladesh as a friendly neighbour of this country. Instead, he is trying to demonstrate certain amount of solidarity of these countries with Pakistan and internalize the issues involved between India, Pakistan, and Bangladesh.'

According to PTI, Jana Sangh members drew the attention of both houses of Parliament to the reported 'indecent' remarks against the Prime Minister Mrs Indira Gandhi, made by Mr Bhutto.

'In the Rajya Sabha, the leader of the Jana Sangh, Mr Pitamber Das said (that) Mr Bhutto was talking like Mr Ayub Khan. This would affect the summit which India wished to be "congenial."

'In the Lok Sabha, Mr Jagannathrao Joshi said the reported remarks might vitiate the talks.'

'In *The Times of India* of 1 June 1972, a news item about the Cricket Club of India's vote to reject President Bhutto says:

'Several members of the CC reacted sharply to the news item ... about an interview reportedly given by President Bhutto to a woman journalist, Oriana Fallaci, which was published in the Italian journal, *L'Europeo*.

'They felt Mr Bhutto's ungentlemanly references to Mrs Indira Gandhi's intellectual attainments were "stupid".'

What India wants out of the summit talks seems apparent from the statements made by the defence minister, Mr Jagjivan Ram and foreign Minister, Mr Swaran Singh, at the recently concluded AICC session. Mr Jagjivan Ram obliquely hinted at a confederal arrangement when he advocated that 'India, Bangladesh and Pakistan should jointly resist any outside interference in the affairs of the subcontinent. Moving the resolution on international situation at the AICC session here, Mr Jagjivan Ram said all the three countries in the subcontinent belong to one group socially and culturally, although they were three separate political entities. The defence minister said whatever be the differences between India and Pakistan, they should be resolved peacefully and through bilateral discussions.'

This report is taken from *The Times of India* of 2 June 1972. In the same report Mr Swaran Singh is reported to have said '... only through bilateral talks, and not through the intervention of third countries, however big they might be, could solutions be found for Indo-Pakistani problems....

'He noted Mr Bhutto's observation that he would recognize Bangladesh after a two-hour talk with the Prime Minister, Shaikh Mujibur Rahman. He pointed out that the Shaikh had made it clear that no talks could precede recognition.

'Describing the attitude of Mr Bhutto as "an amusing and shallow approach to a serious problem", Mr Swaran Singh asked, "If Bangladesh can be recognized after a two-hour talk between Mr Bhutto and Shaikh Mujibur Rahman, why can it not be done two hours earlier?"

Mr Swaran Singh said: "Our own information is that there is now a reawakening and a sense of reassertion among the peace-loving people of Pakistan for normal relations with India, but they have no proper leadership."

A further escalation of this rather dangerous situation that was developing was the news that India was handing over 150 prisoners to the Bangladesh government. But Mrs Gandhi's denial evoked appreciation from Pakistan. A news item in the *Dawn* of 19 June said, 'Sources close to the Foreign Office have expressed satisfaction … These sources said that had the reported decision to transfer such POWs to Dacca been correct, the President would have found it impossible to proceed to Simla. …'

The Changing Political Scene

5 August 1972

Air Marshal Asghar Khan (Retd)

THE political picture in Pakistan has changed a great deal during the last seven months and the mood of the people is very different from what it was on the winter morning of 20 December when Mr Zulfikar Ali Bhutto arrived in Rawalpindi to be sworn in as the President and Martial Law Administrator. It would be fair to say that in spite of recognizing his obvious role in the dismemberment of Pakistan, the people by and large, wished him well in his new office. Being the leader of the largest elected party of West Pakistan, it appeared natural to accept him as the only person who could assume responsibility for their affairs. That this responsibility was not constitutionally conferred—though an important legal issue—is not relevant to the purpose of this article which is to discuss the mood of the people and assess the changing political scene.

Mr Bhutto's reputation as a political manipulator and his experience in the international field lent credibility to his claim to secure an honourable settlement with India and settle the numerous post-war issues. His public condemnation—however belated—of the Tashkent Declaration and his bellicose and—as people discovered later to their cost—indiscreet rejection of the Soviet and Polish proposals of 5 December 1971, for a ceasefire appeared to lend further support to the view, commonly held, that Mr Zulfikar Ali Bhutto was the man of the hour who would pull Pakistan out of the morass of confusion and despair into which he himself had steadily and consistently pushed the country over the previous twelve months.

His rapport with the key military figures in the Yahya regime, which he had assiduously cultivated over a number of years and the fact that he had secured a clear electoral majority in the Punjab—the recruiting ground of the Pakistan Army—lent further weight to his claim for leadership in the traditional power base of Pakistan. The emergence of Mr Zulfikar Ali Bhutto on 20 December as the ruler of what remained of Pakistan, therefore, occasioned no surprise and was generally welcomed throughout the country.

The days that followed, however, highlighted what some of us knew already: that Pakistan was on the threshold of a new chapter of authoritarian rule with all the attendant evils. Scant respect for elected institutions, dictatorial decisions, political victimization, suppression of the press, and organized harassment and assault of political opponents became the rule, and dissatisfaction has therefore begun to mount throughout the country. Rather than change its approach, the government has reacted in the classical authoritarian manner in such situations. More suppression and intolerance of criticizm [*sic*] has hastened the journey towards a fascist society which Mr Bhutto ironically appears to have fixed as the ultimate goal for a people who had voted for democracy and social and economic justice.

Just as the deteriorating law and order situation has affected the people's attitude towards the government, the economic depression and the inadequacy of the so-called reforms has hastened the disenchantment of the public with the party in power. Interference of party workers in the administration has reduced further the effectiveness of the administrative machinery already creaking under the first impact of Mr Bhutto's version of *people's raj*. The dissatisfaction of both the workers and the industrialists with the government's approach towards industry has created an area of instability in a vital sector of society. The students, who had been a powerful factor in the success of the People's Party, have begun to see the contradictions in the promises and the performance of the ruling party and have moved away from it as rapidly as they had flocked to its ranks. The bureaucracy which, however imperfect, provides a framework of administration for the country is being systematically humiliated. Without disciplined party cadres, indiscriminate interference with the normal functioning of the complicated administrative machinery is creating fresh problems which ultimately hit the common man.

The armed forces, whom Mr Bhutto had publicly named as one of the three political powers—the People's Party and the Awami League being the other two—had to be cut down to size in order to ensure the emergence of the People's Party as the unrivaled political force in the country. How this purpose was achieved and the consequences that flow from the method may come to surface in due course of time. Suffice it to say here that the armed forces have ceased to be—for the time being at any rate—a pressure group in the country. Whether they assume this role in the future will depend on the emergence or otherwise of effective democratic institutions and on the creation of a climate of trust and confidence amongst the public in their elected representatives. It is sad but true that the events of the last seven months have not enhanced the image or the reputation of the elected and so-called democratic institutions in the eyes of the people.

It is with this background of the changing political scene that Mr Zulfikar Ali Bhutto embarked on his journey to Simla. The symbol of a policy of confrontation with India cannot, however, easily become an apostle of peace. The contradictions inherent in Mr Bhutto, the sabre-rattling politician, and Mr Bhutto the peace-seeking President, acquiescing in India's grossly unreasonable demands, cannot be easily resolved.

These factors and the composition of the People's Party which has in its ranks both the inveterate reactionaries and revolutionaries of the extreme left has created further divisions within the party. A small but sincere minority is in open revolt and the 'Parties Act' is keeping some of the other elected representatives from voicing their views openly against the anti-people policies of the top party leadership. The People's Party, therefore, presents the picture of a house, widely divided on basic issues and principles.

No wonder then that disenchantment with the ruling party and the mounting oppositon to it should have made itself felt in so short a time. In the Punjab, steady erosion of the People's Party position is taking place and the public is looking for alternative leadership which can be trusted to work honestly for the resolution of the people's problems. In Sind, the acceptability of the People's Party amongst the non-Sindhi population is at its lowest point. Bhutto's partisan attitude in the Sind troubles, the mishandling of the situation by his government and its apparently deliberate policy to flush the non-Sindhis out of Sind, has lost for him the support of almost the entire Urdu-speaking population of the province. Apart from the extremist element amongst the Sindhis, whose numbers now are larger than they were before the People's Party assumed the responsibility for the affairs of the province, the pattern of Sindhi loyalty remains much as it was a year ago. The indiscriminate victimization of the people and the settling of old scores has antagonized a section of the Sindhi population who do not share the responsibility for the sad state of affairs in the province.

Two explanations can be offered for the motive that led the ruling party to create this problem. The first is that this strife was designed to divert attention from the Simla accord, especially in Karachi, which has traditionally been an opposition city and did not generally vote for the People's Party. It was, therefore, expected to react unfavourably to the Simla Agreement. This purpose has been effectively achieved for such has been the nature of the disturbances in Sind that Simla and its disastrous consequences have been pushed into the background and are not a subject of discussion today.

The second is the calculated move of the ruling party to provide economic relief to those people who constitute its main support in Sind. With the party's position visibly shaken in the Punjab, a strong base in Sind is considered essential to the survival of the People's Party. This economic relief could be provided either by radical changes in the economic structure of the province or by depriving the non-Sindhis of their business and property. Since the first, that is radical changes in the economic structure of the province, would have adversely affected the top leadership of the party, it appears to have been decided by them to create conditions in which the non-Sindhi-speaking people would leave the province. There is enough evidence to show that this forcible eviction of settlers was carried out on an organized scale, as for instance, was done in Mr Bhutto's home-town, Larkana, under the direction and in the presence of one of his provincial ministers. The serious law and order situation that has been created as a result of the language dispute has, therefore, been rightly attributed to the Machiavellian role of the People's Party. Otherwise Sindhis had learned to live in good fellowship with their settler brethren. Even now, parts of Sind not dominated by the PPP did not witness any disturbances, such as in Sanghar.

In Baluchistan and the N.W.F.P., the conditions are better but here, the NAP and JUI suffer from the handicap of provincial governments that must rely on the centre for assistance in the implementation of their development plans. The marginal parliamentary majority of the governments in these provinces and the People's Party's antagonism has created political uncertainty which will only be resolved when fresh countrywide elections are held. The People's Party, however, cannot today be considered an effective political force in these two provinces and its position there will be affected in proportion to the change of its fortunes in the Punjab. Considering the erosion in the strength of the People's Party in the Punjab, it can be said with a fair degree of certainty that the People's Party is not likely to show any appreciable recovery in the N.W.F.P. and Baluchistan, at least in the foreseeable future.

The political scene in Pakistan today, therefore, presents an interesting though tragic spectacle. The upshot of Pakistan's first general elections has been the dismemberment of the country and the ushering in of unabashed dictatorship in West Pakistan. But then, democracy and freedom are not easily achieved and freedom is easier won than preserved. If the people of Pakistan continue their struggle and the urge for a change builds up as it is doing today, it will undoubtedly bring us closer to the day when we could successfully build a society on sound democratic lines in which people can breathe freely and exploitation of man by man will be ended. After a disastrous start, we have moved a few steps in the right direction. A long way, however, still remains to be covered. Will we reach the goal? The answer will depend on the basic character and determination of our people. We shall soon know whether we have these simple qualities in the required measure, for without these democracy cannot flourish.

Bhutto Watches the Punjab

9 September 1972

Our correspondent writes:

WHAT is President Bhutto scared of? That he is scared of something is clear from the ambivalent attitude he has adopted on the question of recognizing Bangladesh. It is no longer in any doubt that he wants to go ahead with immediate recognition. But he doesn't. Why?

One reason is the insistence on a prior meeting with Mujib. This may or may not be a principled stand, but if the Government had wanted to, it could have easily got the N.A.'s approval in principle for recognizing Bangladesh during the current session. Things might then have moved forward. Responsibility would not have remained the President's alone and the Bhutto-Mujib syndrome in Pakistan politics might have dissolved somewhat. But the issue was not even referred to the N.A. Instead, there has been the Chinese veto, the abortive telephone call to Claridge's, and ominous-sounding statements from New Delhi. So, why did the Government balk at putting forward a B.D. resolution in the N.A.? Which brings us back to the question whether there is something else besides bloated post-recognition demands by B.D. which is preventing Bhutto from acknowledging Mujib's sovereignty?

For instance, is he afraid of the Punjab? More and more the signs are that he is. The recent right backlash has clearly unnerved the PPP. The first Mochi Gate rally in which Shorish Kashmiri levelled his famous charges against Khar was attended by no less than 40,000 persons—the biggest gathering the right has been able to muster in six and seven years. There have been other manifestations of the backlash—poster campaigns, neatly-printed stickers, daily editorials in the *Nawa-i-Waqt*, Z. A. Suleri's 'raison-de-etre' columns, Tikka Khan slogans.

Combined with general public dissatisfaction with the PPP's performance on the economic and social fronts, the backlash has certainly helped to make Bhutto's bastion of power now sometimes feel like a millstone around the party's neck. But despite this, there is actually less to be scared of than Mr Bhutto appears to think: he seems largely the victim of a self-created fear. If public opinion in the Punjab has been misled on the issue, it is simply because the PPP has not directed it firmly and courageously enough. The field has been left open to the right to exploit, from the moment Bhutto had asked for the pre-Simla national debate. Neither the party as a whole, nor the ministers individually, nor the government-controlled newspapers played their part in the debate. Mr Khurshid Hasan Meer did some public speaking, but that was all. No trouble was taken to work among the student community, and no wonder all major campuses in the Punjab continue to be rightist preserves: how glaring the omission has been is underlined by the decision to keep colleges and universities closed for another month for fear of right-inspired agitations against the government.

Time lost has been time lost. It is said that even Punjab PPP legislators who had at one time advocated acceptance of Mujib's six points are now listening to rightist propaganda on the recognition issue. (Some of the legislators' sneaking loyalty to rightists had already become more open when Bhutto had imported Qaiyum Khan into the cabinet in a sad compromise with reaction.) Chauvinist attitudes are becoming strong again, with the language agitation in Sind having made its own contribution to the process.

But the ground has not been surrendered to the right, which has no alternative to offer except the usual ideology formula. There is a serious realization—and it is growing—that the POWs cannot come home unless Pakistan recognizes Bangladesh. It is also beginning to look increasingly strange that while fences are being mended with India, Bangladesh is being kept at arm's length. The real war was with India, and if we are patching up with New Delhi, why not with Dacca? may be a simplistic way of putting it but the question is being asked.

The situation can still be retrieved in the Punjab from the PPP's point of view. The President's 14 August address to the Assembly was an effort at persuading public opinion to reconcile itself to reality. Further support can be rallied if President Bhutto undertakes a tour of the Punjab. Mochi Gate, unlike (reportedly) Golimar, is not out of bounds for him. He can still take the Punjab along with him. He should, before he concedes more to the right. It would be tragic if the right backlash forced Bhutto again into a position of confrontation.

My People Here I Come

9 September 1972

M. Shahid Alam

*L*OOK *at Mr Bhutto and his motorcade, he neither sees nor is seen; not even Yahya in all his glory could rival him in his entourage and its style.*

Mr Bhutto had stepped in with promises of a *new* Pakistan; a brave new Pakistan with a popular government and popular head of state. Mr Bhutto was merciful enough to elaborate upon the concept of his 'popular president'. He even offered a few dramatic close-ups of what his concept implied.

There would be no protocol, he had promised. Security arrangements would be scaled down, he had assured. A popularly elected figure has nothing to fear from the people. The people would be free to approach him with their grievances, wherever they found him. Hopes were raised high. Public morale got a fillip. Here is our man, all had shouted.

And instances were not wanting when the image was approximated. The President moved freely in the Punjab, stepping out of his Cadillac to meet the masses. And not a few were the public hands he shook, the popular *salaams* he acknowledged, or the proletarian grievances he redressed. It wasn't impossible for a determined petitioner in those days to bring the President's motorcade to a grinding halt and have his petition endorsed. The hopes raised were being fulfilled.

This popularization reached its apogee when the President addressed his first public gathering in Karachi after assuming office. Even in that massive gathering, Mr Bhutto with an air of dramatic sincerity gave up the protection of the speaker's enclosure. That was the height of it!

Well-meaning people were concerned, they had begun to fear for his life. All suggested that it was indiscreet of the President, that he should not expose himself thus. And they were right. But soon the pendulum began to swing in the other direction. And in less than nine month's time, the concept of a popular President had turned full circle, so that now for reasons of security the people cannot see their President, and the President cannot see his people. The President, in a mere nine months, has been depopularized. He is now the 'peoples' President.

Before we go into the causes and implications of such a reversal, it would, be better if we gave an expose of the dramatic changes which attended the protocol of Mr Bhutto's last visit to Karachi.

We may begin with the irksome security measures which were clamped at the Karachi Airport when Mr Bhutto flew in from Rawalpindi. What else could be a better indicator of the tight security than the expulsion of Mr Amanullah Khan, Salaar of Peoples Guard from the airport lounge. Even Mr Minhaj Barna, Secretary of PFUJ, was not allowed in on his personal credentials.

When the President had gone to address the lawyers at Hotel Intercontinental, the entire road leading upto it from Clifton residence was closed to traffic. This road closure has become a regular feature of the President's visit. And people have complained of traffic being held up for as long as half an hour just to let the President's entourage use it for five minutes.

But what is intriguing everyone is the appearance of an entirely novel breed of traffic-policemen who make their appearances only for the President. Their special novelty is a spiked helmet with wide flaps which cover the neck right upto the shoulders. And not a few have been struck by the similarity of this uniform with the outfit in which the Prussian militarists dressed their militia. In fact, when one sees these ominous men one is reminded of Frederick Wilhelm II. My inquisitiveness led me to a police officer on duty. But his answer intrigued me. The steel helmet contains a wireless set, and the pike serves as the aerial.

A study of the security arrangements made for Mr Bhutto's journey to the airport tells its own story. The President was supposed to leave on the morning of 3 September for Lahore. The *Sun* of the same morning carried the news: President yesterday postponed his scheduled departure for Lahore. However, the President left on schedule. One is inclined to ask, was this confusion a security measure!

As early as 6 a.m., truck-loads of police started arriving, and in a few minutes the entire fifteen-mile route from the President's House to the airport had been flanked by policemen of all descriptions. There was one policeman for every fifty yards. The extra security measures were visible in the form of rifle-carrying police, who at places also formed a second line of defence behind the column of their *lathi* wielding brothers. One could also see groups of policemen stationed at 'strategic' points such as bridges, cross-roads, etc.

Calculating on the basis of the above observations one can easily say that no less than a thousand policemen had been mobilized for the President's departure. This figure does not include the additional squads of policemen hiding away in bylanes, and the numberless sergeants, sub-inspectors and inspectors who were commuting up and down in a great flurry.

It is interesting to note that the authorities had taken the further precaution to restrict pedestrian traffic only to the left side of Drigh Road (as one moved north). One pedestrian, who with all decency was keeping to the right was immediately ordered to the left. He protested but I am on the RIGHT side. Never mind, once in a while you have to take the wrong side, and that coming from the horse's mouth.

There was no dearth of plain-clothesmen either, a few of them with their revolvers ill-concealed in their *kurta* pockets. And here and there one found a few traffic policemen in their new tunics making a smart but ominous appearance.

Finally, more than one full hour after the police had taken up its position, the President's entourage was announced by an officer from a speeding jeep. No sooner, all the pedestrian traffic was pushed off into bylanes. One felt that Karachi was a conquered city with the victorious commander making his first appearance.

Never since Adam had Drigh Road been so empty as it was that morning at around 6 a.m. A whistling pilot in blue jersey zoomed past, followed at a distance by a bevy of pilots. Soon, the President followed, flanked on each side by two pilots in blue jersey. The blue jersey and the four pilots flanking the President's car were obviously a new feature. The President's car was followed by vehicles carrying armed police.

One may here recall that during his last visit to Karachi, the first after the language riots, Mr Bhutto, the official press note had claimed, had paid a surprise visit to Lalukhet. What a 'surprise' visit! We all remember. The motorcade carrying the President had zoomed past at 60 mph, flanked on both sides by policemen with drawn rifles.

It may also not be out of place to mention that sometime back the Punjab Police had felt the necessity of addressing a note to each of the MPAs and MNAs of Punjab, requesting them not to embarrass the authorities by bringing along their friends and relatives to places to which only they were invited. It is indeed no mere coincidence that the police took so long to act against uninvited guests. Why hadn't the embarrassment come earlier?

What does all this add up to? Has Mr Bhutto come to realize that his popularity is on the wane? The conclusion is inescapable. Add to it Mr Bhutto's love of regalia and the above pieces begin to fall into place. Authoritarianism can defend itself with only one weapon, more authority. And the process has begun. The de-popularization of the President marks a successful though unfortunate beginning.

Boom in Larkana Town

10 February 1973

Our correspondent writes:

TIME was when little Larkana—one of Sind's many half-forgotten towns—was remembered only as the hometown of Mr M. A. Khuhro or of Kazi Fazlullah. But times change and Larkana has emerged overnight as Pakistan's new in-town, the haunt of kings and presidents, diplomats and dancing troupes. The recent visit of Iran's Shah to Larkana seemed to confirm and legalize, as it were, the city's fancy new status. A new sun has risen in little Larkana.

Larkana's 30,000 or so rice cultivators, petty tradesmen and landowners of various sizes aren't exactly unaware of their town's sudden importance. Larkana has begun to be referred to, and only half facetiously, as Sind's future capital. A few ambitious types even describe it as Pakistan's future seat of power.

The first and most obvious sign of change are the roads. Larkana roads and those leading to it were, till about a year ago, so bad that even truckers used to hesitate to drive through. Today Larkana has smooth metalled roads with imposing signs. No longer is the approach to Larkana the nightmare that it used to be. Today you enter Larkana via a dual carriage highway. The road on which Al-Murtaza stands has been given a new name: Quaid-i-Awam Zulfikar Ali Bhutto Road. When the President is in residence, no traffic is allowed on this road. Even pedestrians can't walk on the pavement alongside Al-Murtaza. Another road is called Sir Shah Nawaz Bhutto Road, complete with title.

In some cases roads have been rebuilt and recarpeted in two short weeks: between the Abu Dhabi ruler's visit and that of the Shah of Iran. The 18-mile stretch between Larkana and Mohenjo-Daro—where the airport is located, is now a dual carriage road.

Advertisements bloom profusely in Larkana. As a rule advertising tends to follow economic development and prosperity. In Larkana it seems to be the other way around. Since development takes time, hoardings and electric pole signs have been put up in anticipation, it would appear.

Ironically, the billboards' bright new paint and gay designs serve only to mock the surrounding dirt and squalor. And their presence seems to heighten the contrast between the modern age, which these ads symbolise, and the primitive state of the whole place. But even these vast hoardings cannot hide the occasional *Bangladesh Namanzur* slogans scribbled on Larkana's ancient walls.

Until lucky Larkana hit the jackpot, it was never given any development priority. Not that it did not deserve a better deal. About the only touch of the 20th century in that region was the Rice Research Institute at Dhokri, some 10 miles away. So rapid has been the change recently that Larkana today boasts a modern stadium called People's Stadium. If you'd gone to Larkana a little while ago, you would have noticed the impressive gates of the stadium being built. On your next visit a few weeks later, you could rub your eyes and gape at the now complete People's Stadium.

The Rs. 25 crores (figures unconfirmed) which have been spent on development have brought about a visible change in the sleepy town. And Larkana will never be the same again. Two new hotels are going up. One is being built by Karachi's Avari chain and the other is a PIA project. Two new bank buildings are shooting up. The banks have been ordered, it appears, to centrally aircondition both buildings. Other banks, too, are going to put up big, impressive looking offices. Whether they are doing so of their own accord, or are being directed to do so, is not known.

Larkana appears determined to enter the jet era speedily. Plans are underway for modernizing Mohenjo Daro airport—at a cost of Rs. 70 lakhs. And here, too, the accent is on speed. The present runway will be extended for jet landings at a cost of Rs. 50 lakhs; it will be finished in six short months. The airport will have completely modern lighting, terminal building, and wide access roads which will be completed in four months at a cost of Rs. 20 lakhs.

Larkana is to have a railway station to match. Its cost: Rs. 1.5 crores, according to one knowledgeable estimate. Thus what used to be an all but inaccessible town is now assured very impressive entrances and exits. The town will be easier to contact from elsewhere. A long distance direct dialling exchange which was to be installed in Sukkur is instead going to Larkana.

The new Larkana will be cleaner, prettier, with more facilities than any of the neighbouring towns. For the Sind Government has upgraded the status of the Larkana Municipal Committee to senior class I. Mr Inayatullah Junejo, formerly Land Manager, Karachi Municipal Corporation, is its new administrator and should be able to help in giving dusty Larkana a newer, cleaner face. A Sui gas pipeline is being laid and a general face lifting of the town has begun. Is it any wonder, then, that land has become more expensive in these parts of late?

Some of the importance of Larkana has rubbed off on nearby Mohenjo-Daro. Great pains are being taken to make the ancient city a tourist attraction. Hence a tourist complex costing Rs. 2.5 crores is envisaged; half of this money is to be collected from UNESCO. This complex is in addition to the 8 million dollar 'save Mohenjo-Daro project' which will fight the twin-headed monster of waterlogging and salinity. This project has been on the drawing board for the last several years. It is being finalized now.

The way Larkana is being developed is quite in the tradition of Ayub Khan who built up a network of roads, industries and big buildings at Haripur, Hazara. The ex-President seemed quite happy with the result—for it made him popular and won him a great deal of local support.

Perhaps Mr Bhutto is aware of this, or maybe he genuinely believes in the maxim: development begins at home.

Not that the President is tight fisted with funds needed for public projects or even to improve and renovate his living quarters in various parts of the country. In fact, the old President's House at Rawalpindi will be discarded and another one is being built at a cost of Rs. 15 crores, according to Air Marshal (retired) Asghar Khan. Actually, the construction was started by Yahya Khan. The air conditioning plant alone for this house is going to cost Rs. 1.5 crores, to requote the grumbling air marshal.

No new building has been made for him in Lahore. But the Governor House where he usually stays has seen some improvement in recent days and four rooms have been redecorated for the President at a cost of Rs. 3.5 lakhs.

Karachi too, has reason to be happy. The road from Clifton bridge to his Clifton residence is being recarpeted and broadened at a cost of Rs. 12 lakhs.

The President enjoys travelling in style. Hence the special executive nine seater *Falcon* jet, which brought him to Karachi on 24 January. The jet, which can climb up to 25,000 feet and has a speed of 600 miles an hour, was piloted by none other than the Commander in Chief of the Pakistan Air Force, who flew down from Peshawar to Larkana specially for this purpose. Mr Bhutto piloted the jet part of the way to Karachi. An air conditioned helicopter is also on order from France.

Two special luxurious, air conditioned saloons have been ordered—one for himself and one for his entourage. The jerking movement of the train will not be felt in these saloons. It is not that some of these amenities are not necessary. The President does keep a very strenuous schedule specially because he keeps close contact with the people all over the country. It is not exactly fair to grudge him a few comforts.

Three Angles on Mr Bhutto: The Psychology of Brinkmanship

31 March 1973

Faheem Anwar

THE late lamented John Foster Dulles was the architect of brinkmanship. Believing that nothing succeeds as effectively as shock tactics whether in hot or cold wars, he assiduously followed a course of deliberately steering a crisis up to the maximum danger point in an attempt to frighten the other side into calling off whatever tactical ploys it was employing for the furtherance of its overall strategy against the interests of the United States. Quite often his methods would surprise his allies more than his enemies. On one occasion when a crisis abated, he announced blandly to a hushed world that they had been on the brink of a third global war only weeks previously. This evoked gasps of incredulity from all corners of the world and forthwith the strategy of brinkmanship came into official existence in the glossary of international power politics while John F. D. became its first accredited exponent.

John Foster has since departed from this earthly realm to make his peace with his Maker, but he has left behind enough food for thought and action to keep the world (or at least a significant corner of it) perpetually astir by the constant employment of his methods and precepts. How far Mr Zulfikar Ali Bhutto is prepared to acknowledge the contribution of Mr Dulles to his political education is open to speculation, it may even be so that he himself is unaware of any overt influence of Mr Dulles on his thinking. But the fact remains that in his own course of action so far, if his first year is any worthwhile guide, he has evinced an understanding of the theory and practice of brinkmanship which, had Mr Dulles been alive today, would have obtained a nod of approval from the master himself. Indeed, he has even gone a step further and added a new dimension to the theory of brinkmanship. This can be simply explained by the following example. Imagine a rider mounted on a docile and trained steed. If he merely gallops or canters to his destination, he achieves his object without any fuss. But is that enough? Would it not be more spectacular and exciting if he pretended to be taming a fiery, uncontrollable bronco and bringing him under control? So he rather needlessly whips the poor animal into a frenzy, digs his rowels hard into its sides, rouses it to a defiant mood, and then, as suddenly, reverses his tactics, talks soothingly to it, relaxes the tight rein, and succeeds in bringing it back to its normally docile and tractable mood. His object achieved, he gallops on, having impressed the onlookers with his equestrian dexterity. What would perhaps have otherwise gone unnoticed as a tedious essay in horsemanship has now registered itself with electrifying impact on the minds of the viewers. The triumphant cavalier bows in courteous fashion to his admirers as he proudly acknowledges their plaudits.

This then, in a nutshell, is the new corollary to brinkmanship rocking the boat, or rockmanship. It is a common prelude to reaching the precipice prior to reining in at its very extremity but it is not an essential step in the process. The objective may as well be and as effectively achieved by unobtrusive methods without necessarily rocking the boat in an obvious manner. Boring a hole in its floor to let the water in is one method that comes to mind in this regard. But then, it would be an unspectacular way of reaching not the brink but the bottom, as the boat would merely sink without affording the boatman an opportunity to show off his skill. Since taking charge of the nation's destiny a year ago, Mr Bhutto has provided many instances where his ability to ride the rapids could be universally appreciated. Starting with the near-crisis caused by his reluctance to let go of his martial law powers, came the labour crisis, again a product of the present regime's equivocal attitudes towards labour, of alternately pampering it beyond all rational limits and thereafter crushing its militant attempts to give practical form to the promises of the PPP. Far more could have been given to the workers than they actually received, and this was possible without demoralizing the entrepreneurs unduly. Similar and even more fruitful results should have been possible provided the regime had operated from a base of composed and objective attitudes vis-a-vis the capitalistic sector. The investors in Pakistan have, for some time now, been aware of the decade old phenomenon of the wind of change, first brought to the notice of the diehards of colonial Africa by Mr MacMillan during his stewardship of Britain's affairs in the sixties. The government could have achieved all its objects by putting its cards on the table and persuading the capitalists to fall in step with the rest of the civilized world in giving to the working classes what was only their legitimate due. The new order could have been brought about in a manner so as to ensure that the working class, secure in the belief that its future was in very safe hands, would not only go on working as usual, but would in actual fact, redouble its efforts to produce more than ever before, since it would be confident of sharing in the new prosperity to be ushered in by the PPP. The capitalist on his part, had, to some extent, resigned himself to spending a trifle more of his enormous profits on the welfare and uplift of the miserable agents of his aggrandizement. He would, perhaps, have protested a little for form's sake, but in the end all would have been well with the labour sector and we would all have been spared the agonies of inflation and the collapse of the share market, which have recently, like Shakespeare's proverbial sorrows, invaded us in battalions and given many solid citizens untimely coronaries besides depriving the middle class of its hard earned savings in one fell sweep.

Unfortunately, all the desired results would have been achieved only if the temptation to show off had been successfully resisted. As is common, knowledge today the champion fell at this fence, taking everything down with him in the process. Brinkmanship had once again claimed its victim. Roughly there can be more than one reason for resorting to brinkmanship as a standard and routine gimmick of day to day statecraft. In the case of Pakistan, and the current exponent of this legerdemain, the following reasons might suggest an explanation for the rather inexplicable preference for this unusual mode of consent in political affairs.

To begin with, Mr Bhutto probably wishes to drive home the fact that in the present scheme of things and amidst the acute scarcity of able, home-grown political leaders, he and he alone, is the one person the nation can never do without—the helmsman and the rudder as it were. To prove this theory, he has so far led the country from repeated crisis to crisis, successfully extinguishing the conflagrant potential of each one before it could reach the danger point. He seems to dare the audience to refrain from applauding him for his dexterity and his political sleight of hand. One minute the crisis is there, the next minute it has disappeared without any trace of ever having been there. Surely, thinks the common mind, here is a leader, who has it within him to vapourize the most insoluble problems into nothingness. Let us, therefore, retain him as our leader and the master solver of our seasonal crises.

A more forceful reason is the famous Napoleonic dictum of attack being the best form of defence. Mr Bhutto believes, and with a fair amount of justification, that even were he to leave the Opposition alone in peace, he himself would yet be deprived of it as they would keep him in a perpetual state of siege and pressure. His answer to this is a pre-emptive strike in which he carries the war to them. By fighting a war of attrition on the territory of the Opposition he loses nothing even if he does not achieve victory. All he has to do is retreat from their territory to his own and thereby give them the illusory impression of having won against him, when in actual fact it has been no more than a drawn battle. Further, his very act of retreating is made to give the impression of a lordly and statesmanlike concession in the overall interests of peace and amity, and the Opposition is thereby presented with a mental block barring the way to the consolidation of its success by invading Mr Bhutto's domain for a change. Before they can get their second wind he is, irrepressibly, on the offensive once again and this time probing a different sector of their defences. And so on and so forth *ad infinitum*. Like a jack-in-the-box Mr Bhutto's ceaseless manoeuverings give his opponents no breathing space at all in which to marshall their faculties and effectively counter-attack. Only Wali Khan showed an ability to do this during the first half of 1972, but thereafter he became flat and stale and failed to rise above the level of a small-time regional politician unable to see beyond the bridge of his nose.

In the creation of a personal image of power and awesomeness, brinkmanship plays no mean a part. A person of unpredictable moods presents a frightening appearance to his detractors and rivals. Each move of his could be a painful surprise for them. Predictability, on the other hand, is the hall-mark of the mediocre. If you can successfully guess your opponent's next move and the one after and the next one after that, you have half won your game of chess. On the other hand, if you are dealing with an unorthodox and mercurial opponent, you will be more intent on saving your king against his brilliant moves than on checkmating him. Politics is very much akin to a game of chess, and it is Mr Bhutto, not Bobby Fischer, who is the Grand Master among all of its exponents.

With such powerful and effective methods at his disposal, Mr Bhutto remains sadly enough, a disillusioned magician. He has demonstrated all his adroitness before his audience only to leave it coldly unmoved. The reasons are quite simple. A hungry and cold wretch needs to be fed and warmed first and entertained later. The price flight upwards has crushed the middle class and the white collar workers who comprise the backbone of the 'country's educated segment. The entrepreneurs and capitalists have decided to do something else somewhere else with their money, while the workers have been led up the garden path, misguided into desperate acts of violence, and then been ruthlessly crushed into mute submission. As for the students, once the vanguard of Mr Bhutto's crusade against Ayub Khan, they are now being told to mind their studies and prepare themselves to take over as leaders of the new utopia which is just round the corner. Very sound advice, but how do you convert a trained hawk to a diet of bird-seed after a lifetime of seeking more adventurous game? Human emotions and attitudes are not mechanical contraptions that you can switch on and off to suit your particular moods and requirements. It takes a brilliant mind to miss such banalities.

Mr Bhutto's attitude towards the immigrants of Sind has been similarly characterized by the now familiar hot and cold tactics. By putting them under the cloud of a linguistic handicap, and later on, by removing the threat by his benign conciliation, he sought to strengthen his hold among the regional supremacists while at the same time appearing as a moderate and a saviour to the despondent settlers. For some reason, hard to understand, the immigrants have failed to appreciate his liberality, and have, instead, considered him to have been as much an author of the language bill as any of his lesser followers. Thus yet another move of his to stabilize his position has gone awry owing to the inability of the captive audience to compliment and respond to his brilliance. Can one blame him, then, for refusing to share power politically and administratively with the urban half of Sind, and for choosing instead the support of feudal barons, politically and mentally and centuries behind the times? Who needs progressives anyway? They only serve to obfuscate simple issues. People like Mr Khar and Jam Sadiq on the other hand, follow instructions loyally and faithfully and these days such traits are more useful than the high faluting mumbo-jumbo of the armchair sophists, who will, anyway, criticize anything that is done for the shirtless *awam*. In a disciplined organization there is room for only one leader, one progressive and fresh mind which will do all the thinking and deciding for the lesser fry. And lest anyone should forget this lesson; let him but once take a look at Mir Rasul Bux Talpur and his predecessors in dissent. Where are Mairaj Mohammad Khan and Hamid Jatoi and Mahmud Ali Kasuri and Ali Ahmed Talpur? Out on a limb, or, in the words of Ahmed Faraz, 'as dried flowers found in the pages of books.'

Bhutto's Political Style

31 March 1973

Nasim Ahmad

MR Z. A. Bhutto is the *product* of the last decade—of dictatorship. He is the creation of Ayub Khan who picked him up from the dust and gave him political glamour and national fame. But while the creator is down and out, disowned by the nation, his creation, curiously enough, still holds the field: determined to go to any length to recover the lost glory and power.

In Mr Bhutto's case public memory seems to be really proverbially short. Today's champion of democracy and the people's rights was, not long ago, the most trusted lieutenant of Ayub Khan whom he now denounces and debunks with all the rhetorical force and skill at his command. Today Mr Bhutto poses as the champion of the downtrodden and assures a gullible public that there is no greater friend of democracy in the country at the moment; but only yesterday he was one of the stoutest defenders of Ayub Khan's dictatorship. Today he wants to establish [a] popular, democratic government; yesterday he loudly sang the paeans of basic democracy. Today he terms the Tashkent Declaration as a betrayal of the Pakistani nation. He, however, conveniently forgets—and thinks that the public would also have forgotten—that only a little before he left the Ayub cabinet, he had made a most impassioned defence of the same document on the floor of the National Assembly. When he was a minister of Ayub Khan, he had thrown a challenge to Sh. Mujibur Rahman for a debate on the Six Points. Though today the country would very much like to see him take issue with the AL chief on the Six-Points, he is curiously reticent on the subject.

By disowning and denouncing Ayub Khan, Mr Bhutto is indirectly denouncing himself—his association with dictatorship, his role in the Ayub government, in short, his entire political past. When the nation had given its verdict against Ayub Khan, it was not only against him, but against his philosophy, his system, his government, his associates, his friends, his aides, and his advisers. The mass movement of early 1969 was a blanket denunciation of the dictator and the paraphernalia of dictatorship. The revolt was not only against Ayub Khan personally, but against everyone associated with him in one way or the other. That is the reason why we saw in those fateful days the mass fury turning against BD members, circle officers and Convention Leaguers. Mr Bhutto was the most important cog in the dictatorial machine that impersonally ruled the country in the last decade. He was the most important member of the Ayub cabinet, he was the Secretary-General of the Convention Muslim League. He cannot disown his responsibility for whatever happened during the last decade. If Ayub Khan is to be accused of committing the crime of dictatorship, Mr Bhutto, more than any other man, should be tried before the bar of public opinion for abetment of that crime.

Mr Bhutto has an unenviable past. Is his present any better? During the last days of Ayub Khan, Mr Bhutto, who was no longer with him, founded his own party and sought to build up his own and his party's image and popularity by trying to sail on the crest of the anti-Ayub movement that had gripped the country at that time. He is a master tactician; during his 8-year old apprenticeship under Ayub Khan he had learned how to tug at the heartstrings of the masses, exploit their sentiments and win popularity. The Tashkent Declaration was considered a document of capitulation in the west wing and was highly unpopular with the man on the street who thought Ayub Khan had betrayed the country. Mr Bhutto, master tactician as he is, pounced upon the opportunity and began to disparage the Tashkent Declaration, conveniently forgetting that he was a party to it and not long ago had forcefully defended it. In the last days of Ayub Khan until martial law, his two main political planks were denunciation of the T.D. and opposition to Ayub Khan.

In the post-martial law period he has stormed the political field with his dubious slogan of Islamic socialism. This is a curious concoction which only Mr Bhutto was capable of. Does he intend to proselytize the socialist system? How is this Islamic socialism different from socialist Islam? Mr Bhutto has not specified in what proportion he will mix up Islam and socialism if he ever gets power. As Hindu socialism or Buddhist socialism will not connote anything, so is the case with Islamic socialism.

Islamic socialism is the slogan of an opportunist. President Nasser was a staunch socialist, and a staunch Arab nationalist. But he never mixed up the two. Islamic socialism is a vague term. It is only sound and fury that signifies nothing. It is, in fact, a clever political slogan to cash in upon the religious and economic sentiments of the people. The overwhelming majority in Pakistan are Muslims; that accounts for the word Islamic. As a result of the gross economic mismanagement in the last 23 years, there is in the country existing today acute economic inequity and the masses are now demanding their share of the economic cake. This accounts for the word socialism in the term. In a moment of truth Mr Bhutto is reported to have told an interviewer that he has concocted the formula of Islamic socialism in view of the state of the mass mind in the two wings of Pakistan.

Mr Bhutto's opportunism is also discernible in the composition and structure of the People's Party. Though he prefers socialism, he is now admitting in his party waderas, feudal lords, and other classes of vested interests who can never subscribe to philosophy that promises to secure the people's welfare and strike at the privileged few. While they are at the moment seeking entry into the party to safeguard their own interests, it may be that in the long run they may capture the levers of the party and prevent Mr Bhutto from realizing his socialist aims, if any. What can explain the entry into the party in hordes of *waderas* and *jagirdars* is the charge that Mr Bhutto is not sincere about his socialist professions and anything goes for him so long as he is sure of capturing power.

One of the biggest landlords of Sind, Mr Bhutto's socialist professions do not fit in with his style of life. He is a *wadera* and in the socialist jargon, a class enemy. And if the socialist theory is not wrong, a class enemy cannot safeguard the interest of the proletariat. He belongs to the exploiters' class, he is not fit to lead the exploited. The leadership of the proletariat will come from among the proletariat. Mr Bhutto has perhaps not carefully studied Marx's *Capital*, the Communist Manifesto and Mao Tse Tung's thought. Otherwise, he would have been aware of the pitfalls ahead of him in the class war that he is trying to spark off. He will be the first victim of the revolution that he is trying to bring, in which if the Marxian logic is to have its way, members of the proletariat will capture power and the class enemies will be liquidated. It seems that Mr Bhutto, in blind pursuit of power, is tragically unaware of the role that he is playing.

Mr Bhutto's political style is a reflection of his political philosophy. His political methodology is inconsistent with the political goal he has set for himself. He has reduced political meetings into fun-packed *tamashas* and the audience into amused and applauding spectators. He has perfected the politics of stunt. For example, during the last nine months, he has been promising his audience to disclose the secrets of the Tashkent Declaration. But he has not so far. Similarly he has been threatening every other political leader with exposure. Recently he threatened to expose Maulana Bhashani. He has held out the same threat to other leaders too, such as Air Marshals Nur Khan, Asghar Khan etc. It seems that Mr Bhutto knows the weaknesses of all politicians in Pakistan. But so far he has not given any evidence of his morbid knowledge. Recently he has been speaking of his probable arrest by the present regime and his threat to boycott the elections. This is a ploy to win popular sympathy as much as his oft-repeated accusation that President Yahya's government is discriminating against his party and is partial to his rivals.

Sometimes in his anxiety to play to the gallery and keep the audience enthralled, he uses very outrageously crude tactics. During his speeches he sometimes sits on the ground, covers the face with a piece of cloth in an effort to mimic other leaders. These antics and histrionics explain the large attendances in his meetings.

Bhutto has set a new style in politicking—a style whose essence is to keep the audience pleased and engrossed in the speaker. While his pleasing public performance, on the one hand, draws large audiences, on the other it shows the weakness of the political stand as it never allows the listeners' mind to dwell on what he says and this hides the weakness of his speech. Anything is fair in love and war. Mr Bhutto's public style proves that anything is fair in politics too.

Mr Bhutto has great personal charm. He is young, talented, and dashing. The younger generation feels closer to him than to any other leader in thought and action. He has both the buoyancy and irresponsibility of youth. His political style also appeals very much to the young mind of youth. He is very popular among students and the young. It is those young men who swell the ranks of his audience and work for the success of his public meetings. But his well-attended meetings are no indication of his probable performance at the polls. For one thing, these young men constitute a small fraction of the total voting population and not all of them are voters. For another, as I have said earlier, the large attendance in his meetings are accounted for by his theatrics and antics and are not a reflection of popular support for him. This fact acquires added significance when we consider that Mr Bhutto's party is almost non-existent in the east wing.

(Reproduced from DAWN, Dated 16-10-1970)

The Odyssey of the PPP

14 July 1973

Mohammad Mian

ACCORDING to Mr Bhutto's own account, before they parted company, Ayub warned him: 'You are compelling me to relieve you of this job'. On his part says Mr Bhutto, 'I was fed up with the government, therefore I readily accepted his suggestion. But Ayub Khan did not stop at it, and said, 'Remember one thing more. Don't indulge in politics in future.' And Mr Bhutto did just the opposite.

From Pindi Mr Bhutto took the train to Karachi. Arriving at the cantonment station, unexpectedly, he found hundreds of National Students Federation members were present there to cheer and welcome him. He was hailed with full-throated slogans as the hero of Tashkent, the man of guts who could stand up to the tyrant Ayub, an anti-imperialist and of course a good friend of China. Within a few days a meeting was arranged at the Dow Medical College. Mr Bhutto addressed Karachi students exhorting them to march forward. It was here that Mr Bhutto discovered the great rhetorical talents of Miraj Mohd. Khan and the magic of mass appeal and mobilization. Next these young men with the help of some local workers organized a public meeting in the Lyari slums of Karachi and invited Mr Bhutto to address Karachi's grimy and emaciated masses for the first time in his own right.

However, Mr Bhutto did not start on his long march all at once. He could hardly take the children's crusade seriously. And Lyari is certainly not the bastion of Pakistan power politics. Certainly Miraj Mohd. Khan and his youthful followers could be made use of to organize meetings and mass contacts. This is what they actually did for Mr Bhutto during the coming years. So Mr Bhutto started making overtures to various political pressure groups that were lying low under the Ayubian masquerade. It is said he even tried to make contacts with Maulanas Bhashani and Maudoodi. Nevertheless, he managed to recruit some of his peers. Dr Mubashir, the Lahore technocrat, was the very first. Mir Rasul Bux Talpur from Mr Bhutto's native Sind readily joined in and was immediately arrested for his indiscretion. The young Khan of Sherpao from N.W.F.P. was one of the early converts. Mr J. A. Rahim joined the group later on. For some time past J. A. had been waging a one-man war against the undemocratic tendencies in Pakistan through the letter page of London's *Economist*.

Between Z. A. and J. A. there was the common bond of their experiences of the corridors of power besides the Anglo-Saxon and Oxbridge training. It is said that most of the documents of the PPP had been drafted by J. A. From Punjab there came Mr Khar, an ex-Convention Leaguer and the NAP dropout Mr Mahmud Ali Qasuri at a later stage. Then there were others of Punjab middle peasant and middle class background, Mr Khurshid Hassan Mir, Mr Miraj Khalid Sheikh Rashid and an ex-Maudoodi lieutenant, Maulana Kausar Niazi. These could have never made a breakthrough in the traditional *Jat*, *Arain* and *Pir* nobility power enclave of the Punjab. Mirza Tahir was the first one from Baluchistan. Abdul Hafeez Pirzada, Taleb El-Maula joined from Sind. Also one of the early arrivals was ex-Major General Akbar Khan. Mr Bhutto is said to have declared Messrs J. A. Rahim, Khurshid Mir, Miraj Mohd. Khan, Dr Mubashir Hassan, Mir Rasul Bux Talpur, and Khan of Sherpao as his first friends who had also been the founder members of the Pakistan Peoples Party.

The PPP held its first convention during 1967 at Dr Mubashir's house in Lahore where the official title Pakistan Peoples Party was adopted out of a list of several names. At this convention the party's 'programmatic principles' were also adopted 'expressing pithily the nature of its ideology', which was condensed: 'Islam is our faith. Democracy is our polity. Socialism is our economy. All power to the people.' It sounds like a convenient exercise in dialectics and offers almost a computerized synthesis of Jamaat and NAP ideologies. No wonder, a new party which had among its elite such extremes as the rightist feudal Taleb El-Maula and the firebrand Maoist-Leninist Miraj could outwit both the Jamaat and the NAP. With these four principles the PPP had taken the wind out of the sails of the Jamaat and the NAP. At the same time it had allowed too much wind to its own sails. The party adopted what Mr Bhutto later termed 'a people's programme' and exhorted party workers to 'take it to workers, peasants, labourers, students, and all the helpless.' He assured them this 'programme would end the monopolies and the robbery of the twenty families.' It had pledged to eliminate the bad influences of feudalism and laid down various long and short term targets. A list was provided of various industries which would be nationalized along with banking and insurance. Parliamentary form of government, adult franchise, various welfare provisions were part of the guiding principles. An end to exploitation of East Pakistan, support for the right of self-determination of the people of Kashmir, and confrontation with the expansionist India were included in the pledges. Besides these guiding principles, the next important party document was its election manifesto which was published in 1970. The manifesto says: 'West Pakistani owners of large estates, the feudal lords, constitute a formidable obstacle to progress.' It had also fixed the land holdings: 'the size of the agricultural estate will be limited by the ceiling, the norm being the ownership of 50 to 150 acres of irrigated land'. It was the 'party's policy for dealing with agricultural problems' and was 'laid down in the programmatic principles' accepted in 1967. Article 6 of the principles says the 'party stands for elimination of feudalism and will take concrete steps in accordance with the established principles of socialism to protect and advance the interests of the peasantry.'

The PPP held its second convention in September 1968 in Hyderabad. On 21 September Mr Bhutto delivered his famous oration to the convention which formed the basis of his mass contact drive and strategy that ultimately led to the overwhelming PPP election victory in 1970; and his own ascendancy to power as the President of Pakistan in 1971. He told the convention: 'We have to overwhelm dictatorship step by step. You are aware that when it gave up the war, one part of it was cut off and fell down. The Tashkent declaration cut off another part and the dictatorship was further weakened. The death of Kalabagh paralysed one of its arms. With my departure it weakened still further. Now the people should throw out this mutilated dead body from the government house.' He proposed 'a suitable candidate' from either East Pakistan or West Pakistan to come forward and challenge Ayub's presidency. 'But if both from East and West Pakistan no popular person comes into the field then reciting the Kalima "*La ilaha il Allaho Mohammadur rasul Ullah*", I would myself jump into the field. Hear, the people of Hyderabad! I swear to God that whatever tyranny and torture I may have to suffer I would confront this dictatorship myself.'

Earlier in the course of the same speech Mr Bhutto analysed the situation: 'Today right from the Khyber Pass to Karachi and from Karachi to East Pakistan, wailing cries are coming from hungry peasants, naked workers, penniless students, and downtrodden people but there is none to listen to them. If these conditions continue to persist the day is not far off when the people will raise the banner of rebellion to defend their rights and then there would be civil war and bloodshed in the country. It is not my prophecy, it is just common sense. It will be said, I am spreading rebellion. If need be, I may do so, I am not afraid of it. So far as I am concerned, I believe in solving the people's problems through peaceful and democratic means. But if you are unable to understand the language of democracy then you should tell us what means we should adopt for achieving the rights of the people. If the need arose I would be the first person to come out in the field. We are not afraid of revolution, we are not afraid of bloodshed.'

Mr Bhutto challenged Ayub: 'Respected Khan Sahib!' 'I am not a coward that I should be afraid of Section 144 and the DPR. I am not scared of the power of your guns either. Bring your guns, the people of Pakistan are with me and the people are more powerful than the atom bomb. You will see that for democracy and socialism I would come out with the people with the shroud around my head. You must also know that I have already burnt my boats. You are responsible for the miseries of the people and your comforts will also be snatched away. The government has antagonized the twelve crore people for the gratification of the twenty families who are sucking the blood of the people. This will be a very costly bargain for the government. Do not judge the nation from its silence and think that the people are cowardly. This nation is not cowardly; its so-called leaders are cowards.'

And the over-inflated 'administrator, bureaucracy or *kamora shahi*' in Sindhi, had some of the deadliest jobs: 'It remains busy day and night praising the ministers and the rulers, disrupting the meetings of the opposition parties and lathi-charging their processions, protecting the goonda elements and detaining good people under the Goonda Act, patronizing the dens of prostitution and gambling and arranging for the bogus voters during the elections, seeing to it that slogans of democracy, socialism, and liberty are not raised from any quarter. I warn the administration of this country that it should immediately change its unconstitutional and undemocratic behaviour.' He warned them, 'I ask the bureaucracy of this country to change its behaviour. We have in our mind the record of the doings of every official from section officers to the secretaries. Remember, one day you have to appear before the court of the people.'

There was an open challenge to the establishment: 'Let them come in the field; let them bring all their money and wealth; let them bring their licences and permits; let them also bring their police. Use your radio, television, and newspapers. We don't have anything. Our hands are empty. You have got the government and power. But remember! We have seen this "powerful" paper tiger from inside. Come out in the field!'

He expressed satisfaction over the progress of the PPP. 'Brethren: I am very happy today because in the short period of one year our revolutionary party has been organized on strong foundations and is working in the people. The party branches are opening in every corner of Pakistan, and the most significant thing is that our party has the following and support of the people.' He exhorted his party members: 'Prepare the nation for a people's struggle. This is a people's programme. Therefore take this programme to the people. This programme is the voice of liberation of all the exploited classes. Therefore take it to workers, peasants, labourers, students and all the poor and the helpless. This programme would end the monopolies and the robbery of the twenty families.'

He was ready for the foundation of a united front. 'We invite all the opposition parties to unite on issues like restoration of democracy, establishment of socialism, civil liberties, fundamental rights of the people, adult franchise, independent foreign policy, independence of judiciary, freedom of press, etc.' This was Mr Bhutto's main arsenal with which he hectored his way to power. While Mr Bhutto busied himself with the formation of his party and the mass contact drive, the autumn 1968 thunder of youth's fury struck the tall oak that was Ayub. All the top soil of Swat which he had gathered around himself could not keep him from falling. Then there was the Yahya interlude. Give the devil his due. Whatever the motives, Yahya did allow a certain amount of political activity and freedom of expression, possibly to let off the steam. But that was the highest level of political freedom this country ever had.

The day Yahya gave a green signal to political parties, the PPP held a huge rally in Karachi. It was one of the biggest ever held in the metropolis. The stage management was controlled by the NSF and Lyari workers, Mr Bhutto arrived in a shiny American limousine that drove right to the stage through the struggling crowd. Among the speakers to warm up the occasion were boyish Mr Abdul Hafeez Pirzada and the pucca saheb ex-General Akbar Khan. The audience was too huge to be managed by the beginners, so they gave up the attempt. Then came Miraj Mohd. Khan haranguing the exploiters and reactionaries in front of a hyptonized audience. As Miraj finished his volcanic piece of rhetoric, an *a la* Bond Street dressed Mr Bhutto stood up from his chair and embraced

Miraj in front of the cheering crowd, the atmosphere was rent with thunderous slogans. Now it was Mr Bhutto's turn. He advanced to the mike. One could think of all the textbooks of politics and rhetoric that would have gone into the mental framework of this full-time politician, probably the second since Suharwardy.

There he stood in front of the huge crowd of greasy, shining black heads, dark, bony, lean, and sunken faced, their eyes shining. It looked like a cluster of ants blazing with a primordial will to live. These are the hands that keep the wheels of industry of this city moving and provide 61% of the total revenue of this country. This is the type that hailed Bhutto all over Pakistani and swept him to victory against his feudalist adversaries. Mr Bhutto was their *messiah*, their Shri Krishna. They applauded him hysterically, gasped and laughed as the maestro went on with his magic, promising them the bonanza and castigating the public enemies. He took off his jacket, loosened his tie, rolled his sleeves and at one stage, turning from his eager audience he asked the potentates on the stage, 'Haven't I improved as a speaker? After a bit more of practice, I will be as good as Khaliquzzaman.'

Mr Bhutto started his election campaign on the wave of such mass support backed by a broad-based party. Its slogans were reduced to the simple demand: *Mang raha hey her insan, roti, kapra aur makan.* (It is the demand of every man. Bread, dress and house.) And the simple folk took him literally. He also promised the landless peasants a parcel of 15 acres of land. He toured the countryside and the cities, especially the heartland of Pakistan's establishment between Multan and Pindi, taking with him a battery of fiery orators and the message was made clear to everyone.

December 1970 elections were a complete surprise to everyone including Yahya and Mr Bhutto. The General must have thought that in West Pakistan several squabbling feudal groups would come to the Assembly over whom he will pontificate. Mr Bhutto could hardly hope for very much against such feudal adversaries as Daultana and Wali Khan with their permanent fiefs in West Pakistan and that man of the masses—Mujib—from East Pakistan. A Bhutto aide commented on the election results, 'Now Mr Bhutto Saheb doesn't know what to do. How to choose between the *wadera* and the *hari*. We never expected more than thirty seats.' The PPP success in Sind rested to a great extent on the support of traditional rural potentates, though the poor *haris* had definitely shown their awakening through their voting pattern. But the rout of the Council Muslim League in the Punjab and Daultana's downfall was completely unexpected.

Immediately after PPP won the elections, the process of alienation between its leadership and the rank and file had started. There were the realities of power politics which took most of the time of its high command, leaving them hardly with any time to attend to the common folk that had voted for the PPP. The 'street power' was mobilized from time to time to put pressure on Yahya and the other parties during the 'Don't go to the Assembly, or your legs will be broken' campaign. During this period the most hilarious exercise of the PPP potential was the 'rat-race' that Mr Bhutto made Mr Daultana run during a train journey through Punjab and Sind when Daultana in sheer exasperation got down the train and took a taxi to reach Karachi from a suburban station.

Naturally, the party started showing the signs of inner rifts between left-right and *wadera*-urban pressure groups. Mr Bhutto was too busy in tackling Yahya, Mujib, Wali Khan, Maudoodi, even Qaiyum.

Then, suddenly things started happening. The trauma of East Pakistan was followed by the ascendancy of Mr Bhutto right to the top. Now the PPP was ruling the roost and in the process the party ceased to be what it was and became yet another version of the Convention League with very strong overtures of the pre-independence Unionist politics of rural Punjab. This time with new recruits from rural Sind as well. The almighty establishment is again masquerading with a lot of fanfare. As a matter of fact the PPP was never ready for the great responsibility that fell to its lot. It had no time to plant its roots deeply and prepare the party apparatus. It seems the party was stunned by the over-reaction of the masses to its slogans and could hardly be expected to go the whole hog. Basically, it was a rural conservative party of disgruntled village potentates who were fed up with the top dogs in the manger. They could hardly hope for what they got out of the blue. This is the predicament of the PPP.

The PPP has a four tier party organization—the ward-village, the town, the province, and the central committee. The organization was the result of personal and mass contacts, traditional pressure groups, and of course, the objective conditions. The masses of West Pakistan, in spite of the parochial poison that was deliberately injected in the society both from inside and abroad, are deeply aware of their lot and earnestly crave for a change for the better. This was proved by the general elections. In East Pakistan the people voted for nationalism. In West Pakistan the majority of the people on the grassroots level voted for economic consideration, the presence of other motives and pressures is not denied here. The PPP that emerged victorious from the elections was the symbol of the common people's aspirations.

The present PPP organization is even weaker than the various Muslim Leagues and stands no comparison to the Jamaat or even the NAP in this respect. Now its mainstay are the traditional pressure groups of the rural area and of course the state apparatus. The central figure of the Central Committee is Z. A. as he had always been. As secretary general, J. A. is the meticulous draughtsman. The party has three Vice-Chairmen—Makhdum Taleb El-Maula of Sind, Mr Taher Mohd. of Baluchistan, Khan of Sherpao from N.W.F.P. and Mr Mahmood Qasuri used to be the fourth from the Punjab. The central committee has 28-30 members. All of them had been nominated. There never had been any elections held on any level. Only the ward parties were the spontaneous growths due to mass protest. They have withered away since long like the grass that grows following the summer rains. Since the left has been completely ousted from the party organization, the field has been left open to the conservatives.

Mr Bhutto is too busy with the 'state-power' and the 'street-power' is being properly looked after by the forces of law and order. The process of alienation has been furthered by inflation, unemployment, law and order situation, and the highhandedness of the administration.

Mr Bhutto has himself acknowledged that he has lost the support of the youth who pushed his wagon at the beginning. The same Nishtar Park of Karachi from where his high-tide of popularity had started, gave him a flat no on the Bangladesh proposition on 3 January of this year.

As the PPP engrosses itself with the realities of ruling the country, the process of its alienation with the people is further deepening and its ties with the establishment, of which Mr Bhutto rendered the severest criticizm [sic] at the beginning of his present political career, continues to become closer with the passing of each day. And now Mr Aziz Ahmed besides bagging the crucial defence and foreign affairs portfolios has successfully made inroads into the party and the Senate. A disgruntled J. A. in exasperation goes protesting to the press on the sneak entry into the PPP of 'Ayub Khan's first Deputy Chief Martial Law Administrator'. 'The rank and file of the party who are progressive and socialist in spite of party bosses, have been considerably agitated by what is taking place. They fear that a coup d'etat within the party is being prepared, and Mr Aziz Ahmed's announcement adds more substance to their fears.' However, J. A. Rahim practically disowned his statement after one meeting with Chairman Bhutto.

Meanwhile Mr Bhutto is surrounded with his new peers and draughtsmen. Besides venerable Aziz Ahmed, others are policemen Mian Bashir, Said Ahmad, and Tiwana and of course Khan Abdul Qaiyum—all adept in looking after the 'street-power' with the sleekest possible, up-to-date police gear. Add to them the village potentates Khar, Pirzada, and wily Pir Ali Mohammad Rashidi with all his intriguing qualities. Between Mr Khar and Mr Mumtaz Bhutto, the Punjab and Sind PPP are tightly controlled. Those who are important in the central party besides Z. A. are Khar, Pirzada, Rafi Raza, Mumtaz Bhutto, Sherpao, and Maulana Niazi. It is said that hardly anyone speaks during the party Central Committee meetings. Mr Bhutto has a great flare to be the board-room patriarch. Hardly anyone speaks in front of him. During the last party convention in Pindi, the opposition had been completely ousted with Miraj Mohd. Khan staying away from the proceedings. Out of some 1,700 cards for the delegates from the Punjab, Sheikh Rashid got only 100, the rest were given to Mr Khar's nominees. From Sind all the 400 cards were distributed at the sweet will of Mr Mumtaz Bhutto. It is said that even some *Jiye Sind* supporters attended as delegates.

Meanwhile, the PPP central office in Karachi has been locked and a couple of guards placed at the entrance. The party secretariat has moved from Karachi to Islamabad. Occasionally, it is opened when some party leader wishes to address a select gathering of PPP workers. Last week there was a meeting. Those gathered vehemently supported J. A. and protested on Aziz-Ahmed's entry into the party. Each speaker complained about the alienation of PPP government from the rank and file. The much repeated refrain was that the benefits from the government are held away somewhere on the top and do not seep down to the ordinary workers and ordinary people. This is one good indication of how the party worker has gone to seed in the slime of petty interest. It bodes ill for the future of the party.

Part III
Afghanistan

The Shape of Pressures to Come

15 April 1972

Askar Ali Shah

PESHAWAR is an ideal vantage point for readings of a sensitive area made ultrasensitive now. There is a new tune on Radio Kabul with an eye on the tribal areas. Nearby, Russia is showing a more than keen interest and, of course, Bangladesh and India have overbusy channels open to Kabul.

Three elements are clouding our horizons. Russia, India, and Bangladesh are apparently in ominous concert; each with its own axe to grind and all intent on cashing in on the military setback we received in December last. In this context Russia's role is particularly perplexing. While India and Bangladesh have some scores to settle, Russia has none such, at least not so visibly. And yet, Russia has played a very potent role in the setback, pointing to some specific purpose. That purpose, of course, is her grand design of coaxing us into an Asian security scheme of her desire. Fine: but for us this is too bitter a pill to swallow.

Russia has been working at it since the days of Tashkent. Indeed, in her reckoning, the Tashkent Declaration was the cornerstone on which the vast agglomerate in South Asia, with herself at the apex, was to be established. That prospect was more or less wrecked by the subsequent agitation which toppled the Ayub regime. If Mr Kosygin was then Russian Premier as he is now, and T.D. was his fond baby, Mr Bhutto was the one who had stifled the baby; and he subsequently had to go to Moscow cast in another role—so very different from that of 1966. With him went, coincidentally Mr Aziz Ahmed, another survivor of the T.D. melodrama. Kosygin must have eyed both with a significant twinkle.

Mr Kosygin should be expected to have made up his mind not to be outdone this time. He seems to have been waiting six long years for the opportunity now so well in his grasp. Three years ago, in 1969, he had made one more try when he managed to persuade the Afghan government to call a five-country (Afghanistan, Iran, Russia, Pakistan, India) conference at Kabul to formulate a unified policy for land transit of trade goods. Pakistan spurned the overture because of the inclusion of India in the list. Russia must have strengthened her resolve to manoeuver us into a more amiable disposition.

And so, when the occasion came, she struck. What happened is now a painful story. We now find ourselves in a most unfavourable bargaining position. Russia holds the key to a great many

349

things, and she knows it. She can not only afford to wait, but also contrive to put more pressure on us. Recent stepping up of Radio Kabul's propaganda seems part of it. The Pakhtoonistan programme has suddenly been stretched from one hour to three hours. Moreover, messages are believed to have been sent to tribal areas for increasing hostile activity (much to the embarrassment of NAP leadership painstakingly building up their image in the wider perspective). All this looks in one piece with Russia's aim to bring us round to her scheme of things.

Very vital issues are involved in this. However, Russia's scheme would have us turn our back on China and thus shut out the only possible corridor that country has to South Asia and to the warm waters of the Indian Ocean. Pakistan eminently provides that corridor. She is also the missing link in the chain aimed at the containment of China—which would result in a marked dissipation of that country's war potential. Russia also wants to oust all other possible rivals in the area, which encompasses such a precious thing as the Persian Gulf oil. If the Arabian Sea-Persian Gulf area becomes a Russo—Indian lake, as is obviously intended, America, and more particularly, Western Europe, will find themselves at a marked politico-economic disadvantage.

Russia thus wants to achieve two objects with one stroke. Pakistan, with her geographical situation and a military potential still capable of being revived, can play a potent role in this, one way or the other. If she can somehow wriggle out of her present predicament, she could still become a factor in the region of South Asia. It is precisely this that both Russia and India want to frustrate. The problem is that both at the moment have the means to keep us pressed down.

Of compassion or consideration we can expect very little. The possible counteractive pull from the side of China and America is not so conspicuously visible. Both these countries apparently have their own reasons for not getting overly involved. Political instability in the country and unpredictability of our future attitudes is perhaps one reason. Another is Russia's unquestioned stranglehold—through India. And then India has her scores to settle, not the least being her obvious desire not only to render us incapable of posing any further threat to her, but also to bring us to some measure of interdependence. And she has Bangladesh to dangle in our faces.

The Bangladesh leaders for their part are expected to be very hard bargainers when it comes to deciding things across the conference table. They have every means of making things difficult. Even if we recognize Bangladesh, the next step might be a huge bill of impossible 'dues' demanded of us. And unless we obliged, Bangladesh might refuse to come to talking terms. It shall need quite some doing for us to get out of this cruel paradox.

On the bargaining counter will feature prominently the prisoners. For us the question of prisoners is not only vital, but is likely to acquire very compelling proportions before very long. Hundreds of thousands of families are, directly or indirectly, affected, and it is possible that after some time these families will begin to get restive. And, the more this happens, the tighter will be the squeeze on us for falling into line. It is this prospect that is causing so many to ask the question whether the country will at all be in a position to get out of the morass.

And, as bad luck would have it, Mr Bhutto was connected with some of the unfortunate sequences that culminated in the blow-up of December last. However much he desires cooperation now, the events of the past do not look like getting effaced altogether. Since we cannot be the ones at the giving end of the bargain, if and when it comes to that, we will have to do quite a lot of convincing (with what effect is a debatable point) at the bargaining counter. Mr Bhutto may have the best intentions in the world now when he is charged with the well-nigh impossible task of cleaning the Aegean stables, but the big question is whether the other side will be convinced that their acquiescence would really be a safe enough bet.

It is significant that quite many of Mr Bhutto's minus points in this particular regard are plus points for Mr Wali Khan. Unlike Mr Bhutto with his pro-Chinese predilections, Wali Khan has in his party men like Mahmudul Haq Usmani and Ajmal Khattak with reputedly pro-Russian bents. And the party has never really pronounced itself decisively for this or that country. As regards India and Mujib, Wali Khan has decidedly more favourable points than, perhaps, has anyone else. But even so, Mr Bhutto is in power and Wali is not. This is a problem which the country has to sort out—of course by constitutional means. And unless that happens the drift is likely to keep us guessing.

A Season for Conspiracies

16 September 1972

Asrar Ahmad

AS if the new London plan was not enough of a conspiracy, the corridors of power here have been stirred deep and wide by the news that Khan Abdul Ghaffar Khan may arrive in Pakistan by 15 September or thereabouts, thus ending his 8-year long self-imposed exile in bordering Afghanistan. The news itself is unconfirmed and the latest on the grapevine is that he may not come after all. It is hard to trace the inspiration behind it but the starting point could be Ghaffar Khan's broadcast from Radio Kabul on 1 September, observed in Afghanistan as Pakhtoonistan Day. Crafty old man! To make his passage back to Pakistan smooth and easy, he made no mention of the Pakhtoonistan demand in his broadcast, instead he offered his cooperation to President Bhutto to build a new Pakistan 'free from exploitation, hatred, reaction, and military pacts'.

The news of the prospective return of the prodigal who, it is said, is always seated next to King Zahir Shah on ceremonial occasions, set 'political circles' here agog with excitement. It is also known that Ghaffar Khan is on very good terms both with India and Soviet Russia. The event was immediately co-related to the latest version of the London plan. The route of his sneaking entry was also speculated upon and enthusiasts even made plans to nab him at some point along the craggy, unwatched frontier. Good luck and good hunting. The administration itself has maintained a shuffling silence on the issue.

Meanwhile, the press, radio, and television, shackled as ever, continued to blow the so-called London plan out of all proportion, throwing revealing light on the government's intentions to crush all conspiracies, hatched and unhatched. The scenario is made the more ominous by the reported massive flow of arms into Frontier and Baluchistan and the generous distribution of arms licenses in the two provinces. Not only the fate of the two provincial governments seems to be hanging by a thin thread but peace in the country itself seems to be in danger.

What is the revised London plan? Is there a plan at all? Only time will tell. Mufti Mahmood, Chief Minister of the Frontier, and Governor Bizenjo, have debunked it in strong terms—a figment of imagination, an airy nothing. There are various versions of the plan, though, and it is interesting to note the variations. The main theme seems to be that the plan aims at a confederation of Bangladesh, India, Pakistan and Afghanistan. It envisages four autonomous states in Pakistan including two Pakhtoon states in the provinces of Frontier and Baluchistan to be linked into a mini-confederation of their own.

The London plan, if true, appears to be more of a straitjacket than the Asian Security Pact tailored by the Soviet Party chief, Leonid Brezhnev, four years ago. It aimed at voluntary regional cooperation comprising India, Pakistan, Ceylon, Afghanistan, Iran, Nepal, and the Soviet Union. Bangladesh, not born then, could be easily accommodated into the pattern. In view of the Indo-Russian treaty of friendship, Soviet domination over the region will become more plausible if either version of the plan is put on the ground. The Russian outfit when it is actually worn shrinks tight, as is known to most of the East European countries.

It is argued by some observers that the London plan, though still lacking in substance, has already delineated its structural moorings with the formation of the two provincial governments in Frontier and Baluchistan. Both governments are under the influence of pro-Moscow NAP headed by Wali Khan.

The team which masterminded the first plan is now reported to be giving final touches to the 2nd plan under the advice of Sh. Mujib. The team, according to press reports, represents all the four provinces of Pakistan. It includes Wali Khan (N.W.F.P.), Ataullah Khan Mengal (Baluchistan), the Haroon brothers (Sind and Karachi), and Malik Ghulam Jilani (Punjab). Other politicians abroad include Akbar Khan Bugti, Ahmad Nawaz Khan Bugti, Sardar Marri, and Zafar Ali Shah of Sind. Except for the Haroon brothers and Akbar Bugti, all others flew to London recently, ostensibly for medical treatment. Wali Khan, before departing for London, is said to have discussed the plan with his father and the Afghan authorities.

President Bhutto has called Governor Bizenjo to Pindi for urgent talks. The Information Minister, Maulana Kausar Niazi, has already sounded the drums. He has taken strong exception to Wali Khan's reported threat to reach for the trigger if his autonomy demand was not conceded in the constitution. Wali Khan is also reported to be willing to concede only defence, foreign affairs and currency to the centre. Maulana Niazi, on Sunday last, promised due retribution to the conspirators. It is understood that plans for a crackdown are underway. But it may be worthwhile to remember that Wali Khan has said harsher things in the past. Wali Khan's recent interviews to the foreign press also indicate that he left the country confused and frustrated as a result of President Bhutto's insistence on introducing the parliamentary form in the provinces and the French-style presidential pattern at the centre.

Later in the week, the whole edifice of the so-called plan caved in and embarrassed spokesmen of the regime were busy with salvage operations. But the wreck seemed to be complete and the debris strewn far too wide to be swept out of the view of a skeptical public.

As for Ghaffar Khan, political analysts are of the view that he has rightly expressed his desire to settle down in the dry and parched hills of Baluchistan, the poorest amongst the four provinces. They expect him to use his charisma to convert those who still waver on the Pakhtoonistan issue. Some of the Persian speaking Baluchi leaders are not so far reconciled to the idea of Pakhtoonistan because of their close affinity with their compatriots inhabiting southern Iran.

Ghaffar Khan will be hard put to convince waverers both in Frontier and Baluchistan to his own concept of Pakhtoonistan. He has always been associated with the 'Kabul brand' of Pakhtoonistan under the hegemony of Afghan rulers. On the contrary, Wali has been giving an impression that he believes in 'Utmanzai (Wali's ancestral home) brand' of Pakhtoonistan which means an autonomous state within Pakistan. It is, however, difficult to confirm whether Wali is still sticking to this idea.

The land-locked Afghanistan, allergic to sharing borders with India, has been vacillating on its concept of Pakhtoonistan ever since Pakistan came into being. Afghanistan's concept of Pakhtoonistan is generally governed by the vagaries of her relations with Pakistan. When the two countries pull on well, Pakhtoonistan remains confined to the bounds of the North Western Frontier. Whenever the relations are on the heat, Pakhtoonistan extends down south up to Mekran coast in Baluchistan with an eye on her imports and exports.

The Afghans Taste their own Brew

28 October 1972

M. I. Laskar

THE Pakhtoonistan stunt has been raised again in the UN General Assembly by Afghanistan, this time with a greater vigour. The Afghan Foreign Minister's statement in the world forum virtually amounted to a claim on the territory inhabited generally by Pashto-speakers on this side of the Durand Line. His contention that the N.W.F.P. and Baluchistan were incorporated into Pakistan against the wishes of their inhabitants is not new; but the tone was different and observers at the UN did not fail to note it.

The timing appears strange. There had been a lull on this front since the flying visit to Kabul by President Bhutto only a few days after his assumption of office. But those who have been following the Afghan government's thinking and the resultant socio-political scene, are not surprised. The revival of the bogey has been necessitated by the country's own survival needs in the face of the divisive forces and ethnic aspirations which themselves are a by-product of the stunt itself.

President Bhutto's visit had a compromising effect. King Zahir Shah's enthusiasm for Pakhtoonistan has cooled off over the years and he would not be sorry to let it die its own death. So, a sort of ceasefire followed at the explicit behest of the monarch. But much water has flowed down the Kabul River in the meantime and it was not easy for his government to withdraw outright. In Afghanistan now, a ministry works full time to keep the issue alive through various propaganda measures including the regular bribing of tribal maliks and the observation of a Pakhtoonistan Day, as a part of the Afghan independence anniversary ceremony, with a large-scale public participation.

The real test for the Afghan Government came with the formation of NAP-JUI governments in N.W.F.P. and Baluchistan. It may not be wide off the mark to say that President Bhutto's compromise with the NAP-JUI coalition including the appointment of party governors in N.W.F.P. and Baluchistan, was prompted more by a desire to rebuff the Pakhtoonistan lobby in Afghanistan and the resultant Soviet withdrawal, once and for all, from Pakistan's western border. The compromise was not conceived as a means to achieve political cohesion within the country.

Whatever may be the case, for the Afghan government it was a difficult time. After the

355

establishment of popular governments in the Pakhtoonistan of Afghan definition, it seemed to have lost the last of the weapons in its armoury. But following Begum Bhutto's visit, things were again going in favour of the Afghan hawks.

Two important developments made a particular contribution to it. One is the uneasy relationship between the PPP government at the centre and the NAP-JUI governments in the two bordering provinces. In the Afghan context, Wali Khan's castigation of Begum Bhutto's visit to Kabul served the hawks' purpose. So also Wali Khan's move to reserve for his party the right to make any overture to Afghanistan. He tacitly maintains that since Pakistan's relations with Afghanistan are based on the Frontier's interest and will always have a direct bearing on the Frontier, any overture from Pakistan should come through the NAP.

The second event of similar import is the central government's far from enthusiastic reaction to the recommendations made by the N.W.F.P. Govt. regarding a project linking Chitral with Peshawar via a land route through Afghanistan. This was also a test case watched with equal eagerness by the governments at Peshawar and Kabul. For the N.W.F.P. governments, it was a cunning move to bring the ball into its own court. And for the Afghans, it was a sign of the Bhutto govt.'s apathy towards the Pakhtoons.

More trouble, however, was in store for the Afghan government. It was the message of goodwill to President Bhutto and the Pakhtoons on this side of the border sent by Bacha Khan in his speech at the Pakhtoonistan Day rally in Afghanistan this year. This was a speech which otherwise should have put an end to anything that remains of the Kabul brand of Pakhtoonistan. And yet came the loud voice of the Afghan Foreign Minister on the floor of the United Nations General Assembly renewing an otherwise dead issue. The reasons are to be found in the cracks developing in the foundation of the Afghan nationhood. The wild wind is blowing back.

The immediate cause of the fall of Afghan cabinet last month was the threat of a no-confidence motion signed by 175 members of the Wolesy Jirga (Lower House) as a chain reaction to the language issue. It all began with an amendment moved by a member of the Wolesy Jirga, a Pashto-speaker and an émigré from Swat, in the government servants conduct rules. The amendment required the officials to know both the Dari (Afghan Persian) and Pashto languages. In the Afghan Constitution, both the languages are declared as national languages. But by convention, Dari continues to be virtually the official language. The amendment thus indirectly seeks the raising of Pashto to the status of an official language. In such a case, however, the Dari-speaking people would be in a disadvantageous position. In Afghanistan, the people speaking Pashto as the mother-tongue simultaneously know Dari language while the Dari speakers generally do not know Pashto.

The subsequent events made the issue a great national controversy and a time came when it seemed that the division of the nation on linguistic basis was complete. At the height of the controversy, an independent newspaper, published the case of the Dari-speakers and left no stone unturned to dig deep into the 'ethnic inferiority' of their rivals. This infuriated the Pashto-speakers who also sent rejoinders in the form of an article to the same newspaper. The paper accepted the article for publication. In Afghanistan, there is no pre-censorship of newspapers, but since there are no private printing presses of worth, the government presses print all newspapers. The article in question was detected in the printing press which is required by law not to print objectionable material and was referred to higher authorities who declared it unsuitable for publication. This prompted the 175 members of the parliament to sign a non-confidence motion which was to be tabled in the Jirga, if within a specified time, the article was not published.

The farsighted King foresaw the inescapable consequences of the controversy. If the article was published, it would hurt the sentiments of the Dari speaking people and the Jirga could not escape its reverberations even then. And if the article was not published, the cabinet faced the no-confidence. So he quietly asked his Prime Minister to resign.

In the whole controversy, one thing was clear and it was that the Pashto-speakers who number about half the population have started making their presence felt on the Afghan scene. The stage has been prepared by nothing other than the Pakhtoonistan bogey which has made the Afghan Pakhtoons conscious of their rights. The authors of the stunt meant them for the Pakhtoons of 'Pakhtoonistan', but now it boomeranged on them. And to counteract it, the stunt is being taken up vigorously again. It is intended both to divert the attention of the Afghan Pathans and to pacify them in the face of great provocations from Persian Afghans.

Nevertheless, within the Afghan society, resistance from the Dari-speaker would be there. The Dari-speaking Afghans comprising three ethnic groups including the Uzbeks, the Tajiks, and the Qizilbash, who all belong to pure Persian stock, have been providing noblemen to the Afghan society for centuries and Afghan democracy has not come to such a stage that the nation can do without them.

A corollary of this situation which may prove dangerous for the Afghan rulers is that the Pashtoon in Afghanistan are rallying around Bacha Khan who has by now become their uncrowned leader. And this is why King Zahir Shah is ill at ease wishing to wash his hands off the bogey. A central Asian monarch, however constitutional he may be cannot coexist with the sort of a leader thrown up by a Pathan confederacy.

The Call of Geography

6 January 1973

Askar Ali Shah

WHILE taking stock of the disaster that has befallen this country some people solace themselves with the thought that with the breaking away of Bangladesh, Pakistan has come on its true bearings. Already eyes are being cast westward more than could be the case before. For what was once East Pakistan had very little interest in what lay to the west of us. It was more or less part of South East Asia while we here are in south central Asia. Not only did the socio-geographic separation of the two wings preclude buildup of a truly permeating nationhood but it also obtruded on the prospect of the country finding equations with some of its more immediate neighbours.

Even the RCD had seemed a strange beast to the East Pakistanis and they never really reconciled themselves to it. They did not openly disown it because the base of power was in Islamabad, but they did have their reservations. Under the circumstances, any further progressions westward from West Pakistan towards cultivation of cultural, economic and, maybe, even political affinities was out of the question. The susceptibilities of East Pakistanis could be taxed only to a limit.

But now East Pakistan is gone. The country is still reeling under the impact of the blow. But even in this distress there are those who say that the position as it has emerged now enables us to pursue what could not be done earlier. A new vista unfolds itself and we can now look west without having to look back. Things may happen if we are able to clear up the mess left by the events of last year. Some pointers do give us the hope that what now appears a colossal tragedy may in the final analysis turn out to be a blessing in disguise.

Towards this end some dropped threads may have to be picked up again and a new direction followed. Even the talk of firm ties—some people even would call it a 'loose confederation'—with Afghanistan is again in the air. And this is not empty talk, for the topic has already been broached on a number of occasions in various contexts.

I remember when I had an interview with King Mohammad Zahir Shah of Afghanistan—some three years ago—he had talked of economic affinities with Pakistan. 'Joint ventures' and mutual trade he had in mind. He said if the rich countries of western Europe out of economic self-interest found it necessary to form an 'economic community' then there was many times more justification for the poor countries to do likewise. The king had waxed eloquent and said 'if Afghanistan and Pakistan did not come to true realization of their economic situation it would be unfortunate.'

The king was saying something not without a perspective. Sometime earlier talks had been held between Pakistan and Afghan officials about the possibility of exploiting the rich and abundant Afghan iron ore at Hajigak, some 80 miles from Kabul. The king during the interview told me that Afghanistan had the ore but not a big enough market to justify a full-sized steel mill whereas Pakistan had the market but no ore; so why not combine the two factors and go for a joint venture.

The talks then had not made much headway, due obviously to still lingering political suspicions. A steel mill is a very expensive proposition and one has to be absolutely sure about a fool-proof source of raw materials as well as of the market before going for it. If the mill was established in Afghanistan the country had to have a fully guaranteed market which in this case was Pakistan; if it was to be in Pakistan then the latter had to be thoroughly convinced that the ore would be coming to it without any hitch. But if the suspicions prevailed then no such satisfaction could be extended or accepted either way. The steel mill talks had faltered and then fizzled out on this score, and little has been heard of it since.

Somewhat similar has been the fate of the proposal for having a transit agreement which would have enabled passage of trade goods through Afghanistan as being safer, quicker, and cheaper. Again 'bad politics' came in and about the time I met the king the projected transit conference in Kabul had failed to get off the ground. The Afghans were unhappy about it, but did not say so.

The idea of some sort of collaboration between the two countries had come early. Even as far back as 1948, less than one year after the advent of Pakistan, late Agha Khan (grandfather of Karim Agha Khan) had mooted it as being the natural follow up of the creation of Pakistan. Shah Wali Khan, uncle of the Afghan king had been associated with this part of it and in an interview he had told me that the Agha Khan actually had a firm proposal which he conveyed to his government. At that time he was Afghan Ambassador in France and the Agha Khan had invited him to his residence where he unfolded his proposal. He conveyed this to his own government which, however, told him that Pakistan was a 'big country and a new one too,' so they better wait and see how the trend went. The matter had ended there.

The question was again agitated in 1958 by Iskandar Mirza but there again nothing happened perhaps because the Afghans were not too sure of Iskandar Mirza's intentions. Also, the One Unit had been formed and the Afghans had apparently been piqued by the way the little autonomy enjoyed by the provinces—and the Pukhtoons—had been taken away.

A lot has happened since. One Unit is now no more and Pakistan is no longer encumbered by an inward-looking east wing. Whatever is left of the country is very much part of south central Asia and can share its politics more truly than ever. Moreover, the traditional bogey of India, flaunted by the Muslim League as being the only means, it believed, of keeping the country intact, has noticeably faded, so that we can view the perspective more objectively. And, no less, we now feel that we can build up a vigorous and comparatively secure hegemony only by entering into some sort of collaboration, or even partnership, with neighbouring Afghanistan.

The interests and affinities of the two countries overlap. No two countries could have more in common. Further, it is also a fact that if one perchance breaks up the other will be breaking up too. If, for instance, the Pukhtoon areas of Pakistan break away, there will almost certainly be a similar breaking away of the Pukhtoons of Afghanistan Similarly, if the Pukhtoons of Afghanistan break away or more precisely, if the Persian-speaking element, the Farsiwans, separated themselves from the rest of the Afghans—the Pukhtoon—then such a Pukhtoon state will almost certainly attract the Pukhtoons of Pakistan.

Safety for both countries and their peoples therefore lies in the prevalence of the present overall position which, besides all else, has a diluting effect on narrower parochialisms. If this concept was conceded then the only way to preserve the present relative positions and yet bring the two countries to a more elevated condition of good-neighbourliness is to bring them closer together and integrate the mutual interests in such a way that not only is conflict excluded but both sides have come by a more reassured sense of security in the region.

It is possible that in both the countries the majority communities may not be so ready to take the concept in full embrace. For in the case of Afghanistan any close collaboration with Pakistan will mean the bringing together of the Pukhtoons of the two countries. Both together could make themselves the second largest community in the enlarged aggregate and politically they would certainly have come by a commanding position as being in the centre of it all. Some ultras among the Farsiwans may not be cherishing this prospect, and so also, perhaps, some in the Punjab.

But among both the Farsiwans of Afghanistan and the people of the Punjab there are also substantial elements craving wider horizons, maybe for their several reasons. The Farsiwan's fear of enlarged Pukhtoon hegemony, occasionally being played up by the Pukhtoonistani ultras in that country, and among the people of the Punjab, the still lurking fear of India and of a possible 'break-up' of the country may have combined to urge them to work for some sort of positive collaboration—may be even union—between the two countries.

It is said that some religious sects, particularly in Pakistan are averse to such a proposition because of the predominant role of Sunni clergy in the affairs of Afghanistan. This is believed to be an insidious but otherwise very potent factor particularly in view of the influence such sects exercise in the affairs of Pakistan. How far the other counter-balancing influences are able to override this sort of sectarianism depends much on how conscious the people of the two countries are of the perils they would have to face.

It is obvious nevertheless that things are not going to be the same in both countries from now on. If normalcy with India comes about at long last there will be almost certainly be no obstacle left in the way of the transit agreement which will enable trade goods to pass in both directions—from

Bangladesh on the one hand and the countries of Europe on the other. Sheer economic necessities will impel this. Once the interests are so integrated there will develop the same urge as in the countries of Western Europe. And then there will be no East Pakistan to be pulling us back from it.

As Kabul Sees It

3 March 1973

Askar Ali Shah

THE drifting scene in this country is viewed by our Afghan neighbour with half consternation and half concern. Indeed, the events have been moving so fast that many of the Afghans were prone to take the stories emanating from here with a certain amount of scepticism. But they nevertheless have reacted, and the end seems not yet.

I reached Kabul the day the report came of arms recovery at the Iraqi Embassy in Islamabad. There happened to be a big function that evening at the Indonesian Embassy in Kabul and there were diplomats in it from nearly 20 embassies. At first the common consensus was that it might have been a 'concoction'. It was only when the BBC and other foreign stations broadcast eye-witness accounts from their correspondents that there was a scratching of heads and puzzlement at what earlier had seemed the incredible.

Political and diplomatic mills thereafter began to grind fast. And then there came the dismissal of the N.W.F.P. and Baluchistan governors, setting off the chain of events that only deepened the dilemma. The one outcome was that the Afghans began to believe that there was no such equation left between them and the Pakistan rulers as to have inhibited their recognition of Bangladesh. Almost immediately they went into a conclave to ponder the pros and cons of the matter.

When I met the Afghan Prime Minister, Mr Musa Shafiq, on 18 February they had recognized Bangladesh that same day. The Premier told me that they had withheld the recognition till the very last, hoping that things would have resolved themselves somehow and Pakistan come to terms with the reality of her circumstances. But with the new upswing in the events that hope too had faded, so that they could not go on waiting any longer.

Mr Shafiq remarked that the Afghans still would desire the people of Pakistan to sort out their differences among themselves. They did not want any serious upsets to the precarious balances in the region. As the saying goes in Pashto, he said, 'If a knot can be untied with hands, it has not to be done so with the teeth.' But, he warned, if the situation went on deteriorating and the Pakhtoons began to be oppressed then the Afghans could have nothing for it but to support such Pakhtoons 'with all the means at our disposal'.

Mr Shafiq was speaking in measured and subdued tones, characteristic of the man. The promptness with which Bangladesh was recognized in the wake of the happenings here and then a team sent next day to Dacca to find a place for housing the embassy bespoke of the practical aspect of the Afghan reaction. The Afghans, moreover, have stepped up radio and press propaganda and Pukhtoonistan leaders who were not given much prominence in these media for a long time suddenly began to hit bold headlines.

But then there have since been some scare stories coming out too. These though are based largely on conjecture and some people's passion for cooking up spicy stories. Report of troops mobilization, movements and that sort of thing are not warranted by facts. The Afghans are known for steadiness in their politics and they are not the ones to be taking rash and precipitate steps as would only have heightened the crisis conditions and caused the point of no return to be reached.

I met several other Afghan officials, and they were reassured on hearing on the radio that the National Awami Party and JUI were still giving a fight on constitutional lines in the National Assembly. One high Foreign Ministry official told me that so long as the constitutional battle was on and the Pukhtoon leaders were hoping that things had not become impossible, the Afghans would be taking it all in their stride. It would be different, however, if possible democratic means had proved unavailing.

Meanwhile, the Afghans have been casting significant looks on the tribal regions which would have proved a key factor in any crisis condition. They believe that, thanks to the happenings of 1971 and subsequent events, Pakistan's image in these regions had begun to somewhat fade. The Afghans seem to have started interesting themselves in the tribal affairs more than they did for a long time before this.

But one potent factor which weighs heavily with the Afghans is the possibility of any large-scale trouble in Pakistan spilling over into Afghanistan. In that case, they believe, events would have forced themselves on them, and they would have few options. What is perturbing them intensely is the possibility of some political elements fleeing from Pakistan and invoking the aid of the people in Afghanistan. That would place the Afghan government in a very difficult situation. If they did not help such people, other sympathetic political elements would, and this in its effect could cause big-power involvement.

There is at least one party in Afghanistan waiting for just such an opportunity. It is the pro-Russian Parcham group, small but highly organized and pledged to overthrow the monarchy and bring in unalloyed socialism. Somehow the group deems itself to be a counterpart of the National Awami Party here and is, as such, in the forefront of the activity whenever any NAP leader happens to be in Kabul.

Not unexpectedly, therefore, the group was the first to react sharply at the ouster of the NAP-JUI ministries here. On 18 February they held a public meeting—not a frequent phenomenon—in Kabul's Zarnigar Park, and the group's leader, Babrak Khan, delivered a tirade against President Bhutto and the sequence of events that had caused the Pukhtoon-led governments in Pakistan's two provinces to go into wilderness. (In Afghanistan 'Pukhtoon' are always equated with Baluchis and so the definition is invariably in its wider context).

The Afghan government does not like any sort of activity by the Parcham; but then it could not stop such an activity either. All it could do was to fix the time of the meeting (an official prerogative) in such a way that by the time this sole speech had ended, dusk had descended on snow-bound Kabul, and there was no occasion left for staging the planned procession after the meeting.

The Afghan government is particularly concerned about the possibility of some NAP-JUI leaders and students taking refuge in Afghanistan and then the Parcham—as also other groups like the 'Khalq' and 'Millet'—proceeding to pre-empt the government in the arousing of the public sympathy for the fugitives and even invoking, perhaps, Russian aid for them. In that case the only way out for the government was to forestall such a design and to take care of such fugitives in every possible way. In that case too the invoking of the Russian help could not be altogether ruled out.

These possibilities are an anathema to the experienced Afghans. They know that any big power involvement in the territories of their weaker neighbours has always gone against the interests of such neighbours. They also know that in case Russia did interest herself in the matter, such an involvement would mean the stretching of Russia's long arm over the entire length of Afghanistan, even upto the ocean. The Afghans have for over a century tried to prevent just this to happen, and they will think twice before they would fall for such a recourse. What is bothering them is the realization that events are moving even faster than their own comprehension and in the sphere of a neighbour with whom her interests are so inextricably interlaced.

Kabul's Big Question Mark

11 August 1973

Askar AM Shah

LAST month's coup in Kabul meant more than a mere change of masters. For one thing it meant the end of the first experiment in parliamentary democracy. It also put an end to the institution of the monarchy which for over two centuries has held together an essentially tribal society. It also may have turned out to be a major slip in the power game which is overtly and covertly being played, and might even be stepped up, in the region of south Asia which harbours vast quantities of oil. The coup may turn out to be much more than it now appears to be.

That it has come about so soon after the Pakistan-Iran entente, with the Shah's clear-cut 'hands-off Baluchistan' warning to all who might be interested, is significant. When this entente was reached and the warning came, there were some who believed there would be a reaction. It is customary in Pakistan to look in the direction of India when there is any talk of threat to the integrity of the country. But India, in this case at least, could easily be ruled out. She probably does not want anything more to do with Pakistan territory, or else she could not have gone for a unilateral ceasefire soon after the end of the hostilities in East Pakistan and then evacuated the occupied areas of West Pakistan at the first opportunity. Probably the Shah also did not mean India when he was serving the notice.

This leaves us with Afghanistan and Russia and by this coup they now find themselves on a more common grid than even earlier. It should not be forgotten, however, that President Daud is not such a Russophile as some people might think. He is essentially an Afghan nationalist—irredentist, if you might call it—with a 'positive' approach to what comes to be called Pakhtoonistan. He has all along made no bones about it. In 1955 when he was Prime Minister he entered into an agreement with Russia for military and economic assistance mainly as a counter to Pakistan's entering into a similar agreement with America. That was a very big thing for an Afghan government to do, for at the back of such hobnobbings with Russia there is always the fear of the great neighbour in the country's north. The Afghans have been watchful of that too and have also been trying to find the golden mean so that while aid from Russia could be coming there was also the watchfulness for seeing that the bear held back his paw.

But now there was this challenge thrown by Iran. Obviously there could not have been qualms in Afghanistan as such, but Afghanistan with Russia at her back and both having a common thinking on the point is something different. There is the Russian dream, dating back to Czarist days, of having access to the warm waters of the Indian Ocean and there are the Afghan inhibitions of being a land locked country and having to depend on not too friendly neighbours for outlet to the sea. The equation is there; it is only that there still are other factors which could have borne on the course of events and which would still have acted as brakes on the developing drama. Firstly, there is the Afghan tradition of not doing anything at anyone else's bidding particularly as such an act will bring in their midst one too powerful to be shown the door. Secondly, there is still the hope that things in Pakistan will stabilize themselves and that a political rather than a military solution can be found to the trouble in Baluchistan.

So the game will still remain one of watching, at least for some time to come. It will be taking fairly long for President Daud and his army junta to have consolidated their hold in a country where the attitude of the tribes still remains an unknown factor. It is still difficult to comprehend how semi-tamed tribes like the Ghelzais, Mengals, Zadrans, Jajis, Shinwaris, Mohmands, and Safis, spread over a vast area to the east and south of Kabul, could take to such an abstract thing as republicanism. To them the king was both secular and temporal head of state. The king stood as a symbol of unity and the Friday *khutba* used to be read in his name in the mosques across the country. Nobody from among these tribes at least had even imagined that the king would be no more on the scene. How these tribes could be brought round to the new concept of governance remains to be seen.

In Afghanistan, politics is rooted mainly in the city of Kabul which alone has a measure of the proletariat. Here too are centred leftist group like Parcham, Khalq, and Shola-e-Javed of which the first named at least was outspokenly pro-Russian. This group is important because it is dedicated and influential and it had openly advocated the overthrow of the monarchy. This is the group, too, which deems itself as more or less the counterpart of the National Awami Party here. Ajmal Khattak was mainly taken care of by this party which now finds itself in the forefront of events. While the government of king Zahir Shah could treat NAP escapees from Pakistan at least as honoured guests, there might be a more pertinent attitude towards them by Kabul's new rulers. But we have yet to wait.

It is conceivable that the new rulers in Afghanistan will be taking longer than is believed in ramming home their concept of state. Democracy itself has failed to come out of its teething troubles in the country and it has crashed only after 8 years of operation. Members of parliament did little more than engage themselves in inconsequential debates and discourses which in the end had meant nothing. Even the budgets over the last three years could not be passed because the members would just talk and talk. It was due to a fortuitous provision in the constitution that if a new budget was not passed the provision of the previous one could continue to operate so that the country's system could continue somehow.

And there was the king's hesitation too in giving the people a fuller measure of what he himself had began. He had brought in democracy and he gave the country a constitution which was all that should be desired. But when the thing got going, he began to falter. The parliament passed the Political Parties Act but for almost ten years he hesitated in giving his assent thinking that this would have meant endorsing of parties which he believed were subversive including of course, the Parcham. But this hesitancy was producing recoils. Although the parties continued to operate with their labels, the members did not know whether they were for or against the government. And so they went on obstructing every measure of the government and articulating local grievances as the next best thing. Since the king had ordered the proceedings to be broadcast live, these members talked and talked to infatuate their constituents back home. In doing so they reduced the National Assembly into virtual ineffectiveness.

Daud Khan in his retreat was watching all this and obviously waiting for conditions to deteriorate enough for him to strike. Meanwhile a new ripple had come to the power game in the region with Baluchistan as the main focus this time, and here the cap seems to fit. Russia obviously wanted some more vigorous regime in Kabul that could preferably be more amenable to her overtures, present or prospective, and she could not have found a time more opportune. Daud is a man of action and he has obsessions too in respect of Pakhtoonistan. He somehow has learnt the knack of getting closer to Russia. While yet seeing to it that the bear's paw was not stretched too far out, and so here he is again on the scene and he probably will be pursuing the same policies over again.

Russia may not have connived at the coup, but those who staged it were probably convinced that if the initial strike was successful, Russia's recognition would be quick in coming and this could certainly have demoralized the pro-king elements. This is precisely what happened. Russia's immediate recognition after the first strike must have given such elements cold feet. This is significant in that while the coup was staged by the troops in Kabul supported by the Russian trained air force, the real strength of the king lay in the provinces. There should normally have been expected a string reaction in the latter, especially in the intensely loyalist Pushto-speaking eastern and southern provinces. But when Russian recognition gave the hint that there was full backing of the big neighbour to the junta, the loyalists must have got confused and demoralized.

Russia should be expected to see to it that the junta stays in power. This will make the latter's consolidation of power a lot easier. And there may begin some eloquent articulation of the Pashtoonistan theme than the ritualistic broadcasts on the Kabul radio. Daud has already pronounced this as the keynote of his policy. Russia for her part has her now familiar aim of pressurizing Pakistan into falling in with her scheme of things vis-à-vis the so-called Asian security plan. Pakistan is a big factor in the matter of this plan in that the country is not only a gap in the line of China's containment along her southern borders but also a potential corridor for the latter's projection southward. Russia apparently has not forgiven Pakistan for being so consistently reluctant. She has acted once and half the country is gone. She may be doing it again.

The climate is congenial for Russia's aim. The British have quit the Middle East, America is upto her neck in the Watergate affair and is not likely to involve herself again in distant venture unless perchance impossibly provoked. So there is, among the buffer countries, India on the scene, and there is Russia in close proximity and she has a workable equation with India. She now has a dependable protégé too in Afghanistan, and so she may be making her next move with a more assured step.

Pakistan in consequence has to watch intently the gathering clouds over her western horizon. She has to work for harmony inside her own borders and try, if possible, to find political rather than military solutions to her problems. There is trouble in Baluchistan and there is a political condition in N.W.F.P. which gives the people there the feeling that they were being treated as the country's second class citizens. Even though Governor Aslam Khattak is filling the stopgap role admirably, but an understanding has nevertheless to be reached with the NAP which hates to be branded as anti-national.

Meanwhile, Kabul has made its position clear. While advocating Pashtoonistan, it yet has towed the line of its predecessors by declaring that it did not have acquisitive aims and that all it desired was an arrangement which the Pakhtoon leadership conceded as acceptable to them. The hint is there. A democratic system with provincial autonomy is indicated. President Bhutto is likely to have his hands too full with his own problems to be going anywhere beyond that. He wants some face-saving, much as his predecessor did.

But this nevertheless will not rule out the possibility of Russia prosecuting her own aims. This eventually could be headed off only by normalization of relations with India with which Pakistan so far has direct involvements. This involvement is not without its grievous effect on the country's economic situation at home and her role in the international field. If the confrontation continues and simultaneously events in Baluchistan and N.W.F.P. keep drifting, the opportunity may come the way of both Afghanistan and Russia for their own respective reasons but with one objective—the pursuance of their designs at the cost of Pakistan.

Walter Schwarz of the *Guardian* wrote from Kabul: 'At first the coup looked like a Soviet-inspired plot carried out by pro-Russia officers…The Soviet Ambassador however confided to a fellow Russian that the coup had taken him completely by surprise. The Tass correspondent in Kabul was not invited to Daud's conference and felt very annoyed. All this may be window-dressing.

'…Daud appeared to be phlegmatic and uncommunicative at the press conference and the only time he showed signs of animation was when someone hinted that his was a foreign inspired coup. He rejected the notion that there was an alien hand in his undertaking. On the seventh day his line on Pakistani Pathans was also changed. He said this dispute would be solved through 'peaceful means', exactly what Zahir Shah's government used to say. On the first day of his coup he ominously omitted this important phrase.

'…Students of Kabul are happy and optimistic about their job and scholarship prospects which until recently were the reserve of those with the right family links.

'The President who is the cousin and brother-in-law of the deposed King has allowed the Queen and her children to join him in Rome. He could have kept them as hostages against the King's good behavior. This kind of blackmail is not practised among the cousins. To the predominantly illiterate countryside the coup is said to be family feud in which President Daud has replaced King Zahir Shah. May be that is the reason why no resistance is forthcoming to the new regime.'

Now president Daud has announced a general promotion for all army officers and personnel, except generals. All the sergeants in the army have been promoted to the rank of second lieutenants while one promotion has been awarded to the other ranks. This only shows that the military will increasingly form the new elite in the country.

The Riposte to Kabul

17 November 1973

A S a natural corollary of his current tour of the Frontier and the tribal areas, the Prime Minister has shifted the limelight to Afghanistan. After his recent pronouncements on Kashmir, this is a sally into another prickly domain, this time with more justification but an eye may as well be kept on the attendant risks.

Certainly, the record of Afghan provocations to Pakistan is long and bizarre enough to warrant a firm riposte. This is one dispute to which Pakistan has made no contribution except to be on the receiving end and, in the process, keep its cool. The recent dismissals of the NAP-JUI governments in Baluchistan and the Frontier may be cited to justify Afghanistan's abrasive behaviour but the tension-ridden relations between the two countries have a different genesis. The dispute long antedates the Bhutto regime and coincides with the very birth of Pakistan. Afghanistan threw in its irridentist wrench into the wheel when the people of the Frontier were deciding, through a plebiscite, whether or not to join the state of Pakistan. Afghanistan's was the lone vote to have opposed the admission of Pakistan into the United Nations.

There have been shifts and turns in the Afghan demands upon Pakistan. What began rather nebulously as support for the Pathans' right of self-determination has lately concretized itself into a definite territorial claim on the Frontier Province and the tribal areas. The Afghan delegate to the UN recently spoke of these areas as having been forcibly severed from the 'fatherland' i.e. Afghanistan. The implications are obvious. In the meantime, the Afghan propagandists would have us believe that a 'Government of Occupied Pakhtoonistan' has been functioning in Kabul for long, exercising jurisdiction over what, for the sake of political convenience, has been divided into southern, central and northern zones of 'occupied Pakhtoonistan'.

All this is not a mere picnic. The Afghans mean business if only they could rake it off and if they could be sure of digesting the hefty morsel without turning the applecart of the precariously balanced Afghan society right on its creaking axle. Afghanistan has yet to discover the 20th century. Likewise, its concern for the prevalence of the writ of democracy in Pakistan lacks conviction. Not that it washes away the sins of Mr Bhutto but a medieval society like Afghanistan can hardly hold the candle. That a well entrenched monarchy has been dusted out does not mean that the sun of democracy has chased away the shadows from under the hills of Afghanistan. Power is still the privilege of a closed circle.

How does it affect us? What happens in Afghanistan is none of our concern. It will find its own political level. The dictates of common sense and of mutual advantage should induce Afghanistan, in the long haul, to move towards accommodation with Pakistan. That day has yet to dawn. Nevertheless, as neighbours and co-sharers in the strategic destiny of this area, they have a claim on our sympathy and our sense of good fellowship. In this Pakistan should not be found wanting. Geopolitical and strategic compulsions will always outlast the regimes of the day. The Afghan monarchy, without having abjured its claims, had evolved a working relationship with Pakistan which, though far from ideal, kept the demons of confrontation at bay. Sardar Daud, on the other hand, is negotiating risky slopes.

Prime Minister Bhutto has twice referred to the possibility of ex-king Zahir Shah being given asylum in Pakistan. This may be fair tactics in the great game of diplomacy and may even be held valid in the court of last resort. Coupled with the 'forward policy' which Pakistan has, with enough justification, initiated in the tribal belt, this could be interpreted as notice to Afghanistan that enough is, after all, enough. A sense of restraint must nevertheless condition Pakistan's graduated response to the Afghan challenge. Pakistan as Mr Bhutto has rightly emphasized, has nothing to gain by stoking the fires of confrontation. Neither will any gain accrue to Afghanistan. It will be the outside powers who will collect the dividend.

It is true that Afghanistan by itself is no threat to Pakistan. The danger lies in Soviet and/or Indian encouragement to the rulers in Kabul. A Soviet military mission has just visited Afghanistan coinciding with the visit of the Indian External Affairs Minister, Sardar Swaran Singh. It will be premature to conclude that decisive policy shifts have already occurred in Moscow or New Delhi. It is incumbent upon Pakistan to mend its fences with Russia and India, keeping in mind the lessons of the 1971 crisis. In this subtle war of attrition, gains and losses cannot be counted over a period of months. This will be a long drawn-out struggle in which internal cohesion will be as important as our relations with the international powers.

It is, therefore, of paramount importance that Prime Minister Bhutto should adjust his sights so as [to] promote the politics of consensus at home and a policy of reconciliation abroad. The more he strives to establish a one-party hegemony inside the country, the more vulnerable he will be to outside pressures. Exaggerated notions of ethnic and cultural distinctiveness and of provincial autonomy, as professed by certain opposition elements, have contributed as much to the current state of divisiveness in the country as Mr Bhutto's quest for unrestrained power. The Prime Minister's responsibility is greater because he has to set the tone and the pace for national politics. The resumption of the dialogue in Baluchistan can be taken as an admission of the mistakes which have been made in the past. Regardless, the dialogue must succeed if the situation in Baluchistan is to be defused. Unfortunately, no such spirit of reconciliation informs the Prime Minister's recent appreciation of the role of the

NAP in the Frontier. The tar brush still delineates the NAP's portrait there. The politics of dissent need not be christened the original sin.

The shadows creeping over from across Afghanistan and beyond are invariably part of this web. The Prime Minister may be playing poker like nobody else can. We would only wish he does not overplay his hand as he did on 25 March 1971.

* * *